Oswald

PAUL WATKINS MEDIEVAL STUDIES
General Editor: Shaun Tyas ~ *Consultant Editor:* David Roffe

1. ANDERSON, Alan Orr, *Early Sources of Scottish History AD 500-1286*; a new edition with corrections, in 2 vols. (1990).

2. HARMER, Florence, *Anglo-Saxon Writs*; a new edition comprising the original work together with her later essay 'A Bromfield and a Coventry Writ of King Edward the Confessor' (1989).

3. STENTON, Sir Frank Merry, *The Early History of the Abbey of Abingdon*; reprinted for the first time since 1913 (1989).

4. SPITTAL, Jeffrey and FIELD, John, *A Reader's Guide to the Place-names of the United Kingdom* (1990).

5. HILL, Sir Francis, *Medieval Lincoln*; reprinted with an introductory essay by Dorothy Owen (1990).

6. PARSONS, David (ed.), *Eleanor of Castile 1290-1990, Essays to Commemorate the 700th Anniversary of her Death: 28 November 1290* (1991).

7. COATES, Richard, *The Ancient and Modern Names of the Channel Islands, a Linguistic History* (1991).

8. FOULDS, Trevor (ed.), *The Thurgarton Cartulary* (1994).

9. ORMROD, W. M. (ed.), *England in the Thirteenth Century*, Harlaxton Medieval Studies I (1991).

10. ANDERSON, Alan Orr, *Scottish Annals from English Chroniclers, 500-1286 AD*; a new edition with corrections (1991).

11. LINDLEY, Phillip, *Gothic to Renaissance: Essays on Sculpture in England* (1995).

12. HICKS, Carola (ed.), *England in the Eleventh Century*, Harlaxton Medieval Studies II (1992).

13. ROGERS, Nicholas (ed.), *England in the Fourteenth Century*, Harlaxton Medieval Studies III (1993).

14. STANCLIFFE, Clare and CAMBRIDGE, Eric (eds), *Oswald: Northumbrian King to European Saint* (1995).

15. ORMROD, W. M. and LINDLEY, Phillip (eds), *The Black Death* (forthcoming, 1995).

16. ROGERS, Nicholas (ed.), *England in the Fifteenth Century*, Harlaxton Medieval Studies IV (1994).

17. DEMIDOWICZ, George (ed.), *Coventry's First Cathedral. The Cathedral and Priory of St Mary, Coventry. Papers from the 1993 Anniversary Symposium* (1994).

18. GROSS, Anthony, *The Dissolution of the Lancastrian Kingship: Sir John Fortescue and the Crisis of Monarchy in Fifteenth-Century England* (forthcoming).

19. THOMPSON, Benjamin (ed.), *The Reign of Henry VII*, Harlaxton Medieval Studies V (1995).

OSWALD

NORTHUMBRIAN KING
TO EUROPEAN SAINT

EDITED BY

CLARE STANCLIFFE

&

ERIC CAMBRIDGE

PAUL WATKINS

STAMFORD

Typeset from the disks and papers
of the authors by the publisher

PAUL WATKINS
18 Adelaide Street
Stamford
Lincolnshire, PE9 2EN

ISBN
Hardback: 1 871615 46 1
Paperback: 1 871615 51 8

Printed on long-life paper

Printed and bound by Woolnoughs of Irthlingborough

TO

THE PEOPLE

OF ST OSWALD'S

FOREWORD

St Oswald's Durham was not alone in wanting to mark the 1350th anniversary of the death of St Oswald, in 1992. In June of that year, I attended a memorable service at St Oswald's, Oswestry, with a sermon to match the occasion from the archbishop of York. In Durham, we organised a series of events; and this included a memorable pilgrimage to Heavenfield, with some of the pilgrims, like the monks of old, walking the distance from Hexham Abbey.

Our most ambitious project, however, was the one day conference, entitled 'Oswald: Northumbrian King to European Saint', which took place on 25 April 1992, in St Oswald's Institute. Seven of the contributors to this volume read papers at the conference; and another three, Alison Binns, Dagmar Ó Riain-Raedel and Victoria Tudor, kindly agreed to join the project at a later date. In addition, Clare Stancliffe has added a short paper on the place of Oswald's death. We thank them all, both for their willing participation in the conference, and for accepting the further demands imposed by the decision to publish. (I am speaking here for St Oswald's Parochial Church Council, which not only sponsored the conference and provided a skilled and hospitable team of helpers on the day, but also agreed to give whatever support was needed in order to achieve publication.) It should also be recorded that the day conference ended, in church, with the singing by the church choir of the twelfth-century vespers for St Oswald's day.

Let me now go back a little in time, if only to show that this project was not conceived in haste. At our annual church meeting in April 1989, I threw out the suggestion of marking this coming anniversary in some way; it was as though a seed had been sown. A year later, I was speaking tentatively of a day conference, 'not too highbrow, making use of local talent, and (I hoped) adding to the sum of knowledge'. By 1991, the date was set.

Soon after that first occasion, Clare Stancliffe, who is an early medieval historian with an interest in Anglo-Saxon Northumbria, gallantly responded to my suggestion and began to explore the possibility of mounting a conference. Her decision may or may not have been influenced by the fact that she is also married to the vicar! Anyway, she duly received the backing of the P.C.C., and then began to plan in more detail, 'making good use of local talent'! Even before the day, and to our great amazement, we were oversubscribed. In the event, more than a hundred and twenty people were squeezed into the hall.

There and then, we tested conference opinion, which was decidedly favourable to the idea of publication. Clare, however, was firmly of the opinion that further contributions were necessary in order to integrate the original papers and to make a satisfactory book. More than six months passed before the present shape of this volume finally emerged.

The editorial task has been shared between Clare Stancliffe and Eric Cambridge; and we are deeply indebted to them both for the care they have taken in bringing these essays together in such a coherent and articulate form. I am the closest observer of the hours the editors have spent on this task; and I marvel at their tenacity.

On behalf of the people of St Oswald in Durham, I thank the editors and all the contributors for giving us this book. It is our hope that, in many other places, Oswald's people will discover it and make it their own.

Ben de la Mare, July 1994
Vicar of St Oswald's, Durham

OSWALD

Northumbrian King to European Saint. Edited by Clare Stancliffe and Eric Cambridge

Paperback with full colour cover: £14.95

St Oswald, king of Northumbria, is a commanding figure whose life and reign dominate our understanding of seventh-century England. Oswald was the ruler who was responsible for introducing the Irish mission to Northumbria which led to its conversion and to a great cultural flowering; it also exerted considerable influence on England as a whole. In battle he was a successful warrior king of his age, recognised as overlord of much of Britain during his eight-year reign between 634 and 642. Finally killed in battle against the pagan Penda, king of the Mercians, his life became the inspiration for legends as his cult spread throughout Europe in the middle ages.

This new volume of eleven essays by leading historians and archaeologists explores the diversity of his life and posthumous reputation. It includes all the papers given at the 1350th anniversary conference (Durham 1992) together with four additional ones commissioned to make a coherant, balanced volume. It is the first book to give full-length treatment of Oswald himself and to examine the development of his cult in England, a subject which has hitherto been strangely neglected. It also covers the continental cult where it complements existing studies and probes further the crucial question of how the cult of St Oswald came to enjoy such widespread popularity on the continent.

The book is 320 pages long, with 9 figures, 24 plates and a full index. After a general introduction by the editors, which discusses the iconography, the 11 essays are:

Rosemary Cramp, The Making of Oswald's Northumbria, pp. 17-32

Clare Stancliffe, Oswald, 'Most Holy and Most Victorious King of the Northumbrians', pp. 33-83

Clare Stancliffe, Where was Oswald Killed?, pp. 84-96

Alan Thacker, *Membra Disjecta*: The Division of the Body and the Diffusion of the Cult, pp. 97-127

Eric Cambridge, Archaeology and the Cult of St Oswald in Pre-Conquest Northumbria, pp. 128-163

David Rollason, St Oswald in Post-Conquest England, pp. 164-177

Victoria Tudor, Reginald's Life of St Oswald, pp. 178-194

Richard N. Bailey, St Oswald's Heads, pp. 195-209

Dagmar Ó Riain-Raedel, Edith, Judith, Matilda: The Role of Royal Ladies in the Propagation of the Continental Cult, pp. 210-229

Annemiek Jansen, The Development of the St Oswald Legends on the Continent, pp. 230-240

Alison Binns, Pre-Reformation Dedications to St Oswald in England and Scotland: A Gazetteer, pp. 241-271

followed by notes on further reading and a comprehensive index.

CONTENTS

LIST OF PLATES

16 King with bird, probably Oswald with raven, statue: 14th C. (Museum der Stadt, Regensburg).

17 Oswald, historiated initial from a collection of saints' Lives and sermons: 2nd half of 12th C. (Munich, Universitätsbibliothek 2° Cod. MS 312, fol. 104^v).

18 Oswald's 'martyrdom', historiated initial from a collection of saints' Lives and homilies: Trier, 14th C. (Darmstadt, Hessische Landes-bibliothek MS 2766, fol. 44^r); photograph, Bildarchiv Foto, Marburg.

19 St Cuthbert holding Oswald's head, historiated initial from Nicholas of Lyra's commentary on the Pentateuch: Durham Priory, 1386 (Durham, Dean and Chapter Library MS A.I.3, fol. 1^r).

20 Oswald holding a covered cup, statue from the Dollingersaal, Regens-burg, Bavaria: late 13th C. (Museum der Stadt, Regensburg).

21 The Dollingersaal statue of Oswald before restoration (cf. Pl. 20): drawing by J. G. Ostermeyer, 1812 (Museum der Stadt, Regensburg).

22 Oswald with raven holding ring on his orb, wing of an altarpiece by the Styrian Master: Styria, Austria, mid 15th C. (Steiermärkisches Landesmuseum Joanneum, Graz, Abteilung Alte Galerie).

23 Raven arriving from heaven with letter and chrism for Oswald's coron-ation: Salzburg school, 2nd half of 15th C. (Bayerisches National-museum, Munich); photograph, Bildarchiv Foto, Marburg.

24 Óðin (Woden) struggling with the wolf Fenrir, with a raven on his shoulder: fragment of stone cross-slab from Kirk Andreas, Isle of Man, 10th C. (The Manx Museum, Douglas).

LIST OF FIGURES

LIST OF CONTRIBUTORS

Rosemary Cramp — University of Durham

Clare Stancliffe — University of Durham

Alan Thacker — Victoria County History

Eric Cambridge — University of Durham

David Rollason — University of Durham

Victoria Tudor — Hitchin

Richard N. Bailey — University of Newcastle upon Tyne

Dagmar Ó Riain-Raedel — University College, Cork

Annemiek Jansen — University of Groningen

Alison Binns — The Open University, Milton Keynes

ACKNOWLEDGEMENTS

Our thanks must go in the first place to St Oswald's church, Durham, and to all our contributors. We would also like to thank our publisher, Shaun Tyas, for his interest and support. We are grateful to the many individuals and institutions who have helped in various ways: in particular to Joan Trowbridge for her skilful word processing, often against the clock; to Drs R. R. A. van Gruting for kindly sending copies of his article; to the University Library and the Dean and Chapter Library, Durham; and to the Bodleian Library, Oxford, one of whose staff was outstandingly helpful.

In the pursuit of medieval representations of St Oswald in connection with the introduction, we have drawn upon the good will and expertise of many people. Dr Kevin Hilliard assisted with correspondence in German. Dr A. I. Doyle, Dr Sally Dormer, and Dr Rosamond McKitterick assisted us in tracking down or checking medieval manuscripts. Dr David O'Connor, Mr Peter Gibson, Martin Stancliffe, and Tim Ayers helped in various ways with our investigation of English stained-glass windows. Jane Cunningham patiently and frequently assisted our research into the iconography of St Oswald; without her efforts the writing of that part of the introduction would not have been possible.

We are most grateful to the following institutions for supplying us with photographic illustrations, and for granting permission for them to be reproduced here: Bildarchiv Foto Marburg (Pls. 18, 23); the trustees of the British Museum (Pls. 1, 3, 6, 7); Cleveland County Council (Pl. 2); Conway Library, Courtauld Institute of Art, London (Pl. 14); the Dean and Chapter of Durham (Pls. 8, 19); Dom- und Diözesanmuseum Hildesheim (Pls. 10, 12); the Manx Museum, Douglas (Pl. 24); Museum der Stadt, Regensburg (Pls. 16, 20, 21); National Museum of Scotland (Pl. 4); the trustees of the Pierpont Morgan Library, New York (Pl. 13); Rijksmuseum Het Catharijneconvent, Utrecht (Pl. 11); the Dean and Chapter of Ripon (Pl. 5); Steiermärkisches Landesmuseum Joanneum, Graz (Pl. 22); Universitätsbibliothek, Munich (Pl. 17). Pl. 15 is reproduced by kind permission of the Dean and Chapter of York.

The publication of this book has been assisted by a grant from the Scouloudi Foundation in association with the Institute of Historical Research; and by a grant from the trustees of the Francis Coales Foundation. The editors and publisher are most grateful to both bodies, as these grants have enabled the book to be illustrated more fully than would otherwise have been possible.

CLARE STANCLIFFE
ERIC CAMBRIDGE
Durham, October 1994

LIST OF ABBREVIATIONS

AASS	*Acta Sanctorum quotquot toto orbe coluntur vel a catholicis scriptoribus celebrantur...* (Antwerp and Brussels 1643-)
AB	*Analecta Bollandiana* (Société des Bollandistes, Paris and Brussels 1882-)
Alcuin, *BKS*	Alcuin, *The Bishops, Kings, and Saints of York*, ed. P. Godman (Oxford Medieval Texts; Oxford 1982)
AMI	*The Age of Migrating Ideas. Early Medieval Art in Northern Britain and Ireland*, ed. R. M. Spearman and J. Higgitt (Edinburgh and Stroud 1993)
Arnold	*Symeonis Monachi Opera Omnia*, ed. T. Arnold (2 vols, RS 75; London 1882-5)
Arnold-Forster	F. Arnold-Forster, *Studies in Church Dedications or England's Patron Saints* (3 vols; London 1899)
ASC	*Anglo-Saxon Chronicle*, ed. C. Plummer and J. Earle, *Two of the Saxon Chronicles Parallel* (2 vols; Oxford 1892)
ASE	*Anglo-Saxon England* (Cambridge 1972-)
Baesecke, *MO*	*Der Münchener Oswald*, ed. G. Baesecke (Germanistische Abhandlungen 28, Breslau 1907)
Bailey, *VAS*	R. N. Bailey, *Viking Age Sculpture in Northern England* (London 1980)
Baker, 'Zug'	E. P. Baker, 'St Oswald and his church at Zug', *Archaeologia* 93 (1949), pp. 103-12
BAR	British Archaeological Reports (Oxford; Br. ser., British series; Int. ser., International series)
BHL	*Bibliotheca Hagiographica Latina Antiquae et Mediae Aetatis* (2 vols (Subsidia Hagiographica, vol. 6) with supplement (Subsidia Hagiographica, vol. 12); Société des Bollandistes, Paris and Brussels 1898, 1901, 1911)
BL	British Library, London
BM	British Museum, London

Brandt, *Kirchenkunst*   *Kirchenkunst des Mittelalters. Katalog zur Ausstellung des Diözesan-Museums Hildesheim*, ed. M. Brandt (Hildesheim 1989)

Butler, 'Dedications'   L. A. S. Butler, 'Church dedications and the cults of the Anglo-Saxon saints in England', in *The Anglo-Saxon Church: Papers on History, Architecture and Archaeology in Honour of Dr H. M. Taylor* (CBA Research Report 60; London 1986), pp. 44-50

CBA   Council for British Archaeology

Clemoes   P. Clemoes, *The Cult of St Oswald on the Continent* (Jarrow Lecture; Jarrow 1983)

CPR   *Calendar of the Patent Rolls Preserved in the Public Record Office (1232-1509)* (52 vols; London 1891-1916)

Craster, 'Patrimony'   E. Craster, 'The patrimony of St Cuthbert', *English Historical Review* 69 (1954), pp. 177-99

Ctl. Shrewsbury   *The Cartulary of Shrewsbury Abbey*, ed. U. Rees (2 vols.; Aberystwyth 1975)

Curschmann, *MO*   *Der Münchener Oswald*, ed. M. Curschmann (Altdeutsche Textbibliothek 76; Tübingen 1974)

Curschmann, *MODSE*   M. Curschmann, *Der Münchener Oswald und die deutsche spielmännische Epik* (Münchener Texte und Untersuchungen zur deutschen Literatur des Mittelalters, 6; Munich 1964)

Domesday Book   *Domesday Book seu Liber Censualis Wilhelmi Primi Regis Angliae* (vols I-II, text, continuous foliation [ed. A. Farley, 1783]; vol. III, *Indices*, 1811)

EYC   *Early Yorkshire Charters*, 12 vols (I-III, ed. W. Farrer (Yorkshire Archaeological Society, Edinburgh 1914-16); IV-XII, ed. C. T. Clay (Yorkshire Archaeological Society, Record Series, Extra Series, i-iii, v-x; Wakefield 1935-65))

Folz   R. Folz, 'Saint Oswald roi de Northumbrie: étude d'hagiographie royale', *AB* 98 (1980), pp. 49-74

Gesta Ottonis   Hrotsvitha of Gandersheim, *Gesta Ottonis*, ed. P. Winterfeld, *Hrotsvithae Opera* (Scriptores Rerum Germanicarum in usum scholarum ex Monumentis Germaniae Historicis separatim editi; new edn, Berlin and Zurich 1965)

HBS	Henry Bradshaw Society
HDE	*Historia Dunelmensis Ecclesiae*, by Symeon of Durham, cited by book and chapter; ed. Arnold I, 3-169
HE	*Bede's Ecclesiastical History of the English People*, ed. and trans. B. Colgrave and R. A. B. Mynors (Oxford Medieval Texts; Oxford 1969)
HR	*Historia Regum*, cited *sub anno* or by chapter; ed. Arnold II, 3-283
Ideal and Reality	*Ideal and Reality in Frankish and Anglo-Saxon Society: Studies Presented to J. M. Wallace-Hadrill*, ed. P. Wormald (Oxford 1983)
LR	*Liber Regis, vel Thesaurus Rerum Ecclesiasticarum*, ed. J. Bacon (London 1786)
MGH	Monumenta Germaniae Historica
Morris, *Churches*	R. Morris, *Churches in the Landscape* (London 1989)
Origins	*The Origins of Anglo-Saxon Kingdoms*, ed. S. Bassett (Leicester 1989)
pb edn	paperback edition
Plummer	*Venerabilis Baedae Opera Historica*, ed. C. Plummer (2 vols.; Oxford 1896)
Reginald, *VO*	Reginald of Durham, *Vita Sancti Oswaldi*, ed. Arnold I, 326-85
Relics	*The Relics of Saint Cuthbert*, ed. C. F. Battiscombe (Oxford 1956)
RS	Rolls Series (Rerum Britannicarum Medii Aevi Scriptores or Chronicles and Memorials of Great Britain and Ireland during the Middle Ages)
St Cuthbert	*St Cuthbert, His Cult and His Community to AD 1200*, ed. G. Bonner, D. Rollason, and C. Stancliffe (Woodbridge 1989)
SS	Surtees Society
Two Lives	*Two Lives of St Cuthbert*, ed. and trans. B. Colgrave (Cambridge 1940; reprinted 1985)

VCA	*Vita Sancti Cuthberti Auctore Anonymo*, the anonymous *Life of St Cuthbert*, cited by book and chapter; ed. and trans. *Two Lives*, pp. 59-139 and notes, pp. 310-40
VCol	*Adomnán's Life of Columba*, ed. and trans. A. O. and M. O. Anderson (new edn, Oxford Medieval Texts; Oxford 1991)
VCH	Victoria County History (The Victoria History of the Counties of England (London 1900-))
VCP	*Vita Sancti Cuthberti Auctore Beda*, Bede's prose *Life of St Cuthbert*, cited by chapter; ed. and trans. *Two Lives*, pp. 141-307 and notes, pp. 341-59
VW	*The Life of Bishop Wilfrid by Eddius Stephanus*, cited by chapter; ed. and trans. B. Colgrave (Cambridge 1927; reprinted 1985)
Wallace-Hadrill, *Comm*	J. M. Wallace-Hadrill, *Bede's Ecclesiastical History of the English People: A Historical Commentary* (Oxford Medieval Texts; Oxford 1988)

Introduction

CLARE STANCLIFFE & ERIC CAMBRIDGE

Oswald of Northumbria is a commanding figure. For a brief eight years he was a successful warrior king of his people; and, although he was cut down on the field of battle, his achievements in this sphere were far from negligible. His most significant act, however, was his turning to the monastery of Iona for a bishop to bring Christianity to his people. It was this which inaugurated the Irish mission which was primarily responsible both for converting Northumbria, and for making an important contribution to the Christianisation and the culture of England as a whole. Thus, while many other seventh-century warrior kings are now of interest only to historians who study the period in its own right, Oswald is a figure of more general concern: his action contributed, in a perceptible way, to the subsequent history of north-east England.

If the history of Oswald himself is one of continuing interest both to the specialist and to a wider circle, the history of his cult is equally intriguing. First, in a world in which the vast majority of those who won recognition as saints were churchmen or professional religious, whether bishops or hermits, monks or nuns, Oswald belongs to that select band of royal saints. The Christianisation of the barbarian successor states to the Roman Empire was, as Rosemary Cramp notes below, bound up with their transformation into more stable political entities under the rule of kings; and it has been noted that king-saints often appear at the formative point in the history of a people. An obvious parallel to St Oswald is the Norwegian King Olaf, who was killed in battle in 1030 and rapidly thereafter venerated as a saint. Quite why saint-kings appear at this point in the history of some peoples, but not others, is a matter for further research. But the case of St Oswald, which is presented below in some detail, is of considerable relevance. It also has bearings on other matters of interest: the question of whether it is possible to reconcile the ideals of Christianity and the demands of political leadership; or the use to which the cult of a saint-king might subsequently be put. For instance, it seems that Athelstan, the tenth-century West Saxon king who sought to unite the whole of England under his rule, may have tried to make the most of an indirect kinship link between the West Saxon royal house and Oswald of Northumbria in order to boost his claim to rule in the north; while simultaneously, on the continent, German kings who intermarried into the West Saxon royal house sought to bolster their position by emphasising their kinship ties with Oswald as one who had been both king and saint.

This leads on to a second reason why the cult of St Oswald is so significant: that is its remarkable success, viewed in terms both of its

1

geographical spread and of its continuing life and adaptability right through the middle ages. If one is trying to understand the dynamics of saints' cults, and the reasons that led to one particular saint becoming recognised beyond his own locality as a saint of national and even international importance, then Oswald is an obvious candidate to study. Not only was he the first Anglo-Saxon Christian to receive any widespread recognition as a saint in his own country; he also became the most widely venerated Anglo-Saxon saint on the continent, and, of medieval English saints as a whole, he ranks second only to St Thomas à Becket in popularity in German-speaking countries. The reasons for his rise and continuing popularity are explored in several papers in this volume, which highlight the immediate dismemberment of his body and consequent wide dispersal of his relics; the skill of Bede's advocacy; the promotion of his cult by important churches and powerful royal ladies; and the way in which different groups were able to re-interpret the figure of Oswald to suit their own current needs. In turn, he could be portrayed as the founder of the Northumbrian church, as a generous patron of foreign Christians, as a crusader figure, as a romantic hero of a vernacular romance, and as a potent bringer of good harvests, fertility and health amongst the peasantry.

This last prompts consideration of another significant aspect of the cult of St Oswald: its appeal at a popular level, both in England and in the Alpine countries; and, seemingly linked with this, its intriguing relationship to pre-Christian practices in these areas. Of course, it is widely recognised that when Christianity replaced the nature religions that we class as paganism, the expectations of the mass of the population were not transformed overnight; instead, people were persuaded to look to Christian saints for the this-worldly help and healing that they had formerly sought from pagan deities. The possible links between the cult of St Oswald and pre-Christian practices are, however, more specific than this. There is the relatively high incidence of holy wells associated with St Oswald in Britain, a phenomenon which appears to have pagan Celtic roots; there is also the complex question of whether Oswald was seen by his people, whose grasp of Christianity would at this stage have been tenuous, as being in some sense a sacral king, possibly one with a special relationship to Woden. Although much remains unknown, we may surmise that the fact that Oswald was a king who died a violent death when leading his people in battle lent itself to this interpretation. Woden was a Germanic war god, who used ravens as his messengers, and to whom both ravens and the ash tree were sacred (Pl. 24); and there are instances of kings being dedicated to Woden in battle. Small wonder, then, that some scholars have seen a special significance in the sacred ash tree above St Oswald's well at Oswestry and the associated story of a raven-like bird, or in the appearance of a raven as the king's companion in the vernacular legends that developed about Oswald in medieval Germany.

For all these reasons, Oswald is a figure of considerable interest. In view of this, it is perhaps surprising that up till now only certain aspects of his cult and legend have been considered in any detail. The only scholarly attempt to survey the whole subject hitherto has been an article by a French scholar which appeared in 1980 and provides a helpful overview.[1] Apart from this, attention has concentrated on two specific areas: the development of his cult on the continent, and the vernacular German legends about St Oswald. The present book seeks to redress the balance and fill the gaps. The starting point is the historical Oswald in his seventh-century setting, seen here from the complementary perspectives of an archaeologist and a historian. Detailed studies then follow of the development of the cult of St Oswald in England, both before and after the Norman Conquest, with contributions by historians and archaeologists. Also included here is the first ever study of the *Life of St Oswald* written by Reginald, a monk of Durham in the twelfth century, and a gazetteer of all pre-Reformation dedications to St Oswald in England and Scotland.[2]

On the continental side, we have not attempted complete coverage, as that would have involved the replication of subjects adequately treated elsewhere. As regards the continental cult, an overview was recently provided by Peter Clemoes in the Jarrow Lecture for 1983, while two older, detailed articles by E. P. Baker provide excellent coverage of the spread of the cult from Weingarten, a Welf monastery in southern Germany, through the Alpine countries and down into Italy.[3] We have therefore preferred to concentrate our efforts on probing what seemed to be the main questions still awaiting resolution: how, when and why did the cult of St Oswald win its popularity on the continent? The studies of Alan Thacker and Dagmar Ó Riain-Raedel have brought new light to bear on this, suggesting that the crucial phase was not the early development of the cult, but rather its successive reinvigoration at various later dates. In particular, Ó Riain-Raedel's focus on the role of royal ladies has approached the subject from a fresh angle, and confirmed the crucial role of Judith, one time wife of Tostig of Northumbria, who later married Welf IV of Bavaria. It was through her that the cult of St Oswald was transmitted to the powerful Welf family, rivals in power to the German emperors themselves. This provides the back-

---

[1] Folz.

[2] Owing to the constraints of time and of other commitments, Dr Binns was not able to include Wales. This has at least one Oswald dedication, at Jeffreyston, Pembrokeshire. Cf. also *Historia Brittonum*, ch. 65, 'sanctum Oswaldum' (edn. cit. below, p. 46, n. 61); and Rollason, below, p. 164.

[3] Baker, 'Zug'; and E. P. Baker, 'The cult of St Oswald in northern Italy', *Archaeologia* 94 (1951), pp. 167-94.

ground to the subsequent spread of the cult through Welf lands, studied by Baker.

Together with a further Welf-English marriage and the intriguing role of Irish monks, this also explains how the cult of St Oswald became popular in twelfth-century Regensburg, since the latter was very much a Welf city; and it was apparently in late twelfth-century Regensburg that a German poet transformed the Oswald story into popular romance. The ramifications of the German vernacular literature on St Oswald have been studied in detail by German scholars, but hitherto virtually nothing has been published in English. Annemiek Jansen's paper therefore seeks to provide a general survey of this literature to introduce non-Germanists to this entertaining subject, while probing further the fascinating question of the relationship between St Oswald, his raven, and the cult of Woden.

Closely bound up with the cult of St Oswald is his portrayal in pictorial or iconographic form. Hitherto attention has focused on the continental iconography of the saint, while the English evidence has been strangely neglected.[4] The contributions of David Rollason and Richard Bailey in this volume do something to redress the balance, while Annemiek Jansen's paper sketches the context for the emergence of the most distinctive continental attribute of all, the raven. It may, however, be helpful if we here survey the development of the iconography of St Oswald from a general perspective, so that readers may gain an overall view of how the saint came to be portrayed in the two major and distinct areas of his cult, that is, England on the one hand, and Germany, the Alpine countries and northern Italy on the other. We will include mention of the English examples known to us, as this material has not previously been collected together.

The Changing Image of St Oswald

The earliest surviving representations of St Oswald date from the twelfth century. There are wall paintings at the Stift Nonnberg in Salzburg and in the Galilee Chapel of Durham Cathedral; there are portrayals in manuscripts from St Winnoc's, Bergues, in Flanders, and from southern Germany (e.g. Pl. 17); there is a chasuble, probably from the Tyrol, and there is the splendid metalwork head-reliquary, which was produced for the Welf duke, Henry

---

[4]   A. Vizkelety, 'Oswald König von Northumbrien', in *Lexicon der christlichen Ikonographie*, ed. E. Kirschbaum and others (8 vols., Rome etc. 1968-76), VIII, cols. 102-3, is helpful, but brief. A. Vizkelety, 'Der Budapester Oswald', *Beiträge zur Geschichte der deutschen Sprache und Literatur* 86 (1964), pp. 107-88, at pp. 131-40, catalogues medieval portrayals of Oswald; this makes a good starting point, but England is poorly served. See also Curschmann, *MODSE*, pp. 169-93; and Baker's two articles (as n. 3), which are good on the south German, Swiss and north Italian developments, and well illustrated.

the Lion, and is now at Hildesheim (Pl. 12).[5] This work, which seems to include both English and German features,[6] can be taken as typifying the earliest surviving representations of St Oswald. Besides the three-dimensional crowned head of Oswald on the top, which may be a slightly later addition, the saint also appears on one of the panels below. Here he is shown seated on a throne, crowned and haloed, and holding orb and sceptre as symbols of his royal dignity. In this it is typical of the twelfth-century representations. What is striking is that in all these different places, and in all these different media, the portrayal of Oswald is essentially the same: that of a king, with royal attributes, but no other distinguishing characteristic – save for a martyr's palm in two south German or Austrian instances.

The crucial step in portraying Oswald as an individual, rather than a representative of a type, was apparently first taken at the Benedictine monastery of Weingarten in southern Germany in the late twelfth or early thirteenth century. Its masterpiece is the missal executed for Berthold, abbot from 1200 to 1232, and this includes a full page illustration of one of Bede's stories about King Oswald (Pl. 13; cf. *HE* III, 6). Here we see Oswald, on the left, sitting at a feast with Aidan. The artist has caught the moment when the king is on the point of sending out the silver vessel and its contents to be shared amongst the poor, who crouch pathetically in the foreground; and Bishop Aidan is in the act of blessing Oswald for his generosity: 'may this hand never perish'. Another, probably slightly earlier, depiction of this story comes in the Gradual and Sacramentary of Henry the Sacristan, also from Weingarten, which includes the same scene in a historiated initial. What is so significant about the portrayal in the Berthold Missal, however, is that there, the vessel to be given to the poor has metamorphosed from Bede's 'dish' (*discus*) into a covered cup. Possibly this reflects the influence of the popular German minstrel's tale about Oswald, which transformed Bede's original story.[7] In all events, the covered cup was to become one of St Oswald's

---

[5] Vizkelety, *Beiträge* 86, pp. 131-2; and, for the Durham fresco, see Rollason, below, p. 177.

[6] The niello spiral decoration (as in the background to the Oswald panel) and the depiction of the rivers of paradise appear as hallmarks of works produced for Henry the Lion in Germany, while some of the features of the portrayal of the human figures together with the selection of so many Anglo-Saxon saint-kings point to English influence. Perhaps it was produced in Germany after Henry the Lion's exile in England had forged close links there. See P. Lasko, *Ars Sacra 800-1200* (Harmondsworth 1972), p. 207; J. Geddes, 'The twelfth-century metalwork at Durham Cathedral', in *Medieval Art and Architecture at Durham Cathedral*, ed. N. Coldstream and P. Draper (London 1980), pp. 140-8 at pp. 142-5; Brandt, *Kirchenkunst*, p. 135. For an alternative suggestion, see Ó Riain-Raedel, below, p. 223.

[7] On all this, see Baker, 'Zug', pp. 115-16, and plate XXII b-c; cf. Curschmann,

identifying attributes on the continent (e.g. Pls 20-1); and this is its earliest known portrayal, while the context in which it appears reveals its origin. Although no such representations of fully developed scenes are known to survive in England from this period, that same story from Bede must lie behind what is in all probability a statue of King Oswald on the west front of Wells Cathedral. There, in addition to wearing a kingly crown, the saint holds a dish as his identifying attribute (Pl. 14).[8] This statue is virtually contemporaneous with the Berthold Missal, dating from around 1220-40.

At this period, then, there are no very obvious differences between the English and the continental representations of St Oswald. In both areas Oswald is portrayed either in accordance with the standard iconography used for kings, or in a scene or with an attribute derived from Bede's story of his generosity to the poor. There are, however, two qualifications which may tentatively be made regarding the parallelism between English and continental representations of St Oswald, even at this early period. The first is that Oswald appears to have been a more popular subject for iconographical representation on the continent, particularly in manuscripts. The number of representations of St Oswald in manuscripts from Swabia and Bavaria, above all from the monastery of Weingarten,[9] was not matched by English centres such as Durham. This imbalance may reflect the more pronounced interest in royal saints in Germany, as compared to England. It would, however, be rash to make too much of this contrast at the moment, given the extensive losses of saints' images in England suffered at the Reformation, and in view also of the lack of any systematic attempt to identify iconographic representations of St Oswald in this country; perhaps this publication may stimulate others to fill the gap.

A second possible difference in emphasis between the continent and England is that there seems to have been a greater readiness on the continent to regard Oswald as a martyr, who accepted death for the sake of the Gospel, than we find in England. Of course, Oswald is regularly grouped with the martyrs and explicitly designated as such in tenth-century calendars from England;[10] but it is interesting that Ælfric presents his death exactly as Bede had done: 'he was killed in defence of his people'. Contrast this with his German contemporary, Hrotsvitha of Gandersheim, who writes that 'he

---

MODSE, pp. 178-80, who regards the Henry the Sacristan MS (Pierpont Morgan Library, M. 711) as later than the Berthold Missal (Pierpont Morgan Library, M. 710); but M. Harrsen, *Central European Manuscripts in the Pierpont Morgan Library* (New York 1958), pp. 27-8, would date it earlier.

[8] L. Colchester, *The West Front of Wells Cathedral* (4th edn; Wells 1974), p. 7 (no. 207). The motif may recur in the early fourteenth-century glass of the presbytery clerestory (a point kindly drawn to our attention by Mr Tim Ayers).

[9] Vizkelety, *Beiträge* 86, pp. 132-3; Curschmann, *MODSE*, p. 176.

[10] See Thacker, below, pp. 124-5.

yielded himself to death for the sake of Christ's name', and Drogo of Bergues, who in the mid eleventh century was the first to write explicitly of Oswald's 'martyrdom'.[11] A generation later, Manegold of Lautenbach sought to justify warfare against pagans and heretics on the grounds that those who died in battle against pagans were regarded as 'martyrs' by the catholic church – the prime example being Oswald.[12] The most remarkable verbal statement, however, occurs in the inscription on the Hildesheim head-reliquary: 'Oswald gave himself ... to Christ, and his head to the executioner...'[13] Whoever was responsible for the production of this object, the inscription presumably reflects the concerns of its patron, Henry the Lion. Now, two twelfth-century continental portrayals of Oswald do, as we have seen, include the martyr's palm amongst his attributes.[14] Far more remarkable, however, is an actual martyrdom scene in a fourteenth-century manuscript containing saints' Lives and homilies that comes from Trier (Pl. 18). Here we see Oswald kneeling before an executioner, who has already cut off his arms and is about to behead him. This is no battle scene: Oswald is shown unarmed, in civilian dress, and wearing his crown. It is totally unhistorical, but appears to reflect the sort of thinking apparent in the inscription on the Hildesheim head-relic.

This portrayal of Oswald's death as a martyrdom seems to have found no imitators. In the later middle ages artists continued to represent Oswald as a king,[15] and on the continent they sometimes portrayed him with the

---

[11] Ælfric, *Lives of Three English Saints*, ed. G. I. Needham (London 1966), pp. 35, 36; for Hrotsvitha and Drogo, see below, pp. 213-14; p. 126 and n. 188.

[12] C. Erdmann, *The Origin of the Idea of Crusade* (Eng. trans. Princeton 1977), p. 236.

[13] The inscription is quoted in full in Latin, below, p. 223 n. 59, and in English, p. 202.

[14] Vizkelety, *Beiträge* 86, nos. 4 and 6 (pp. 131-2). Cf. also nos. 50 and 63, dating from c.1500.

[15] In addition to the continental examples in Vizkelety, *Beiträge* 86, note, for England: the Madresfield Hours, fol. 52ᵛ, dated c.1320-30, reproduced in J. Backhouse, *The Madresfield Hours* (Roxburghe Club, Oxford 1975), pl. 26; the (14th-c.?) edge painting added along the top of a Durham Priory MS, now Durham A.IV.35 (*Two Lives*, pp. 32-3; Rollason, below, p. 176 and n. 56); the images and stained-glass windows in Durham Cathedral, destroyed at the Reformation (Rollason, below, p. 177 and *Rites of Durham*, ed. J. T. Fowler (SS 107, Durham 1903), esp. pp. 114, 116, 117, 119); the 'royal window' in the antechapel of All Souls College, Oxford, datable to the 1440s (F. E. Hutchinson, *Medieval Glass at All Souls College* (London 1949), pl. XXI); the late medieval sculptured panel in St Oswald's Methley, Yorks. and the 1533 east window at Wragby church, Yorks. (N. Pevsner, *The Buildings of England, Yorkshire: the West Riding* (2nd edn, Harmondsworth 1967), pp. 364, 560; cf. Binns, below, pp. 263, 267). For the stained-glass windows in York Minster, see below, pp. 9-10.

covered cup. Meanwhile, two English manuscripts and a French one, as well as the lost medieval stained glass in Durham Cathedral, included represent-ations of other Bedan scenes, such as the battle in which he was killed.[16] The most significant developments, however, are the emergence of separate iconographical traditions in England and on the continent, neither of which derived from Bede, and each of which came to have a major influence in its respective sphere.

In England, Durham developed its own iconography which brought together its two pre-eminent native saints: St Cuthbert was now portrayed holding the head of St Oswald (which rested in Cuthbert's coffin in Durham Cathedral).[17] The earliest surviving example at Durham is a statue, now in the feretory of the cathedral, which on stylistic grounds must date to the early fourteenth century. Interestingly, however, the same motif also occurs at this date in a stained-glass window in the chapel of St Lucy, Christ Church Cathedral, Oxford.[18] This implies a slightly earlier origin for this distinctive motif in Durham itself. Later in the fourteenth century the motif appears in Durham manuscripts (Pl. 19), and it was also represented, alongside portrayals of Oswald in his own right, in Durham stained-glass windows that were destroyed at the Reformation.[19] In addition, it has been noted in stained glass from further afield: not only in York Minster, Methley (Yorkshire), and Edenhall (Cumberland), all in areas open to Durham's influence,[20] but also in

16   E.g. BL MS Royal 2 B VII, fols. 258ᵛ, 259ʳ; the former is reproduced in G.
      Warner, *Queen Mary's Psalter* (London 1912), p. 49, pl. 262. See also Vizkelety,
      Beiträge 86, nos. 35 and 27 (pp. 135, 134): no. 35, Paris, Bibl. nat. MS lat. 17294,
      fols 533ʳ-34ʳ, illustrates Oswald enthroned, three battle scenes, two healings,
      Oswald feasting, and two scenes with Oswald's relics. For the Durham windows
      which portrayed Oswald's death and translation, see *Rites of Durham*, ed. Fowler,
      p. 119, and cf. J. Haselock and D. E. O'Connor, 'The medieval stained glass of
      Durham Cathedral', in Coldstream and Draper, op. cit. (n. 6 above), pp. 105-29,
      esp. p. 111 and pl. XVIA.
17   See Rollason and Bailey, below, pp. 177, 195-6.
18   P. A. Newton in J. Sherwood and N. Pevsner, *The Buildings of England,
      Oxfordshire* (Harmondsworth 1974), p. 79. We are grateful to Mr Ayers for
      drawing our attention both to this, and to the glass in Kempsey church,
      mentioned below. A late medieval statue with this iconography from the tower of
      St Mary the Virgin, Oxford, is now in the cloisters of New College: ibid, p. 172,
      and information from Jane Cunningham.
19   *Rites of Durham*, ed. Fowler, pp. 47-8, 114, 115, 116, 118; Rollason, below;
      Haselock and O'Connor in Coldstream and Draper, op. cit. p. 111 and pl. XVIB.
20   The York window, which is still extant, was a gift from a Durham bishop: P.
      Gibson, *The Stained and Painted Glass of York Minster* (Norwich 1979), p. 27,
      illustrated in Coldstream and Draper, op. cit. pl. XVIIA. The 15th-century
      Methley glass is described by J. Fowler, 'On the painted glass at Methley, part II',
      Yorkshire Archaeological and Topographical Journal 2 (1873), pp. 226-45, esp. pp.

Oxford, as we have seen, and in mid-fourteenth-century glass in the church at Kempsey, Worcestershire. Indeed, this Durham type appears to have influenced what is thought to be the latest sculptural representation of St Oswald that is known from pre-Reformation England, that in Henry VII's Chapel, Westminster Abbey. This portrays a king crowned, with a sceptre in his right hand, but also holding his own crowned head in his left as his identifying attribute.[21] This oddly illogical iconography seems best understood as a portrayal of King Oswald, influenced by the tradition of showing Oswald's head held by St Cuthbert.

We must bear in mind that, even at Durham, the number of portrayals of Oswald on his own in stained-glass windows far outnumbered those where Cuthbert appeared holding Oswald's head.[22] In other words, Oswald continued to be portrayed as a saint-king in his own right. Generally, as we have seen, these portrayals keep to standard types for royal saints or to incidents told by Bede, although the lost glass from Durham Cathedral apparently included scenes of Oswald 'blowing his horne', and of St Cuthbert (sic) appearing to St Oswald.[23] Equally intriguing is a late thirteenth-century stained-glass window from York Minster, which has happily survived. Here Oswald, who is identified by a partially legible inscription, appears as a crowned king, with a bird on his wrist which he is apparently feeding (Pl. 15).[24] It is worth considering this representation carefully since, as we shall see, a raven becomes the distinctive attribute of St Oswald in continental portrayals in the late middle ages, although the York window is too early for iconographic influence from Germany to be plausible. Is Oswald's bird a raven, or in any way related to the continental portrayals? Taken in isolation the bird could be interpreted as a raven, since

226-8; the Cuthbert figure (with three others) has not survived the moving of this glass from the chancel to the Waterton Chapel east window. The Edenhall glass has also been lost: Bailey p. 195 and Fig. 7.

[21] J. T. Micklethwaite, 'Notes on the imagery of Henry the Seventh's Chapel, Westminster', *Archaeologia* 47 (1883), pp. 361-80, at p. 374.

[22] The ratio is *c.* 12 to 5: see *Rites of Durham*, ed. Fowler, pp. 47-9, 109-19.

[23] Ibid., p. 118, and for the horn as a Durham relic, p. 291; cf. Haselock and O'Connor, as n. 16 above.

[24] The window is in the vestibule leading to the chapter house, just off the north transept: CH n.IX (on *Corpus Vitrearum* numbering); or 50, on York Minster's own numbering scheme: J. Toy, *A Guide and Index to the Windows of York Minster* (York 1985), p. 45; Gibson, op. cit., p. 35. Note the arms at the bottom of the right light, beneath Oswald and an unidentified king: Gules, a cross flory, Or. While doubtless those of the Latimer family (Toy, loc. cit.), they are also one of the arms attributed to St Oswald (F. C. Husenbeth, *Emblems of Saints*, ed. A. Jessopp (3rd edn, Norwich 1882), appendix II, p. 30; Baker, 'Zug', p. 114 n. 3) – though seemingly not in York Minster (Y. E. Weir, *A Guide to the Heraldry in York Minster* (York 1986), pp. 16-17).

it resembles the undoubted crow or raven (*corvus*) which figures in a story represented in the later Cuthbert window in the minster's south choir transept, and the blue-grey colouring of the bird is similar.[25] It is, however, risky trying to identify medieval depictions of birds purely on the basis of their appearance, as medieval artists frequently do not provide realistic portrayals; and in any case, the bird in question makes a more convincing bird of prey. The latter interpretation is strengthened by the context of Oswald's bird in York Minster, since an unidentified king immediately beneath Oswald holds a virtually identical bird. In addition to this, the adjacent window of the same date includes a clear instance of a queen holding a pale bird, which is certainly not a raven, and a possible example of a king holding a falcon.[26] The most plausible interpretation, therefore, is that the York window shows Oswald and the unidentified king holding birds of prey, and that, as in the adjacent window, these are used rather randomly, not as specific identifying attributes.[27] Elsewhere in York Minster glass, Oswald appears simply as a king, without any distinctive attribute.[28] There is, then, no convincing evidence that the raven iconography for St Oswald was known in England in the middle ages,[29] although more detailed research than we were able to undertake is needed before this can be regarded as certain. It may well be that when the Winn family of Nostell Priory in the early nineteenth century imported a miniature panel from Switzerland depicting Oswald with covered cup, on which perched a raven with ring, they were introducing this motif to England for the first time.[30]

How had this iconography originated on the continent? We have already seen how the covered cup became an attribute of St Oswald there, having

25 On *Corpus Vitrearum* numbering, s.VII; Gibson, op. cit. no. 15 and p. 27, dating the window to *c*.1440. The scene is no. 57 in Toy, *Guide*, p. 23; cf. *VCP* ch. 20.

26 CH n.VIII (or no. 51), bottom left-hand and right-hand corners. Toy, *Guide*, p. 45; discussed by D. O'Connor in *Age of Chivalry*, ed. J. Alexander and P. Binski (London 1987), p. 198, who compares the design on the Chertsey tiles, where a queen holds a squirrel (ibid. no. 367, p. 360).

27 We are very grateful to David O'Connor for his help both with this point, and with confirming the identification of Oswald in this window.

28 North choir clerestory window N.X (Gibson, op. cit. C18), dated 1410-20; and probably in the great east window, bottom row (dated 1405-8).

29 The east window at Greystoke, Cumberland, is too jumbled to bear the Oswald and raven interpretation suggested by P. Nelson, *Ancient Painted Glass in England* (London 1913), p. 67, and in any case the bird is white, and therefore presumably a dove. We are grateful to the rector, Richard Frank, for his help with this. As for the Oswald, raven and ring which appear in a stained-glass window in the north aisle of St Michael-le-Belfrey, York, this is a 1960s creation by Peter Gibson, working at the behest of Dean Milner-White: information from Mr Gibson.

30 The panel is now in Wragby church, in the north chancel aisle, the second window from the east.

metamorphosed out of the dish which Oswald presented to the poor. The most interesting development, however, is the appearance of the raven, a feature which derives from the minstrel's tale about Oswald, as Annemiek Jansen explains below. In the iconographic sphere, the earliest possible examples of St Oswald with a raven come from Regensburg, which is probably also where the German poem on Oswald originated. Here, in the late thirteenth century, the Dollinger family placed a group of monumental sculptures inside a hall in their newly-built house to commemorate the legendary feat of one of their ancestors, who overthrew a pagan knight on behalf of his king.[31] On one side of the jousters was the German king, Henry the Fowler, mounted on horseback, with a cross in his right hand and a falcon on his gloved left hand; on the other side stood King Oswald of Northumbria. The original statue of St Oswald still survives (Pl. 20), though comparison with a drawing made in 1812 suggests that some of its key features have since been lost (cf. Pl. 21). The king appears crowned, holding a sceptre, the symbol of his royal authority, in his right hand, and in his left, a covered cup, symbolising his generosity to the poor (cf. Pl. 13). The chief innovation, however, is that the drawing shows a raven with a ring in its beak perched upon the covered cup. The raven and ring were certainly there in 1555 when Wiguläus Hundt described the statue; they seem to have disappeared in the 1840s. It is, then, not possible to verify that the raven and ring were part of the original sculpture,[32] but they may have been. The sceptre obviously was, and has also disappeared.

If we discount the raven and ring that were formerly attached to the Dollinger hall statue, then it becomes difficult to say when the raven first became associated with St Oswald in continental iconography. There is a late thirteenth-century statue of a king with a bird on his arm, which used to stand on the gate-tower of the old bridge at Regensburg. But the king is wearing a glove, and the bird does not look very raven-like, so we should probably interpret it as a king holding a bird of prey, as with the York Minster portrayals.[33] Perhaps, however, the existence of such models facilitated the transition to representations of St Oswald with a raven. A second, fourteenth-century statue of a crowned king with bird on his left hand, sceptre in his right, has hitherto generally been accepted as Oswald with his raven (below, Pl. 16).[34] This may well be correct, as the sceptre in

---

[31] On this and what follows see K. H. Göller and H. W. Wurster, *Das Regensburger Dollingerlied* (Regensburg 1980), esp. ch. 2 and pp. 23-5. K. H. Göller and J. Ritzke-Rutherford, 'St Oswald in Regensburg: a reconsideration', in *Bavarica Anglica*, vol. I: *A Cross-Cultural Miscellany Presented to Tom Fletcher* (Frankfurt am Main 1979), pp. 98-118. Cf. Clemoes, p. 12.

[32] Vizkelety, *Beiträge* 86, pp. 140-1, suggests that the raven was a later addition.

[33] Illustrated by Clemoes, p. 4; cf. Curschmann, *MODSE*, p. 189.

[34] Vizkelety, *Beiträge* 86, p. 134, no. 26, where a date of *c*.1370 is given. Clemoes

the right hand might suggest that we have here a formal attribute, rather than just a king holding a bird. It has to be admitted, however, that we do not know how securely the king may be identified as Oswald, as opposed, say, to Henry the Fowler. In fact it is only near the end of the fourteenth century that we encounter an unquestionable portrayal of Oswald with a raven: in this instance, a wood carving of the king, now in the museum at Graz, which portrays the raven sitting on King Oswald's orb.[35] This is patently no posture for a hawk, whereas it recurs in a subsequent portrayal of St Oswald, this time with the added feature of the raven holding a ring in its beak, a feature which obviously derives from the Oswald legend (below, Pl. 22).[36]

To sum up, then. In southern Germany or the Alpine areas, in the late thirteenth or the fourteenth century, the raven which had for some time been Oswald's companion in the vernacular literature first made its appearance in the iconography of the saint. Initially, this may have been in secular contexts; but by the early fifteenth century, the raven had begun to appear in ecclesiastical contexts also, and, as Jansen explains below, the church found a new role for the raven (Pl. 23). During the fifteenth century and beyond, the raven, with or without a ring in its beak, became a widespread attribute of St Oswald right through southern Germany and the Alpine countries, and down into northern Italy.[37] Eventually, in the nineteenth and twentieth centuries, the raven as an attribute of St Oswald made its appearance in northern England, where it was integrated into the indigenous tradition. Since this book took its origin in a conference sponsored by St Oswald's Durham, it is appropriate to end by recalling that one of the windows in the north aisle of this church, dating from c.1910, depicts St Cuthbert holding Oswald's head in the left light, and in the right-hand light, King Oswald clad in armour, with the raven on his wrist.

---

dates it to the early 14th century: p. 14, pl. 5.

[35] Vizkelety, *Beiträge* 86, p. 134, no. 28.

[36] Ibid. p. 135, no. 38. Cf. Jansen, below.

[37] See Vizkelety, *Beiträge* 86, pp. 135-40, for examples; Clemoes; and Baker, 'The cult in northern Italy'.

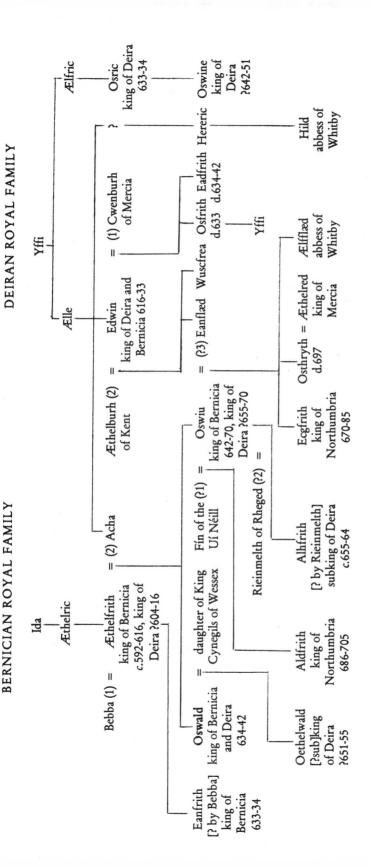

Figure 1: The Bernician and Deiran Royal Families in the Seventh Century

Note: Siblings are not necessarily shown in order of birth. Both the nature and the timing of Oswiu's relationship to Fín are uncertain: Bede regarded Aldfrith as illegitimate.

Figure 2: Oswald's World

Explanatory Note: The Peoples of Britain

In the seventh and eighth centuries, the period relevant to the first four papers in this book, the political divisions within Britain were rather different from the Scotland, England and Wales of later centuries. The island of Britain was then divided between four major peoples: Britons, English, Picts, and Irish (*Brettones*, *Angli* and *Saxones*, *Picti*, *Scotti*, and variants).

The Britons or British – the words are used interchangeably in the following papers – had formerly occupied the whole area south of the Forth/Clyde isthmus for many centuries, and seen the Romans come and go. They spoke a Celtic language, of the Brythonic or P-Celtic branch: modern Welsh is a linear descendant. From the fourth century they had been under attack by the other peoples, of whom the English proved the most devastating. These attacks, which continued during Oswald's lifetime, were restricting their areas of political independence to kingdoms in western Britain, e.g. Strathclyde, Rheged, Powys and Gwynedd, although Elmet survived east of the Pennines up till the reign of Oswald's predecessor, and the Gododdin were probably conquered by Oswald himself.

The English, or Anglo-Saxons, were Germanic incomers who were colonising what is now eastern England from the fifth century, at the expense of the Britons. The Angles and the Saxons spoke closely related dialects of a Germanic language, Old English, of which modern English is the linear descendant. They established several originally independent kingdoms within Britain, and the general trend was for the more successful of these kingdoms to conquer and absorb the less successful ones, as well as British kingdoms. This process can be illustrated from Oswald's lifetime by the attempt to unite the formerly independent kingdoms of Bernicia and Deira into a single kingdom of Northumbria. The latter is not named on the map, because in Oswald's own lifetime people would still have thought in terms of a king of Bernicia and of Deira, rather than of a single Northumbrian kingdom. The term is nevertheless used in the following essays in early seventh-century contexts, both as a convenient short-hand, and because Northumbria can justifiably be regarded as having been in the process of formation at that period. The map makes no pretence at naming all the small Anglo-Saxon kingdoms in existence in Oswald's day, but only those relevant to the papers which follow: Bernicia, Deira, Lindsey, Mercia, East Anglia, Essex, Kent, Sussex, Wessex, and the Hwicce.

The area north and west of the Forth/Clyde line was occupied by the Picts and the Irish. The Picts were the longer established, and had been pushed back from the south-west of this area by the Irish; their main power base lay in eastern Scotland. Little is known of their language, but it appears to have had at least a Brythonic Celtic component, and it may well have been

Brythonic. Meanwhile the Irish from mainland Ireland had been colonising Argyll, in western Scotland, perhaps from the fifth century. In Oswald's lifetime this area, together with the north-east tip of Ireland, formed the single kingdom of Dál Riada. It was ruled by one king at least up to 637, and probably beyond; and those of its inhabitants who lived in Argyll were not distinguished from those living in mainland Ireland by contemporary writers such as Adomnán and Bede: they were all termed *Scot(t)i*, Irishmen. Thus Iona, in Argyll, should be classed as an Irish monastery at this period. Ireland itself was then divided between a very considerable number of small kingdoms, grouped successively under overkings in pyramid fashion. A king of the powerful Uí Néill dynasty was – or sought recognition as – the ultimate overlord of much of the northern half of Ireland, although the provincial king of the Ulaid retained his independence over a reduced province in north-east Ireland. The Irish were another Celtic-speaking people, but belonged to the Goedelic or Q-Celtic branch: Scots Gaelic and modern Irish are both descendants of the Old Irish language spoken at this period.

Although both the Britons and the Irish spoke languages of the Celtic family, these were so different in the early middle ages that these two peoples had no conception of them both being 'Celtic' languages, or of themselves as 'Celts'. Thus they did not regard themselves as being more closely related to each other than to the Anglo-Saxons.

The Making of Oswald's Northumbria

ROSEMARY CRAMP

I

To characterise the 'culture' of Oswald's life and reign – the art, the styles of architecture, the whole appearance of his environment – is an impossible task in our present state of knowledge. This is not only because we have so little evidence, but also because we cannot place in time the evidence from Northumbria which we do have as belonging precisely to the period of Oswald's life-span (c.605-642), or even to the half century 600-650. The historical evidence for the events of Oswald's life is no less limited, almost entirely dependent as it is on the writings of Bede.[1] Nevertheless, I feel that it is possible to sketch in an interim account of some aspects of the Northumbrian cultural environment which had developed by the beginning of the seventh century, and I will try to demonstrate how the special circumstances and the contacts of Oswald's life may have brought about new developments.

II

To understand the circumstances of Oswald's reign one must look briefly at the formation of the kingdom of Northumbria, and at the preoccupations and achievements of the two kings who preceded him there, his father, Æthelfrith, and his uncle, Edwin. Northumbria was initially formed from two separate groupings of people, the Bernicians in the north and the Deirans in the south. Each of these groups formed a kingdom of its own (Fig. 3).[2] Oswald was descended from the Bernician rulers of Northumbria, Æthelfrith being the last pagan king of that line, a line which, according to the *Moore Memoranda*, started with Ida (c.547-59); there are six other names before that of Æthelfrith, who took over the kingdom c.592 and held it until his death in 616.[3] It may be remembered, though, that late British traditions record that the first settlers of Northumbria were linked to the Kentish settlement,[4] and

---

[1] See in particular *HE* III, 1-3, 6-7, 9, and specific references below.

[2] See Stancliffe, below, pp. 36, 43-6.

[3] The difficulties of establishing the chronologies for the reigns of the northern kings are well known and often discussed. For a recent discussion, see D. P. Kirby, *The Earliest English Kings* (London 1991), pp. 67, 83, fig. 7, p. 226; cf. B. Yorke, *Kings and Kingdoms of Early Anglo-Saxon England* (London 1990), p. 72. For the Bernician and Deiran genealogies, see Fig. 1, above, p. 13; and D. N. Dumville, 'The Anglian collection of royal genealogies and regnal lists', *ASE* 5 (1976), pp. 23-50.

[4] *Nennius's History of the Britons*, chs. 38, 56; ed. A. Wade-Evans (London 1938), pp. 60-1, 74-5.

it appears from archaeological evidence that there were probably Anglo-Saxon settlers in the northern regions before this royal family took over.[5]

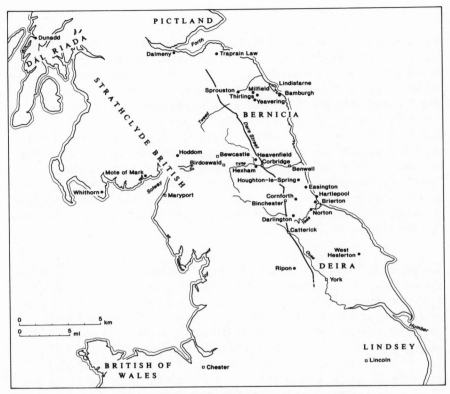

Figure 3: The Making of Oswald's Northumbria

The first half of the sixth century was the period when the British strove amongst themselves to establish their own rulers in territories carved out in the second half of the fifth century in the aftermath of the collapse of the Roman system. It was the time of their major successes in confining the Germanic mercenaries and their relations to the eastern parts of Britain, and also when the Picts were pushed back from southern Scotland and the power of the newly established Dalriadan Irish rulers was extended into what is now Argyllshire in western Scotland (Figs 2-3).[6] The second half of the sixth

5   B. N. Eagles, *The Anglo-Saxon Settlement of Humberside*, I (BAR, Br. ser. 68(i); Oxford 1981), pp. 66-73.
6   L. Alcock, *The Neighbours of the Picts: Angles, Britons and Scots at War and at Home* (Groam House Museum Trust 1993), ch. 1.

century was characterised by the wars waged against the newly settled Anglo-Saxons by the peoples already established in Britain. These were truly a fight to the death. The British, Irish, Pictish, and Anglo-Saxon tribes in the north were all simultaneously concerned with developing their own identities and trying to establish frontiers, and it is noteworthy that in this period some tribes of Britons and of Anglo-Saxons assisted each other in these aims, against their own ethnic groups.

The two constituent kingdoms that were to form Northumbria, Deira and Bernicia, have Celtic names,[7] and it is usually assumed that they were native foundations, later taken over by the Anglo-Saxons. We can, though, only define their extent by looking at the distribution of evidence, notably place-names and burials, which is characteristic of Anglo-Saxon settlement – and even then the boundaries of the two kingdoms remained fluid throughout the sixth and seventh centuries, the border between them being the debateable land of County Durham (see further below).

In the first half of the sixth century the native British rulers seemed able to contain their English enemies in Bernicia in the prime farming areas of the coastal plain and the Tyne valley, but Æthelfrith put an end to that: 'He ravaged the Britons more extensively than any other English leader and overran more of their territory than any other English king or chief, exterminating or enslaving their people, extorting tribute and annexing their lands for the English'.[8] These successes aroused Áedán, the king of the Dalriadan Irish, who seems to have expanded into the territory of central lowland Scotland while the north British rulers had been concentrating on containing the English invaders in the east; he thus came into direct conflict with Æthelfrith on the latter's northern border. In 603, the eleventh year of Æthelfrith's reign, Áedán attacked him but suffered a terrible defeat at a place called *Degsastan.* Bede noted that 'from that time no Irish king in Britain has dared to make war on the English to this day'.[9] Perhaps after the defeat Æthelfrith made peace and treaties with the Dalriadan Irish,[10] because in the second half of his reign he seems to have concentrated his efforts to the south and west of his kingdom, ravaging as far down as Chester (Fig. 3), where, before a battle, he is credited with slaying 1200 monks who were

[7] K. Jackson, *Language and History in Early Britain* (Edinburgh 1953) pp. 419-21, 701-5.

[8] *HE* I, 34.

[9] *HE* I, 34. A new interpretation of the site of the battle as Addinston in Lauderdale has been proposed in a wide ranging study: I. M. Smith, 'The Archaeological Background to the Emergent Kingdoms of the Tweed Basin in the Early Historic Period' (unpublished Ph.D. thesis, University of Durham, 1990), pp. 310-34.

[10] *HE* I, 34. It is interesting to note that only thirteen years later the sons of Æthelfrith fled for protection from the rival Anglo-Saxon dynasty to those same Dalriadan Irish.

supporting the British by their prayers.[11] If to Bede he was a conqueror worthy of comparison with Saul, to the Britons he was known as *Flesaur* ('the Twister'). They recorded many of his exploits, including the fact that he reigned twelve years in Bernicia and twelve in Deira.[12] He seems to have married twice: first Bebba; and then Oswald's mother Acha, the daughter of King Ælle of Deira, thus cementing his and his children's claim to that part of Northumbria (see family tree, Fig. 1). During his reign over Deira, Edwin, Acha's brother and the Deiran heir, was a fugitive wandering throughout many of the kingdoms of Britain; but eventually he found an ally in Rædwald, king of the East Angles, and with his help defeated and killed Æthelfrith on the southern borders of Northumbria in 616. Now it was the turn of the sons of Æthelfrith (including Oswald) to flee for their lives and they, together with a considerable retinue, went into exile amongst the Dalriadan Irish and the Picts.

In the reign of Edwin (c.616-33), Northumbria was significantly transformed. He already had contacts in the south and he cemented them by marrying (as his second wife) the sister of the king of Kent, Æthelburh. Kent was the most sophisticated and continentally orientated of all the English kingdoms, and the only one with a Christian king; indeed, one of the terms of the marriage was that Edwin should himself become a Christian.[13] He had already encountered Christianity, possibly in the British west as well as during his exile in East Anglia, although it had not been deeply accepted by his host there.[14] The acceptance of Christianity by the barbarian kings of Europe at this time was very much bound up with the establishment of larger units of territory and power and the validation of their right to rule in the eyes of a wider group, through their attachment to late Roman traditions. It was perhaps this appeal of Roman tradition as much as the Christian marriage and the efforts of the queen's chaplain, Bishop Paulinus, which eventually converted Edwin and many of his people also. Edwin had to think long and hard about the acceptance of the new faith; the centre of his power was Deira, where the Anglo-Saxons had been settled since the fifth century and had well established traditions of their own, as well as pagan shrines and sacred places. Like other expatriates, some of the Anglo-Saxons seem to have intensified their homeland traditions as they became established in their new territories, and this intensification may have extended to their pagan religious beliefs and practices.[15]

11   *HE* II, 2.
12   Nennius, *History*, chs. 57, 63; ed. Wade-Evans, pp. 76, 81.
13   *HE* II, 9.
14   *HE* II, 12 and 15; Stancliffe, below, p. 38.
15   This can be seen in the more ostentatious use of barrow burials in the late sixth and seventh centuries. See J. Shepard, 'The social identity of the individual in isolated barrows and barrow cemeteries in Anglo-Saxon England', in *Space,*

Edwin maintained a firm and peaceful government within Northumbria but pursued Æthelfrith's policy of securing control over the west, particularly over the western seaways. Bede tells us that he brought the islands of Anglesey and Man under his control as well as much British territory,[16] and this was a direct threat to the Britons of Wales, whose capability to form a pan-Celtic block from Scotland to Wales had already been maimed by Æthelfrith (Fig. 2). In the end it was a coalition of Cadwallon of Gwynedd and Penda of the royal house of Mercia which overthrew Edwin.[17] There may have been personal as well as political animosity here (though Penda was politically expansionist as well as a pagan); for Edwin had once married into the Mercian royal family, and (according to Welsh traditions) had been sheltered at the court of Cadwallon's father, Cadfan, during his time of exile, yet now was seizing territory in that region.[18] Both of these contacts could have provided a personal edge to the conflict.

The peace and prosperity of Edwin's reign was rudely shattered by his death. For a year Cadwallon took a terrible revenge for the humiliations and defeats of his people by the English, and in the words of Bede 'raged through their land meaning to wipe out the whole nation from the land of Britain, nor did he pay any respect to the Christian religion which had sprung up amongst them'.[19] On Edwin's death the two constituent kingdoms of Northumbria again fell apart: Deira was ruled by Edwin's cousin, Osric, and Bernicia by the eldest of Æthelfrith's sons Eanfrith who, together with his brother Oswald and others, had returned from exile as soon as they knew their enemy Edwin was dead. Meanwhile, Edwin's children by his second marriage were whisked off to Kent and to the continent by their mother, out of reach of the new regnal line.[20] According to Bede, both of the new kings reverted to paganism, and both were killed by Cadwallon: Osric in battle, and Eanfrith by treachery.[21] The continuation of the blood feud, and indeed the preservation of English power in the north, now fell to Eanfrith's brother, Oswald. As is well known, he triumphed and destroyed Cadwallon

---

Hierarchy and Society: Interdisciplinary Studies in Social Area Analysis, ed. B. C. Burnham and J. Kingsbury (BAR, Int. ser. 59; Oxford 1979), pp. 47-59. See also M. Carver, 'Kingship and material culture in early Anglo-Saxon East Anglia', in *Origins*, pp. 141-58.

[16] *HE* II, 9.

[17] *HE* II, 20; cf. Stancliffe, below, p. 47.

[18] *HE* II, 14. For a discussion of Edwin's Mercian connections, see Plummer, II, 103, and for his possible Gwynedd connections, see Stancliffe, below, p. 38.

[19] *HE* II, 20.

[20] *HE* III, 1; II, 20.

[21] *HE* III, 1; see Kirby, *Earliest English Kings*, p. 87.

and his army at Heavenfield (Fig. 2), and in so doing put an end to the attempts of the Britons to drive out the English from the north.

Oswald accomplished a great deal in his short reign of eight years (634-42). He could lay claim to Deira through his mother, and this helped his efforts to reunite the Northumbrian kingdoms. He was recognised as an overking by some of the other English tribes, as Edwin had been: his power extended as far south as Wessex, and indeed he married into the West Saxon royal house.[22] Such royal marriages, as we have seen in the cases of the earlier kings, always had a reason. Edwin had turned his attention to the expansionist activities of Mercia on the east. Oswald, having defeated the British of Wales, now needed to prevent their ever joining with Mercia again, and to protect his southern flank he backed the southern enemy of Mercia, Wessex. The question of who was ruling in the west midlands in Oswald's reign is still contested. It has long been recognised that the names of the rulers of the west midland kingdom of the Hwicce are identical with those of the Bernician royal house, although recently the Northumbrian connection has been somewhat played down.[23] Charles-Edwards has noted that the English kings did not follow the pattern of territorial expansion combined with segmentation of dynasties as the Irish did.[24] But Oswald had been an 'Irish' prince during the formative years of his exile in Dál Riada (from about the ages of eleven to twenty-eight), and he may well have adopted this practice in his overlordship of the western provinces, which could provide him with a western passage from his northern kingdom to Wessex.[25] It has been said that the overthrow of British power in 577 at the battle of *Deorham* (generally identified with Dyrham in Gloucestershire), when the British kings of Bath, Cirencester, and Gloucester, were defeated, 'had little effect further north and west'.[26] I would suggest that it did, and that Oswald's grand design was to be overlord of a territorial bloc which ran from southern Scotland to the English Channel (Fig. 2). He apparently was in a strong position vis-à-vis his northern neighbours,[27] had broken the military power of the British in Wales, married into the West Saxon dynasty, and thus only needed to establish client British states with English rulers in the west midlands in order to complete his security. No wonder that it was probably in the latter area that he was killed, at Oswestry (Fig. 2),[28] by a coalition of

22 See Stancliffe, below, pp. 44-5, 52-3.
23 S. Bassett, 'In search of the origins of Anglo-Saxon kingdoms', in *Origins*, pp. 3-27, at p. 6, p. 238, note 19.
24 T. Charles-Edwards, 'Early medieval kingships in the British Isles', in *Origins*, pp. 28-39, at pp. 36-8.
25 Cf. Stancliffe, below, pp. 55-6.
26 K. Pretty, 'Defining the Magonsæte', in *Origins*, pp. 171-83, at p. 175.
27 Cf. Stancliffe, below, pp. 48-9, 58-60.
28 Traditionally the site of the battle of *Maserfelth*, in which Oswald met his death,

enemies west and east of that central bloc; both would have had much to lose if his work had been consolidated.

III

In attempting to understand the age of Oswald, the importance of contacts through wars, diplomatic marriages, and exile, as well as the fragile state of the Christian religion in its various centres, needs to be continually borne in mind. I will now speculate a little about the world in which Oswald lived and which formed him, concentrating mainly on material evidence. I will first look at the differences between the Anglo-Saxon Northumbrians and their Celtic neighbours, and then at what evidence for Christianity in Northumbria may be postulated for the *floruits* of Edwin and Oswald.

The main difference remarked by Bede between the British, Irish, Pictish, and English tribes in north Britain was that they spoke distinct languages. The Britons and English may have early reached some accommodation and it is possible that the British language was supplanted in the eastern part of the island not just as a consequence of political dominance but also because the Britons had been used to accommodating to alien languages for four hundred years, whilst at least some of the English were not so tolerant.[29] Since Oswald had to serve as an interpreter for Aidan, it is clear that the Irish needed linguistic help when undertaking the conversion of the English. Nevertheless, the many monks who came from Ireland in the next generation must have learnt Old English; likewise, the English who flocked for education in Ireland must have learnt Irish.[30] Of course, for the literate of the seventh century and later, Latin was a *lingua franca*. This obviously aided cultural fusion, as did the comparable social and economic structures of these peoples. The similarity of the social organisation of the native and invading peoples in Britain and Ireland has received much recent discussion; for present purposes, it is worth noting that, by Oswald's day, there seems to be no doubt that a tribal structure, based on leaders of warrior élites who enriched their followers with the loot and territorial gains of conquest and who ruled over mainly subsistence communities, was a common feature of all the ethnic groups. It remains difficult, however, to distinguish the material culture of these groups archaeologically; at present the Britons are the most

---

has been equated with Oswestry, a view supported still by P. Sims-Williams, *Religion and Literature in Western England, 600-800* (Cambridge 1990), p. 29. Doubts have, however, been cast on this identification by Margaret Gelling, for a critique of which see Stancliffe, below, pp. 84-96. To my mind this site, which marks a boundary, is a perfectly appropriate one for the battle if one accepts the political framework for Oswald's activities in the west and south of his kingdom as I have outlined it above.

[29] *HE* I, 1; *HE* III, 7.
[30] *HE* III, 3, 27.

invisible, largely because of the lack of the clothed burials which tell us a certain amount about the personal adornment, weapons, and armour of the Anglo-Saxons. In fact we currently lack sites which tell us much about the Britons, dead or alive.[31]

Besides the imbalance in the archaeological evidence as between British and Anglo-Saxons, there is also at present an imbalance in the archaeological evidence for the Anglo-Saxons in the two parts of the Northumbrian kingdom: burials furnished with grave-goods are much more common south of the Tees, though recent discoveries in County Durham, at Darlington, Norton, and Easington (Fig. 3), indicate that the contrast should not be too strongly drawn.[32] The scanty literary evidence that settlement occurred in Deira by the middle of the fifth century and in Bernicia by c.500 is supported by the wealth of early Deiran burials, both in York (the former centre of the Roman northern military command) and in eastern Yorkshire.[33] The distribution of burials in the latter area is concentrated quite markedly east of the important north-south Roman road known as Dere Street and in areas which controlled the eastern seaways (Fig. 3).

There is no doubt that there is a substantial difference between the big Deiran burial-grounds containing cremations, and the smaller groups buried in a variety of ways in Bernicia; the implications of this variation in mortuary practices are, however, much less certain. It has been too readily assumed that Bernicia was less Germanicised than Deira and that the population remained largely native British, ruled over by a small Anglo-Saxon élite, largely on the grounds of the sparseness of burials which conform to the type known from Deira and other Anglo-Saxon kingdoms. But other explanations are possible. For example, Pretty has interpreted a comparable situation in the west midlands as implying that the strength of British Christianity in those areas was such that the incoming Saxons were quickly converted;[34] yet, if the Bernician evidence is to be interpreted in this way, Christian British centres still remain to be identified archaeologically. Alternatively, it may be that the Anglo-Saxons arrived in Bernicia only after they had already been converted elsewhere; yet burials which are like other sixth-century pagan burials have been found there, for instance, at Corbridge, or Milfield (Fig. 3).[35] The above explanations presume, moreover, that burial

---

31 For one view of this problem, see N. Higham, *The Kingdom of Northumbria AD 350-1100* (Stroud 1993), pp. 72-5.

32 For Norton, see S. J. Sherlock and M. G. Welch, *An Anglo-Saxon Cemetery at Norton, Cleveland* (CBA Research Report, British ser. 82; London 1992); for Easington, J. Pickin, 'An Anglo-Saxon cemetery at Easington, Co. Durham', *Archaeology North* 2, p. 16.

33 Higham, *Northumbria*, fig. on p. 69.

34 Pretty, 'Magonsæte', p. 175.

35 For Corbridge, see R. J. Cramp, 'Anglo-Saxon settlement', in *Settlement in North*

customs and religion are invariably connected, which is not necessarily so. Native Germanic religious practices seem to have been based on specific locations, such as groves or lakes, and when migrating overseas the incomers would have had to find new and probably similar sites in which to locate their cults. It is possible that the Bernicians used the old cult sites of the native Britons. It is also possible that some modified their burial practices to conform with indigenous customs whilst others maintained their continental practices. Hope-Taylor's perceptive analysis of the difficulty of transporting a type of religion based on sacred places is applicable to all areas of Anglo-Saxon England, though, and not just to Bernicia.[36] It may be that Bernicia was in fact more sparsely settled than Deira (perhaps because its land could only support a smaller population); but the most plausible explanation of the archaeological evidence may be rather that social customs were modified more quickly than belief, especially in those areas occupied by a number of different races. In this context, the lack of a high-status burial from Northumbria is also noteworthy; this may be because leaders changed their social customs more readily than their followers. Certainly the recent excavation of the royal burial ground at Sutton Hoo in Suffolk, which contained the burial of a clothed boy with his horse, several cremations, boat burial, coffin burial, possible human sacrifices, and rich deposits with silver marked with Christian emblems, shows how fluid high-status burial practice was in the first generations of Anglo-Saxon settlement.[37] Æthelfrith's burial would no doubt have been as rich as some of the Sutton Hoo graves.

Many of the early Anglo-Saxon cemeteries in Northumbria are associated with prehistoric ritual sites. The most recently examined one in Deira, excavated under modern scientific conditions, is at West Heslerton (Fig. 3), where there are both cremations and inhumations; the earliest inhumations are perhaps a cluster of burials containing weapons and laid out in rows within a hengiform enclosure.[38] These may be compared with the recently published late sixth-century burials within one of the henges at Milfield in Bernicia.[39] Another characteristic location for pagan burials is within the

---

Britain, 1000 BC-AD 1000. Papers presented to George Jobey, Newcastle upon Tyne, December 1982, ed. J. C. Chapman and H. C. Mytum (BAR, Br. ser. 118; Oxford 1983), pp. 263-97, at p. 268; for Milfield, see C. J. Scull and A. F. Harding, 'Two early medieval cemeteries at Milfield, Northumberland', *Durham Archaeological Journal* 6 (1990), pp. 1-30.

36   B. Hope-Taylor, *Yeavering, An Anglo-British Centre of Early Northumbria* (London 1977), pp. 248-67.

37   M. Carver, 'Kingship and material culture', pp. 150-1.

38   D. Powlesland, 'West Heslerton, 1989, the Anglian settlement: an interim report' (unpublished, but see summary in *Medieval Settlement Research Group, Annual Report* 5 (1990), p. 46).

39   Scull and Harding, 'Milfield'.

confines of Roman forts. Examples have been found at Benwell, Binchester, Birdoswald, Catterick, and Corbridge.[40] Did this custom originate amongst the British? We shall never be able to answer this question satisfactorily until we have excavated more Roman cemeteries and seen whether or not they continue into the post-Roman period, and, if so, in what form; besides, we have no means of knowing how far people were prepared to transport their dead to a preferred place of burial in ideal circumstances, and so to what extent the archaeological evidence is atypical within its area. Yet we may perhaps begin to identify a mixture of social custom: in Catterick, British people were buried clothed;[41] this may also be the implication of the nineteenth-century records of burials in slab-lined graves (the latter traditionally perceived as a Christian British practice) found as far south and east as County Durham, at Brierton (near Hartlepool), Houghton-le-Spring, and Cornforth, where two were accompanied by spears in the Anglo-Saxon manner (Fig. 3).[42] If Oswald had not become a Christian, would he have been buried with some such mixture of rites?

Another cultural indicator, especially among illiterate peoples, is forms of dress (tribal costume and its adornment). It was necessary to be able to recognise quickly anyone's social or ethnic group, and in times of stress or conflicts such differences are especially important. It is possible that the earliest Anglo-Saxon leaders of the fifth century, and the Britons also, continued to look like late fourth-century Roman soldiers, but by the sixth century many of the British leaders had probably taken up native costume and had begun to wear again the distinctive ring brooches which had never gone out of fashion amongst their Celtic kinsmen and allies. Hand pins and ring brooches have been found on Roman sites in the north, whereas the distinctive long brooches of the Angles are found in the Anglo-Saxon graves of the Yorkshire Wolds, as well as, for example, at Catterick (Pl. 1), Norton (Pl. 2), or Corbridge. It is possible also that the showy square-headed brooches of the Angles stimulated the development of more elaborate penannular brooches among the Celts. In the fortresses of the Britons, such as the Mote of Mark along the Solway, moulds for making such brooches have been found.[43] Metalworking debris there is dated sixth to early seventh century, and the interlace ornament is of the same type as in metalwork throughout Anglo-Saxon England, just as the peltas and spirals of Celtic art

---

[40] Cramp, 'Anglo-Saxon settlement', at pp. 267-8.
[41] A. N. Wilson, pers. comm.
[42] R. Cramp, Dalrymple Lectures for 1994 (forthcoming).
[43] N. Swindells and L. Laing, 'Metalworking at the Mote of Mark, Kirkcudbright, in the 6th-7th centuries AD', in *Aspects of Early Metallurgy*, ed. W. A. Oddy (London 1977), pp. 121-8; see also L. Laing, *A Catalogue of Celtic Ornamental Metalwork in the British Isles c.AD 400-1200* (Nottingham Monographs in Archaeology no. 5; BAR, Br. ser. 229; Oxford 1993), pp. 56-8.

were quickly absorbed into the repertoire of the Anglo-Saxon smith.[44] Perhaps also the taste for ring brooches with bird-head terminals, which are found in some Anglo-Saxon graves in Northumbria as well as on moulds from the Dalriadan site of Dunadd, represent an accommodation of Celtic and Germanic taste (Pl. 3).[45] A good deal of new work on the metalwork from the fortresses of the Dalriadan Irish as well as of the Britons is in course of publication, and because the working debris has been dated scientifically these results will be very valuable in demonstrating when and how styles were transmitted between the northern peoples.[46] What is needed in Northumbria is the comparable discovery and excavation of more Anglo-Saxon production sites.

The aspiration of Germanic leaders all over Scandinavia and Europe by the beginning of the seventh century was to emphasise their right to rule by looking like the east Romans (Byzantines) in their use of gold and garnet jewellery. This taste would surely have been shared by Northumbrian rulers such as Edwin and Oswald. The evidence is scanty, but the garnet pyramid discovered near Dalmeny in East Lothian (Pl. 4) is often compared with the pyramids which decorated the strap of the Sutton Hoo sword,[47] and the round garnet brooches of Kent seem to have become the fashion in the north, if the testimony of the Ripon brooch (Pl. 5) and the Franks Casket (Pl. 6) can be accepted. The warrior figures on this whalebone box carry swords which could be intended to represent sword hilts like the one found in Cumberland (Pl. 7). The warriors of the Franks Casket are still the most plausible model for how Oswald might have looked in battle (even though it is normally dated to c.700). On the other hand, when one considers that the formative years of his life were spent amongst the Irish of Dál Riada, one wonders what impact this might have had on his personal taste, and hence what difference it might have made to his personal appearance.

---

[44] For an example, see G. Speake, *A Saxon Bed Burial on Swallowcliffe Down* (Historic Buildings and Monuments Commission Archaeological Reports 10; London 1989).

[45] For a mould from Dunadd for a bird-headed penannular brooch and its Northumbrian analogues, see E. Campbell in *The Work of Angels*, ed. S. Youngs (London 1989), no. 181 (p. 191), and E. Campbell and A. Lane, 'Celtic and Germanic interaction in Dalriada: the 7th-century metalworking site at Dunadd', in *AMI*, pp. 52-63, at pp. 54-5. Among surviving brooches the one most closely related to these Dunadd moulds was also found in Dál Riada (at Clogh, Co. Antrim): see Pl. 3, and S. Youngs in *The Work of Angels*, no. 182 (p. 192).

[46] Campbell and Lane, 'Metalworking site at Dunadd', pp. 58-60.

[47] R. L. S. Bruce-Mitford, 'Six interesting pieces of cloisonné jewellery', in idem, *Aspects of Anglo-Saxon Archaeology* (London 1974), pp. 262-80, at p. 268, pls. 86e-f, 87.

Houses may also be a sign of status, aspiration, and sometimes also of tradition. The most eloquent argument for a Bernician architectural style which combined Romano-British and Germanic traditions was made by Hope-Taylor after his famous excavations in the mid 1950s of the royal site of Yeavering (Fig. 3).[48] This site was not published until 1977, and within two years some of his conclusions had been challenged in the light of new evidence which had accumulated since his dig. The validity of his chronology based on linking archaeological events in the ground with the scanty historical evidence which survives for this period (for example, that a burnt level represented the burning of the site by Penda, or that a new architectural style was the result of new contacts when Oswald returned from Dál Riada) was challenged by Miket;[49] and many archaeologists, myself included, would consider that this is an unsafe chronological method. The assumption that the earliest building phase of the site is British rather than Anglo-Saxon was also challenged by Miket on grounds which have been reinforced in a recent article by Scull.[50] To quote Miket's conclusion: 'Before Yeavering became a royal centre it consisted of a settlement of rectangular timber buildings. That they stemmed from good Anglo-Saxon traditions cannot be denied on chronological grounds, and it has yet to be convincingly demonstrated that rectangular forms were part of the north British repertoire.'[51] It is still uncertain when the British changed from round to rectangular buildings, but in the earliest phases at Whithorn (that is, earlier than the seventh century), the buildings are sub-rectangular, with rounded ends,[52] and on the whole the seventh century seems to be the point of change. On the other hand, rectangular buildings of closely similar type, ranging in date from the sixth to the eighth centuries, are now a commonplace Anglo-Saxon form on sites as far apart as Mucking in Essex, West Heslerton in Yorkshire, and Thirlings in Northumberland.[53] At West Heslerton these rectangular buildings exist

[48] Hope-Taylor, *Yeavering*.

[49] R. Miket, 'A restatement of evidence for Bernician Anglo-Saxon burials', in *Anglo-Saxon Cemeteries 1979*, ed. P. Rahtz, T. Dickinson, and L. Watts (BAR, Br. ser. 82; Oxford 1980), pp. 289-305.

[50] C. Scull, 'Post-Roman Phase I at Yeavering: a re-consideration', *Medieval Archaeology* 35 (1991), pp. 51-63.

[51] Miket, 'Restatement', p. 301.

[52] The post-excavation process at Whithorn is still continuing, but see P. H. Hill, *Whithorn 4: Excavations at Whithorn Priory 1990-91* (Whithorn 1992).

[53] For Mucking, see H. Hamerow, *Excavations at Mucking, II: The Anglo-Saxon Settlement* (Historic Buildings and Monuments Commission Archaeological Reports, 21; London 1993); for West Heslerton, see D. Powlesland, C. Haughton, and J. Hanson, 'Excavations at Heslerton, North Yorkshire, 1978-82', *Archaeological Journal* 143 (1986), pp. 53-173; for Thirlings, see C. O'Brien and R. Miket, 'The early medieval settlement of Thirlings, Northumberland', *Durham Archaeological Journal* 7 (1991), pp. 57-91.

alongside structures with a sunken area or cellar, and excavations have shown that such huts constitute an industrial area of the site. West Heslerton is a very large and 'managed' site with different zones of activities, although so far with no large building in the centre and no defensive enclosures. Similar groupings of buildings at sites revealed by air photography in Bernicia do have enclosures, such as at Milfield, or at Sprouston in the Tweed valley (Fig. 3).[54] These could well represent a process of Anglian colonisation of British lands, taking the form of estate centres containing major halls, with subsidiary huts and houses (perhaps for the retainers of the local lord) grouped around them. Buildings very similar to the Yeavering great halls have also been excavated in Hampshire at Cowdery's Down and others have been identified by air photography in the west midlands and up the east coast of Scotland.[55] Yet there are small differences between these sites, and in my view Hope-Taylor was correct in seeing some of the large hall types as deriving from the fusion of Romano-British and Anglo-Saxon characteristics. This view has been accepted by other archaeologists, although it is now apparent that the phenomenon is not confined to Bernicia. Nevertheless, there is a continuous tradition in the north of large timber halls, such as those discovered recently which had been built over the Roman granaries at Birdoswald (Fig. 3).[56] At Yeavering, the amphitheatre, together with the great scale of the fortified enclosure, set that site apart even today; so this region may indeed have possessed its own Roman-derived traditions of building. We are still a long way from being able to work out the architectural details of what really distinguish timber buildings from one another, for the distinctive features are not likely to have been their ground-plans so much as their superstructures; as Hope-Taylor pointed out, it was possibly the decorative details which distinguished regional or even ethnic styles.[57]

54 For the latest publication of this important crop-mark site see I. M. Smith, 'Sprouston, an early Anglian centre of the eastern Tweed basin', *Proceedings of the Society of Antiquaries of Scotland* 121 (1991), pp. 261-94.

55 S. James, A. Marshall, and M. J. Millett, 'An early medieval building tradition', *Archaeological Journal* 141 (1984), pp. 207-12.

56 T. Wilmot, 'Birdoswald', *Current Archaeology* 112 (1988), p. 158; idem, 'Birdoswald', *Current Archaeology* 116 (1989), pp. 288-91.

57 For a useful summary of the literary evidence for the form and decoration of Northumbrian timber buildings, see C. Karkov, 'The decoration of early wooden architecture in Ireland and Northumbria', in *Studies in Insular Art and Archaeology*, ed. C. Karkov and R. Farrell (American Early Medieval Studies 1; Oxford, Ohio 1991) pp. 27-48.

IV

Let us now turn to consider the material evidence for Christianity, or rather, its apparent absence. It is generally supposed that the British in the north were Christian from the Roman period onwards, and a few grave-stones, as well as long-cist cemeteries, testify to the presence of the faith,[58] but churches have proved extraordinarily difficult to find. Their walls are assumed to have been of wood or dry-stone, but only at Yeavering has an excavated structure been identified as a possible timber church, and this for the time of Oswald.[59] Let us consider the account of the scene in Bernicia before the battle of Heavenfield, as Bede tells it to us. Oswald decided to pray for help to God and '...when a cross had been hastily made and the hole dug in which it was to stand, he seized the cross himself in the ardour of his faith, placed it in the hole, and held it upright with both hands until the soldiers had heaped up the earth and fixed it in position'.[60] He then exhorted them to kneel and pray for God's defence. Learned Christians later might see this as a parallel to the activities of Constantine, the first Christian emperor,[61] but this gesture may have been to encourage his soldiers by erecting a wooden symbol which would remind them of the cult posts familiar to them from their pagan religion.[62] The settings for such posts have been remarked on several Anglo-Saxon sites, but especially at Yeavering, where their use as reference points was seen by Hope-Taylor as being of cultic significance.[63] We do not know, though, what such posts looked like. Bede also relates that members of the community at Hexham were later accustomed to celebrate the vigil of St Oswald's feast, first by the cross at Heavenfield, and then in a church which 'has lately been built there; ...and rightly so: for, as far as we know, no symbol of the Christian faith, no church, and no altar had been erected in the whole of Bernicia before that new leader of the host, inspired by his devotion to the faith, set up the standard (*vexillum*) of the holy cross when he was about to fight his most savage enemy.'[64] How did Bede reach that conclusion? We know that church building was begun in Deira in the reign of Edwin – even though his major stone church in York had to be finished by Oswald.[65] It has been suggested that Bede's statement was based on Hexham tradition.[66] It is possible, though, that Edwin had left no permanent

58 For references, see Stancliffe, below, pp. 76-7, notes 195-6.
59 Hope-Taylor, *Yeavering*, pp. 73-82, 278-9.
60 *HE* III, 2.
61 Cf. Wallace-Hadrill, *Comm*, pp. 88-9.
62 D. Maclean, pers. comm.
63 Hope-Taylor, *Yeavering*, p. 258.
64 *HE* III, 2.
65 *HE* II, 14.
66 Wallace-Hadrill, *loc. cit.*.

memorial in Bernicia, and neither the Dalriadan-Irish church of Lindisfarne nor the more continentally minded clerics such as Wilfrid or Bede were disposed to take into account the timber or dry-stone buildings of their British predecessors, which might in any case have vanished by their time. The late- and sub-Roman church in the north does seem to have left some traces datable to the fourth or fifth centuries at a variety of sites, whether Roman, like Maryport in Cumberland, or native, like the great hill fort of Traprain Law in Lothian (Fig. 3), both of which have produced objects with a Chi-Rho symbol, while at the latter there is a long building which has recently been identified as a possible church by Ian Smith.[67] Its appearance as he draws it up is somewhat bizarre, but it is not unlike the famous late Roman church excavated at Colchester in Essex,[68] and there are other smaller D-ended buildings in the north in the British area of Cumbria, which seem to be post-Roman.[69] It is, then, possible that Roman settlements in the north, such as Birdoswald or Bewcastle, continued for a time as Christian foci, as others elsewhere, such as Lincoln (Fig. 3), certainly did.[70] I do not yet know what to make of the building recently discovered at Hoddom in Dumfriesshire (Fig. 3), which has been claimed as a possible baptistery. It is almost square (6m by 5.4m), with low stone walls containing many reused Roman stones, supporting a timber superstructure; associated radio-carbon samples have provided a probable date of AD 525-625.[71]

It is possible that, under the Anglo-Saxon hegemony before Edwin, the borders of permitted public expressions of the Christian faith were quite firmly drawn. I pointed out long ago the real cultural divide on either side of Dere Street, the great Roman route from Yorkshire north to the Tweed (Fig. 3).[72] If the Christian faith had to go underground in the sixth century in areas under Anglo-Saxon control, the memory of earlier churches in areas which had been dominated by the pagan Anglo-Saxons could have been lost by Bede's day. Thus, when Edwin became Christian, he first built a church in wood at York, a former Roman town (possibly in the legionary fortress).

[67] C. Thomas, *Christianity in Roman Britain to AD 500* (London 1981), pp. 106-8, 102; cf. Smith, 'Archaeological Background' (as n. 9), pp. 104-15, fig. 5.5.

[68] W. J. Rodwell, 'Churches in a historic town', in *Historic Churches – a Wasting Asset*, ed. W. J. and K. Rodwell (CBA Research Report 19, London 1977), pp. 24-41.

[69] Smith, 'Archaeological Background', fig. 4.19.

[70] K. Steane and A. Vince, 'Post-Roman Lincoln: archaeological evidence for activity in Lincoln from the 5th to the 9th centuries' in *Pre-Viking Lindsey*, ed. A. Vince (Lincoln 1993), pp. 71-9.

[71] C. E. Lowe, 'New light on the Anglian "minster" at Hoddom', *Transactions of the Dumfriesshire and Galloway Natural History and Antiquarian Society*, 3rd series 66 (1991), pp. 11-35, at pp. 20-3, fig. 5.

[72] Cramp, 'Anglo-Saxon settlement', pp. 266-70.

There was, apparently, no tradition at York by his time of churches built by the Romans, despite the fact that York is known to have had a bishop in the late Roman period;[73] this situation contrasts with that at Canterbury at the end of the sixth century.[74]

The organisation of the Christian church in north Britain before Oswald's reign must have been as precarious and individualistic as that of the evolving secular kingdom. The individual missionary efforts of Paulinus, backed by James the Deacon, had been linked to royal centres and to the ruler's backing, but teaching was dependent on a peripatetic bishop who had to traverse a large area, perhaps in the same fashion as shadowy British precursors like Ninian or Kentigern. Aidan likewise used royal centres as he travelled around his huge diocese; but at the same time, the church was established in a more durable way. For Oswald's foundation of Lindisfarne as an episcopal and monastic centre with a colony of dependencies produced a more stable missionary network, which enabled native boys to be trained up as clerics, and Christianity to take root.

V

The swift development of Oswald's cult as a saint should not blind us to the fact that he was trained as, and lived as, a warleader of his people. There can be little doubt that many of his political achievements, though impressive, proved ephemeral. No other Northumbrian king extended his power so far from base as Oswald did, and the rising power of Mercia was soon to sever the links he had established with Wessex. Friendly relations with the Picts and the Dalriadan Irish were also soured in later reigns. In contrast to the rapidly changing political situation, from the point of view of its material culture the making of Oswald's Northumbria was a slow and by no means monolithic process about which all too little is yet known. The region was varied in its cultural mix and its development, but the contacts which Oswald fostered, particularly his turning to the Dalriadan Irish of Iona to re-establish Christianity in his kingdom, were to bear fruit in the next generations. This was perhaps the most important achievement of his life, for it is surely no exaggeration to say that, without the contacts established in Oswald's reign, the development of Insular art in the later seventh century would not have been possible. Ultimately, therefore, Oswald had a profound and lasting impact on the religious and cultural life of the northern English.

[73] J. M. C. Toynbee, 'Christianity in Roman Britain', *Journal of the British Archaeological Association*, 3rd series 16 (1953), pp. 1-24, at p. 4.
[74] *HE* I, 26 and 33, and notes. Cf. N. Brooks, *The Early History of the Church of Canterbury* (Leicester 1984), pp. 17-21.

Oswald, 'Most Holy and Most Victorious King of the Northumbrians'[1]

CLARE STANCLIFFE

I

Interpreting Bede's Portrayal of Oswald

Oswald's life was the stuff of which legends are woven. He was born the son of the great Bernician king, Æthelfrith, who had annexed the kingdom of Deira to his own and thus laid the foundations for Northumbria's greatness, and of Acha, sister of the dispossessed Deiran prince. He grew up at a time when his father was waging war on the native Britons; and later, his own victory against the British King Cadwallon of Gwynedd ended for ever hopes of a British return to rule over what is now north-east England. In 616, when he was about eleven, his fortunes suddenly changed: his father was killed by his mother's brother, the Deiran Edwin, and Oswald and his companions fled north-west to the kingdom of Dál Riada in western Scotland. He was to spend seventeen long years amongst the Irish people of Dál Riada. Here, he first encountered Christianity; and here, he grew expert in the craft of war, probably even fighting for his Irish hosts in battles on the Irish mainland. When Edwin was killed in 633, Oswald's elder brother Eanfrith attempted to return; but he in his turn was killed by Cadwallon and his Mercian ally. Then Oswald set out to avenge his brother's death and win back his father's kingdom. With a small army, entrusting his cause to the Christian God, he fought the battle of Heavenfield (634). Victory was his, and Cadwallon was slain. Oswald then ruled for eight years over his father's kingdom, establishing the church, wedding a princess from Wessex, and extending his power both south and north over other peoples. In 642 he was killed in battle at the hands of the Mercians and the British of Wales. But his name was to live far on into the future.

However briefly told, the story is a good one, and we can see why Tolkien thought that it would have gone well in Old English verse: Oswald has the makings of a hero of a well-wrought tale.[2] To our knowledge,

---

[1] 'Sanctissimus ac victoriosissimus rex Nordanhymbrorum': *HE* III, 7. I am very grateful to Dr T. M. Charles-Edwards for his helpful comments on a draft of this paper.

[2] J. R. R. Tolkien, 'Beowulf: the monsters and the critics', *Proceedings of the British Academy* 22 (1936), reprinted as a separate booklet (London 1958), at p. 34. Oswald's life fits with certain key themes of the widespread story pattern of the hero's 'expulsion and return': cf. T. Ó Cathasaigh, *The Heroic Biography of Cormac mac Airt* (Dublin 1977), pp. 2-9, esp. p. 9 (citing G. Murphy).

however, it was not till the twelfth century,[3] and then in distant Germany, that the poets got to work on the story of King Oswald; and the features they then highlighted were different from those that would have attracted an Anglo-Saxon bard. Instead, Oswald's story was told in Latin prose by an Anglo-Saxon historian, Bede, whose selection of material and portrayal of Oswald as a Christian king underlie all subsequent attempts to interpret Oswald and his reign. There are, indeed, some other sources available, particularly those stemming from the monastery of Iona in Dál Riada, which at this period was effectively an Irish monastery (Fig. 2, above, pp. 14, 16). Its ninth abbot, Adomnán, composed a *Life of St Columba* c.700, a generation before Bede wrote his *History*; and in it he included an account of the battle of Heavenfield, as well as reference to Oswald's exile and baptism amongst the Irish.[4] Iona was also making brief annalistic entries from an early period, many (or all) of which were later incorporated into the 'Chronicle of Ireland', and thence transmitted to us via *The Annals of Ulster* and the Clonmacnoise group of Irish annals, especially those of Tigernach.[5] On the British side, the later 'Welsh Annals' (*Annales Cambriae*) include for this period a small number of entries which probably originated as marginal notes entered on Easter tables somewhere in north Britain;[6] and the early ninth-century compilation known as the *Historia Brittonum* incorporates some further information which appears to derive from north British sources, although its reliability is open to question.[7] All this means that, even without

[3]   *Pace* F. Klaeber's speculation, 'King Oswald's death in Old English alliterative verse', *Philological Quarterly* 16 (1937), p. 214. For the German poem, see Jansen, below.

[4]   *VCol* I, 1, discussed below, pp. 50-2; J.-M. Picard, 'The purpose of Adomnán's *Vita Columbae*', *Peritia* 1 (1982), pp. 160-77 at pp. 166-9, 172-7; M. Herbert, *Iona, Kells and Derry* (Oxford 1988), chs. 1, 3 and 12.

[5]   J. Bannerman, *Studies in the History of Dalriada* (Edinburgh 1974), pp. 9-26; K. Hughes, *Early Christian Ireland: Introduction to the Sources* (London 1972), ch. 4, esp. pp. 99-107, 115-28, 142-8. For editions of the Irish annals, see below, notes 76 and 118. Neither the 'Chronicle of Ireland' nor the original Iona annal entries survive in their original state.

[6]   K. Hughes, *Celtic Britain in the Early Middle Ages* (Woodbridge 1980), chs. 5 and 6, esp. pp. 91-4; K. Jackson, 'On the Northern British section in Nennius', in *Celt and Saxon: Studies in the Early British Border* (Cambridge 1964), pp. 20-62, at pp. 48-9; D. N. Dumville, 'Sub-Roman Britain: history and legend', *History* 62 (1977), pp. 173-92 at p. 176. For the edition used, see below, n. 65.

[7]   The fundamental discussion remains Jackson, art. cit. His suggestions about the date and nature of the sources used by the *Historia Brittonum* have been criticised by D. N. Dumville, 'On the North British section of the *Historia Brittonum*', *Welsh History Review* 8 (1976-7), pp. 345-54; but Dumville's own article, while valuable in some respects, is open to criticism, and does not do justice to Jackson's full and circumspect discussion. For the edition used, see below, n. 61.

Bede, we would know the salient events of Oswald's life: his descent from
Æthelfrith, his exile, his victory over Cadwallon and subsequent
overkingship, the foundation of the monastery on Lindisfarne, and some
military engagements, including that in which he was killed. But there is
little else that one can say on the basis of these sources alone, and any
interpretation of Oswald must rest largely on what Bede tells us in his
Ecclesiastical History. For this reason it is important to begin by reminding
ourselves of the limitations and the probable areas of bias that affected Bede's
portrayal of Oswald.

Bede has generally enjoyed a good reputation as a historian, and rightly
so. We do, however, need to remember three important points when reading
his account. First, he was selective in what he chose to say: he wrote with a
didactic purpose, and he presented Oswald as one of the great heroes of his
Ecclesiastical History, a king who was simultaneously 'most holy' and 'most
victorious'.[8] He will, then, have been careful in what he chose to say about
Oswald; and, equally so, in what he chose not to say.

Secondly, Bede was writing a century after the reign of Oswald. This
raises the obvious question of how well informed Bede was, and by what
channels information about Oswald was transmitted to him.[9] Besides the
recognised role of the monasteries of Hexham (in Bernicia) and Bardney (in
Lindsey),[10] the royal centre of Bamburgh is a possibility. Oswiu had St
Oswald's incorrupt arm enshrined here in the church of St Peter, and, as the
dynastic capital, Bamburgh might have been of considerable importance in
handing on information about Oswald as king. Its traditions might have been
transmitted to Bede via the nearby church of Lindisfarne, or possibly via
Hexham.[11] All this means that much of Bede's information on Oswald will
have come from ecclesiastical cult sites with an interest in stories portraying
Oswald as a saint, although Bede also appears to have been able to draw on

---

[8]   When one realises that Oswald and Aidan do not appear in the summary account
of the conversion of Northumbria which Bede wrote in 725 (Thacker, below, p.
112), just six years before his *History*, one cannot help wondering about the
artificiality of the role which the *History* assigns to Oswald.

[9]   In addition to the principal sources discussed here, see below, pp. 72-3, for the
question of the transmission of information on Eadfrith's death, and whether
Oswald was behind it.

[10] Hexham (via Bishop Acca): *HE* III, 2 and 13; IV, 14. Bardney (probably via the
abbot of neighbouring Partney): *HE* III, 11-12. See D. P. Kirby, 'Bede's native
sources for the *Historia Ecclesiastica*', *Bulletin of the John Rylands Library* 48
(1965-6), pp. 341-7 at pp. 350-1. Dorothy Whitelock, 'Bede and his teachers and
friends', in *Famulus Christi*, ed. G. Bonner (London 1976), pp. 19-39 at pp. 26-7.
Thacker, below.

[11] *HE* III, 6; Thacker, below, pp. 100-1, 110. On Bede's links with Lindisfarne, see
Kirby, art. cit. pp. 344-5; Whitelock, art. cit. p. 31.

more widespread oral traditions about Oswald of a popular nature, particularly from the site of *Maserfelth* where he fell in battle.[12]

The transmission of Oswald material, however, is only one factor we need to bear in mind when recalling the long gap between Oswald's death and Bede's date of writing. We must also be aware that Bede will have interpreted Oswald and his world through eighth-century eyes, not those of a strict contemporary. One obvious instance of this is his appellation of Oswald as king of the Northumbrians, *rex Nordanhymbrorum*. Of course, Bede tells us that the Northumbrian people (*gens*) had in bygone times been divided into two *provinciae*, if not two *regna* (kingdoms): that of the Deirans in the south, ruled by a royal dynasty represented by Edwin; and that of the Bernicians in the north, with a separate royal family represented by Æthelfrith, Oswald's father.[13] But for all that, his habitual usage of 'king of the Northumbrians' for Æthelfrith, Edwin and Oswald can lull the unwary into imagining that even in the early seventh century there was some conception of a Northumbrian identity; that the men of Deira felt more kinship with those of Bernicia than they did, say, with those of Lindsey, just to the south of the Humber. Such a supposition is almost certainly false. Some early texts speak of 'Humbrians', not 'Northumbrians'; and Lindsey was generally under 'Northumbrian' domination right up to 679, just as separate subkings of Deira are found alongside the (Bernician) overkings of 'Northumbria' to the same date.[14] Bede may not have coined the term *Nordanhymbri*, but he was responsible for popularising it;[15] and in referring to the Bernicians and Deirans as one people when writing about the early seventh century, he was certainly guilty of anachronism.

A third caveat is that Bede was an Anglo-Saxon and a monk; and, for all his appearance of studied impartiality, his background inevitably imposed its own spectacles through which Bede looked at the past.[16] So, just as Bede's

---

[12] *HE* III, 9, 10 and 12. Thacker, below, p. 98. On the likelihood of the transmission of *Maserfelth* traditions to Bede via Bardney see Stancliffe, below, pp. 94-5.

[13] *HE* III, 1; family tree, above, p. 13. See T. M. Charles-Edwards, 'Bede, the Irish and the Britons', *Celtica* 15 (1983), pp. 42-52 at pp. 49-51; and Charles-Edwards and P. Wormald *apud* Wallace-Hadrill, *Comm*, pp. 226-8.

[14] See D. P. Kirby, *The Earliest English Kings* (London 1991), pp. 64-5, over against P. Hunter Blair, 'The Northumbrians and their southern frontier', reprinted from *Archaeologia Aeliana* 4th ser. 26 (1948) in his *Anglo-Saxon Northumbria* (London 1984), no. IV, pp. 98-126, esp. pp. 102-4. On the Deiran subkings Oethelwald, Alhfrith, Ecgfrith and Ælfwine, see Kirby, op. cit. pp. 8, 103; Plummer II, 120; *VW* 17 and 24.

[15] Cf. Hunter Blair, art. cit. pp. 99-104; Charles-Edwards and Wormald, loc. cit.

[16] Patrick Wormald, 'Bede, "Beowulf" and the conversion of the Anglo-Saxon aristocracy', in *Bede and Anglo-Saxon England*, ed. R. T. Farrell (BAR Br. ser. 46; Oxford 1978), pp. 32-95. Cf. W. Goffart, *The Narrators of Barbarian History (A.D. 550-800)* (Princeton N. J. 1988), ch. IV.

views will not always have been those of Anglo-Saxons living a century earlier, neither will they always have been those of Anglo-Saxon laymen of his own day, nor even necessarily those of all other Anglo-Saxon churchmen – let alone those of British or Irish churchmen. There are two related areas relevant to this paper where Bede's hostility or silence, stemming from this background, are in danger of blinding us to important aspects of the early seventh century: one concerns relations between the Anglo-Saxons and the Britons; the other, the heroic society common to the warrior aristocracies of these two peoples.

Bede was hostile to the Britons; and this hostility was probably sharpened by his perception of them as backsliding Christians, who had waywardly refused to join the Gregorian missionaries in preaching to the English, and who now refused to accept the authority of Rome. This meant that Bede, like modern historians, tended to see the history of the preceding centuries in part in terms of Anglo-Saxons versus the Britons. How far these very general racial perceptions were operative in early seventh-century society at large, however, is a very nice question. Counterbalancing Bede's 'them and us' approach, we have, of course, from the British side sources such as Gildas and the Synod of Victory canons,[17] which portray the Anglo-Saxon invaders as the bitter enemies of the indigenous Britons. Nonetheless, both sources also imply that there were some Britons who sided with the Anglo-Saxons, or were prepared to ally themselves with them.[18] It looks as though the churchmen on both sides, who are the ones who have left us with written sources revealing their own viewpoint, were hostile to the concept of a British alliance with Anglo-Saxons – not least, because their religion served to give them a common identity over against those who stood outside its fold.[19] Reading between the lines, however, it becomes apparent that relations between the two peoples were not uniformly antagonistic.

[17] Gildas, *De excidio Britonum* 23-6; ed. and trans. M. Winterbottom, *Gildas: The Ruin of Britain and Other Works* (Chichester 1978), pp. 26-8, 97-8. *Sinodus luci victorie* §4 assigns the heaviest penance to those 'who afford guidance to the barbarians'; ed. and trans. by L. Bieler, *The Irish Penitentials* (Dublin 1963), at pp. 68-9, and cf. p. 242. The *barbari* are generally taken as the Anglo-Saxons because they are implicitly identified as non-Christians.

[18] *Sinodus luci victorie* §4; Gildas, *De excidio* 23,1; 92,3 (pp. 26, 97; 69, 133). The latter is discussed by D. N. Dumville, 'The chronology of *De Excidio Britanniae*, book I', in *Gildas: New Approaches*, ed. M. Lapidge and D. Dumville (Woodbridge 1984), pp. 61-84 at pp. 81-2.

[19] See N. Higham, *The Northern Counties to AD 1000* (London and New York 1986), p. 275; cf. H. M. and N. K. Chadwick, *The Growth of Literature*, vol. I (Cambridge 1932), p. 158 n. 3: 'It has not been sufficiently appreciated that the anti-British feeling so frequently displayed in the *Hist. Eccl.* is primarily odium theologicum; there is no reason for supposing that such feelings were generally shared by the princes on either side.' Cf. the way in which, on the continent, the

Sixth-century British society, after all, was not dominated by churchmen of Gildas's stamp;[20] and, religion aside, British and Anglo-Saxon – and Irish and Pictish – societies had much in common with each other. Britain south of the Clyde/Forth isthmus was divided into a number of rival kingdoms, some larger, some smaller; some British, some Germanic in leadership. All of them were dominated by a ruler and his warrior élite, who lived, in theory, at least, by a heroic code of honour, and who were supported in their lifestyle in part by food rents of peasants, and in part by the booty carried off through warlike expeditions against rival kingdoms, and tribute exacted therefrom. What is important to realise is that the values that ruled this society were shared between Britons and Anglo-Saxons;[21] and that, as well as Britons fighting Anglo-Saxons, we find Britons fighting Britons, Anglo-Saxons fighting Anglo-Saxons, and Britons and Anglo-Saxons allying with each other against rival Anglo-Saxons. The peasant farmers who supported such warriors no doubt had very local horizons; but royalty, and the warrior nobility, often had far-flung links with other kingdoms and peoples. Sometimes these were forged through intermarriage, sometimes through exiles from one kingdom seeking refuge elsewhere. In south-east England, such links are found with Frankia, while further north, they occurred between the Anglo-Saxon and the Celtic peoples of Britain. Some of the royal exiles from Deira, after its seizure by Æthelfrith, took refuge in the British kingdom of Elmet, and Edwin possibly did the same in Gwynedd.[22] Conversely, as we have seen, on Æthelfrith's death, Oswald and Oswiu fled with their retinues to the Irish of Dál Riada, a kingdom that straddled the sea between north-east Ireland and western Scotland, while the eldest son, Eanfrith, sought refuge amongst the Picts of central and eastern Scotland. Eanfrith married into the Pictish royalty; meanwhile his younger brother, Oswiu, appears to have inter-married at various stages of his life into the important mainland Irish dynasty

---

Arian form of Christianity practised by most of the Germanic invaders served to isolate them from Roman society, not integrate them: see P. Brown, *The World of Late Antiquity* (London 1971), pp. 112, 122-5.

20 *De excidio*, passim. The gap between the ideals of British heroic society and those espoused by Gildas is epitomised by the latter's attack on the panegyrists of Maelgwn of Gwynedd: *De exc.* 34, 6, discussed by Patrick Sims-Williams, 'Gildas and vernacular poetry', in *Gildas*, ed. Lapidge and Dumville, pp. 169-92, esp. pp. 174-5.

21 E.g. see T. M. Charles-Edwards, 'The authenticity of the *Gododdin*: an historian's view', in *Astudiaethau ar yr Hengerdd: Studies in Old Welsh Poetry*, ed. R. Bromwich and R. B. Jones (Cardiff 1978), pp. 44-71.

22 *HE* IV, 23; Triad 26 W, ed. and trans. R. Bromwich, *Trioedd Ynys Prydein* (2nd edn Cardiff 1978), pp. 46-8, and cf. pp. 54, xcvii f. Guthlac was in exile amongst the Britons later in the 7th century: *Felix's Life of Saint Guthlac*, ed. and trans. B. Colgrave (Cambridge 1956), ch. 34.

of the Uí Néill overkings, into the British royal dynasty of Rheged, and finally with the daughter of Edwin – herself the great-granddaughter of a Frankish king.[23] As regards the limitations of the *Ecclesiastical History*, we might note that Bede tells us directly only of the last of these three marriages of Oswiu.

The point to be further emphasised here is that, while the heroic values according to which both the British and the Anglo-Saxon warrior élites lived appear to have been identical, they will have been very different from those of Gildas or Bede, who were both churchmen. Fortunately, there are other sources which can help us here. Despite controversy, there is good reason to regard the Old English poem *Beowulf* as providing us with an insight into the mentality of the Anglo-Saxon warrior élite that can usefully complement the viewpoint of churchmen.[24] The poem transports us to a world of drinking and feasting in a kingly hall, where there is boasting and glorying in the individual's prowess, although the fragility and impermanence of good fortune are often alluded to. The tone is set by Beowulf's words: 'It is better for anyone that he should avenge his friend, rather than mourn greatly. Each of us must await the end of life in this world; let him who can, achieve glory before death.'[25] Beowulf, eager for fame, lives up to his boast, 'I shall achieve this deed of heroic courage, or else meet my final hour in this mead-hall',[26] in his combat against the monster Grendel. Victory in single combat is rewarded with rich gifts, horses, weapons and twisted gold. From the many allusions in the poem we are able to build up a picture of the 'good king' who is brave and generous, and therefore able to attract loyal retainers to his service, and so win victory in battle, imposing tribute on the defeated.[27] The poem is, however, subtle, and can be seen as questioning as well as celebrating the heroic ideal, particularly when a warrior bears responsibility

[23]   See Fig. 1. *HE* III, 1; Kirby, *Earliest English Kings*, p. 87. If Æthelfrith only married Oswald's mother after annexing Deira c.604, then it is likely that Eanfrith had a different mother (Bebba?). On Oswiu's wives see *HE* III, 15; *Historia Brittonum*, ch. 57, discussed below, p. 57; H. Moisl, 'The Bernician royal dynasty and the Irish in the seventh century', *Peritia* 2 (1983), pp. 103-26 at pp. 122-3.

[24]   Wormald, 'Bede, *Beowulf*'. Problems arise not just because the date of *Beowulf* is disputed, but also because so is its interpretation: in particular, how far does its attitude to heroic values arise from a later, Christian perspective? Cf. C. Chase, 'Saints' Lives, royal lives, and the date of Beowulf', in *The Dating of Beowulf*, ed C. Chase (Toronto 1981), pp. 161-71 at pp. 161-2. The *Gododdin* provides similar insights into the British heroic age: Charles-Edwards, 'The authenticity'.

[25]   Lines 1384-8. The standard edition of *Beowulf* is that by F. Klaeber (3rd edn Boston 1950). I quote the translation in the parallel edition by M. Swanton, *Beowulf* (Manchester 1978), p. 101.

[26]   Ibid. lines 636-8.

[27]   E.g. lines 1-25, 64-81, 2633-60. The antitype is Heremod, lines 1709-22.

for his people as their king.[28] Was Beowulf being gloriously heroic, or rash and putting the well-being of his people in jeopardy, when he went forth as an old man to meet the dragon in single combat?

To read *Beowulf* is to feed the imagination, so that we can attempt to enter the thought-world of Oswald. One can gain an additional dimension by pondering some of the archaeologist's findings such as the treasure from Sutton Hoo, or the royal complex at Yeavering. But my concern here is primarily with literary sources; and with Oswald himself, the picture is complicated by the fact that from the ages of about eleven to twenty-eight he and his younger brother were growing up and gaining experience in Dál Riada. During this period they and their companions were baptized on Iona; but most of their time was probably spent at the Dalriadan royal court, whose principal stronghold, Dunadd, has revealed jewelry work implying Anglo-Saxon/Celtic links in the seventh century.[29] The Anglo-Saxon æthelings (or princes) also appear to have taken an active role in fighting on their Dalriadan host's behalf on the Irish mainland.[30] Oswald and Oswiu became fluent Irish speakers,[31] and they would have been open to influence from Irish models of kingship and tales of heroism. These may have provided a more varied fare than the Old English poems, and Irish kings were also encouraged to show moral, non-martial qualities, such as the pursuit of justice and truth, in a way that may not have been expected from their Anglo-Saxon counterparts prior to their conversion; but delight in feats of valour was certainly common to both traditions.[32]

The challenge of interpreting Oswald's personality and achievements should by now be apparent: the only written sources directly informing us about Oswald's reign are by churchmen, and they leave whole areas of his life as a Germanic warleader to our imagination. Of these churchmen, only Bede tells us much; and he will have looked at the past through his own spectacles, and filtered out of the record all that did not fit with his aims. We

[28] J. Leyerle, 'Beowulf the hero and the king', *Medium Ævum* 34 (1965), pp. 89-102. Cf. T. A. Shippey, *Beowulf* (London 1978), pp. 34-41; T. A. Shippey, *Old English Verse* (London 1972), ch. 2, esp. pp. 28-9, 51; Swanton, *Beowulf*, pp. 19-27.

[29] E. Campbell and A. Lane, 'Celtic and Germanic interaction in Dalriada: the 7th-century metalworking site at Dunadd', in *AMI*, pp. 52-63; Cramp above, p. 27.

[30] Moisl, art. cit., esp. pp. 105-12.

[31] *HE* III, 3 and 25 (pp. 220, 296).

[32] E.g. Cú Chulainn's feats in the *Táin Bó Cúalnge*. For Irish guidance on kingly behaviour, see *Audacht Morainn*, ed. and trans. F. Kelly (Dublin 1976); *De duodecim abusivis saeculi*, ed. S. Hellmann, *Texte und Untersuchungen zur Geschichte der altchristlichen Literatur* series 3, vol. 4 (vol. 34 of the whole run; Leipzig 1909/10), part 1, pp. 43-5, 51-3. Cf. also Ó Cathasaigh, *Heroic Biography*, pp. 9-11, 62-8.

must also realise that Bede faced a peculiar difficulty in writing about Oswald: Oswald is the one figure in his *History* who is presented unambiguously as a saint, while also being a successful king. There are, of course, plenty of cases of kings who laid aside their kingship for the sake of Christianity, but that is something very different: first they were kings, then they devoted themselves to the religious life or pilgrimage to Rome. There are also some examples of kings who were, to varying degrees, actively involved in Christianity, and commended for this by Bede. Those of them who met violent ends in battle at the hands of a pagan, or as murdered innocents, had the potential to attract a cult, becoming honoured as 'martyrs',[33] and Oswald obviously had much in common with them. But although by Bede's day there was some cult of Edwin, and possibly of Oswine too, Bede does not mention this, nor write about either explicitly as a 'saint'.[34] In contrast, not only does he call Oswald *sanctissimus, Christianissimus*, and a *miles Christi*;[35] he also includes the story of how the monks of Bardney, 'etsi sanctum eum nouerant', did not wish to receive his bones until persuaded by a miracle,[36] and several other Oswald miracles. Most decisive of all, after one of these he comments, 'It is not to be wondered at that the prayers of this king, *who is now reigning with the Lord*, should greatly prevail.' Again, a further Oswald miracle slotted into his *History* at a late stage also shows Oswald as a powerful intercessor in heaven.[37] Thus, while some of Bede's contemporaries may have regarded Oswald's status as similar to Edwin's, and in time both certainly became regarded as 'martyrs', Bede himself regarded Oswald, and Oswald alone, as a saint-king – and a saint thanks to the life he lived as a king, not to a life lived after laying aside royal power, nor yet thanks to dying a martyr's death.[38] Bede never used the

[33] In general, see J. M. Wallace-Hadrill, *Early Germanic Kingship in England and on the Continent* (Oxford 1971), pp. 80-91; F. Graus, *Volk, Herrscher und Heiliger im Reich der Merowinger* (Prague 1965), ch. V, 5, at pp. 415-25 for the Anglo-Saxon kings, and pp. 428-30 for these three categories. On the first, see further C. Stancliffe, 'Kings who opted out', in *Ideal and Reality*, pp. 154-76. On the last, see D. W. Rollason, 'The cults of murdered royal saints in Anglo-Saxon England', *ASE* 11 (1983), pp. 1-22.

[34] Edwin: *The Earliest Life of Gregory the Great*, ed. B. Colgrave (Cambridge, pb edn 1985), chs. 16, 18, 19; Wallace-Hadrill, *EGK*, pp. 80-3; below, pp. 105-7, and cf. p. 152. Oswine: *HE* III, 14; Plummer II, 164; Rollason, art. cit. p. 3 and n. 6; C. Chase, 'Beowulf, Bede, and St Oswine: The hero's pride in Old English hagiography', in *The Anglo-Saxons: Synthesis and Achievement*, ed. J. D. Woods and D. A. E. Pelteret (Waterloo, Ontario, 1985), pp. 37-48 at p. 41.

[35] 'Most holy', 'most Christian', and 'soldier of Christ': *HE* III, 7 and 9; *HE* IV, 14.

[36] 'Although they had known that he was a saint/holy man': *HE* III, 11.

[37] *HE* III, 12 (my italics); IV, 14.

[38] On this last point, see now V. A. Gunn, 'Bede and the martyrdom of St Oswald', *Studies in Church History* 30 (1993), pp. 57-66.

word 'martyr' about Oswald. He narrates Oswald's death in an unadorned sentence which simply gives the 'facts', as a historian.[39] This is separated, by three chapters, from popular stories told about Oswald's death, and Bede there makes clear the hearsay nature of what he tells: 'It is commonly known (*vulgatum est*), and has become a proverb, that he even ended his life in prayer. For when he was surrounded by warriors and enemies, and realised that he was about to perish, he prayed for the souls of his own army. So the proverb runs, "May God have mercy on their souls, said Oswald as he fell to the earth."'[40] Legend was clearly at work on Oswald's death, and one can glimpse something of how Oswald would be transformed into a martyr:[41] but not by Bede.

The interest of Bede's picture of Oswald as both active king and saint is that it is unusual, if not unique, for its time. There was no Life of a saint-king for Bede to draw ideas from, no clear exemplar.[42] Of course there were figures like King David in the Old Testament, or the Emperor Constantine from the late Roman Empire; and of course, Bede was not attempting to write a formal Life. Nonetheless, the novelty of what Bede set out to do should not be overlooked. Nor should its inherent difficulties. To write about a royal martyr would have been a relatively simple proposition: with martyrs, it was not the life they lived, but their actual death that was the crucial feature; and any shortcomings in the martyr's previous life were readily expiated through his death, a baptism of blood. But to present the sanctity of someone who had lived as a king so Christianly that he should be honoured as a saint was to enter a minefield.[43] In the martyrs' acts, it is normally the secular powers which *persecute* Christians; and even in the fourth century there lingered the idea that government service, with its routine use of torture, defiled its officers to such an extent as to unfit them for ordination. Worse still, what of warfare? From one angle, killing remained killing, however just the cause – a feeling that is reflected among

---

[39] *HE* III, 9.

[40] *HE* III, 12. Bede's practice here parallels that of his account of Gregory's mission to England: first we have the historian's account; then, much later, and with ample warning of its hearsay nature, comes the story of Gregory's encounter with the Deiran slave boys in Rome: *HE* I, 23; II, 1 (pp. 132-3). Cf. Wallace-Hadrill, *Comm*, p. 51.

[41] I owe this point to the unpublished work of Victoria Gunn, of Glasgow University; cf. also Chase, 'Saints' Lives, Royal Lives', pp. 164-6.

[42] Graus, op. cit. pp. 392-3. *Vitae* of saint-kings appear only in the 11th century: ibid. pp. 425-33. J. Nelson, 'Royal saints and early medieval kingship', *Studies in Church History* 10 (1973), pp. 30-44, at p. 41.

[43] It may be significant that all the miracles attributed to Oswald are posthumous ones: the life of the warrior king was probably not perceived as 'saintly' at the time. Cf. Thacker, below, p. 97.

the newly-converted Anglo-Saxons by the prescription of short penances even for killing someone in battle.[44] How, then, could Bede convincingly portray Oswald as a saint, when he had had to fight and kill even to win his kingdom, and in a society where warfare was an every-day occurrence in a king's life?

Bearing all these problems in mind, let us begin where any historian of Oswald must begin: that is, with Bede's portrayal of Oswald in book III of his *Ecclesiastical History*. First, we might note Bede's artistry in his selection and deployment of material about Oswald. Book II of his *History* had ended bleakly, with Edwin's achievement of a Christian Northumbria in ruins, and the very existence of the Roman mission there hanging on the slender thread of James the Deacon. The first chapter of book III opens with the relapse of 'Northumbria' into Deira and Bernicia, and of its Christian rulers into paganism; but, by the end of the chapter, Oswald's victory has been reached. The battle of Heavenfield and the miracles later wrought by Oswald's cross are then given full treatment in chapter two, and followed by an account of how Oswald immediately sent to Iona for a bishop to bring Christianity to his people, of Aidan's arrival and the foundation of Lindisfarne, and of how Oswald took an active role in backing Aidan's mission.[45] This enabled a striking contrast to be drawn between the apostasy of Osric and Eanfrith, followed by their death at Cadwallon's hands, on the one hand; and, on the other, Oswald's victory in the sign of the cross, followed by the successful conversion of his people. Oswald himself is shown playing an active role in this, 'diligently seeking to build up and extend the Church of Christ in his kingdom', and acting as Aidan's interpreter when the Irish bishop was preaching.[46] Bede then turns to sketch in the history of Iona, and Aidan's praiseworthy example of living out the Gospel which he preached, tucking in the story about Aidan's unsuccessful predecessor in such a way that one does not think of it as a failure; rather, it serves to enhance our admiration for Aidan. 'With such a bishop to instruct them', Oswald and his people

> learned not only to hope for the kingdom of heaven...; but also, Oswald gained ... greater earthly realms than any of his ancestors had possessed. In fact he held under his sway all the peoples and kingdoms of Britain, divided among the speakers of four different languages, British, Pictish, Irish and English.[47]

Bede contents himself with this general statement about Oswald's political success, eschewing any details or examples. Instead, he plunges

---

[44] J. E. Cross, 'The ethic of war in Old English', in *England before the Conquest*, ed. P. Clemoes and K. Hughes (Cambridge 1971), pp. 269-82, at pp. 280-1.

[45] *HE* III, 3.

[46] Loc. cit.

[47] *HE* III, 6.

straight into the story of how Oswald gave away his Easter feast to the poor, and ordered the dish on which it was served to be broken up and distributed amongst them. Bede was obviously concerned to drive home the lesson that despite Oswald's political success, he remained 'wonderfully humble, kind, and generous to the poor and to strangers.' The chapter ends with his successful healing of the strife between Deira and Bernicia, and presents Oswald as Edwin's 'heir' to both his Christianity and his kingdom.

The following chapter serves as a bridge between Bede's account of Oswald, and his more general concern with the conversion of the Anglo-Saxons. It opens by telling how Birinus came from Italy on the pope's advice to help to convert the English, and found himself amongst the heathen Gewisse, whom Bede regarded as identical with the West Saxons.[48] Oswald conveniently appears visiting King Cynegils of the Gewisse at the time of the latter's conversion. He acts as godfather to the king and joins with him in donating Dorchester-on-Thames to Birinus for his episcopal see, while an incidental reference to his marriage to Cynegils's daughter is also slipped in. Bede's narrative then turns to the subsequent history of Wessex, and, in the following chapter, to that of Kent. After this, Bede returns once more to King Oswald, assigning him a nine-year reign – which included the unmentionable year 633-4 when the apostate kings reigned – and then giving a brief account of his death in battle at *Maserfelth* at the hands of the pagan Mercian leader Penda. Oswald died on 5 August 642, at the age of thirty-seven.[49] This, however, does not mark the end of Bede's interest. On the contrary, Oswald's death is followed by some five chapters containing seven miracle stories wrought by virtue of Oswald's relics. This means that Oswald and his posthumous miracles dominate the first half of book III of Bede's *Ecclesiastical History*, and indeed play a significant role in the *History* as a whole.[50]

It is not, however, the quantity of Oswald material that is as significant as its selection and presentation. Thus, Oswald's victory at Heavenfield is highlighted by the contrast with the dark days of Osric, Eanfrith and Cadwallon; by the allocation to it of a whole chapter; and by the fact that it is the single example of Oswald's military prowess which Bede describes. Oswald surely fought many other battles; but of these, Bede has chosen to say nothing. What is more, he is very careful to show Oswald fighting only just wars. At Heavenfield, he puts into Oswald's mouth an exhortation to prayer 'that God... may, of his mercy, defend us from the proud and fierce enemy; for he knows that we are fighting a just war for the *salus* of our

---

[48] *HE* III, 7. Kirby, *Earliest English Kings*, p. 48.

[49] *HE* III, 9.

[50] At a late stage in its composition, an additional Oswald miracle was slotted in at *HE* IV, 14; cf. *HE* pp. xl-xli; and p. 326 note a.

people.' St Augustine himself could hardly have expressed it better.[51] Again, in his account of the battle where Oswald was killed, Bede says that he was 'fighting for his native land' – another justifiable case for warfare.[52] These are the only two battles which Bede mentions Oswald as fighting. Instead, he chooses to present Oswald, once in power, as turning his attention to the work of conversion. This, in its turn, is portrayed as an unalloyed success: the false start of the first bishop sent by Iona returning after failure[53] does not appear in its chronological place, where it would have marred Bede's presentation of a success story.

Then, there is the likelihood that Bede over-emphasises Oswald's role in helping to establish the church in Wessex. Oswald may, as overking, have acted as godfather to a subordinate king, and in this respect played the sort of role which one associates with Byzantine emperors;[54] but since missionary and overking came from opposite directions, this can hardly be seen as the overking initiating the conversion process. Birinus was presumably already preaching in Wessex when Oswald arrived, and Oswald's primary motive in travelling to Wessex was probably to reach a friendly understanding with another king who had good reason to oppose Penda,[55] and to cement this alliance by marrying his daughter. No doubt Oswald did encourage Cynegils to embrace Christianity, and he showed his active support by acting as his baptismal sponsor; but Bede has surely slanted his account of Oswald's visit. As for both kings being responsible for the donation of Dorchester, this remains a puzzle: how could Oswald, king of Bernicia and Deira, have had any rights over land in Wessex?[56] If all he did was to attest a charter, one would expect Bede and Bishop Daniel, his probable informant, to have been familiar with this procedure, and not confuse attestation with donation. Has Bede rewritten the story in order to demonstrate Oswald as actively involved in establishing the church in Wessex?[57]

[51] *HE* III, 2: *salus* can mean both 'well being' and 'salvation', and probably carries both meanings here; cf. Colgrave and Mynors's translation, and Wallace-Hadrill, *Comm*, p. 89. For Augustine's teaching on *iusta bella*, the very words that Bede uses, see Cross, 'Ethic of war', p. 271.

[52] *HE* III, 9. Cross, loc. cit.

[53] *HE* III, 5.

[54] Cf. A. Angenendt, *Kaiserherrschaft und Königstaufe* (Berlin and New York 1984), pp. 5-11, 176-86.

[55] *ASC s.a.* 628. B. Yorke, *Kings and Kingdoms of Early Anglo-Saxon England* (London 1990), p. 136.

[56] See Wallace-Hadrill, *Comm*, pp. 98, 231.

[57] T. M. Charles-Edwards has made the interesting suggestion to me that Bede may have wished to show Oswald being instrumental in a successful mission to the West Saxons that was blessed by the Pope, not simply in the Ionan mission of Aidan; and further, that this concern might go back to Wilfrid who had strong links with Wessex (*VW* 42), and who was active both in promoting Roman over

A further probable instance of Bede's disingenuous shaping of his Oswald material is his reference to how Oswald promoted the unification of Deira and Bernicia so that they became one people, and his acclaim of Oswald's aptness to inherit Edwin's religion and kingdom, since he was Edwin's nephew. In reality, however, the feud between the Deiran and Bernician dynasties was by no means over, while Bede's designation of Oswald as Edwin's 'heir' has been described as 'a diplomatic quarter-truth'.[58] One would also like to know more of how Edwin's obvious heir, his son Eadfrith, met his end. In book II Bede had told of how Eadfrith had survived the battle of Hatfield Chase by surrendering to Penda, only to be murdered by him later, during Oswald's reign. Did responsibility lie with Penda, or with Oswald? Bede's narrative is opaque at this point.[59]

Clearly, Bede did not set down a straightforward account of Oswald's main achievements; rather, his portrayal of Oswald is a deliberate construct, put together to record those aspects of Oswald's achievements and character which Bede wished to bring to the notice of his own contemporaries and future generations – not least, kings.[60] Oswald is Bede's most convincing example of an Anglo-Saxon king who took his Christianity seriously, but at the same time remained a king, and indeed a successful king. He could thus be held up as a model for future generations to imitate. By the same token, however, if we are to obtain something approximating to a true picture of Oswald, we must seek to go beyond and behind Bede's portrayal. Given the gaps in our source material, there is much that we can never know. But on two important questions, we can make some progress: that is, on Oswald's political achievement, and on his role as a Christian king.

II
Oswald's Political Achievement

Oswald's reign comes in the middle of a line of successful seventh-century kings of Northumbria, and it is often difficult to assign particular achievements to individual kings. His father, Æthelfrith, laid the foundations by uniting Deira and Bernicia, thus bringing the whole area between the Tweed and the Humber under his direct control. He may also have compelled British kingdoms further afield to acknowledge his overlordship.[61]

---

against Ionan practices, and also in fostering the cult of Oswald (see Thacker below, pp. 107ff.).

58 *HE* III, 6. Charles-Edwards, 'Bede' (as n. 13), p. 50.
59 *HE* II, 20. Cf. below, pp. 71-5.
60 See Bede's prefatory letter to King Ceolwulf: *HE*, p.2; and Wallace-Hadrill, *EGK*, ch. 4, esp. pp. 78-87.
61 *Historia Brittonum*, ch. 63, ed. from Harleian MS 3859 by E. Faral, *La légende arthurienne: études et documents*, part I, vol. III: *Documents* (Bibliothèque de l'École des Hautes Études, 257), pp. 1-62 at p. 43. *HE* I, 34. Cramp, above. For

So much is implied by the reaction of the king of Dál Riada, who marched against him only to be defeated (c.603); and by his victory over the British of Powys at the battle of Chester (c.615/616). Clearly Æthelfrith had a long arm; and he was only defeated and killed in 616 when Rædwald attacked suddenly, without allowing him time to assemble his whole army.[62]

On Æthelfrith's downfall and replacement by Edwin, the centre of gravity would naturally have shifted south, to Deira. Edwin continued with Æthelfrith's expansionary policies. Near home, he took the British kingdom of Elmet (in west Yorkshire) under his direct rule, expelling its king, Ceretic.[63] Further afield he asserted claims of overlordship, winning a victory against Wessex, intermarrying into the still powerful royal family of Kent, and, after his own eventual conversion to Christianity, prevailing upon the king of the East Angles to follow suit.[64] But his most dramatic expansion was into Wales. He conquered Anglesey and Man, besieging King Cadwallon of Gwynedd on a little island off south-east Anglesey.[65] This was to strike at the heartland of Gwynedd, threatening its independent existence; and it was probably he, rather than Æthelfrith, who was responsible for cutting off the Britons in Wales from their compatriots in northern Britain.[66] Edwin's aggressive action, coming on top of Æthelfrith's attack on Chester, would have convinced the kings of both Gwynedd and Powys[67] that Northumbria was the chief threat to their existence, and would thus have prepared the ground for the Welsh alliance with Mercia which is one of the leitmotifs of the mid seventh century. According to the evidence of a late Welsh triad, and of a probably contemporary panegyric in honour of Cadwallon, the king of Gwynedd took refuge in Ireland. He returned to make a triumphant come-back against Edwin, fighting a major battle at Meigen in Powys, and then, in alliance with Penda of Mercia, carrying the war across England into the southern approaches to Deira, where Edwin was actually killed (at Hatfield

---

[62] Elmet, see n. 63; but Rheged and Gododdin are also possibilities.
Kirby, *Earliest English Kings*, pp. 63, 72-3.

[63] *Hist. Brit.* ch. 63. Æthelfrith had probably already reduced Ceretic to a dependent position, as Edwin's nephew had been poisoned there while seeking refuge: *HE* IV, 23. Cf. G. R. J. Jones, 'Early territorial organization in Gwynedd and Elmet', *Northern History* 10 (1975), pp. 3-27 at pp. 25-6.

[64] Kirby, *Earliest English Kings*, pp. 77-8.

[65] *HE* II, 5 and 9 (pp. 148-50, 162); *Annales Cambriae s.a.* 629, ed. E. Phillimore, 'The *Annales Cambriae* and Old-Welsh genealogies', *Y Cymmrodor* 9 (1888), pp. 141-83, at p.157. Triad 26W, ed. and trans. Bromwich, *Trioedd*, pp. 47-8, and cf. 293-6.

[66] See *HE* II, 16, citing as proverbial that in Edwin's day a mother and baby could walk *from sea to sea* unharmed.

[67] Powys appears to have fought alongside Gwynedd at Meigen: J. Rowland, *Early Welsh Saga Poetry* (Cambridge 1990), pp. 128-9.

Chase in 633, according to Bede).[68]

The aftermath of the battle of Hatfield Chase is far from clear. Edwin's cousin, Osric, certainly became king of Deira, though whether with or without Cadwallon's compliance we do not know; Cadwallon appears to have allowed Æthelfrith's eldest son, Eanfrith, to become king of Bernicia.[69] Was Cadwallon's aim that of 'divide and rule': splitting the too-powerful kingdom of Northumbria between the two rival royal families, and intending them to be subordinate to him as Edwin had tried to subordinate Gwynedd? Some historians would go further, and speculate that there was a prior alliance between Cadwallon and Æthelfrith's sons, and that the latter were probably supported by Dalriadan and Pictish troops.[70] In all events, the various parties soon fell out with each other. Osric dashingly went on the offensive against Cadwallon, his cousin's slayer, and was killed by him. This appears to have unleashed Cadwallon's fury against the Anglo-Saxons in Bernicia as well as Deira, and Eanfrith was killed when he tried to ask for terms. It was against this background that Oswald fought the battle of Heavenfield in 634. Adomnán explicitly emphasises the smallness of Oswald's army by comparison with that of Cadwallon.[71] It is likely that, in addition to his own warband, Oswald also had some military assistance from Dál Riada;[72] but, even so, Cadwallon would probably have had a larger army, and Oswald's victory against the leader who had so recently slain Edwin, Osric and Eanfrith was a significant achievement. Cadwallon himself was killed, and this enabled Oswald to step into his shoes and claim both Bernicia and Deira. From the point of view of Bede's portrayal of Oswald as a model ruler, and possibly even from the point of view of Deirans at the time, Cadwallon's ruthless interregnum had performed a notable service: it meant that Oswald could be presented as a deliverer, as the rightful successor not just of his brother, but also of his Deiran rival, Edwin.

Oswald did not simply succeed Edwin to the north of the Humber. In a famous passage, Bede listed seven Anglo-Saxon kings who sequentially attained overlordship (*imperium*) over other kings south of the Humber. The

68 Bromwich, *Trioedd* no. 29; pp. 57, 151-2, 293-6, 339. *Annales Cambriae s.a.* 630. *HE* II, 20. Rowland, op. cit. pp. 127-9, 169-72. Jackson, 'Nennius' (as n. 6 above), p. 43; D. P. Kirby, 'Welsh bards and the border', in *Mercian Studies*, ed. A. Dornier (Leicester 1977), pp. 31-42 at pp. 33-5, and *Earliest English Kings*, pp. 85-6.

69 Bede says that, on Edwin's death, Æthelfrith's sons were 'allowed' back to Bernicia, where Eanfrith became king (*HE* III, 1); and Cadwallon is the obvious person to have been in a position to allow or deny this.

70 Kirby, *Earliest English Kings*, p. 87. Cf. M. Miller, 'Eanfrith's Pictish son', *Northern History* 14 (1978), pp. 47-66, at p. 57.

71 *VCol* I, 1, at 9b.

72 Moisl, art. cit. (above, n. 23), p. 116.

first four were all from southern England, but the last three were the Northumbrian kings Edwin, Oswald, and Oswiu. Whereas the South-umbrian kings had exercised overlordship only over other Anglo-Saxon kingdoms, and only south of the Humber, the pattern changed thereafter: not only did the Northumbrian kings' power obviously include their own kingdom, but also they are credited with rule over other peoples within Britain: 'Edwin... ruled over all the inhabitants of Britain, English and Britons alike, except for Kent only', and this is backed up by a reference to his conquest of Anglesey and Man. Oswald is portrayed as ruling 'within the same bounds' as Edwin; and Oswiu, as maintaining almost the same territory for some time, and then making tributary the Picts and the Irish in northern Britain.[73] For the historian of Oswald, this passage poses two challenges: first, it seems incompatible with Bede's statement elsewhere that it was Oswald, not Oswiu, who extended Northumbrian rule over the Picts and the Irish – a point we will return to later;[74] more fundamentally, the whole question of what this overlordship might have consisted of is at the moment the subject of sceptical scrutiny.[75] Were these seven any different from other Anglo-Saxon kings who were also overkings over other kingdoms? Were they known by any particular title, viz. the 'Bretwalda' attested in the ninth-century *Anglo-Saxon Chronicle*, or is this a later and perhaps idiosyncratic usage?

It is not my purpose here to enter this general debate, but rather to concentrate on Oswald and, insofar as is relevant, his predecessor and successor. Perhaps, however, this will throw a sidelight onto the debate at large, in that for Edwin and Oswald we are not restricted to Bede. For, emanating from the monastery of Iona, we have two additional sources: an annal entry, and a passage in Adomnán's *Life of Columba*. The *Annals of Tigernach*, recording Edwin's death in battle, say: 'The battle of Edwin son of Ælle, king of the Saxons, who ruled all Britain'.[76] By the 630s, the monastery of Iona was entering regular annal entries; and although these annals have not survived in their original form, there is good reason to accept that they lie behind this entry, as behind most others from this period.[77] In particular, I

---

[73] *HE* II, 5. On the implications of *imperium* cf. S. Fanning, 'Bede, *Imperium*, and the Bretwaldas', *Speculum* 66 (1991), pp. 1-26; and Charles-Edwards, 'Bede' (as n. 13 above), pp. 46-9.

[74] *HE* III, 6, cit. above, p. 43; cf. below, pp. 58-60.

[75] See e.g. P. Wormald, 'Bede, the *Bretwaldas* and the origins of the *Gens Anglorum*', in *Ideal and Reality*, pp. 99-129, esp. pp. 101-19; Fanning, art. cit.

[76] 'Cath Etuin maic Ailli reghis Saxonum, qui totam Britaniam regnauit, in quo uictus est a Chon rege Britonum et Panta Saxano': ed. W. Stokes, 'The Annals of Tigernach. Third Fragment', *Revue celtique* 17 (1896), pp. 119-263, at p. 181.

[77] Above, p. 34 and n. 5. See also A. P. Smyth, 'The earliest Irish annals', *Proceedings of the Royal Irish Academy* 72 C (1972), pp. 1-48; Moisl, art. cit. (above,

can see no reason why a later Ionan or Irish redactor should have wished to add the details about Edwin's rule and this battle; it is far more likely to reflect the interest of a contemporary annalist on Iona, particularly when we recall that Æthelfrith's sons were in exile in Dál Riada and Pictland because of Edwin's rule, and that relations between Northumbria and Dál Riada were closer in the seventh century than subsequently. What is intriguing is that we appear to have a contemporary source – and one with no motive for flattering Edwin or his descendants – recognising Edwin's rule in a clause, 'totam Britaniam regnauit', which conveys much the same import as Æthelbald of Mercia's 'rex Britanniae' in the witness list of the famous Ismere charter of 736, or even the much-suspected term 'Bretwalda', probably to be interpreted as 'Britain ruler'.[78] One should also add that a Welsh poem in honour of Cadwallon, *Moliant Cadwallon*, seems to portray Edwin and Cadwallon himself in similar terms.[79] Obviously rule of 'all Britain' should not be taken literally. Nonetheless, this annal entry does provide independent confirmation for Bede's attribution to Edwin of *imperium* over Britons and English.

For Oswald, we have a more extended passage in the introductory chapter of Adomnán's *Life of Columba*. Adomnán asserts that Columba's prayers were able to obtain victory for kings in battle, even after the saint's death, and the example he adduces is the battle of Heavenfield. He reports Oswald as having a vision before the battle in which St Columba assured him of his support, and foretold his victory over Cadwallon, encouraging him in words borrowed from the book of Joshua. Oswald's army, who were virtually all heathen, promised that they would accept baptism after the battle. They advanced against Cadwallon and won the victory, and Oswald, 'the victor, returning from battle, was afterwards ordained by God as emperor of the whole of Britain.'[80] Adomnán adds that he had heard the story from his predecessor, Abbot Failbe, who had been present when Oswald himself told a previous abbot of the vision. How much here is due to Adomnán? The details concerning the battle of Heavenfield as described by Bede agree only in that both authors show Oswald fighting explicitly as a Christian. But while Bede has stylised Oswald as a Constantine figure,[81]

---

n. 23), pp. 106-8.

78   Ismere charter: Wormald, 'Bede, *Bretwaldas*', pp. 106-7; photograph in *The Making of England*, ed. L. Webster and J. Backhouse (BM, London 1991), p. 197, no. 152. On the interpretation of *Bretwalda*, see Fanning, art. cit. pp. 22-3, where he argues that the variant form *brytenwalda* is only a spelling variant, not a separate word with a different etymology.

79   Kirby, 'Welsh bards', p. 34.

80   'Totius Brittanniae imperator a deo ordinatus est', *VCol* I, 1, at 9a.

81   *HE* III, 2, with the story of Oswald erecting 'the sign of the holy cross' before battle, and committing his cause to God. See below, p. 63 and n. 145; Wallace-Hadrill, *Comm*, p. 89.

Adomnán casts him more in an Old Testament guise. Given that Adomnán heard the story at only one remove from Oswald himself, I think we should accept that Oswald attributed his victory to the intercession of Columba.[82] But the casting of Oswald as another Joshua, and the detail that Oswald was then 'totius Brittaniae imperator a deo ordinatus est' are surely due to Adomnán: they chime with his description elsewhere of the Uí Néill overking Diarmait mac Cerbaill as 'totius Scotiae regnator deo auctore ordinatus' – again, a bombastic claim rather than an accurate description.[83] A recent study has argued that Iona in the late seventh and early eighth centuries was interested in developing an ordination rite for kings, modelled on Old Testament precedents, and that the chapters in Adomnán's *Life of Columba* on the relationship of saint and various kings are pure propaganda, aimed at contemporary kings.[84] Undoubtedly there are propagandist elements in the Life, but it is not pure propaganda in the sense that, say, Muirchú's *Life of Patrick* is.[85] As regards the relationship between Columba, kings, and warfare, I am inclined to regard it as something which dates back to Columba, who was the close relative of several Uí Néill kings, rather than being invented by Adomnán, another Uí Néill churchman, but one known to have been keenly concerned to limit the cruel effects of war on non-combatants.[86] I would, however, accept that the Oswald story was told by Adomnán with an eye to the contemporary Northumbrian king, Aldfrith, who ruled from 685 to 705. Like Oswald himself, Aldfrith had spent much time in exile amongst the Irish, some of it on Iona, and he is here being reminded of the efficacy of St Columba's intercession – perhaps with an eye to outbidding the claims of Northumbria's own St Cuthbert.[87]

Given this background, how do we interpret Adomnán's portrayal of Oswald as 'totius Brittanniae imperator a deo ordinatus est'? The Irish parallel warns us against taking Adomnán's words too literally, for Diarmait was never ruler of all Ireland. With these titles we are undoubtedly in the realm of aspiration, rather than actual achievement.[88] But Adomnán's

---

[82] On the testimonies about Columba in *VCol* see Herbert, *Iona, Kells, and Derry*, pp. 18-26. I find it more convincing to think of Adomnán shaping and using an existing story rather than inventing it, as suggested by M. J. Enright, *Iona, Tara and Soissons* (Berlin, New York, 1985), pp. 59-62.

[83] *VCol* I, 36, at 36b. This is obviously not historically accurate: see F. J. Byrne, *Irish Kings and High-Kings* (London 1973), pp. 94-7, 255, 259.

[84] Enright, op. cit., pp. 5-78.

[85] Cf. Herbert, op. cit., pp. 138-48.

[86] Herbert, op. cit., pp. 50-1.

[87] See Picard, 'The purpose' (as n. 4 above), pp. 172-5. Cf. C. Stancliffe, 'Cuthbert and the polarity between pastor and solitary', in *St Cuthbert*, pp. 21-44, at pp. 22-3 and n. 7.

[88] Byrne, *Irish Kings*, pp. 255, 259.

wording, particularly his use of *imperator* and reference to 'all Britain', does suggest that he saw Oswald as more than a king of Northumbria: the implication is that he ruled over more peoples than just his own.[89] Further, *totius Brittanniae imperator*, coupled with the annal entry describing Edwin's rule, do seem to fit with Bede's portrayal of these kings as having a far-flung *imperium* which set them apart from other contemporary Anglo-Saxon kings; and the very wording cannot but remind one of the Ismere charter and the Bretwalda titles. The Ionan evidence thus provides helpful, and independent, confirmation of Bede's general portrayal of Oswald's political power; but it does not take us further in understanding the actualities of that power. 'All Britain' is clearly a rhetorical flourish; and for the purposes of discovering how far Oswald's power actually extended, we need to piece together the evidence for ourselves, beginning with what can be deduced from Bede's narrative.

Oswald's victory at Heavenfield will have given a favourable start to his reign, enabling him to take over the kingdoms of both Bernicia and Deira. Unlike his successor, he was able to retain sole rule over Deira throughout his lifetime: it was only on his death that a king of Edwin's line reappeared there.[90] To the south, he conquered Lindsey.[91] He forged a marriage alliance with Wessex; and here, the fact that King Cynegils accepted his religion implies that Oswald was the dominant partner: one might contrast Edwin's agreement to the king of Kent's preconditions before he was allowed to marry a Kentish bride.[92] As regards Kent itself, Oswald appears to have been able to make his power felt here in a way that Edwin had not, for Edwin's widow thought it necessary to send Edwin's young male descendants to Frankia for their safety, 'out of fear of Kings Eadbald and Oswald'.[93] As Eadbald of Kent was her own brother, the source of her fear must have been

[89] Cf. Fanning's discussion of *imperium*, *Speculum* 66, pp. 6-26. The Ionan use of the same expression, *tota Britania*, for Edwin's area of rule, means that we cannot assume that Adomnán is here backing up the claim that Oswald ruled over the Irish and Picts as well as the Britons and Anglo-Saxons. (Cf. *HE* II, 5 (above, p. 49), whose limitation of Edwin's overlordship to the Britons and Anglo-Saxons is corroborated by the Bernician æthelings finding safety from Edwin's reach amongst the Picts and Irish.)

[90] *HE* III, 14.

[91] *HE* III, 11.

[92] Above, pp. 44-5; *HE* II, 9. I would see Oswald's standing godfather at a baptism ceremony performed by an Italian missionary as evidence that differences between 'Roman' and 'Ionan' Christianity were not, at that period, regarded as of overriding significance. I therefore do not accept N. J. Higham's interpretation of this event (*The Kingdom of Northumbria, AD 350-1100* (Stroud 1993), p. 129). To see Oswald's Christianity as 'heretical' is anachronistic for the 630s: such a perception belongs rather to the archiepiscopate of Theodore.

[93] *HE* II, 20; cf. II, 5 and below, pp. 58, 71-2.

Oswald, who was presumably powerful enough for her to feel that he would threaten Eadbald in the way that Æthelfrith had formerly threatened Edwin's protector, Rædwald.[94] As regards Sussex, too, there is evidence that Oswald's overlordship extended there.[95]

The most crucial relationship, however, is that between Oswald and Mercia. In 633 Penda of Mercia in alliance with Cadwallon of Gwynedd had defeated and slain Edwin; nine years later, Penda and the king of Powys slew Oswald.[96] Thereafter, Penda remained a thorn in the side of Oswald's successor, Oswiu, raiding and burning into the heartland of Bernicia – once apparently driving Oswiu to take refuge as far north as Stirling – until Oswiu succeeded in defeating him at the battle of the Winwæd in 655.[97] If one considers Mercia's geographical position, it could obviously threaten Northumbrian control over southern England. Would a Northumbrian king be able to collect tribute from Wessex, Sussex and Kent, and return with it in safety north of the Humber, if an unsubdued Mercia lay adjacent to and threatening the road he must take? (See map, p. 14.)

Penda's reign was crucial for the consolidation and expansion of Mercia, but unfortunately the chronology of events within it is uncertain.[98] There is, however, a danger that our knowledge of Penda's later success in Oswiu's reign may lead us to exaggerate his strength vis-à-vis Oswald. According to Bede, at the time of his and Cadwallon's victory over Edwin in 633, Penda was then a prince of royal blood, and he appears to have become king of the Mercians as a result of this victory. Bede comments that, from that date, he ruled over the Mercians for twenty-two years 'with varying success'.[99] This implies that Penda's fortunes had their downs as well as their ups; and, since the 640s and early 650s saw a powerful Penda harassing the East Angles and West Saxons as well as the Northumbrians, and Penda's success then appears to have continued unbroken till his death in 655, the presumption must be that his unsuccessful period(s) had come earlier, i.e. in Oswald's reign.[100]

---

[94] HE II, 12; *Earliest Life of Gregory*, ed. Colgrave, ch. 16.
[95] HE IV, 14.
[96] HE III, 9 and below, p. 56.
[97] HE III, 16, 17 and 24. *Historia Brittonum*, chs. 64 and 65. Jackson, 'Nennius' (as n. 6 above), esp. pp. 35-8. On the identification of *urbs Giudi* see further K. Jackson, 'Varia: I. Bede's *Urbs Giudi*: Stirling or Cramond?', *Cambridge Medieval Celtic Studies* 2 (1981), pp. 1-7.
[98] Two important recent contributions are N. Brooks, 'The formation of the Mercian kingdom' and D. Dumville, 'Essex, Middle Anglia, and the expansion of Mercia in the South-East Midlands', both in *Origins*, pp. 159-70 and 123-40.
[99] HE II, 20.
[100] HE III, 7 and 18. Brooks, art. cit. esp. pp. 165, 167. Kirby, *Earliest English Kings*, pp. 88 and 108-9 n. 26, attempts to date Penda's attack on the East Angles as early as c.636, relying on the late *Liber Eliensis*; but this is scarcely compatible with the

If we could be sure that Oswald pressurised Penda into killing Edwin's son, Eadfrith, this would be excellent evidence of Oswald's power over Penda. There are, however, serious problems in interpreting Bede's non-committal wording about Eadfrith's death in this way: we shall return to this point later.[101] In any case, we must tread warily when attempting to understand the motives of men who lived in another age. To us, it seems self-evident that it was in Penda's interests to keep Eadfrith alive, so that he could try and weaken or overthrow Oswald through him.[102] But it is just as likely that Penda killed him, despite his oath, because as long as Eadfrith was alive he also represented a threat to Penda. We must remember that Penda had been joint leader of the army which was responsible for killing Eadfrith's father and brother, and that Eadfrith would therefore have regarded it as his duty to take vengeance for them on Penda. Eadfrith was in a very similar position to Hengest, in the story told in the Finnsburg episode in *Beowulf*: both men were forced to come to terms with the leader of their enemies; but the shame inherent in such a position is openly hinted at in the poem, and Hengest was already turning over the possibility of taking vengeance when the placing of a sword in his lap spurred him to action.[103] Penda might simply have been seeking to forestall a similar attack from Eadfrith; and we must also remember that Eadfrith was descended via his mother from a former Mercian king, Cearl, who belonged to a different royal lineage (or branch thereof) from Penda.[104] He might well have had relatives among the Mercian nobles who were on the lookout for an opportunity to seize the kingship for themselves. We therefore cannot assume that Penda slew Eadfrith out of deference towards Oswald, rather than for his own reasons.

---

evidence of the 7th-century *Vita S. Fursei*, chs. 25-9 (ed. W. W. Heist, *Vitae Sanctorum Hiberniae* (Brussels 1965), at pp. 48-9), particularly if the *Annals of Ulster* date of 627 for Fursey's vision is accepted. Cf. Plummer II, 168-9, 173. The *AU* date seems plausible, and could not have been calculated on the basis of the information in the *Vita Fursei*. As for the *Liber Eliensis*, Roman numerals are notoriously liable to corruption; and one could suggest, for instance, that its compiler or his source had misread Anna's reign as lasting for xix rather than xiv years.

101 Below, pp. 71-5.
102 So Charles-Edwards, 'Bede' (as n. 13 above), p. 51.
103 *Beowulf*, lines 1068-1159, esp. 1095-1106, 1138-59. For an outline of the story (also known from an independent poetic fragment) see Swanton, *Beowulf*, p. 196; cf. also the discussion by Shippey, *Old English Verse*, pp. 19-30. The importance of exacting vengeance is amply attested from historical sources as well as poetry: see D. Whitelock, *The Audience of Beowulf* (London 1951), pp. 13-19.
104 *HE* II, 14. Penda's genealogy survives, and there is no trace of Cearl in it: D. N. Dumville, 'The Anglian collection of royal genealogies and regnal lists', *ASE* 5 (1976), pp. 23-50.

Even if we leave the Eadfrith episode aside, however, it seems likely that Oswald was able to dominate Mercia for much or all of his reign. Bede's lack of explicit information means nothing: it is only on the basis of indirect information, largely furnished by chapters detailing Oswald's support for the church or subsequent miracles, that we are able to prove his overlordship over Lindsey, Wessex, Kent and Sussex. We have no information about various other kingdoms such as East Anglia and Essex. For Mercia, however, we are at least able to gain some idea of the probable position of its ruler in the 630s. First, Penda was only establishing himself in power in Mercia after the battle of Hatfield Chase in 633, and he would not have been left in a strong position when Oswald conquered and slew his chief ally the following year. On top of that, we know for certain that Oswald was able to conquer Lindsey, the most obvious bone of contention between Mercia and Northumbria in the seventh century; and the Mercian leader would not have had the resources to match himself against the king of Bernicia and Deira at a time when he had yet to conquer the smaller midland peoples whose lands lay between Mercia and East Anglia.[105]

In an interesting recent paper, Nicholas Brooks has reviewed the evidence for Penda's early career, and, taking into account the evidence of the *Historia Brittonum* in addition to Bede and the *Anglo-Saxon Chronicle*, he has put forward the hypothesis that Penda was not even king of the Mercians uninterruptedly from 633.[106] He suggests that the Mercian king, Eowa, a brother of Penda's who fell in the same battle as Oswald, might have been not a joint king with Penda, but rather their only king at that time, and one who was subservient to the Northumbrian overking and fighting on his side. On this scenario, Penda would have been fighting for Mercia's independence from Northumbrian control – an achievement which the *Historia Brittonum* does indeed credit him with. The corollary is that, during his lifetime, Oswald was most certainly able to dominate Mercia; and Brooks further suggests that Oswald might have been responsible for taking the Hwicce out of Mercian control and establishing a Bernician dynasty over them, thus effectively reducing the area over which Eowa ruled.[107] Although the

[105] Cf. Dumville, 'Essex, Middle Anglia', pp. 128-33.

[106] Brooks, 'The formation', pp. 164-8.

[107] See also H. P. R. Finberg, *The Early Charters of the West Midlands* (Leicester 1961), pp. 167-70; and Cramp, above, p. 22. Brooks's and Cramp's attribution to Oswald of a formative role in the creation of the Hwicce is far more plausible than Finberg's hypothesis – particularly as we now know that the Bernician princes and their warband were fighting in Ireland in 628, so would not have been available to Penda: see Moisl, art. cit. (above, n. 23) pp. 105-12. As regards Bassett's questioning of the relationship between the rulers of the Hwicce and of Bernicia (*Origins*, p. 238 n. 19), note (a) that there is positive, albeit late, evidence for such a relationship – it does not rest purely on inference drawn from the

evidence is not sufficient to allow firm conclusions to be drawn, as Brooks himself realises, this hypothesis does have the merit of enabling all the various pieces of the jigsaw which we possess to slot into place in a way that makes good sense. I would conclude that Oswald was probably able to dominate Mercia for all or most of his reign; and that he may indeed have been strong enough to oust Penda, have Eowa in a dependent relationship, and place the Hwicce, a recent conquest of Penda's at the expense of Wessex, under direct Bernician overlordship. (Cf. map, p. 14.)

Finally, we may turn to Oswald's relationship with the various British kingdoms. Unfortunately, Bede is silent here. As regards Gwynedd, we have no means of knowing whether Cadwallon's successor acknowledged Northumbrian overlordship. As regards Powys, our only evidence here is the fact that its king fought alongside Penda in the battle of *Maserfelth*, where Oswald was slain.[108] The traditional identification of *Maserfelth* is Oswestry, then probably still in Powys – an identification which may well be correct, though it cannot be conclusively proved.[109] If *Maserfelth* is correctly identified with Oswestry, then clearly Oswald was the aggressor: he may have been trying to meet a threat posed to his domination of Mercia by a hostile alliance between Penda and Powys.

Coming further north, we must again recognise that we do not have the sort of evidence which would enable us to say under which Northumbrian king the pre-1974 counties of Lancashire, Westmorland and Cumberland were incorporated into Northumbria. The scarcity of pagan Anglo-Saxon burials from these areas, coupled with the existence of the independent British kingdom of Elmet as late as Edwin's reign, suggests that their conquest should be placed later than Æthelfrith's reign.[110] On the other

similar names (see Finberg, op. cit. p.170); (b) that his suggestion that the survival of the Hwiccian dynasty throughout the seventh century would be easier to explain if they were of Hwiccian stock is not conclusive: rulers placed by the Carolingians over outlying peoples appear to have 'gone native' very rapidly. Finally, we should note that there are interesting ecclesiastical links between the Hwicce and Northumbria in the later seventh century, particularly with Whitby: *HE* IV, 23; P. Sims-Williams, *Religion and Literature in Western England 600-800* (Cambridge 1990), pp. 92-3, 101-3, 184-90.

108 Rowland, *Early Welsh Saga Poetry*, pp. 123-5, 445, 494. Cf. also *Marwnad Cynddylan*, line 28 (ibid. pp. 176-7), although this may not relate to the battle of *Maserfelth/Cogwy*.

109 See below, pp. 84-96.

110 Recent overviews are provided by D. Kenyon, *The Origins of Lancashire* (Manchester and New York 1991), pp. 79-97; D. O'Sullivan, 'Cumbria before the Vikings: a review of some "Dark Age" problems in north-west England', in *The Scandinavians in Cumbria*, ed. J. R. Baldwin and I. D. Whyte (Edinburgh 1985), pp. 17-35, esp. pp. 24-9; and, for west Yorkshire, M. L. Faull and S. A. Moorhouse, ed. *West Yorkshire: An Archaeological Survey to A.D. 1500* (3 vols,

hand, the Ribble and Dent valleys were clearly in Northumbrian hands by the 670s, and Cartmel and Carlisle by 685. Evidence for the former occurs in the *Life of Wilfrid*, which tells of extensive endowments for Wilfrid's church at Ripon of lands in west Yorkshire and northern Lancashire, representing 'those holy places in various districts which the British clergy had deserted, when fleeing the battle line of the hostile sword wielded by our own nation'.[111] This implies that the Anglo-Saxon take over was of fairly recent origin at that date, viz. the 670s, although other interpretations can be offered.[112] The only other evidence of significance is that Oswiu was married to a British wife, Rieinmelth: presumably during the reign of Oswald, before he married Edwin's daughter Eanflæd.[113] Our source is the *Historia Brittonum*, but confirmed by the Durham *Liber Vitae*; and since the *Historia Brittonum* gives her genealogy, naming her grandfather as 'Rum', and since it shortly after mentions a 'Rum' son of Urien as the baptizer of Edwin, she has been plausibly identified as a princess of the British kingdom of Rheged, whose late sixth-century king, Urien, was famed in poetry.[114] As has been pointed out, the implication is that Rheged was still an independent kingdom at least up to Oswald's reign, 'since the young Northumbrian prince is not very likely to have married a representative of a ruined and landless dynasty'.[115] It could have been conquered by Oswald, with this marriage the equivalent to that between Oswald's own parents, stemming from Æthelfrith's annexation of Deira. Alternatively, and, given the *Life of Wilfrid* evidence, more probably, it could have been annexed under Oswiu, or even at the beginning of Ecgfrith's reign in the early 670s.[116] In this scenario, we might interpret Oswiu's marriage to Rieinmelth as a northern counterpart to Oswald's alliance with Wessex, securing a well-disposed ally to protect an

---

Wakefield 1981), I, pp. 179-86.

[111] *VW* ch. 17; see Hunter Blair (as n. 14 above), pp. 122-4. K. Jackson, *Language and History in Early Britain* (Edinburgh 1953), pp. 213-18.

[112] Viz. that their conquest from the Britons occurred earlier, but that the flight of the British clergy occurred only after the synod of Whitby; or after these areas were reincorporated into Northumbria, having meanwhile been in Mercian hands: M. L. Faull, 'British Survival in Anglo-Saxon Yorkshire' (2 vols. unpublished Ph.D thesis, University of Leeds 1979), I, p. 59.

[113] For the date, see Kirby, *Earliest English Kings*, p. 90.

[114] *Historia Brittonum*, chs. 57, 63; Jackson, 'Nennius' (as n. 6 above), pp. 41-2, 32-3; Rowland, *Early Welsh Saga Poetry*, pp. 86-7. Rum is probably a mistake for Run, modern Rhun; a Run is listed among Urien's sons in *Bonedd yr Arwyr* §7, ed. P. C. Bartrum, *Early Welsh Genealogical Tracts* (Cardiff 1966), p. 87.

[115] Jackson, 'Nennius' (as n. 6 above), p. 42.

[116] Cf. Jackson, loc. cit.; A. P. Smyth, *Warlords and Holy Men: Scotland AD 80-1000* (London 1984, pb edn), pp. 23-6, who is surely correct in arguing that Rheged will have been conquered, not acquired peacefully through Oswiu's marriage.

important flank.[117]

Finally, we may turn to the north British kingdom of Gododdin, which had suffered a famous defeat at Catterick some decades previously, but appears to have continued its separate existence in the Lothians up to Oswald's reign. Irish annals, which here again represent those written on Iona, place the siege of Edinburgh in 638;[118] and, as Edinburgh appears to have been the royal stronghold of the Gododdin, who disappear from the historical record around this time, this laconic annal probably marks the overthrow of the independent kingdom of the Gododdin.[119] The victors of this siege were presumably the Bernicians under Oswald, for a reference in the *Historia Brittonum* implies that Oswiu was sufficiently well in control of former Gododdin territory to flee northwards to Stirling when under pressure from Penda in the early 650s.[120] Thus Oswald appears to have been responsible for pushing the northern frontier of Northumbria up to the Forth, where the Anglo-Saxons would come up against the Picts to their north, and the resilient British kingdom of Strathclyde to their west.

We may now return to the more general question of how we should interpret Oswald's political achievement. Clearly, much remains unknown; but for all that, we do have enough detailed indications to be able partially to fill out the generalisations of Bede and Adomnán. We know that Oswald's overlordship was felt in Lindsey, Wessex, Sussex and Kent, and that in the north it was he, in all probability, who annexed the kingdom of the Gododdin. He was probably also able to assert his overlordship over Mercia, and quite possibly over Rheged. Even this limited amount of information enables us to improve upon Bede's general statement that Oswald ruled 'within the same bounds' as Edwin.[121] Edwin may have had more power over Gwynedd, and possibly Powys; but Bede excepts Kent from his control, and his northern frontier probably ran along the Tweed.

What of overlordship over the Picts and Dalriadan Irish, which Bede attributes to Oswiu in his general overview of Southumbrian overkings, but

---

[117] Cf. Kirby, *Earliest English Kings*, p. 90.

[118] *The Annals of Ulster s.a.* 638, ed. S. Mac Airt and G. Mac Niocaill, part I (Dublin 1983), p. 120: 'obsesio Etin'; 'Annals of Tigernach', ed. Stokes (as n. 76), p. 184; *Chronicum Scotorum s.a.* 637, ed. W. M. Hennessy (London 1866, RS 46), p. 84. Given that the Irish annals place Oswald's death in the following year, the capture of Edinburgh should probably be dated c.638 x 641.

[119] K. H. Jackson, *The Gododdin: The Oldest Scottish Poem* (Edinburgh 1969), pp. 75-8, 105-6 (B. 19, B. 21), 122 (A. 17); K. H. Jackson, 'Edinburgh and the Anglian occupation of Lothian', in *The Anglo-Saxons*, ed. P. Clemoes (London 1959), pp. 35-42.

[120] Jackson, 'Nennius', pp. 35-8; Kirby, *Earliest English Kings*, p. 90; above, p. 53.

[121] *HE* II, 5.

to Oswald elsewhere?[122] As so often, the evidence is teasing, and can be read in support of either claim.[123] One possibility worth mooting is that Oswald achieved theoretical recognition as overlord from Dál Riada and the Picts, but that Oswiu later re-established or redefined this in more oppressive terms, requiring them to render tribute, the badge of subjection to a foreign king.[124] Given Oswald's long apprenticeship from approximately the age of eleven to that of twenty-eight in Dál Riada, he may indeed have been ready to follow an Irish model in his relationships with other kingdoms,[125] particularly with Dál Riada itself. One can, then, hazard the suggestion that he might have concluded an agreement with Dál Riada and the Picts of a type known from Irish sources which would have required a limited amount of military service, under specific conditions, and perhaps some entitlement to hospitality, but which would have been perceived as honourable and therefore acceptable even by the subject peoples in a way that the tribute-exacting overlordship asserted later by Oswiu and Ecgfrith was not.[126] If interpreted in this general sense, Bede's claim that Oswald had Britons, Picts, Irish and English under his authority is plausible enough. It certainly should not be rejected on the grounds that it conflicts with what Bede said in book II about Oswald's ruling over the same area as Edwin, as we have already seen that this is inaccurate. Further, the Ionan evidence we have examined provides a convincing context for envisaging Oswald entering into some kind of agreement with Dál Riada and the Picts. His victory over the Gododdin would have brought him into contact with the Picts; and if former Gododdin territory was indeed annexed by Northumbria, it is quite likely that this achievement led the Picts to acknowledge Northumbria's overlordship. As for Dál Riada, given its defeat in Ireland in 637, it may well

---

[122] Cf. *HE* II, 5 and III, 6; cf. above, pp. 43, 49.

[123] Moisl, art. cit. (as n. 23 above), pp. 117-20, provides a balanced discussion.

[124] Cf. the wording of *HE* III, 6, where he says that Oswald 'in dicione accepit' the four peoples of Britain, with the wording of *HE* II, 5, where he says that Oswiu 'Pictorum quoque atque Scottorum gentes... maxima ex parte perdomuit ac tributarias fecit'. See J. Campbell, 'The debt of the early English Church to Ireland', in *Irland und die Christenheit (Ireland and Christendom)*, ed. P. Ní Chatháin and M. Richter (Stuttgart 1987), pp. 332-46 at pp. 335-6. On the negative connotations of tribute, see T. Charles-Edwards, 'Early medieval kingships in the British Isles', in *Origins*, pp. 28-39, esp. pp. 30-1.

[125] As suggested by Cramp, above, p. 22.

[126] Cf. the generous terms of what was due from the Airgialla to the Uí Néill, or from some of the kings in Munster to the Eóganacht overkings: M. O Daly, 'A poem on the Airgialla', *Ériu* 16 (1952), pp. 179-88, discussed by Charles-Edwards, 'Early medieval kingships', p. 38; Byrne, *Irish Kings*, pp. 196-9; and, in general, M. Gerriets, 'Kingship and exchange in pre-Viking Ireland', *Cambridge Medieval Celtic Studies* 13 (1987), pp. 39-72, at pp. 39-52. I am grateful to T. M. Charles-Edwards for drawing my attention to this material.

have been ready to acknowledge Northumbrian overlordship in exchange for a defensive alliance against Strathclyde, on its southern flank.[127] One tantalising detail is that its king was killed shortly after Oswald's death by the Strathclyde British in *Strathcarron*, i.e. to the west of the Firth of Forth.[128] Domnall of Dál Riada's intervention there, in territory which was borderland for Northumbria, Strathclyde, and the Picts, suggests that his campaign was part of a wider strategy, not a simple raid on Strathclyde. Had Strathclyde sought to take advantage of Oswald's death, and was Dál Riada here intervening, unsuccessfully, on behalf of Northumbria?[129] It may well be that Oswald succeeded in establishing recognition from Dál Riada and the Picts only for his lifetime; that it lapsed after his death and defeat at *Maserfelth*, and was re-established by Oswiu in a more tangible and oppressive form.

The Irish annals contain one further item of interest: fairly early in Oswald's reign, they record a 'congregacio Saxonum contra Osualt';[130] in other words, a hostile banding together of the Anglo-Saxons against Oswald. We can guess at the scenario. Once established in both Bernicia and Deira, Oswald will have sought to re-establish Edwin's overlordship over the Anglo-Saxon kingdoms south of the Humber, and presumably met with some success. This *congregatio* was the reaction of the Southumbrian kingdoms, an attempt to shake off Northumbrian overlordship before Oswald's power was entrenched. Presumably it failed, for Oswald would scarcely have been remembered as an effective overlord in so many Southumbrian kingdoms if his power had been checked this early in his career. Indeed, it may well have been Oswald's victory here which confirmed his *imperium* over the Southumbrian kingdoms.[131]

Oswald should thus be seen as an effective contributor to Northumbrian greatness; as one in a line of remarkable kings which begins with Æthelfrith and Edwin, and continues down to Ecgfrith. Undoubtedly there was a hiatus around the middle of the century, when Penda of Mercia dominated the other Southumbrian kingdoms, and Oswiu seemed powerless in the face of

---

[127] Smyth, *Warlords*, p. 120. An excerpt from a fragmentary mid-seventh-century Life of Columba (*apud VCol* at 108a, pp. 188-90) laments that from that 637 defeat to the time of writing, Dál Riada is subject to foreigners; but since the 'foreigners' could be either the Strathclyde British or the Northumbrians, its evidence is riddlingly ambiguous. Moisl, loc. cit.

[128] *Annals of Ulster, s.a.* 642; Stokes, 'Annals of Tigernach', p. 186; *Chron. Scot, s.a.* 640.

[129] Cf. Kirby, *Earliest English Kings*, p. 90. The Irish annals record a war between Oswiu and the Britons in the same year as the battle of Strathcarron.

[130] Stokes, 'Annals of Tigernach', p. 183, placed two years after Heavenfield, three years before the siege of Edinburgh, and four before Oswald's death.

[131] Cf. the events of nearly forty years later, outlined in *VW* ch. 20.

his attacks. This period of weakness, however, began with Oswald's defeat and death at the hands of Mercia and Powys – there is no evidence of it from his lifetime. Also, there was no swift collapse: it says much that Oswiu was able to make a successful raid for his brother's remains into enemy territory the very year after *Maserfelth*.[132]

Up to this point we have been concentrating on the Oswald of whom Bede said relatively little: the successful warleader of his people who fought his way to the kingship, and then to the re-establishment of Northumbrian overlordship over the Southumbrians, while also expanding his kingdom to the north. We must now face the question: was Oswald nothing but a warlike seventh-century king, no more of a 'saint' than, say, Edwin or Oswiu? Is Bede's portrayal of him as a devout Christian king misleading?

III

The Christian King

In view of the scarcity of other sources, our interpretation of Oswald as a Christian king has to rest almost wholly on the evidence of Bede. Before we examine this, however, we might note the interesting point that Oswald received an honourable nickname from the British, who would have had no motive for hushing up any unpleasant characteristics. Whereas his father was known to them as Æthelfrith *Flesaur*, the 'Twister' or 'Artful Dodger', and whereas Edwin was regarded as 'deceitful', Oswald's Welsh nickname was *Lamnguin*, 'Bright Blade'.[133] It suggests a doughty warrior who won the respect of his enemies, rather than a man of unpleasant character.

Turning now to Bede's portrayal of Oswald, there are, of course, the general laudatory epithets: he was a 'man beloved of God', a 'most Christian king', a 'soldier of Christ'.[134] More specifically, Bede concentrates on Oswald's possession of four Christian virtues: his faith; his humility; his generosity to the poor and strangers; and his concern to establish and extend the church.[135] How far is Bede here portraying Oswald's own qualities, or how far is he presenting us with an image of the ideal Christian king?[136]

---

[132] *HE* III, 12; Plummer II, 157. Thacker, below, p. 100.

[133] *Historia Brittonum*, chs. 57, 63 (Flesaur); ch. 64 (*Oswald Lamnguin*); see Jackson 'Nennius', pp. 32-4, 39, and cf. 43 (Oswiu 'White Brow'). Edwin is called 'deceitful' in the early *Moliant Cadwallon*: see Bromwich, *Trioedd*, p. 294, and cf. p. 338.

[134] *HE* III, 1; II, 5 and III, 9; IV, 14; cf. above, p. 41.

[135] *Fide fervens*; *quanta fides in Deum*: *HE* III, 2 and 9 (pp. 214, 242). '[Aidani] admonitionibus humiliter ac libenter in omnibus auscultans, ecclesiam Christi in regno suo multum diligenter aedificare ac dilatare curauit': *HE* III, 3 (p. 220). 'Pauperibus et peregrinis semper humilis benignus et largus fuit': *HE* III, 6 (p. 230).

[136] Cf. G. Tugène, 'Rois moines et rois pasteurs dans l'*Histoire Ecclésiastique* de Bède', *Romanobarbarica* 8 (1984-5), pp. 111-47 (121-2); Wallace-Hadrill, *EGK*, pp. 79-87.

My own reading of the *Ecclesiastical History* is that Bede did not have a single stereotyped ideal of 'a Christian king' to which every individual had to be fitted in the same way. Rather, he took account of the various personalities and actions of the kings he wrote about and used these as a basis for drawing a series of portraits in which sometimes one quality is uppermost, sometimes another;[137] but all are shaped by the presuppositions which he drew from his reading, most notably that God is the ultimate disposer of all that happens in this world, and that the virtuous behaviour of rulers would lead to earthly prosperity, while sin would be punished.[138] The most striking differentiation amongst his praiseworthy Christian kings lies between those who laid aside their kingship for the sake of the religious life, and those who remained at the helm as Christian kings. Even amongst the latter, however, there is considerable variation, as we see in his portrayals of Edwin and Oswald. Both kings are assigned a significant amount of space, and presented in idealised terms: Edwin's reign, for instance, is recalled as a golden age of peace.[139] Yet in their attitude to Christianity they offer a striking contrast: Edwin is continually portrayed as hesitating whether or not to accept the new religion, while his royal pride baulked at the humility of the Christian cross.[140] Oswald, by contrast, is so committed a Christian that we never see any indecision, and he is explicitly praised for his humility.[141] In giving us full-length treatment of these two kings, Bede is doing two things simultaneously: on the one hand, he is presenting us with two stages in the conversion of Northumbria.[142] From this angle, Edwin's hesitations serve to emphasise the weighty significance of the Christian commitment which he eventually takes on himself and his people, while Oswald belongs to the next stage: as a committed Christian, he is shown as largely responsible for establishing the church throughout Northumbria on a secure footing. Secondly, Edwin, with his royal pride and his indecision, acts as a foil for Oswald, throwing his whole-hearted commitment to all that Christianity stood for into strong relief.

---

[137] Cf. H. Mayr-Harting, *The Coming of Christianity to Anglo-Saxon England* (London 1972), p. 255; below, n. 146.

[138] One might single out the Old Testament, Eusebius's *Ecclesiastical History*, Gildas, and Gregory the Great as particularly influential: see Wallace-Hadrill, *EGK*, pp. 72-8; J. M. Wallace-Hadrill, *Early Medieval History* (Oxford 1975), pp. 103, 105-6.

[139] *HE* II, 16.

[140] *HE* II, 9, 12.

[141] *HE* III, 2, 3, 6.

[142] *HE* II, 9, first sentence attributes this to Edwin; but *HE* III, 2 presents the battle of Heavenfield as the beginning of the Christianisation of Bernicia, while the near total collapse of Paulinus's mission after Edwin's death and the apostasy of his successors makes Heavenfield a second start: cf. above, n. 8 and p. 43.

Oswald is thus presented with the faith and humility which may be inferred of Bede's kings who entered the religious life; but, unlike them, he is shown making full use of his position as king to initiate and promote the conversion of his people. In this, Bede's Oswald is the embodiment of the teaching which Gregory the Great had urged upon King Æthelberht of Kent:

> Almighty God raises up certain good men to be rulers over nations in order that he may by their means bestow the gifts of his righteousness upon all those over whom they are set... So, my most illustrious son, watch carefully over the grace you have received from God and hasten to extend the Christian faith among the people who are subject to you. Increase your righteous zeal for their conversion; suppress the worship of idols; ...strengthen the morals of your subjects by outstanding purity of life, by exhorting them, terrifying, enticing and correcting them, and by showing them an example of good works; so that you may be rewarded in heaven by the One whose name and knowledge you have spread on earth... It was thus that Constantine, the most religious emperor, converted the Roman State...[143]

Bede had the greatest respect for Gregory the Great, and he made Gregory's teaching on Christian kingship his own. Despite his commendation of kings who abdicated for the sake of the religious life, he shows considerably more interest in those who used their position as king to further the church.[144] In addition, his emphasis on Oswald erecting 'the sign of the holy cross' before giving battle, and praying to God for a Christian victory, looks very much as though he is here stylising Oswald as a Constantine figure.[145] There is, therefore, a case for regarding Bede's Oswald as an embodiment[146] of Bede's ideal Christian king (an ideal drawn from Gregory the Great): one who

[143] HE I, 32, at pp. 110-13. Cf. Tugène, art. cit. esp. pp. 119, 125-34; C. E. Stancliffe, 'Kings and conversion', Frühmittelalterliche Studien 14 (1980), pp. 59-94, esp. pp. 60-1.

[144] Bede's monk-kings and pilgrim-kings get at most a chapter for this part of their lives (e.g. Sigeberht, HE III, 18), and sometimes only a bare mention (e.g. Æthelred of Mercia: HE V, 24, s.a. 704). This contrasts with the space allotted to Edwin and Oswald. Cf. Stancliffe, 'Kings who opted out', pp. 154-5, 176; Tugène, art. cit., esp. p. 144.

[145] As Adomnán, our earlier source, does not mention the cross, it is possible that Bede (and/or popular tradition) had interpreted a cross erected later to mark the site of the battle as having been set up before the battle by Oswald: cf. above, pp. 50-1.

[146] 'An' rather than 'the' embodiment, because an ideal can be embodied in various ways, and no single individual is likely to shine in all of them equally. For instance, Æthelberht and his grandson are credited by Bede with legislating, respectively, to protect the church, and to ban paganism, thus fulfilling part of Gregory's recommendations to Augustine in a sphere where no action is recorded of Oswald: HE II, 5 and III, 8. Cf. above, p. 62.

united the personal Christian virtues of faith and humility with an active concern for others, as shown in his desire to bring the Gospel to his own people and to others over whom he exercised *imperium*.

This makes it all the more important to investigate what relationship Bede's portrayal of Oswald bears to the actuality of Oswald's Christian kingship. In fact, Bede's own account includes enough circumstantial details to confirm his attribution to Oswald of three out of the four virtues he endows him with. First there is Oswald's Christian faith. Whatever we may think of the story of Oswald seizing the cross and helping to get it erected before joining battle with Cadwallon, there can be little doubt that Oswald did explicitly entrust his cause at Heavenfield to the Christian God: on this, both Adomnán and Bede are in agreement. Now, Edwin's Christianising of Northumbria, and particularly of Bernicia, where this battle was fought, appears to have been limited, superficial and short-lived. This means that all Oswald's Bernician supporters except those who had accompanied him into exile will still have been pagan. On the other hand, their hated enemy, Cadwallon, was a Christian. In view of this, Oswald's explicit entrusting of his cause to the Christian God cannot be dismissed as the action of a man out to curry favour with his future subjects: rather, it must reflect his own conviction. Further, while all warleaders are likely to appeal to whatever deity seems most likely to guarantee them victory when fighting with the odds against them, Oswald did indeed follow up his victory by sending straight away to Iona for missionaries to convert his people.[147] Finally, Bede reports that Oswald 'very often continued in prayer from mattins until daybreak; and because of his frequent habit of prayer and thanksgiving, he was always accustomed, wherever he sat, to place his hands on his knees with the palms turned upwards. It is also a tradition which has become proverbial, that he died with a prayer on his lips.'[148] Bede's source here was popular

147 The Irish (i.e. Ionan) annals place the foundation of Lindisfarne in the same year as Oswald's victory over Cadwallon (although the latter has come down to us in a confused entry, which seems to run together what may originally have been two entries, one on Eanfrith's battle against Cadwallon, the other on Oswald's battle against Cadwallon): Stokes, 'Annals of Tigernach', p. 182; cf. *Annals of Ulster s.a.* 632. Contrast Edwin's hesitations of many months despite his victory over Wessex: *HE* II, 9-14.

148 *HE* III, 12; cf. IV, 14 (p. 378) from an ecclesiastical milieu: 'pro eis quasi pro suae gentis aduenis supplex orabat ad Dominum'. W. A. Chaney's attempt to interpret Oswald's cross and his practice of prayer in relation to Germanic paganism strikes me as far-fetched: *The Cult of Kingship in Anglo-Saxon England* (Manchester 1970), pp. 5, 117 (and cf. Cramp above, p. 30). As indicated above (n. 145), I am by no means sure that Oswald *did* actually set up a cross; but if he did, Ionan usage (below, p. 91) seems to me to provide a more relevant context than Anglo-Saxon pagan practices. As regards prayer, the significant question is, to what deity did Oswald address himself? Here, I see no scope for divergent views. On the other

tradition. In the course of a century it may well have exaggerated the hours spent by Oswald in prayer, but it is unlikely to have invented this trait – perhaps less unlikely than traditions handed down in an ecclesiastical milieu.

Oswald's Christian commitment is further evident in his active concern to establish Christianity amongst his people. It is one thing to give a foreign missionary permission to preach, as Æthelberht did with Augustine; it is another to initiate the whole mission, and to identify oneself with the missionary's preaching to the extent of acting as his interpreter, as Oswald on occasion did with Aidan.[149] It is also worth noting the way in which Oswald and Oswiu put their own resources at the service of Aidan. Aidan actually owned only his church and a small amount of land on Holy Island. Elsewhere he was based on royal estates, where he had a church and a pied-à-terre.[150] Royal support was thus crucial in enabling the success of Aidan's mission. Finally, although we cannot interpret Birinus's mission to Wessex as due to Oswald, by acting as King Cynegils's godfather Oswald was certainly using his position to encourage him to adopt Christianity.

A third Christian trait which Bede attributes to Oswald, his kindness and generosity to the poor and to peregrini, is confirmed by the story of how Oswald was just sitting down to a meal on Easter Day when he heard that a crowd of poor people was outside, asking for alms.[151] Oswald's instant reaction was to send out to them the feast prepared for himself, and even to order the breaking up and distribution amongst them of the silver dish on which it was served. A detail worth noticing is that the man who reported the presence of the paupers to the king was 'an officer, who had been allotted the task of looking after the poor'. This implies that royal generosity to the poor was regarded as a regular duty. Oswald's spontaneous gesture, however, clearly went beyond the ordinary call of duty.

The fourth trait which Bede attributes to Oswald is humility. Bede mentions this in two contexts, that of Oswald giving heed to Aidan's teaching, and that of his care for the poor in the story we have just discussed. However, Bede does not include any specific example to illustrate Oswald's humility, unless we regard it as exemplified in Oswald's acting as interpreter while Aidan preached.[152] If we rephrase this quality, and say that Oswald

---

hand, that some of his Anglo-Saxon subjects regarded Oswald, in life and in death, in the way that they were accustomed to regard sacral pagan kings seems entirely plausible; but this is evidence for the beliefs of his subjects, not of Oswald himself.

[149] HE III, 3.

[150] HE III, 17.

[151] HE III, 6. Colgrave and Mynors translate peregrini as 'strangers', but it could equally well denote (Irish) Christian ascetics who had left their homeland out of a desire to abandon all earthly security for the sake of Christ. Cf. below, p. 82, n. 224.

[152] So Tugène, art. cit. pp. 123-4.

was free from the sort of kingly pride which would have led many to refuse to take on themselves the secondary role of interpreter, then we can accept Bede's point. If, however, we take it to mean that Oswald was always ready to do what his bishop told him, as Bede seems to imply, then I think it very doubtful; and if we take the dictionary definition of 'having a lowly opinion of oneself', then almost certainly Oswald does not qualify; and, indeed, it is difficult to conceive of how any successful seventh-century king could be humble in that sense. It is here that Bede's monastic background makes itself felt, in the emphasis he gives to humility, and in his apparent failure to realise that, on its own, it was inappropriate for leaders.[153] One might contrast his mentor, Gregory the Great, who understood that a leader must balance inner humility with the need to exercise authority towards others.[154] When King Oswine of Deira threw himself down at Aidan's feet, asking his pardon for having remonstrated with him about his gift of a fine steed to a beggar, Aidan's comment is significant: 'I know that the king will not live long; for I never before saw a humble king.'[155] Incidentally, this also reveals that Aidan did not think that Oswald had been a 'humble' king.

For all the need to reject or qualify the sense in which Oswald can be understood as possessing humility, it remains that Bede's other claims about his virtues as a Christian ruler have been shown to have some foundation: he clearly was a convinced Christian himself, a man of faith and prayer; and he used his position to promote the conversion of his people, assisting his bishop in a way which associated him intimately with the work of evangelisation. He also showed himself ready to extend his generosity beyond the circle of his *comitatus* followers to the poor who clustered at his gate. In view both of his personal qualities and of his role as the effective instigator of the conversion of Northumbria, he seems well-qualified for recognition as a saint. Why is it, then, that some scholars feel that he 'cuts a curious figure as a saint'?[156] Essentially it is because of the problem of reconciling this image of a *rex Christianissimus* with the Germanic warrior king we were studying some pages back, who avenged his brother's (and his father's?) death and won back their kingdom, and who fought aggressive campaigns to conquer neighbouring peoples and reduce them under tribute. The Germanic warrior society to which Oswald belonged did have its code of ethics, but it was not the same as that which we associate with Christianity. Above all, the tone is

---

153 Ibid. pp. 122-5, esp. n. 28. Mayr-Harting, *Coming*, pp. 255-6. As, with Gregory the Great, pride had become the cardinal sin, so one can see how humility was emphasised to balance it.

154 Stancliffe, 'Kings and conversion', p. 93; M. Reydellet, *La royauté dans la littérature latine de Sidoine Apollinaire à Isidore de Séville* (Bibliothèque des Écoles françaises d'Athènes et de Rome, vol. 243; Rome 1981), p. 470.

155 *HE* III, 14.

156 Thacker, below, p. 97. Cf. Campbell, *Essays*, p. 14.

warlike: to win personal glory through feats of arms, to show courage and loyalty, to triumph over one's enemies, and to avenge the wrongs done to one's kinsmen or lord. This was the world to which Oswald belonged; surely, then, there is something phoney about his Christianity?

Underlying this question is an unspoken assumption about the nature of the Christian calling. One must emphasise, however, that different generations have interpreted this in different ways. Our present task is not to try and judge Oswald against some *a priori* Christian standard, but rather to understand how he and the world he lived in viewed his role as a Christian king. The first thing we must realise is that Christianity had changed markedly since the early Christian period. Once it had become the religion of the Roman emperor and of Germanic kings, it had had to come to terms with the need for warfare.[157] Jesus had set an example of non-violence for his own individual disciples; but how far was it appropriate for a state, or for those acting in an official capacity to uphold justice and maintain accepted norms in society? Churchmen responded to this challenge in two complementary ways. One, pioneered by Ambrose, was to turn to classical Roman authors, particularly Cicero. The second was to turn to the Old Testament. Here, they found not just that the chosen people of God had fought, but that God himself had fought for them, against their enemies. With all this behind them, the concern of churchmen became not to condemn warfare, but rather to try and canalise military aggressiveness into acceptable channels. Augustine of Hippo had allowed as 'just wars' those that were defensive, those that were fought to avenge injuries, and those undertaken to punish cruel and savage behaviour, and to crush human pride. Gregory of Tours and, in one instance, Gregory the Great went further, and positively commended warfare that was undertaken to extend (catholic) Christianity. By the seventh century, the Frankish and Visigothic churches had set rituals for blessing the king and his army as he set out for war.[158]

Oswald's own Christian formation took place when he was in exile in Dál Riada. The early Irish church appears to have been much less ready to endorse Christian warfare than the Frankish church, and at least some strands of Irish ascetic thought were condemnatory.[159] But the annals reveal

[157] For what follows see C. Erdmann, *The Origin of the Idea of Crusade* (Eng. transl. Princeton 1977), pp. 3-34; D. H. Green, *The Carolingian Lord* (Cambridge 1965), ch. 9, esp. pp. 295-8; Cross, 'Ethic of war' (as n. 44 above); Wallace-Hadrill, 'War and peace in the early middle ages', reprinted in his *Early Medieval History*, pp. 19-38.

[158] J. N. Hillgarth, ed. and trans., *Christianity and Paganism, 350-750: The Conversion of Western Europe* (2nd edn Philadelphia 1986), pp. 90, 93-5.

[159] Stancliffe, 'Kings who opted out' (as above, n. 33), pp. 174-5. Further work is needed to explore the divergent views towards kings and their warfare in Irish sources.

that warfare was a regular part of life in Ireland, as elsewhere; and once kings accepted Christianity, the church had to come to terms with this. Irish writings on kingship from a little later than Oswald's reign teach that the king should trust God and be personally devout, feed the poor, help and defend the church, and judge justly; the importance of the king's justice is strongly emphasised in Irish sources. One treatise adds the need to punish wrong-doers, to protect strangers, widows and orphans, and to defend his country bravely.[160]

The attitude taken to warfare here appears muted in comparison with what we have seen elsewhere in Europe, but two important riders must be added. First, Oswald will have witnessed Christian warrior kingship in action in his years spent in Dál Riada; and Scottish Dál Riada was, of all kingdoms of the Irish, the one that had most need to fight simply to establish its right to exist. This means that Oswald's initial encounter with Christianity will have been within a context which regarded it as perfectly compatible with warrior kingship. Secondly, whatever doubts about such compatibility were entertained by Irish churchmen or women elsewhere, the church of Iona at least seems to have had no qualms in this respect. Its founder, Columba, was first cousin to one Uí Néill overking, and only a little more distantly related to others. Most succeeding abbots, including Ségéne, whom Oswald knew personally, also belonged to the royal line of the northern Uí Néill.[161] It is possible that Columba's decision to leave Ireland and settle on Iona was in some way bound up with his support for his kindred, who in 561 had defeated the then overking, from the rival branch of the southern Uí Néill; 'they prevailed through the prayers of Colum Cille', according to the Annals of Ulster.[162] Certainly Adomnán's Life of Columba shows him involved with kings in his period on Iona. He frequently predicts their futures or has second sight about battles, sometimes actively involving himself in their outcome. According to Adomnán: 'in the terrible crashings of battles, by the power (virtus) of prayer, he obtained from God that some

---

[160] Collectio Canonum Hibernensis 25, ch. 15 and ch. 4 (the latter citing the De xii abusivis saeculi, ed. Hellmann (as n. 32 above), pp. 51-3): ed. H. Wasserschleben, Die irische Kanonensammlung (2nd edn Leipzig 1885), pp. 81, 77-8. On the king's justice (or 'truth': Old Irish fír) see Audacht Morainn, ed. Kelly (as n. 32 above), esp. §§ 6-7, 12-21, 23-8.

[161] Byrne, Irish Kings and High-Kings, tables on pp. 258, 283. VCol I, 1 at 9b.

[162] Sub anno 561; but we do not know when this entry was written – it is most unlikely to be strictly contemporary. For arguments on Columba's possible involvement see Smyth, Warlords, pp. 92-9, but note T. M. Charles-Edwards's comments in Cambrian Medieval Celtic Studies 26 (1993), pp. 70-2; for a more cautious view, Herbert, Iona, Kells, pp. 27-8; however, Columba was not simply 'censured' (loc. cit.), but excommunicated by an Irish synod (Adomnán, VCol III, 3).

kings were conquered, and others were conquerors.'[163] As we have seen, Oswald appears to have attributed his victory at Heavenfield to St Columba's prayers, and Adomnán tells a similar story set in Columba's own lifetime: the saint summoned his monks to the chapel to pray for King Áedán of Dál Riada as he was going into battle against the Miathi, desisting only when victory had been granted to him.[164] As this battle appears to have been fought on Miathi territory, to the west of the Firth of Forth, it looks as though Áedán was the aggressor. This makes Columba's intercession on his behalf the more noteworthy.[165]

This was the Christian tradition to which Oswald was introduced during his exile in Dál Riada. Essentially it means that the Ionan tradition of Christianity saw no necessary divorce between successful warrior kingship and a genuine commitment to Christianity. On the contrary, it appears to have pioneered a *modus vivendi* between the two; and one might speculate that it, more than Gregory the Great, may have laid the foundations which would enable Old English poets to develop the theme of Christ as the warrior lord, surrounded by his *comitatus* of apostles.[166] Certainly the profound religious sensibility apparent in *The Dream of the Rood*, the greatest of these poems, shows that one must not *a priori* dismiss such a heroic interpretation of Christianity as evidence of superficial or insincere Christianisation. Nor, by the same token, should we dismiss the Christianity of Oswald himself as superficial or insincere. If Bede, Adomnán and the Old

---

[163] *VCol* I, 1, at 8a.

[164] *VCol* I, 8. No line of transmission is given for this story, which means we cannot know whether it is based on a genuine occurrence of Columba's lifetime; whether it was attributed to him by Cumméne the White around the early/mid 7th century; or whether it was attributed to him by Adomnán *c*.700. The parallel instance of the British monks praying for the victory of their own side *c*.615 (*HE* II, 2) suggests that the theme could well antedate Adomnán.

[165] Adomnán, loc. cit., simply notes the battle; but it is plausibly identified with the battle of Manau in the *Annals of Ulster* (*s.a.* 582, 583) by Anderson, *VCol*, at pp. xix-xx. Of course Áedán could have been retaliating for a Miathi raid on Dál Riada, but it seems more likely that he was seeking to expand his kingdom – which would explain why he later attacked Æthelfrith (*Annals of Ulster s.a.* 600; *HE* I, 34).

[166] Cf. Green, *Carolingian Lord*, pp. 286-98. God is referred to as *dryctin* already in the poetry of Cædmon of Whitby: *HE* IV, 22; R. Hamer, *A Choice of Anglo-Saxon Verse* (London 1970), p.122. Hild, abbess of Whitby, was frequently visited and instructed by Aidan: *HE* IV, 23. For a parallel suggestion of Irish influence on Old English poetry see C. Donahue, 'Beowulf, Ireland and the natural good', *Traditio* 7 (1949-51), pp. 263-77; *idem*, 'Beowulf and Christian tradition: a reconsideration from a Celtic stance', *Traditio* 21 (1965), pp. 55-116.

Testament could see a link between holiness and victory in battle,[167] then it is likely that Oswald himself thought of the two as interrelated, not opposed.

There remain two areas where we may still feel that the evidence contradicts Bede's presentation of Oswald as *sanctissimus*: Oswald's possible involvement in attempts to assassinate Edwin's male heirs, and his wars of aggression. Neither case, however, is clearcut. We will begin with the latter. If a seventh-century king was to be successful, then he needed to be aggressive.[168] Kingdoms did not exist in a stable state, as wholly independent entities: their relations were in a continual state of flux. The successful king was he who attracted loyal warriors to his service with gifts, and with the aid of these warriors won victories which compelled his neighbour kingdoms to render tribute. It was no use simply allowing one's warriors to while away their time feasting, drinking, and receiving royal gifts: when the treasure had run out, the warriors would take themselves elsewhere. Although kings owned land of their own and were also owed food renders from within their kingdoms, it is likely that tribute levied upon neighbouring peoples also played a significant role.[169] Thus aggressive warfare was a normal part of successful kingship, and the church probably recognised this fact. Peace could only be established by a strong king, and maintained by the threat of force. I doubt if Aidan was overjoyed at Oswald's conquest of the Gododdin; but it may be significant that he was appointed precisely because he was prepared to reach some compromises with the *homines indomabiles et durae ac barbarae mentis*, as Aidan's unsuccessful predecessor described the Northumbrians.[170] In any case, a culture which interprets victory in battle as a sign of divine favour, as appears to have been the case both with Ionan and with Anglo-Saxon Christianity, would have seen Oswald's success as its own justification.

[167] One should, however, note that in Adomnán it is the power of Columba's prayers, not Oswald's, that brings the victory: cf. the story told in *VCol* I,1 at 9b.

[168] Cf. Campbell, *Essays*, pp. 92-5.

[169] Historians of Anglo-Saxon England have concentrated more on the food renders paid to kings by their own people: Charles-Edwards, 'Early medieval kingships in the British Isles', in *Origins*, pp. 28-39; Yorke, *Kings and Kingdoms*, pp. 157-67, 169. But a recent study illustrating the importance of tribute and plunder for Carolingian kings is suggestive of their importance for early Anglo-Saxon kings: T. Reuter, 'Plunder and tribute in the Carolingian empire', *Transactions of the Royal Historical Society* 5th series, 35 (1985), pp. 75-94. The Tribal Hidage is obviously relevant here (ed. D. Dumville in *Origins*, pp. 225-30); and, for booty, cf. the Penitential of Theodore, I, vii, 2, ed. A. W. Haddan and W. Stubbs, *Councils and Ecclesiastical Documents relating to Great Britain and Ireland* (3 vols. in 4; Oxford 1869-71), III, pp. 173-204, at p. 182.

[170] 'Untameable people of harsh and savage outlook': *HE* III, 5. Cf. St Cuthbert's inability to dissuade King Ecgfrith from aggressive warfare against the Picts: *HE* IV, 26.

As for Bede, he was perhaps not so far divorced from the warrior mentality of *Beowulf* as one might imagine. He celebrated the exploits of the pagan Æthelfrith, 'a very brave king and most eager for glory', delighting in his conquests at the expense of the Christian Britons.[171] He would certainly have had no qualms about Oswald's conquest of the British Gododdin; nor, one suspects, about the re-establishment of Northumbrian supremacy over the kingdoms south of the Humber, since that gave an opening for a Christian king to promote the spread of Christianity there. He acclaimed the days of Theodore and Hadrian not least because at that time the English, 'having such brave Christian kings, were a terror to all the barbarian nations'.[172] This view fits with that of the author of *Beowulf*, whose 'good king', Scyld Scefing, struck terror into neighbouring warriors.[173] I would therefore suggest that Bede was more realistic about what was involved in successful warrior kingship than he is often credited with being. When he celebrated Oswald as *sanctissimus ac victoriosissimus rex Nordanhymbrorum*, he was indeed pointing to the intimate relationship between the two attributes, viz. that God gave Oswald victory because of his exemplary Christian life; but Bede was also aware that in order to win battles, it was not enough to be devout: the fate of Sigeberht of East Anglia showed that.[174] No: to be victorious one had also to be brave and to have a sufficiency of well-armed warriors.[175]

As regards the fate of Edwin's male heirs, the supposition that Oswald was involved rests solely upon inference. Bede tells us that Edwin and one son were killed in battle: 'alter Eadfrid necessitate cogente ad Penda regem transfugit, et ab eo postmodum, regnante Osualdo, contra fidem iurisiurandi peremtus est.'[176] Next we hear of Penda and Cadwallon's slaughter amongst the Northumbrians, and of the burial of Edwin's head at York. Then comes the flight to Kent of Edwin's widow, children and grandchild, 'whom afterwards their mother, for fear of Kings Eadbald and Oswald, sent to Gaul, to be brought up by King Dagobert, who was her friend. Both the children died there in infancy.'[177] There are two ways of interpreting this information. As suggested above, Penda may have been acting for good

---

[171] 'Rex fortissimus et gloriae cupidissimus': *HE* I, 34, and n. 1; II, 2. Cf. Shippey, *Beowulf*, p. 19.

[172] 'Dum et fortissimos Christianosque habentes reges cunctis barbaris nationibus essent terrori': *HE* IV, 2.

[173] *Beowulf*, lines 4-11.

[174] *HE* III, 18.

[175] Cf. Bede's letter to Ecgberht, §11, ed. Plummer I, 414-15. Cf. also J. McClure, 'Bede's Old Testament kings', in *Ideal and Reality*, pp. 76-98, at pp. 87-90.

[176] *HE* II, 20, paraphrased above, p. 46.

[177] *HE* II, 20. See above, pp. 52-3.

reasons of his own when he killed Eadfrith;[178] and Edwin's widow, Æthelburh, was clearly taking a precautionary measure. She may well have been motivated by an understandable fear that Oswald would behave towards the Deiran princes in the same way that his father had towards Edwin and Edwin's less fortunate nephew.[179] The alternative interpretation is that Oswald bribed or browbeat Penda into killing Eadfrith, and Æthelburh's action could then be seen as a response to this. Either way it is clear that Æthelburh acted out of fear of what might happen. The chief question, therefore, is who was responsible for Eadfrith's death. On the one hand, to impute blame to Oswald is to read into the text something that is not there; on the other hand, given Bede's known practice of sometimes suppressing material that he regarded as unedifying,[180] it is highly likely that, even if Bede knew that Oswald was responsible, he would not have said so. This case raises a number of complex questions, which we will consider in turn. Our starting point must be to try to understand how Oswald and his contemporaries would have viewed the issues.

'According to the practical wisdom of the day... the only safe member of a rival dynasty was a dead one.'[181] The Oswald/Eadfrith case, however, is peculiarly complicated: on the one hand, Oswald would have had good reason to seek the death of Edwin's son, since he would thereby have avenged the death of his own father and simultaneously eliminated a dangerous rival; on the other hand, Eadfrith was also Oswald's first cousin, so taking blood vengeance would have involved killing a kinsman. (See family tree, above, p. 13.) In such circumstances, compensation was frequently preferred; and we can be reasonably sure that Aidan would have condemned any attempt by Oswald to procure his cousin's death:[182] that would have been regarded as a serious sin, such as might well have merited public rebuke and expiation. From a secular viewpoint, however, his

---

[178] Above, p. 54.

[179] *HE* II, 12 and IV, 23. As Oswald had been in Dál Riada or Ireland throughout Æthelburh's time in Northumbria, she can have known nothing of him personally before she fled to Kent; but she will have heard harrowing tales of Edwin's plight from Edwin himself.

[180] Campbell, 'Bede I' in his *Essays*, esp. pp. 19-22.

[181] Campbell, *Essays*, p. 77. Cf. D. N. Dumville, 'The ætheling: a study in Anglo-Saxon constitutional history', *ASE* 8 (1979), pp. 1-33 at p. 19.

[182] Aidan could be forthright at times: 'neither respect nor fear made him keep silence about the sins of the rich, but he would correct them with a stern rebuke (*aspera inuectione*)'. (*HE* III, 5.) Cf. *HE* III, 14, for a rebuke to King Oswine. Note too that the Lindisfarne-trained Cedd instilled the Gospel teaching about forgiving one's enemies into an East Saxon king, with unfortunate results for the latter: *HE* III, 22, and cf. Wallace-Hadrill's interpretation, *EGK* p. 93.

behaviour would be condoned, although again some form of compensation might well be thought appropriate.

If Oswald were responsible, would this have become public knowledge? And would memory of it have survived down to Bede's lifetime? It would have been difficult for Oswald to escape suspicion; and the person who is likely to have been concerned at Eadfrith's death and tried to discover the true circumstances is his cousin Hild; and the place which would have kept alive his memory is her monastery of Whitby.[183] This was a veritable mausoleum of the Deiran royal family, whose dynastic history would have been cherished by the line of abbesses of royal Deiran blood: Hild herself; Eanflæd, half-sister of Eadfrith and one-time wife of Oswiu; and their daughter, Ælfflæd.[184] Nor would such knowledge necessarily have passed into oblivion with Ælfflæd's death c.714, since it would have been of considerable interest to the Whitby community in the early eighth century when they were fostering the cult of Edwin, while Bardney to the south was promoting that of Oswald.[185] It is difficult not to think in terms of rivalry between the two cults at this date,[186] and Whitby would obviously have been interested in a detail concerning Edwin's son which reflected badly on the reputation of the chief rival, Oswald. Now Bede was in touch with Whitby, which provided him with most of the Deiran material for his *History*.[187] He was apparently well informed about the deaths of Edwin and his sons, differentiating as he does between the fate of Eadfrith and that of Edwin's other son killed with Edwin in battle, and specifying that it was during Oswald's reign that Penda killed the former.[188] Further, Bede elsewhere shows himself perfectly capable of getting at the truth, however distasteful, behind the 'official version' of Northumbrian history.[189] Thus, while there

---

[183] *HE* IV, 23. See P. Hunter Blair, 'Whitby as a centre of learning in the seventh century', in *Learning and Literature in Anglo-Saxon England: Studies presented to Peter Clemoes*, ed. M. Lapidge and H. Gneuss (Cambridge 1985), pp. 3-32, esp. pp. 3-17.

[184] *HE* III, 24, and as preceding note. Family tree, above, p. 13. Cf. the role of female religious houses in Ottonian Germany as preservers of family traditions: Ó Riain-Raedel below, p. 212 and n. 11.

[185] Cf. Thacker below, pp. 105-6. Edwin's cult is clearly of interest to the Whitby author of the early 8th-century *Life of Gregory*, esp. chs. 18-19.

[186] For a different view, see Thacker and Cambridge below, pp. 106, 141-2.

[187] Kirby, 'Bede's native sources' (as above, n. 10) at pp. 351-4. The only reason adduced for doubting Whitby's role as Bede's principal Deiran informant is his failure to make obvious use of the Whitby *Life of Gregory*; but this is no argument that he did not know the work: see Goffart, *Narrators*, pp. 265-6; Thacker, below, p. 105, n. 56.

[188] *HE* II, 20. Contrast the less accurate information in the *Historia Brittonum* ch. 61, ed. Faral p. 41.

[189] *HE* III, 1.

can be no certainty, it is likely that Bede would have known if Oswald himself was behind the killing of Eadfrith.

Is there, then, a likelihood that Bede knew that Oswald was responsible, but withheld the information because it was so unedifying? The problem here is that Bede, as we have seen, had no qualms about presenting Oswald unambiguously as a saint. He calls him not just *sanctus*, but *sanctissimus*, *Christianissimus*, in a way that is unparalleled in his accounts of any of the other active kings he writes about. Could he have used such language if he knew that Oswald had been responsible for Eadfrith's murder? The crucial evidence here is Bede's attitude to Oswiu's assassination of Oswine.[190] The two scenarios are comparable, though not identical in every respect. In both cases, a Bernician king would have been responsible for killing a Deiran rival and relative not in person or in battle, but indirectly, through assassination. Now Bede leaves us in no doubt about his detestation of Oswiu's deed: Oswiu slew Oswine 'with most wretched murder': *miserrima hunc caede peremit*. Certainly the treachery of Oswine's trusted thegn who betrayed his own lord is execrated; but so also is Oswiu's role, and it is he who is seen as responsible: 'Oswiu killed him... by the hand of his reeve Æthelwine *detestanda omnibus morte*.'[191] Bede could not have made his own feelings plainer; and although Oswiu is elsewhere treated with respect, being shown as 'trusting in Christ as leader' when he fought a crucial battle against Penda, and using his position of authority to commend Christianity to subordinate kings and to watch over the church, nonetheless he is never portrayed as a saintly king.[192] The contrast with Bede's portrayal of Oswald is striking.

There is, then, a very real problem about assuming that Bede regarded Oswald as responsible for Eadfrith's death, and simply omitted an explicit reference so as not to let his chosen hero appear in a bad light. In view of Bede's attitude to a closely comparable killing, to jump to this conclusion is to assume that Bede was utterly cynical about the means he used to promote his ideal of Christian kingship. For the unique example in the whole of his *History* of a non-ecclesiastical, non-martyr saint, he would have taken someone whom he knew to be guilty of serious sin, that is, of procuring the death of his cousin; and he would have held up this same person as 'most holy', 'most Christian', the rightful 'heir' of the king whose true heir he had assassinated, and presented him as already reigning in heaven.[193] Why? Surely

---

[190] *HE* III, 14.

[191] 'By a death which is abhorrent to all': loc. cit.

[192] *HE* III, 24; III, 21-22; III, 25, 29. Chase is wrong when he says, adducing no evidence, 'From villain, Oswy has become hero and saint of Bede's account': '*Beowulf*, Bede, and St Oswine', p. 40. See, rather, Wallace-Hadrill, *EGK*, p. 86.

[193] One could be pardoned for thinking that Bede does something very similar with Cædwalla of Wessex, who is presented as slaughtering the inhabitants of the Isle of Wight in *HE* IV, 16, but in *HE* V, 7 as abdicating, going to Rome for his

it would have been preferable to have made much more of other, less problematical kings: Oswine, for instance? In my view, therefore, the balance of probability is against our inferring from Bede's account that he regarded Oswald as responsible for Eadfrith's death, and simply suppressed this information.

We have wrung what insights we can into Oswald as a Christian king, given the limited nature of our single source. As regards Eadfrith's death, we have to recognise that there is insufficient evidence for us to come to a firm conclusion either way; I do, however, regard it as inconceivable that Bede himself could have thought that Oswald had anything to do with it; and fairly likely that Bede was well-informed. If we set aside the Eadfrith case as being unproven, then it would appear that Oswald has stronger claims to be considered as a saint than Æthelberht of Kent, or Edwin, or Oswiu. In the last resort, however, we must recognise the inadequacy of our sources. Bede does provide us with positive evidence of the seriousness of Oswald's Christian commitment and his desire to convert his people, but we have no means of knowing what characteristics he may have omitted. All we can do is to realise that Oswald may have been a rougher diamond than one could ever guess from Bede's polished account.

IV

Some Consequences

It remains briefly to draw out the long-term significance of some of Oswald's actions. On the political side, it may well be that his victory at Heavenfield was more important than we customarily assume. Even if Cadwallon had succeeded in keeping Deira and Bernicia as separate, subordinate kingdoms for only a decade, it is not difficult to envisage a different scenario from the Northumbrian success story we are used to. In ten years Penda would have been able to consolidate his control in Mercia, and might then have been in a position to draw Deira permanently into its orbit, as he appears to have been doing in the years preceding the battle of the Winwæd; and without the southern kingdom, Bernicia might not have been strong enough to defeat the neighbouring British, and beyond them, Irish and Pictish kingdoms. We should not exaggerate Oswald's role here: Æthelfrith had set the stage by annexing Deira to Bernicia; but every succeeding king down to Ecgfrith

---

baptism, and shortly afterwards dying and joining the blessed in heaven. The events of IV, 16, however, occurred while Cædwalla was still a pagan; he was later baptized in Rome on 10 April 689, and died ten days later. The church's teaching was that all sins were remitted in baptism, and Bede is simply reflecting this and the interpretation of his Roman epitaph, which Bede quotes. It is no parallel with Oswald, who was baptized on Iona before he became king. Note also that Bede evinces no warmth towards Cædwalla in IV, 16 (or even V, 7), despite his generous donation to the church.

played a significant part in ensuring that a powerful kingdom of Northumbria came into being in the seventh century. It could well not have done so.

It is, however, in the religious and cultural spheres that Oswald's actions were to have their most significant and lasting effects. True, Oswald or no Oswald, we may assume that Northumbria would have become converted to Christianity in the course of the seventh century: it was already established in Kent, and at some stage the mission to York would probably have been re-established. But if it had, subsequent history would have been different. What Oswald did, which was of long-term importance, was to turn not to Kent, but to the Irish monastery of Iona for his missionaries. The effects of his decision reach far beyond the simple fact that Holy Island in Bernicia, rather than the former Roman city of York in Deira, became for a time the episcopal base for all Northumbria. Two consequences, in particular, are worth dwelling upon: first, the implications for the former British Christian population in north Britain; and secondly, the significance of the Ionan contribution to the Anglo-Saxon church and its culture.

Owing to Bede's hostility and silence, coupled with the difficulty of tracing them in the archaeological record, we know all too little about the Christian Britons and their interaction – or lack of it – with the invading Anglo-Saxons. The Britons we are concerned with here are those who lived in relative independence down to Edwin's reign, at least, and were then absorbed into Anglo-Saxon Northumbria later in the seventh century. I think we may assume that these Britons were Christians. That is certainly the conclusion to be drawn from our literary sources, although these are all problematical in one way or another;[194] and for some areas we can add in the evidence of Christian memorial stones and of Eccles place-names.[195] On the archaeological side, the evidence is at least compatible with a Christian

---

[194] The one accusation which Gildas does not level at his British countrymen in the mid-sixth century is that they were still pagan: *De excidio*, passim. Similarly, paganism is nowhere mentioned in British synodical canons or penitentials (although these are in any case mostly aimed at monks or clerics): *Irish Penitentials*, ed. Bieler, pp. 60-72. The problem is that we generally do not know what area these writings refer to. The *Gododdin* does make it clear that that people was Christian (K. Jackson, *The Gododdin* (Edinburgh 1969, pb. edn. 1978), p. 37); but it does not survive as an absolutely unchanged *c*.600 text in the 13th-century manuscript in which it is transmitted: see Charles-Edwards, 'The authenticity' (as n. 21 above); cf. L. Alcock, *Economy, Society and Warfare among the Britons and Saxons* (Cardiff 1987), p. 248.

[195] A. C. Thomas, 'The evidence from north Britain', in *Christianity in Britain, 300-700*, ed. M. W. Barley and R. P. C. Hanson (Leicester 1968), pp. 117-21; cf. [A.] C. Thomas, *Christianity in Roman Britain to AD 500* (London 1981), ch. 11, esp. pp. 291-3. On *Eccles* names, see below.

population, and may indeed indicate it, although unambiguous archaeological evidence for Christianity is largely absent.[196] However, there is also an absence of explicit archaeological evidence of paganism,[197] and we might expect that to show up in the record more clearly than Christianity. Given, then, this general premise, that in the seventh century the Anglo-Saxon kingdoms of Bernicia and Deira conquered and in time absorbed Christian British kingdoms north of the Tweed (Gododdin), in the Pennines (Elmet), and west of the Pennines also, it is surely important to realise that from the arrival of Irish missionaries early in Oswald's reign right through to the synod of Whitby thirty years later, there was no barrier between the Christianity of the Britons and that of the Irish and their Anglo-Saxon disciples. The Irish had been converted to Christianity largely by British Christians, and relations were close right through the sixth century and beyond, turning sour only as Irish churches began to adopt Roman practices for matters such as calculating the date of Easter, and with them, a perception of the British Christians as wrong-headed. The first Irish churches to adopt Roman methods were in southern Ireland, and they did so around the beginning of Oswald's reign. Iona, however, remained faithful to the traditional methods which they shared with the British churches right through the seventh century and beyond.

The Ionan Irish, as a third party on good terms with both the other two peoples, were thus well-placed to act as a bridge between the Anglo-Saxons and the Britons, and this will have been particularly important in areas where there was substantial British survival at all levels of the population, as in those that concern us here. We have very little explicit evidence about what happened to the British church in areas conquered by the Anglo-Saxons. We can, however, surmise that its prospects under Æthelfrith would have been bleak;[198] and an interesting passage in Stephen's *Life of Wilfrid* suggests that it will not necessarily have fared much better later in the seventh century when

---

[196] Thomas has drawn attention to the long-cist cemeteries of south-east Scotland: 'The evidence', pp. 107-8; cf. [A.] C. Thomas, *The Early Christian Archaeology of North Britain* (London 1971), ch. 3. But on its own (i.e. without positive supporting evidence of Christianity, such as an inscription or chi-rho symbol), such burial evidence is not conclusive. For recent surveys, see E. Alcock, 'Burials and cemeteries in Scotland', in *The Early Church in Wales and the West*, ed. N. Edwards and A. Lane (Oxford 1992), pp. 125-9; Higham, *The Northern Counties*, pp. 258, 274 ff. Cf. Cramp, above, pp. 30-1.

[197] Except at Yeavering, most notably the structure D2 in post-Roman phases II and III, apparently a pagan temple, and the nearby Western Cemetery: B. Hope-Taylor, *Yeavering: An Anglo-British Centre of Early Northumbria* (London 1977), pp. 97-102, 108-16, 158-62, 244-5; but here, it is not clear that the paganism was British, rather than being Anglo-Saxon: see Cramp, above, p. 28.

[198] Cf. *HE* I, 34; II, 2 (at p. 140). Cf. Cramp, above, pp. 19-20, 31-2.

the Romanising Wilfrid was bishop. At the dedication of his new church at Ripon in the 670s, Wilfrid enumerated those lands which had been donated. Included were 'those holy places in various districts which the British clergy had deserted, when fleeing the battle line of the hostile sword wielded by our own nation.'[199] What happened in this instance was that British church sites were respected, in that they were assigned to an Anglo-Saxon church; but the personnel had fled, so there was no continuity there, while the assignment of their churches to a major Anglo-Saxon monastery also means that there will have been a break in their institutional status: they were reduced to dependency on Ripon.

This is not the place for a detailed examination of the evidence, but I would like to suggest that the survival of five certain, and one possible, Eccles place-names from the area between the Tweed and Stirling on the Forth suggests the survival of Christian British churches in the Gododdin territory conquered by Oswald.[200] What is more, the fact that four out of the five well-attested Eccles churches in this area retained their position as 'mother churches',[201] compared with only two out of the nine Eccles sites in Elmet,[202] does imply continuity at a deeper level than we may infer for the sites assigned to Wilfrid's Ripon. In other words, in the area conquered by Oswald there appears to have been continuity at an institutional level of church organisation. We might add that since this area was conquered within some three years of Aidan's arrival, it is highly likely that there was also continuity of personnel: Iona would then have been concentrating its resources on evangelising the huge area covered by Bernicia and Deira, and in any case probably saw no need to substitute Irish churchmen for British ones in former Gododdin territory.

The Tweed valley, in addition to its continuing parish church at Eccles, five miles west of Coldstream, has two other sites of interest for the question

[199]   VW ch. 17: 'Ea loca sancta in diversis regionibus quae clerus Bryttannus, aciem gladii hostilis manu gentis nostrae fugiens, deseruit.' On this see Hunter Blair, art. cit. (above, n. 14), pp. 123-4.

[200]   Names in Eccles and its compounded forms (e.g. Ecclesfield) derive ultimately from the Latin *ecclesia*, 'church'. In general, see K. Cameron, 'Eccles in English place-names', in *Christianity in Britain* (as n. 195 above), pp. 87-92. For the Scottish ones, see G. W. S. Barrow, 'The childhood of Scottish Christianity: a note on some place-name evidence', *Scottish Studies* 27 (1983), pp. 1-15. The certain sites are Eaglescairnie, Eccles (just north of the Tweed), Ecclesmachan, Falkirk (formerly Egglesbrech), and St Ninians (formerly Eccles) by Stirling. The possible site is Eglis.

[201]   G. W. S. Barrow, *The Kingdom of the Scots* (London 1973), ch. 1, esp. pp. 28-30, 36-9, and art. cit., the four being Eccles, Ecclesmachan, Falkirk and St Ninians. Eaglescairnie is in the parish of Bolton, and the possible site, Eglis, in the parish of Penicuik.

[202]   Faull, 'British Survival in Anglo-Saxon Yorkshire', I, p. 245.

of British Christian survival in Anglo-Saxon Bernicia. Melrose, a little further up the valley, is a British (or Cumbric) name, *Moelros*, 'the bare moor', which has passed virtually unchanged into English usage.[203] Both the anonymous biographer of St Cuthbert, writing at Lindisfarne c.700, and Bede, shortly afterwards, name the site as *Mailros* rather than giving it an Anglo-Saxon name.[204] This is unusual: 'other evidence of the kind of Celtic spoken in the Tweed Valley before the arrival of the Angles is very scanty indeed';[205] and the vast majority of churches in Bede's writings have Old English names. Thomas, who drew attention to this fact some years ago, suggested that the survival of British names at *Luel* (Carlisle), *Mailros* and *Aebbercurnig* (Abercorn) might be due to these places having had important British churches which continued into Christian Northumbria.[206] This is an interesting hypothesis, and in the case of Melrose the argument can be strengthened by pointing to the intriguing fact that nowhere, in any of our three Lives of St Cuthbert, are we told anything about the foundation of Melrose; and yet the monastery was apparently flourishing so greatly by 651 that Cuthbert preferred to enter that monastery rather than Lindisfarne.[207] The anonymous *Life* does not even name the monastery in the chapter describing Cuthbert's entry into the religious life, implying rather that he first became a monk at Ripon; it does, however, let slip the name of Melrose later.[208] Now it is of course true that in his *Ecclesiastical History*, Bede frequently mentions monasteries without bothering to record the circumstances of their foundation.[209] One would, however, expect him to say something of Melrose's origins in his prose *Life of Cuthbert* if it had been founded as a result of Aidan's mission, given that its foundation would have been within only a few years of Cuthbert's entry. True, by 651 its abbot was a Lindisfarne-trained Anglo-Saxon, Eata, and its prior was the Anglo-Saxon monk Boisil;[210] but we should at least keep an open mind to the possibility that Melrose had started out as a British monastery: that would account for Bede's and the anonymous monk of Lindisfarne's reticence over its foundation.

---

[203] W. F. H. Nicolaisen, *Scottish Place-Names* (London 1976, pb. edn 1986), p. 6.
[204] VCA II, 3, 4; VCP chs. 6, 7, etc. (*Two Lives*, pp. 78, 82, 172, 176.)
[205] Nicolaisen, loc. cit.
[206] Thomas, 'The evidence', pp. 115-16.
[207] VCP 6. It was, of course, nearer to where Cuthbert had been shepherding: cf. VCA I, 5.
[208] VCA II, 1 and 2, and cf. II, 4. Similarly, Bede's metrical *Life of St Cuthbert*, §7, lines 180-1, ed. W. Jaager, *Bedas metrische Vita sancti Cuthberti* (Palaestra 198; Leipzig 1935), p. 71. On their discrepancy with VCP see Stancliffe, 'Cuthbert' (as above, n. 87), p. 23.
[209] Campbell, *Essays*, p. 51.
[210] VCP ch. 6; HE III, 26.

Higher up the Tweed again, in the hills, lies Peebles. Here, a Christian memorial stone was rediscovered in 1967. It is a kite-shaped boulder, bearing on one side a cross, and on the other, a cross and an inscription NEITANO SACERDOS, presumably a memorial 'to Neitan, priest/bishop'.[211] In general type, it belongs with the other Christian inscribed memorial stones from north Britain in the post-Roman period,[212] which are themselves related to the far more numerous ones in Wales. The particular interest of the Neitan stone is that its lettering suggests a date in the late seventh or early eighth century.[213] If this dating is correct, it provides us with firm evidence for a cleric bearing a British (or Pictish) name long after the Anglian occupation of the upper Tweed; and, what is more, one who was commemorated with a traditional British type of memorial. In these instances, then, we have pointers to probable continuity between the British and Anglo-Saxon churches in the area conquered by Oswald, a continuity which Bede, we may infer, chose to remain silent about; but one which Oswald's approach to the Irish church of Iona would have facilitated.

The second reason for stressing the significance of Oswald's turning to Iona for his missionaries is more obvious: in so doing, he was responsible for initiating a large-scale Irish mission to Anglo-Saxon England, whose long-term effects are so great that they are, quite literally, incalculable. Of course, there would have been some Irish churchmen at work in Anglo-Saxon England in the seventh century, even without Aidan's mission: Fursey, for instance, arrived quite independently in East Anglia.[214] For all that, Irish *peregrini* in general were birds of passage, as was Fursey himself. They arrived; they might establish monasteries; they might preach; they might move on. It tended to be very individualistic. They moved when they felt an inner call to do so, regardless of the consequences for those they left behind;[215] and, even if they stayed, their monastic life did not necessarily

---

211 K. A. Steer, 'Two unrecorded Early Christian stones', *Proceedings of the Society of Antiquaries of Scotland* 101 (1968-9), pp. 127-9 and plate 9a. *Sacerdos* is an ambiguous term at this period.

212 These are mapped by Thomas, 'The evidence', p. 102.

213 Steer, art. cit. p. 128. The letter forms are largely half-uncial, including a sloping rounded form of d. Note, however, Ken Dark's recent questioning of the dating of such stones, 'Epigraphic, art-historical, and historical approaches to the chronology of Class 1 inscribed stones', in *The Early Church in Wales and the West* (as n. 196 above), pp. 51-61. The standard work on epigraphical forms, albeit based on the Welsh monuments, is V. E. Nash-Williams, *The Early Christian Monuments of Wales* (Cardiff 1950).

214 *Vita S. Fursei* ch. 26 (as n. 100 above). He was probably from Louth: J.-M. Picard, 'Church and politics in the seventh century', in *Ireland and Northern France AD 600-850*, ed. J.-M. Picard (Blackrock 1991), pp. 27-52 at p. 34.

215 *Vita S. Fursei* chs. 28-9; *HE* IV, 25.

lead to the conversion of those amongst whom they were living. We see this, for instance, in the case of the little Irish community at Bosham, set in the midst of the continuingly pagan South Saxons.[216] All this is very different from Aidan's mission, which arrived in answer to King Oswald's summons with the explicit intention of evangelising his people, with his aid. This deliberate concentration on missionary work and close partnership with the king is something which, as far as the Irish were concerned, appears to be unique to the Lindisfarne mission and its daughter missions, and there can be little doubt that both factors were important for its success.

For successful, the Irish missionaries certainly were. They and their Anglo-Saxon disciples were basically responsible for the conversion not just of Northumbria, but also of Mercia and the Middle Angles, while continuing Paulinus's work in Lindsey, and reconverting the apostate East Saxons.[217] Of course, the Irish input was not the only one amongst any of these peoples: in Northumbria itself, quite apart from the possibility of a British contribution, the significance of links with Gaul and Italy should never be underestimated. But one telling indication of the primacy of the Irish[218] contribution is the evidence of the script adopted. 'Show me how you write and I'll tell you who your teacher was', is one of the palaeographer's maxims;[219] and it is surely significant that even the Wearmouth/Jarrow monks, for all their impressive achievement in producing the Codex Amiatinus of the Bible in an uncial script so perfectly modelled on Roman uncial that it long passed as an Italian production, should nonetheless relapse into Insular minuscule, the script the Anglo-Saxons learnt from the Irish, when writing under pressure.[220]

This is not the place to attempt to assess the debt of Anglo-Saxon Christianity to the Irish church, initiated principally through the Ionan mission to Northumbria and beyond. One can but mention the artistic achievements of the Hiberno-Northumbrian style,[221] as seen, for instance, in the Lindisfarne Gospels. Underlying all the arguments about which masterpieces should be attributed to Northumbria, which to Iona, and which

---

[216] *HE* IV, 13.

[217] *HE* III, 21-2, 24 (at p. 292).

[218] Or perhaps more accurately, Irish and British. We have no direct evidence for British palaeographical practices at this period, but they probably lie behind certain characteristically Irish ones: see the interesting suggestions of Julian Brown in *A Palaeographer's View: The Selected Writings of Julian Brown*, ed. J. Bately, M. Brown and J. Roberts (London 1993), pp. 179-95, 221 ff.

[219] E. A. Lowe, 'Handwriting', in *The Legacy of the Middle Ages*, ed. G. C. Crump and E. F. Jacob (Oxford 1926), pp. 197-226, at p. 208.

[220] M. B. Parkes, *The Scriptorium of Wearmouth-Jarrow* (Jarrow Lecture 1982).

[221] The term coined by Hope-Taylor in lieu of the commoner 'Hiberno-Saxon' in order to include the Bernician British as well as the Germanic contributions to the art style: *Yeavering*, pp. 313-24.

to mainland Ireland, is the striking closeness of the links between these different areas during the seventh century – something which has led one scholar to talk in terms of seeing Northumbria 'not so much as simply "influenced" by Ireland but rather as being part of a continuum with it'.[222] From the Irish, too, the Anglo-Saxons derived much that gave their Christianity its distinctiveness: the penitential tradition, with all the scope for the formation of a Christian conscience that regular contact with a confessor gave;[223] and the tradition of *peregrinatio*, self-imposed exile as a form of Christian renunciation, although here, the Anglo-Saxons gave it a particular twist in their eagerness to go to Rome, and their more systematic attempts to convert Germanic peoples on the continent who were still pagan.[224] Interestingly, behind both the penitential and the *peregrinatio* traditions lay a British contribution which had been taken further by the Irish.[225]

One interesting suggestion as to why the Irish were so successful in converting the Anglo-Saxons has been made by Patrick Wormald.[226] The Irish, he argues, had already had some experience of adapting Christianity to a barbarian society, and they were therefore able to present Christianity to the Anglo-Saxons in a more readily assimilable form. For instance, they understood the needs of a kin-based society, and one might add that they had already adapted the organisational side of the church to a tribal and rural society. In the context of this paper, I would stress how significant it is that the mission to Northumbria came from Iona; for its close links with the Uí Néill dynasty in Ireland, discussed earlier, may well have led it to preach a more palatable form of Christianity to the Anglo-Saxons than would have been the case with *peregrini* from certain other Irish churches. In particular, it appears to have been more ready to come to terms with the needs of warrior

[222] J. Campbell, 'Elements in the background to the Life of St Cuthbert and his early cult', in *St Cuthbert*, pp. 3-19, at p. 4. Cf. Julian Brown in *A Palaeographer's View*, p. 150.

[223] See A. J. Frantzen, *The Literature of Penance in Anglo-Saxon England* (New Brunswick, New Jersey 1983).

[224] Cf. T. M. Charles-Edwards, 'The social background to Irish *peregrinatio*', *Celtica* 11 (1976), pp. 43-59, and works cited ibid. n. 1; H. von Campenhausen, *Tradition and Life in the Church* (Eng. trans. London 1968), pp. 231-51.

[225] Frantzen, op. cit. p. 19; and, in addition, the *Uinniaus* or *Uinnianus* who was the author of the Penitential of Finnian may well have been British: D. N. Dumville, 'Gildas and Uinniau', in *Gildas*, ed. Lapidge and Dumville, pp. 207-14. For St Patrick's role in the development of the Irish *peregrinatio* tradition see Charles-Edwards, 'Social background', pp. 54-7.

[226] In an unpublished seminar paper of 1976, 'Iona and early Irish Christianity', which he kindly allowed me to read. Cf. also his 'Bede, "Beowulf"' (cited above, n. 16), p. 64.

kings than were some other Irish churchmen. It was thus able to present Christianity to Oswald in a form in which he could adopt it whole-heartedly, while yet living and dying as a warrior – as befitted a successful Anglo-Saxon king of his age.

Where Was Oswald Killed?

CLARE STANCLIFFE

Since the twelfth century, the site of the battle where Oswald met his death has generally been identified as Oswestry in Shropshire. If this identification is correct it is a matter of some importance, because it would indicate that Oswald was sufficiently sure of his position to be carrying the battle far afield, into the kingdom of Powys. This traditional identification, however, has recently been challenged by a distinguished place-name scholar.[1] It may therefore be helpful to re-examine the evidence.

Record of the battle was handed down both in English and in Welsh sources, and each people knew the battle under a name in their own language. The evidence therefore divides into an English branch, and a Welsh branch. Bede, writing c.730, names the site as *Maserfelth*, and this name is found virtually unchanged in the Old English translation of his work made at Alfred's behest in the late ninth century, and in Ælfric's *Life of St Oswald*, written c.1000.[2] On the British side, the *Annales Cambriae* give *bellum cocboi*.[3] In their present form, these annals only began to be kept regularly from the 790s, at St David's in Wales. However, either then or some time between c.790 and 954 the annals were extended backwards to make them run from the mid fifth century onwards.[4] The framework of the earliest entries came from the Irish annals, but from 573 onwards there are a number of entries specific to Britain; and there is a general consensus that these were probably drawn from entries of contemporary events written into the margins of Easter tables, apparently in north Britain.[5] The notice on the

---

1   M. Gelling, 'The early history of western Mercia', in *Origins*, pp. 184-201, at pp. 188-9; Margaret Gelling, *The Place-Names of Shropshire*, part I: *The Major Names of Shropshire* (English Place-Name Society vol. 62/63; 1990), pp. 229-31. I am grateful to Eric Cambridge and Thomas Charles-Edwards for commenting on a draft of this paper.

2   *HE* III, 9. *The Old English Version of Bede's Ecclesiastical History of the English People* III, 7, ed. and trans. T. Miller (2 vols, Early English Text Society, original series, vols. 95 and 110; London 1890, 1898), vol. I, p. 176: *Maserfeld*. Ælfric, *Lives of Three English Saints*, ed. G. I. Needham (London 1966), p. 36: *Maserfeld*.

3   Entry attributed to 644: 'Bellum cocboy in quo osuuald rex nordorum et eoba rex merciorum corruerunt.' (*Cocboy* is an alteration from the original spelling, *cocboi*.) Ed. E. Phillimore, 'The *Annales Cambriae* and Old-Welsh genealogies from Harleian MS 3859', *Y Cymmrodor* 9 (1888), pp. 141-83 at p. 158 and n. 1.

4   See K. Hughes, *Celtic Britain in the Early Middle Ages* (Woodbridge 1980), chs. 5 and 6.

5   Ibid. pp. 91-4; K. Jackson, 'On the northern British section in Nennius', in *Celt and Saxon: Studies in the Early British Border*, ed. N. K. Chadwick (Cambridge 1964), pp. 20-62, at pp. 48-9. D. N. Dumville, review of K. Hughes, *The Welsh*

battle of *Cocboi* probably derives from such an entry. The same source is also likely to lie behind the sentence on the *bellum Cocboy* in the *Historia Brittonum*, a compilation which was probably written in the 820s in north Wales.[6] A third Welsh source is a stray Welsh *englyn*, possibly dating from the ninth century, which is appended as stanza 111 to *Canu Heledd*. This names the site as *maes Cogwy*, 'field of Cogwy', and mentions the participation of Cynddylan, king of Powys.[7] Finally, a Welsh poem written by Cynddelw, a Powys poet of the second half of the twelfth century, has *gweith Gogwy*, 'battle of Cogwy', a more developed form of the same name. This implies that traditions about this battle were handed down orally in Powys.[8]

Neither Bede's narrative nor any of our Welsh sources afford much precision on the likely area of *Maserfelth*. We can say that, since the encounter was between a Mercian/Powys force and a Northumbrian one, it is likely to have lain somewhere in Powys, Mercia, Northumbria, or the north-east midlands area. That Oswiu came with an army the following year to carry off his brother's head and arms, exhibited on stakes at Penda's command, initially suggests that the battlefield lay outside Northumbria; but this argument is not watertight, as Penda could have carried off the remains from Northumbria to exhibit them at one of his own royal centres.[9] However, it is likely that at least by the time that Osthryth, Northumbrian-born queen of King Æthelred of Mercia, was translating her uncle's remains to Bardney, that is between c.679 and 697, *Maserfelth* was under Mercian control.[10] It is inconceivable that a Northumbrian king would have allowed the relics of one

---

Latin Chronicles, in *Studia Celtica* 12/13 (1977/1978), pp. 461-7, at pp. 466-7. D. N. Dumville, 'Sub-Roman Britain: history and legend', *History* 62 (1977), pp. 173-92 at p. 176.

[6] *Hist. Brit.* ch. 65: '[Penda] fecit bellum Cocboy, in quo cecidit Eoua, filius Pippa, frater ejus, rex Merciorum, et Oswald, rex Nordorum...'; ed. E. Faral, from the earliest MS (BL MS Harleian 3859), in *La Légende arthurienne* (3 vols, Paris 1929), vol. III, p. 44. On the composition of the *Hist. Brit.* see D. N. Dumville, 'Some aspects of the chronology of the Historia Brittonum', *Bulletin of the Board of Celtic Studies* 25 (1972), pp. 439-45.

[7] J. Rowland, *Early Welsh Saga Poetry* (Cambridge 1990), pp. 445 (text), 494 (translation) and 125, 168-9 (discussion). Rowland, p. 169, n. 172, says: 'In language and form the Cogwy *englyn* could also [i.e. as well as stanzas 112-113] be a fragment of a bardic praise poem.' Jackson suggests a possible ninth-century date, art. cit. p. 39.

[8] *Gwaith Cynddelw Brydydd Mawr*, vol. I, ed. N. A. Jones and A. P. Owen (Cardiff 1991), no. 3, line 118 (p. 24). (A reference I owe to T. M. Charles-Edwards.) Ifor Williams, 'A reference to the Nennian Bellum Cocboy', *Bulletin of the Board of Celtic Studies* 3 (1926/1927), pp. 59-62.

[9] *HE* III, 12. Thacker, below, p. 99.

[10] Plummer II, pp. 154-5; cf. Thacker, below, pp. 104-7.

of his ancestors, who was already regarded as a saint and credited with miracles, to be transported out of his kingdom and enshrined in the sphere of influence of his chief rival.

As far as place-name experts are concerned, neither the English nor the Welsh version of the name appears to have given rise to a name which can be located on a map. We should not allow ourselves to be detained by the claims recently put forward for Makerfield and Romano-British *Coccium* in Lancashire, by D. Kenyon and N. J. Higham. As Kenyon admits, 'the place-name evidence is not conclusive but there are obvious superficial similarities between *Maserfelth* and Makerfield'.[11] 'Superficial similarities' are no doubt the reason for the popular tradition in the neighbourhood for locating Oswald's battle site there; but they carry no weight with place-name specialists.[12] This lack of a modern descendant of Bede's or the Old Welsh name is probably due either to the site falling into oblivion, and carrying the name with it, or to the name of the site changing. Now the site was well known in Bede's day; nor was Oswald forgotten later in the Anglo-Saxon period.[13] *Prima facie*, therefore, the second explanation would seem the more likely.

The Claims of Oswestry

The identification of Bede's *Maserfelth* with Oswestry, just on the English side of the border with Wales, was made explicitly by Reginald of Durham, writing c.1165.[14] Reginald writes of the 'white church' built on the site of Oswald's 'martyrdom', and, at a distance of one-and-a-half bowshots, a well and a sacred ash tree, whose leaves and branches were credited with miraculous healing properties: this was 'Oswald's tree', whence he derived the name Oswestry.[15] Similarly, Gerald of Wales writes: 'Oswaldestroe, id est, Oswaldi arborem'.[16]

11   D. Kenyon, *The Origins of Lancashire* (Manchester 1991), pp. 77-8, at p. 77. N. J. Higham, *The Kingdom of Northumbria AD 350-1100* (Stroud 1993), p. 129.

12   On Makerfield, see E. Ekwall, *The Place-Names of Lancashire* (Manchester 1922), pp. 93-4; on *Coccium*, cf. Jackson, 'Nennius', p. 39: 'impossible philologically'. I am grateful to Victor Watts, of Durham University, for confirming in a letter to me of 18 October 1993 that neither the *Coccium* nor the Makerfield hypothesis is viable, given our knowledge of phonetic developments. Of Makerfield, he writes: 'It consistently had a "hard" *k* and Bede could never have represented it by a spelling such as *Maserfelth*.'

13   *HE* III, 9; see Thacker, below pp. 119-27.

14   *VO* I, chs. 12, 14, the latter quoted below; on *VO* see Tudor, below.

15   'Arborque ipsa sancti Oswaldi fraxinus ab omni populo terrae nominatur', *VO* I, 14. Reginald's identification of the church built 'for the honour of [Oswald's] name' as *alba ecclesia* is confirmed by documents in the Shrewsbury cartulary: see Binns, below, p. 258.

16   'Oswaldestroe, that is, Oswald's tree.' *Itinerarium Kambriae* II, ch. 12, ed J. F.

The derivation of Oswestry from an Old English *Oswaldestrēow*, 'Oswald's tree', is endorsed by place-name specialists.[17] But recently, Margaret Gelling has argued that the original 'Oswald's tree' was probably an ordinary boundary marker named after a local Oswald, not the Northumbrian king. In Domesday Book, the large estate in which Oswestry lies is called *Meresberie*, the name of a settlement in the southern part of this estate. (Incidentally, she stresses that there is no reason to connect *Meresberie* with Bede's *Maserfelth*.)[18] The estate's centre of administration appears to have shifted from *Meresberie* (modern Maesbury) in the south to Oswestry in the north of the estate, following the construction of a Norman castle in the northern area; and Gelling suggests that, as a result of this shift, the estate began to be called after a boundary marker near the castle known as 'Oswald's tree', a name first attested in the later twelfth century. As for the dedication of the church near the castle to St Oswald, which is attested as early as 1121, she seems to think that the church was only built after the Norman Conquest, and that 'the place-name suggested him as the appropriate saint'. In other words, the dedication arose from the place-name, and the place-name originally had nothing to do with the Northumbrian St Oswald.[19]

There are, however, three points which Gelling appears to have overlooked. First, she makes no mention of Reginald's evidence, although he is in fact the earliest – albeit indirect – source for the name of Oswestry, and explicitly for its association with the Northumbrian Oswald. Writing in 1165, Reginald says:

> Indeed the actual field, which merited to be consecrated by the most sacred blood of the holy king, has up to this day kept the name *Maserfeld*. That place is about one and a half miles from Offa's dyke, which divides England from northern Wales, and a good seven miles from Shrewsbury.[20]

The chain of attestation from Bede's *Maserfelth* (c.730), the Old English Bede's *Maserfeld* (c.890s), Ælfric's *Maserfeld* (c.1000) to Reginald's *Maserfeld* in 1165 does deserve some recognition as a continuous chain; and if Reginald says that the site is still called *Maserfeld*, we should take his testimony seriously. He does appear to be well informed about the site at Oswestry, including the fact that its 'white church' now belonged to an abbey in Shrewsbury.[21] He also provides, as we have seen, the earliest evidence for the name of

---

Dimock, *Giraldi Cambrensis opera* (6 vols, RS 21; London 1868) vol. VI, p. 142. Gerald's journey was made in 1188 and his account published in 1191: ibid., pp. xxxiii-iv. Cf. Tudor, below, pp. 190-1.

[17] Gelling, *Place-Names of Shropshire* I, pp. 229-31; Gelling, art. cit. pp. 188-9.

[18] Gelling, *Place-Names of Shropshire* I, pp. 192-3.

[19] As n. 17.

[20] *VO* I, 14 (p. 353); cf. also I, 12.

[21] See Tudor, below, p. 191.

Oswestry, and he thus bridges the divide between the two quite distinct place-names. Further, I find it difficult to believe that the extensive legends he records about St Oswald's well, the tree, and the role of the large bird (raven?) in carrying Oswald's arm to the tree, had all arisen between the dedication of a Norman church and 1165.[22] If the association between the Northumbrian saint and the church were of recent, Norman, origin, 'fostered by the priests who served there', then one would expect stories showing a far closer derivation from Bede, the obvious source of information on St Oswald for twelfth-century clerics – not the folklore type of story which we actually have, which shows no sign of being of recent clerical origin; rather, it smacks of covert paganism. Indeed, I doubt whether the priests attached to the church would have encouraged people to resort to a holy tree and holy well some quarter of a mile distant, rather than to the actual church building, where they would have been able to control the cult in a way that was impossible at an open-air cult site.

Secondly, Gelling appears to envisage Oswestry church, whose dedication to St Oswald is attested in 1121, as a recent, Norman, foundation.[23] But the Oswestry estate already figures in Domesday Book under the name *Meresburie*; and, as well as documenting Rainald's building of a castle there, Domesday Book also mentions a church and a priest.[24] Indeed, the church had been given to Shrewsbury Abbey between 1086 and 1102 – the 1121 document simply mentions this fact.[25] But if the church whose dedication to St Oswald is attested in 1121 is the same as the church mentioned in Domesday Book, *prima facie* one would expect its dedication to date back to that period also. (Of course, the Normans might have rebuilt and (or) rededicated the existing church to St Oswald, but that must be very hypothetical.[26]) If the church and its dedication date back to the period before the Norman castle was built, and so to the period when the centre of the estate was still Maesbury a couple of miles south, then Gelling's

---

22 See Rollason and Tudor, below, pp. 170-1, 190-1.
23 *Place-names of Shropshire* I, p. 231.
24 *VCH Shropshire* I, p. 316. On the relationship between *Meresburie* and Oswestry, see Gelling, *Place-names of Shropshire* I, pp. 192-3.
25 Binns, below, p. 258.
26 As Cambridge notes (below, p. 140), the 1121 wording implies that the dedication was then well established. U. Rees writes: 'Oswestry is not mentioned [in Domesday Book] but Rainald held the manor of Maesbury within which was the church of St Oswald (Eyton X, 320). This was transferred to the spot known as Oswestry where Rainald built his castle and which became the head of the honor.' (*Ctl. Shrewsbury* I, p. 38.) Rees's wording is somewhat ambiguous as to whether it was the church or the manor that was transferred from Maesbury to Oswestry: the latter certainly occurred; there is no reason that I know of to think that the site of the church changed too.

hypothesis that a boundary marker called Oswald's tree inspired the dedication to St Oswald begins to seem somewhat far-fetched. In any case, the assumption that 'Oswald's tree' refers to a boundary marker is itself open to question, since Oswestry is not on any known boundary.[27] If 'situation on a boundary is a marked characteristic of these names',[28] that is, names compounded of an English personal name plus *trēow* ('tree'), then Oswestry seems rather anomalous.[29]

A third reason for querying Gelling's interpretation of the evidence is that it does not account for why the Welsh version of Oswestry denotes not 'Oswald's tree', but 'Oswald's cross': *Croesoswald*. The Old English *trēow* can mean either 'tree', its primary meaning, or 'wooden cross': it is, for instance, one of the words which the Old English translation of Bede uses for the wooden cross set up at Heavenfield.[30] The Welsh *croes*, on the other hand, simply means 'cross'; it cannot mean 'tree'. *Croesoswald* must therefore have been coined at a time when the interpretation of *Oswaldestrēow* was 'Oswald's cross'. As we have seen, however, both Reginald and Gerald are quite explicit that in the second half of the twelfth century, Oswestry was interpreted as Oswald's tree, *arbor*. Now, *Croesoswald* is first attested in 1254,[31] within eighty years of Reginald, sixty-five years of Gerald; and, given the continuity in the stories told about Oswald even as late as John Leland's visit in the 1530s,[32] it is very unlikely that all knowledge of Oswald's miracle-working tree, to which Reginald devotes a whole chapter, had been forgotten as soon as 1254. It therefore seems more likely that *Oswaldestrēow* was originally understood as 'Oswald's cross', and that the Welsh *Croesoswald* was coined at that period (although not attested till the thirteenth century).[33]

In view of all this, it will, I think, be conceded that the arguments in favour of identifying *Maserfelth* and Oswestry are strong. What I would particularly emphasise here is that we are not faced with a total gulf between Bede's *Maserfelth* in 730, and the Oswestry of Reginald and Gerald in the late twelfth century. Reginald's reference to *Maserfeld*, along with others we have looked at, bridges the gap; and so, arguably, does the history of the cult. As

---

[27] It is certainly not on the boundary of the local hundred, whose centre was at Maesbury: see the map in VCH *Shropshire* III, p. 8.

[28] Gelling, *Place-names of Shropshire* I, p. 231.

[29] See M. Gelling, *Place-names in the Landscape* (London 1984), pp. 211-18 for a helpful discussion of this class of names, and p. 218 for Oswestry not fitting very obviously. Gelling there suggests that the tree might have been an internal boundary marker.

[30] O. E. *Bede* III, 2, ed. Miller I, p.156 lines 5, 22, 27.

[31] Gelling, *Place-Names of Shropshire* I, p. 230.

[32] See Tudor, below, p. 191.

[33] On Cynddelw's continued use of 'Gweith Gogwy' see below.

noted above,[34] *Maserfelth* was presumably in an area under Mercian control by the late seventh century, when Osthryth translated Oswald's relics to Bardney, and one can trace the existence of Oswald's cult in Mercia from that early period. It was clearly flourishing when Bede was writing, both at *Maserfelth* and at Bardney. Its popularity was still there in the late eighth century, as is apparent from the fact that the Mercian King Offa enriched his tomb at Bardney.[35] A century or more later, the importance of St Oswald to the rulers of the early tenth century is clear from Æthelflæd's determination to translate his body from Bardney, now in the Danelaw, to Gloucester, and this importance also seems to be reflected under Athelstan.[36] When, therefore, Bede's *History* was translated into Old English somewhere in Mercia shortly before the translation under Æthelflæd,[37] there is every chance that the reference to Oswald's death at *Maserfeld* would still have been understood: people would have known the site. The cult appears to have remained active in Mercia in the late Anglo-Saxon period, being linked to the royal martyr cults which were promoted by Oswald, archbishop of York and bishop of Worcester, in the late tenth century.[38] Finally, we can point to the translation of Oswald's relics at Gloucester under Thomas, archbishop of York, between 1108/9 and 1114.[39]

So much for the general background. I turn now to consider the cult specifically at *Maserfelth*. Clearly, there are gaps in the evidence here; but it may still be helpful to offer a hypothetical sketch of the development as I envisage it, expanding upon a brief, but perceptive, note by Plummer.[40] We may distinguish three phases of the cult.

The earliest phase is described by Bede.[41] The first miracle he records at the site of Oswald's death, the healing of a sick horse, is dated to 'not long after' the king's death. The rider of that horse erected a sign (*signum*) to mark the exact site; and earth removed from the site was so popular a cure that by Bede's time of writing, *c*.730, a hole the depth of a man's height had been hollowed out. All this is attested by Bede.

As regards the second phase: I would suggest that, given the popularity of the site, the first traveller's makeshift 'sign' was in time replaced by a wooden cross. The use of free-standing crosses was very common in areas

---

34 See pp. 85-6.
35 Alcuin, *BKS* lines 388-91. In general, see Thacker, below, p. 113, who draws attention to the space which Alcuin allots to Oswald.
36 See Thacker and Ó Riain-Raedel, below, pp. 120-1, 213-16.
37 *O.E. Bede*, ed. Miller, I, pp. xxxiii-lix.
38 See Thacker, below, pp. 124-5.
39 See Rollason and Tudor, below, pp. 168-9, 193.
40 Plummer II, pp. 152-3.
41 See *HE* III, 9, and cf. 10.

evangelised by Irish missionaries,[42] which include Mercia. One was set up at Wilfrid's monastery of Oundle, then part of 'Greater Mercia', to mark the miracle-working site where Wilfrid's corpse had been bathed, and the water poured away.[43] There is also evidence from Iona of their use to mark the spot where St Columba's uncle died, and where the saint was standing at that time.[44] Wooden crosses were probably commoner than stone crosses, at least initially, but their chances of survival are infinitesimal. However, there is indirect evidence of their use in Ireland (including Iona), Wales, and England.[45] In the latter, Oswald's famous miracle-working cross at Heavenfield would in any case have served as the prototype. Because the site of Oswald's death now became famous on account of the miracles worked there, people began to refer to it as *Oswaldestrēow*, with the sense of 'Oswald's cross'; or in Welsh, *Croesoswald*. In time, this supplanted the older names of *Maserfelth*, *Cocboy*.

The third phase was marked by the building of a church on the site, perhaps in the tenth or eleventh century: there was certainly one by 1086, which, as we have seen, was given to the abbey of Shrewsbury between 1086 and 1102. Its dedication to Oswald is attested in 1121.[46] Presumably the church building superseded the cross at the site of Oswald's actual death. In the meantime, however, legend was at work concerning St Oswald's well, a quarter of a mile to the west of the church, and a venerable ash tree there: it linked this site with that of the actual death through the story of the bird which had carried one of Oswald's arms to that tree, and then dropped it, causing the spring to break out. The story recorded by Reginald in the late twelfth century now explained the place-name *Oswaldestrēow* as referring to this ash tree as 'Oswald's tree'.[47]

---

[42] R. Hill, 'Christianity and geography in early Northumbria', *Studies in Church History* 3 (1966), pp. 126-39 at pp. 133 ff. citing Huneberc's Life of Willibald; M. Swanton, ed. *The Dream of the Rood* (Manchester 1970), pp. 45 ff. esp. p. 47, citing Boniface's complaint that worship at crosses was detracting from church attendance.

[43] *VW* ch. 66. Cf. *Felix's Life of Saint Guthlac*, ed. B. Colgrave (Cambridge 1956), ch. 5, p. 74.

[44] Adomnán, *VCol* I, 45.

[45] N. Edwards, *The Archaeology of Early Medieval Ireland* (London 1990), p. 163; M. Seaborne, *Celtic Crosses of Britain and Ireland* (Princes Risborough 1989), pp. 13, 46ff; R. Cramp, 'The artistic influence of Lindisfarne', in *St Cuthbert*, pp. 213-28, at p. 223. (I do not know why she assumes that Cuthbert's cross was necessarily made of stone, not wood, though availability of local materials was presumably important.) R. Cramp, 'A reconsideration of the monastic site of Whitby', in *AMI*, pp. 64-73 at p. 69.

[46] See Binns, below, p. 258.

[47] So also Plummer II, p. 153.

So much by way of an outline of the Oswestry hypothesis. There are some additional factors which strengthen the case, although on their own they would not carry weight. To begin with, there is the general plausibility of Oswestry as the site of *Maserfelth*: it fits well with battles fought by Oswald's predecessors, Æthelfrith, at Chester, and Edwin, who fought at Meigen (near modern Welshpool), and also with the participation of Powys alongside Mercia at the battle, and the fact that memory of it was handed down in Powys at least till the late twelfth century.[48] In strategic terms, Oswestry lies on the western edge of rolling hill country, a few miles from where the Welsh mountains begin to rise, just beneath the still impressive Iron Age hill fort of Old Oswestry, and only two miles east of the line that would soon be taken by Offa's Dyke. This border situation also explains why Osthryth preferred to translate Oswald's remains to distant Bardney, in Lindsey, rather than build a church on the actual site of Oswald's death. Oswestry was probably in Powys in 642, and it long retained its Welsh character, although the siting of Offa's Dyke to its west implies that it had by then been incorporated into Mercia, perhaps in the late seventh century. Relations between Mercia and Powys probably deteriorated in the later seventh century, once the Northumbrian threat receded, and Mercia's own increased power became apparent.[49] A richly endowed church on the Mercian/Powys border would have invited Welsh raids.

One additional point also fits with the Oswestry interpretation. Bede narrates three miracles wrought at the site of Oswald's death: two of them were due to the rider whose horse was cured, while the other concerns a Briton.[50] Of course, there might have been Britons travelling freely around further east, where the English had long been dominant; but it would fit more plausibly with a location at Oswestry on the border of Powys.

Finally, we must deal with possible objections to the Oswestry hypothesis. First, if I am correct in arguing that the Welsh form, *Croesoswald*, was probably coined before the Norman Conquest, and certainly well before Reginald's period, why is it that the Powys poet Cynddelw still recalls the battle where Oswald fell as 'gweith Gogwy', even in the late twelfth century? The answer lies, I would suggest, in the conservative nature of the Welsh poetic tradition of which Cynddelw was a master practitioner. He wrote

[48] See map, Figure 2, above, p. 14, and Cramp and Stancliffe, above, pp. 22-3, n. 28, and pp. 47, 56.

[49] Cf. Rowland, *Early Welsh Saga Poetry*, pp. 120-41, esp. 137-8; and Gelling, art. cit. pp. 190-1, 199. Besides the problematical attack by Cynddylan on Lichfield, alluded to in the *Marwnad Cynddylan*, note the Welsh/Mercian antagonism evident in Coenred's reign, 704-9: *Felix's Life of Saint Guthlac*, ch. 34, pp. 108 and 185. Hostile feelings may also have developed after the conversion of Mercia and the synod of Whitby. For positive reasons for choosing Bardney, see n. 55 below.

[50] *HE* III, 10.

praise poems in a tradition which looked back to the days of Aneirin and Taliesin.[51] As a master of tradition, it is understandable that he would have preferred to retain the old name for this battle, rather than adopt a name of more recent – and popular – coinage.

A second query arises from Bede's words that Oswald died 'fighting for his fatherland'.[52] In the context of Bede's portrayal of Oswald, his *patria* must mean Northumbria.[53] But could a battle fought in distant Oswestry be portrayed as being fought 'for Northumbria'? Is not a defensive action, perhaps warding off an invasion from the south, implied? It is here that Bede the patriotic Northumbrian and Bede the apologist for his king-saint join forces and triumph over Bede, the exact historian. As I have argued above, Bede was very careful to portray Oswald as fighting only 'just wars', and he omits all Oswald's battles fought between Heavenfield and *Maserfelth*, when Oswald was probably fighting aggressive wars to assert his supremacy.[54] Bede, however, could scarcely have omitted the battle in which Oswald fell. Instead, he included it, but added his own gloss: it, too, was a just war, for it was fought *pro patria*. In other words, we should take Bede's words, *pro patria dimicans*, as indicating the view which Bede wished to convey, rather than interpreting them literally. Given Bede's subtle, even disingenuous, use of language elsewhere, this interpretation of Bede is fully justified.

Thirdly, there are the reservations implicit in Thacker's interpretation, that 'Oswald would not have been remembered with affection at a site deep within territory held by his Mercian foes', and therefore that somewhere 'on the northern boundary of Lindsey, in some border region freely accessible both to Britons and Oswald's own people', would make better sense than Oswestry.[55] But since one of the two early beneficiaries of the post-mortem Oswald miracles described by Bede was a Briton, one cannot argue that the

[51] Cf. Gwyn Williams, *An Introduction to Welsh Poetry* (London 1953), pp. 71-2, 77-8.

[52] 'Pro patria dimicans': *HE* III, 9.

[53] Cf. Wallace-Hadrill, *Comm*, p. 103, who wonders if Northumbria or heaven is meant. But Bede nowhere portrays Oswald as a type of crusader, fighting on behalf of Christianity; if he had, he would not have refused Oswald the title of martyr.

[54] See above, pp. 44-5, 56-61, 70.

[55] Below, p. 99. Thacker's further comment, that a site in Lindsey would help to explain Bardney's role in disseminating the cult, seems to me a *non sequitur*: once Bardney had received Oswald's relics, wherever they had come from, it would have acquired an interest in disseminating his cult. Conversely, the reason why Bardney was chosen, and not a monastery closer to Oswestry, was surely because Bardney was already marked out as a major dynastic monastery by Æthelred and Osthryth (*HE* III, 11, at p. 246); and Oswald, linked as he was via his relationship to Osthryth (see Fig. 1, above, p. 13), could cast an aura of sanctity over the Mercian dynasty: cf. Ó Riain-Raedel, below, pp. 213-16.

cult could only have developed among Oswald's own people; and the parallel case of St Olaf of Norway shows that even former political enemies could recognise a fallen king as a saint just a year after his death.[56] In any case, even the northern confines of Lindsey lie between seventy and one hundred and fifty miles south of Oswald's own people, the Bernicians, who would presumably have preferred to visit Heavenfield or Bamburgh. It is highly doubtful whether the Deirans, in the generation following Oswald's death, regarded Oswald as their rightful king: *prima facie* they would have been more likely to frequent the site of King Edwin's death.[57] Indeed, one could stand Thacker's argument on its head by suggesting that neither the British nor the Anglo-Saxon peoples around Oswestry – presumably, at this mid-seventh century date, the *Wreocensæte*, or possibly the *Meresæte*[58] – would have had any particular reason to harbour hostile feelings towards Oswald. This area was certainly not part of Mercia proper at the time of Oswald's death; it was probably only incorporated in the following half century. The peoples here are unlikely ever to have felt the hated onus of Northumbrian demands for tribute as acutely as the people of Lindsey, who were more vulnerable because of their immediate proximity, just south of the Humber (see Fig. 2, above, p. 14). We do, after all, have Bede's explicit statement that the inmates of Bardney, in the heart of Lindsey, were reluctant to receive Oswald's bones, because 'although they knew that he was a holy man, nonetheless, because he belonged to another kingdom and had conquered them, they pursued him even when dead with their former hatred'.[59] On these grounds, even the northern confines of Lindsey seem less plausible than the confines of Powys.

The final question we ought to consider is whether, if *Maserfelth* is indeed Oswestry on the Welsh border, Bede would have been so well informed about the miracles that he records as taking place there. The popular story about Oswald's last words as he was cut down on the field of battle could well have derived from oral tradition, originating with members of Oswald's army.[60] But for the post-mortem miracle stories, it is likely that Bardney in Lincolnshire served as the intermediary. Osthryth will probably have told

---

[56] *HE* III, 10. On St Olaf: G. Turville-Petre, *Origins of Icelandic Literature* (Oxford 1953), ch. 6, esp. pp. 142-3; R. Folz, *Les saints rois du moyen âge en occident (VIe-XIIIe siècles)* (Subsidia hagiographica 68; Brussels 1984), pp. 53-4.

[57] Cf. Stancliffe, above, p. 36. Deiran sentiment is still visibly alive in the early eighth-century Whitby *Life of Gregory*, with its depiction of King Edwin being driven out of his *patria* by the tyrant Æthelfrith: *The Earliest Life of Gregory the Great*, ed. B. Colgrave (Cambridge 1968), ch. 16, and cf. chs. 18-19.

[58] See Gelling, art. cit., esp. pp. 192, 199-201, and cf. N. Brooks, 'The formation of the Mercian kingdom', in *Origins*, pp. 159-70.

[59] *HE* III, 11.

[60] Cf. above, pp. 35-6, 42.

the inmates of Bardney about the miracles reported at the site of Oswald's death, when she was trying to persuade the community to receive Oswald's remains as honoured relics. Clearly she succeeded, and Bardney, having made Oswald's cult its own, will thereafter have been a source for disseminating stories of Oswald's miracles; moreover, it was almost certainly one that Bede was in contact with, probably through the abbot of the neighbouring monastery of Partney.[61]

The way thus lies open for the identification of Oswestry and *Maserfelth*, though we must recognise that the case for identifying the two is not proven beyond a peradventure. If we refer back to the phases outlined above, the uncertainty lies in phase two. I do regard it as likely that a site as popular as that described by Bede should have been marked with a cross; and I also think that we are justified in arguing back from the place-name *Oswaldestreow/Croesoswald* that Oswestry must have had a St Oswald cross before it had a church, and had it for a sufficiently long period for that to become an established place-name. Since Oswestry had a church by Domesday Book, this probably carries the erection of the cross back at least as far as the tenth century. There is, however, no means of knowing whether the hypothetical cross erected at the site of Oswald's death was in the same place as the hypothetical cross which gave rise to the place-name Oswestry.

There are two reasons which can be put forward to support the identity of the two. The first is the testimony of Reginald, presumably reflecting popular traditions in Oswestry around the mid twelfth century. However, popular traditions which cannot be verified are not a reliable source for historians. All we can say is that we would expect the site of Oswald's death, which seems to have seen a popular cult developing, to have been remembered locally, and probably to have given rise to stories. Oswestry is not the only place to be remembered in popular tradition as the site of Oswald's last battle.[62] However, its traditions are recorded earlier; they clearly do not arise in any direct sense from Bede's narrative; and there is also the interesting point that the cult site there was a 'split site'. If popular legends developed simply from a cross and then church dedicated to Oswald, together with a well in the locality, would they not have made the tree and well the site of Oswald's death? The legend about the bird flying off to the tree with Oswald's arm has surely arisen to explain why the well is not at the site of his death, where one would expect it, which implies that there was a strong tradition already in existence which identified the church site as the place where he died.

---

[61]   *HE* III, 11-12. Stancliffe, above, p. 35 and n. 10.

[62]   E.g. Gelling cites such a tradition at Oswald's Tump, Gloucestershire (*Place-Names of Shropshire* I, p. 231); and Kenyon refers to a tradition in the Makerfield area of Lancashire (*Origins of Lancashire*, pp. 77-8).

The second reason for favouring the Oswestry hypothesis is that it does provide us with an explanation for what, otherwise, remains a puzzle: namely, that Bede's *Maserfelth* has apparently vanished from the historical record, despite the likelihood that people in that area continued to resort to it as a popular place for seeking healing miracles right through the Anglo-Saxon period and beyond. Even if we envisage *Maserfelth* as lying in eastern England, in an area attacked and settled by pagan Scandinavians in the ninth and tenth centuries, it is unlikely that all consciousness of such a site would have fallen into oblivion. The Scandinavians settled amongst the existing Anglo-Saxons, and in time adopted their religious customs; indeed, the death site of a saint-king who fell in battle would probably have appealed to them. I therefore think it likely that the memory of the battlefield where Oswald fell was kept alive; and probable that in the course of time a cross, and perhaps even a church, were erected on that site. By far the neatest explanation for why none of the St Oswald dedications listed below by Alison Binns occurs at a place called by a modern version of *Maserfelth* is that the site changed its name; and Oswestry must be the obvious candidate.[63]

[63] The instability of name forms for Oswestry (*Blancmonasterium* and variants, *Oswaldestroe/Croesoswald* and variants, and cf. also *Luvre*: Gelling, *Place-Names of Shropshire* I, pp. 193, 229-30) would fit with a change of name. Is it significant that the English (vernacular) name is always attested as *Oswaldestroe* and variants? Cf. ibid. p. 311, though note Leland's 'White Minster' usage: Tudor, below, p. 191.

Membra Disjecta: *the Division of the Body and the Diffusion of the Cult*

ALAN THACKER

The Origins of the Cult in England

Oswald, *rex christianissimus*, cuts a curious figure as a saint. Try as he might, Bede (who is almost our sole source for his life and eight-year reign)[1] could scarcely disguise the lineaments of the Germanic warrior-hero, which lay only just beneath the surface of his carefully contrived portrait.[2] Almost by accident he reveals that the patron of Aidan and the Ionan mission was thought capable of pursuing the bloodfeud against the descendants of his predecessor Edwin. After Edwin's defeat and death at Hatfield, his widow and her family fled to Kent, from whence his infant son and grandson were sent abroad to Frankia for fear of Oswald's vengeance.[3] Those Christian princes, it should be remembered, were Oswald's cousins.[4] The story sits ill with Bede's attempts to present Oswald as Edwin's legitimate heir, and reveals something of the *parti pris* which informs his account of his favourite king.[5]

The origins of Oswald's cult lie not in his life, however saintly, but in his violent end, cut down on the battlefield of *Maserfelth*, fighting valiantly against his people's hereditary enemies. Because the still pagan Mercians were numbered among his foes, Oswald could be presented as dying for the faith;[6] the inconvenient fact that they also included – were perhaps predominantly – the Christian British could be overcome by presenting the latter as heretical barbarians.[7] The process of sanctification was assisted by the treatment of the remains. The body was hacked to pieces and the head and arms affixed to stakes, perhaps as some form of sacrificial offering, at the command of the pagan Penda.[8] That dismemberment was significantly to affect the early development of the cult.

[1] See esp. *HE* II, 5; III, 1-3, 5-7, 9-13; IV, 14; above, Stancliffe, pp. 33-46.
[2] Cf. J. Campbell, *Essays in Anglo-Saxon History* (London 1986), p. 14.
[3] *HE* II, 20.
[4] Edwin's sister Acha was Oswald's mother: *HE* III, 6; above, p. 13 .
[5] Cf. T. M. Charles-Edwards, 'Bede, the Irish and the Britons', *Celtica* 15 (1983), pp. 42-52, at pp. 50-1. But for a different view see Stancliffe, above, pp. 71-2.
[6] Bede never, however, goes so far as to call him a martyr: below (n. 97).
[7] Though this attitude towards the British characterised *HE* as a whole, Bede did not expressly mention their participation in the battle of *Maserfelth*.
[8] *HE* III, 12. This view, which is argued strongly by W. Chaney (*The Cult of Kingship in Anglo-Saxon England* (Manchester 1970), pp. 115-19), finds some support in the fact that the agent is expressly said to be 'the king who slew him'

It might well be thought that it was in the interest of the Northumbrian ecclesiastical hierarchy, which owed its origins to Oswald's summoning of a bishop from Iona, to encourage devotion to their patron. But the signs are that they did not initiate it. Of the miracle stories recorded by Bede, many do not appear to have originated in an ecclesiastical milieu, especially those focused on the place where Oswald fell in battle. Dust from that place, suffused with the hero's blood, had healing properties when mixed with water and taken as a drink. Indeed, such was the fame of the site that, as Bede relates, a hole the size of a man's stature was excavated there by devotees anxious to carry off the sanctified earth.[9] Yet as far as we know, no ecclesiastical community had guardianship of the site or controlled the dispensing of the wonder-working dust. Bede tells of a traveller whose horse fell sick and was cured by rolling on the sacred spot, and of an innkeeper whose paralysed granddaughter was taken thither on a cart. At the time those stories circulated, which Bede expressly says was not long after Oswald's death, the battle site was clearly in the open air, and access could be had to it without ecclesiastical mediation. The people involved appear to have been of modest social status and even included a Briton.[10] All this bears out Bede's statement that Oswald's death, and the fact that he prayed for his enemies as he fell, were so well known among his people as to be proverbial.[11]

Very similar are the early phases of the cult site at Heavenfield, where Oswald set up his wooden cross before his victory over the British in 634. That too seems initially to have been unguarded and in the open air. It focused upon the cross itself, the wood of which performed miracles of healing,[12] and evidently was well frequented; the wonders are reported by Bede, like those from *Maserfelth*, in narratives whose impersonal 'generalised passive' constructions imply that they were so widely told as to be unattributable to a single source.[13] One reason for its popularity may be that the cult site fitted into a more familiar context than is often imagined. A significant element in pagan shrines of the period was apparently a central wooden post upon which graves might be orientated and votives, including

---

(i.e. Penda: *HE* III, 9) and not the Christian Cadwallon. See also Folz, p. 51; D. R. Wilson, *Anglo-Saxon Paganism* (London 1992), p. 34. A similar point was made by A. Meaney, in a communication at the conference of the International Society of Anglo-Saxonists (hereafter ISAS), Oxford 1993.

9 *HE* III, 9. A similar story is told of Bishop Hædde of Winchester: *HE* V, 18.
10 *HE* III, 9-10; D. W. Rollason, *Saints and Relics in Anglo-Saxon England* (Oxford 1989), pp. 101-2.
11 *HE* III, 12.
12 *HE* III, 2.
13 A point well made by Prof. John McNamara in his communication at the ISAS conference 1993.

animal heads, displayed;[14] clearly such totems provide an analogy for the arrangements at Heavenfield.[15]

The location of these open-air sites is a matter of considerable significance. Heavenfield has been securely identified: it lay deep within Northumbria immediately to the north of Hadrian's Wall, a few miles from the administrative centre (*caput*) of a major royal estate where some forty years later Wilfrid was to build his great monastery of Hexham.[16] The location of the death site, perhaps the earliest of the Oswald cult centres, is, by contrast, probably irrecoverable. Known to Bede as *Maserfelth* and to the Welsh as *Cogwy*, it has traditionally been identified with Oswestry in Shropshire.[17] A good case can be made in defence of that view,[18] and, as we shall see, the strongly pagan character of the cult there, in particular its association with a holy well, accords nicely with the evidence from other centres. Nevertheless, the traditions are undeniably late,[19] and in many ways Bede's account makes better sense if the battlefield is thought of as in or near the north midland province of Lindsey rather than on the Welsh border at Oswestry. Such a location would go a long way towards explaining the role of the community at Bardney in Lindsey as the principal early disseminator of the cult.[20] But if *Maserfelth* lay in Lindsey, it was probably only at the periphery. It is highly unlikely that in the aftermath of his defeat Oswald would have been remembered with affection at a site deep within territory held by his Mercian foes.[21] The fact that part of his remains were recovered by his successor Oswiu in a raid on enemy soil has little bearing upon the location; they may have been carried off as trophies to one of Penda's pagan sanctuaries. Despite the claims of Oswestry there are, therefore, strong reasons for placing *Maserfelth* on the northern boundary of Lindsey, in some border region freely accessible both to Britons and Oswald's own people.[22]

---

[14]   Dr John Blair in a communication at the ISAS conference 1993. Cf. Wilson, *Anglo-Saxon Paganism*, pp. 45-7, 57-8.

[15]   *HE* III, 2. The site itself is now marked by a small church dedicated to St Oswald.

[16]   *HE* III, 2; *VW* 22.

[17]   *HE* III, 9; Plummer, II, 152-3.

[18]   Stancliffe, above, 'Where was Oswald killed?'

[19]   M. Gelling, 'The early history of western Mercia', in *Origins*, pp. 184-201, at pp. 188-9; and see below for further discussion of these traditions.

[20]   On Bardney see below. It seems likely that the king's mutilated torso, which was eventually brought to Bardney, was buried near the battlefield. His predecessor Edwin was certainly buried near where he fell in Hatfield Chase: *The Earliest Life of Gregory the Great*, ed. B. Colgrave (Kansas 1968), ch. 18.

[21]   For the chequered history of the overlordship of Lindsey see Plummer II, p. 155.

[22]   For the possible British background to the kingdom of Lindsey see B. Yorke, 'Lindsey: the lost kingdom found?', in *Pre-Viking Lindsey*, ed. A. Vince (Lincoln 1993), pp. 141-50, at p. 143.

It seems then that Oswald's cult began early, perhaps immediately after his death, at open air and primarily secular sites. The story of the cure of the horse at *Maserfelth* points in that direction and also suggests a milieu conditioned by pagan beliefs. In particular, the horse's crucial role in detecting the place where Oswald fell accords with the strong associations which horses had with death and the afterlife among the Germanic peoples; besides being sacrificed and buried as companions and protectors in their masters' graves, they were also psychopomps who conducted the soul to paradise.[23] There is, perhaps, more than a grain of truth in the traditional view that the origins of devotion to Oswald lie as much in Germanic attitudes to kings and to heroic deaths in battle as in the teachings of the church.[24] Interestingly, too, the cult incorporates distinctively Celtic features. As we shall see, the special significance which the Celts attributed to the severed head and the associated veneration of holy wells left their mark.[25] It may therefore be significant that Britons were involved in the cult in its early stages.

Nevertheless, despite the strong impetus from below, Oswald's cult was never the special property of the common people. In 643, a year after the king's death, his brother and successor Oswiu recovered the severed head and arms. The latter were taken to Bamburgh where at some point before the 730s they were enshrined in a silver reliquary and where the right hand and arm, which Aidan had declared would never perish, were reputed incorrupt.[26] According to Alcuin, who apparently had access to additional information,[27] the enshrinement was made upon the orders of Oswiu himself and indeed the king founded the church of St Peter on the rock at Bamburgh to accommodate the relics.[28] If so, Oswiu was making a dramatic and highly unusual gesture. In the Latin west the traditional focus of a saint's cult was

---

[23] E. Salin, *La civilisation mérovingienne* (4 vols, Paris 1949-59), IV, pp. 23-9, 148-9. For evidence of a horse cult among the pagan Anglo-Saxons, see Wilson, *Anglo-Saxon Paganism*, pp. 101-3.

[24] This point is made most forcefully by Chaney, *Cult of Kingship, passim*, but esp. pp. 115-20. For more judicious arguments see E. Hoffmann, *Die heiligen Könige bei den Angelsachsen und den skandinavischen Völkern* (Neumünster 1975), pp. 32-8, 46-56. For the view (rejected here) that clerical sponsorship preceded the development of the 'popular' cult see F. Graus, *Volk, Herrscher und Heiliger im Reich der Merowinger* (Prague 1965), pp. 417-20; J. M. Wallace-Hadrill, *Early Germanic Kingship in England and on the Continent* (Oxford 1971), pp. 83-5.

[25] A. Ross, *Pagan Celtic Britain* (London 1967), pp. 20-33, 61-126; below.

[26] *HE* III, 6.

[27] He also relates that the nails continued to grow.

[28] Alcuin, *BKS*, lines 304-9 (pp. 28-30). Bede, it should be noted, is less explicit about who was actually responsible for the enshrinement. Cf. Cambridge, below, pp. 137-8.

the tomb which enclosed his corporeal remains.[29] By the late sixth century its centrality had been reinforced by the papacy, which, in an attempt to defend its own vast heritage of holy bones, had evolved the doctrine that the sacred grave and the relics it contained were inviolable, and that interference was likely to bring disaster and even death upon intruders. Those views had most impact, of course, in Rome. In Gaul, which took a considerably more relaxed attitude, there was from the mid seventh century a growing interest in holy incorruption and in the detachment from those so preserved of such modest appendages as teeth, nail-parings, and hair clippings. Nevertheless, saints' remains were rarely, if at all, divided and there was absolutely no precedent for the solemn enshrinement of a substantial portion of the body outside the tomb.[30] Even by such relatively advanced continental standards, therefore, the treatment of the uncorrupted arm was remarkable. In English terms, if it really occurred in Oswiu's time, it was truly amazing, pre-dating the other earliest known examples of incorruption by well over a generation.[31]

The unusual nature of Oswald's end offered exceptional opportunities to the impresarios of his cult. At Bamburgh the most was made of the royal arms, and they were soon reputed the agents of miracles.[32] At Lindisfarne, the resting-place of the king's head, the procedures were, however, very different. Although it remained a valued object, and according to Symeon was taken from Lindisfarne together with the body of St Cuthbert in 875,[33] the relic seems never to have been the focus of wonders.[34] Bede's account implies that it was not exposed for veneration but quietly interred in the monastic cemetery.[35] The reasons for the comparative reserve are complex. It cannot be attributed to any lack of interest in the enshrinement of mortal remains,[36] for we know that the monks of Lindisfarne cared sufficiently for Aidan's bones to translate them to the south side of the altar, and (remarkably enough) even defied Latin tradition and took a portion with

---

[29] For a fuller treatment of what follows see A. T. Thacker, 'The making of a local saint', forthcoming in *Local Saints and Local Churches*, ed. R. Sharpe and A. T. Thacker (Oxford forthcoming).

[30] Ibid.

[31] *HE* IV, 19; IV, 30; A. T. Thacker, 'Lindisfarne and the origins of the cult', in *St Cuthbert*, pp. 103-22, esp. p. 106.

[32] *HE* III, 6; Alcuin, *BKS*, lines 308-11 (p. 30).

[33] *HDE* II, 6 (p. 57). For difficulties with Symeon's story see Bailey, below, pp. 197-9.

[34] No credence can be attached to Reginald of Durham's fantastic account of miracles wrought by the head in the cemetery of Lindisfarne and its consequent removal to Bamburgh: Reginald, *VO* I, 13 (p. 351). See Tudor, below, pp. 188-9.

[35] *HE* III, 12. Significantly Alcuin makes no reference to the head in his poem.

[36] As at Iona: Thacker, 'Lindisfarne and origins', pp. 108-9.

them upon their departure after their defeat in the Paschal controversy.[37] Oswald's severed head, which could have been taken with greater convenience and propriety, was left behind. That may, of course, have been because it did not matter sufficiently to the monks of Lindisfarne; more plausibly, however, it was because it mattered too much to the Northumbrian establishment.

One possible explanation for the difference between Bamburgh's and Lindisfarne's treatment of the king's remains may lie in the nature of the two communities. Bamburgh was a dynastic foundation, set up expressly to house Oswald's relics; it was not like Lindisfarne the seat of a bishop.[38] At the see of Aidan (and later of Cuthbert), the cult of a king, however holy, was bound to take second place to those of the leaders of the ecclesiastical hierarchy. Perhaps a more potent factor, however, was the strong reverence for the human head in Anglo-Saxon and more especially Celtic paganism.[39] Among the Celts in particular severed heads were believed to possess protective power and their display, enshrined in temples or suspended from gateways or on ramparts, brought good fortune. Interestingly, they could also be buried.[40] Clearly Oswiu's gift may have raised some very sensitive issues for the Irish community at Lindisfarne in the 640s.[41]

A surprising aspect of Oswald's cult is its strong association with holy wells, to be found, for example, at Oswestry (Shropshire), Elvet (Durham), Winwick, Warton (both Lancashire), Astbury (Cheshire), Kirkoswald (Cumberland), Grasmere, Burneside (both Westmorland), and perhaps at Cathcart (Renfrewshire)[42] and Heavenfield, near turret 25b on the Roman

[37] *HE* III, 17, 26. It is worth noting that the partitioning of Aidan's bones in 664 was not necessarily primarily connected with a desire to see them enshrined in a worthy new resting-place. In the early Irish canons the permissible reasons for relocating a body were to reunite someone with his family or (in the case of martyrs) when persecution threatened or the burial-place was vexed by the society of evil-doers: *Collectio Canonum Hibernensis*, ed. H. Wasserschleben, *Die irische Kanonensammlung* (2nd edn Leipzig 1885), 18, 7; 49, 8 (pp. 58, 206). I am grateful to Dr Stancliffe for drawing my attention to this point.

[38] The large parish focused on Bamburgh suggests that Oswiu's foundation was a great royal minster. But cf. Cambridge, below, pp. 138-9. On the differences between episcopal and minster communities see A. T. Thacker, 'Kings, saints, and monasteries in pre-Viking Mercia', *Midland History* 10 (1985), pp. 1-25, at 17-18.

[39] Wilson, *Anglo-Saxon Paganism*, pp. 92-5; Chaney, *Cult of Kingship*, pp. 95-6; A. W. Smith, 'The luck in the head: a problem in English folklore', *Folklore* 73 (1962), pp. 13-24; idem, 'Some further observations', *Folklore* 74 (1963), pp. 396-8; Ross, *Pagan Celtic Britain*, pp. 61-126.

[40] A. Ross, *The Pagan Celts* (London 1986), pp. 119-23.

[41] Cf. the similar treatment of Oswald's predecessor Edwin's head, buried at York after his death in Hatfield Chase: *HE* II, 20.

[42] R. C. Hope, *The Legendary Lore of the Holy Wells of England* (London 1983), pp.

Wall.[43] That too may owe something to Celtic beliefs. Sacred springs and wells formed a significant element in Celtic religion, often, it seems, linked with veneration for the head.[44] That this left its impact upon Christian cults in areas dominated by the British church is apparent from the legends and sites associated with the saints of Devon and Cornwall. There, healing wells linked with local saints abound.[45] Particularly interesting are the stories of the decapitation of SS Juthwara and Sidwell, in which it is related that a healing spring gushed forth where the head struck the ground.[46] A similar association of the sacred well with the shedding of holy blood also appears in late traditions relating to the wells at Oswestry and Winwick. The well at Winwick was supposedly upon the site where Oswald fell, while that at Oswestry was said to mark the spot where his right arm fell to earth after having been carried off by a raven from its adjacent place of exposure.[47] Such analogies raise the possibility that the existence of so many wells at Oswald cult sites may reflect ancient patterns of Celtic devotion.[48]

---

[43] 84-5, 143-4; H. Taylor, *Ancient Crosses and Holy Wells of Lancashire* (Manchester 1906), pp. 210, 364; VCH *Lancashire* VIII, p. 153; Morris, *Churches*, 87; Rollason, below, pp. 170-1; Binns, below, pp. 244, 249, 252-3, 258-9.

Charmian Woodfield, letter to Clare Stancliffe, 30 April, 1992: 'It occurred to me that it ought to be recorded that the place from whence we fetched our water when working at Turret 25b, St Oswald's, at Heavenfield (although then appearing rather unromantically as a fairly modern pipe, leading, presumably from a spring, into some sort of equally fairly modern tank) was known as the White Well. The name puzzled me at the time, but I do now wonder whether the spring had not been at some time associated with a Holy Well. It was, from memory, about 50 yards westwards along the military road past St Oswald's, on the south side. It might have been a little further – it was some 35 years ago.' (Mrs Woodfield's excavation of turret 25b on Hadrian's Wall took place in 1959 and was published in *Archaeologia Aeliana* for 1965.)

[44] Ross, *Pagan Celtic Britain*, pp. 104-12; A. Ross, 'Severed heads in wells: an aspect of the well cult', *Scottish Studies* 6 (1962), pp. 31-48.

[45] *Nicholas Roscarrock's Lives of the Saints: Cornwall and Devon*, ed. N. Orme (Devon and Cornwall Record Society, new series, 35 (Exeter 1992)), esp. pp. 33, 41, 62-4, 71-3, 77-9, 81-2, 84-9, 94-8, 101-4, 113, 122-3, 130, 136-41, 143-4, 146-51, 153, 160-3, 168, 170-2, 176. Cf. Ross, 'Severed heads in wells', pp. 37-40. I am grateful to Dr B. Yorke for drawing my attention to this evidence.

[46] *Roscarrock's Lives*, pp. 81-2, 113, 143-4, 170-2.

[47] Hope, *Legendary Lore of Holy Wells*, pp. 84-5; Reginald, *VO* I, 18 (pp. 357-8).

[48] A similar association was made in Gaul, where of course there was also a Celtic substrate, in Gregory of Tours's account of Julian of Brioude. The place at which Julian was killed was noted for its spring, which acquired healing powers after the martyr's head was immersed in it: *De Passione et Virtutibus Sancti Iuliani Martyris* (MGH, Scriptores Rerum Merovingicarum 1, i; 2nd edn Hanover 1969), ch. 3 (pp. 115-16).

Lindisfarne's reaction to its royal relic was therefore almost certainly a complex one. Clearly, burial by the community was a relatively prudent response to such a highly charged object. While in accord with traditional custom, it removed the head from public worship, an altogether more ostentatious concession to ancestral values. Such caution was perhaps necessitated by Oswald's kingly status. Although cultic honours were accorded to members of royal kin on a lavish scale in the sixth- and seventh-century Latin west, the cult of kings themselves was very unusual and probably aroused distrust among church leaders. Suspicion would have rested especially upon the cult of the holy warrior, who surrendered his life in battle against his people's foes, because of its obvious appeal to those who wished to preserve the sacrality which Germanic paganism traditionally attributed to its leaders.[49] Indeed, that type of holy king was unknown before the mid seventh century and almost certainly originated in England, with the cult of Oswald himself or of his predecessor Edwin.[50] By burying its relic, Lindisfarne was in a sense hiding it. The pattern is in fact fairly clear: Oswald's cult, impregnated as it was by traditional beliefs and custom, was primarily secular and dynastic, exciting more enthusiasm among the king's own people and especially his close relatives than among the leaders of the church.

The next – and perhaps the most crucial – phase in the establishment of Oswald's reputation as a saint was the work of Oswiu's daughter Osthryth, the wife of King Æthelred of Mercia. Some time in the late seventh century, between 679 and her assassination in 697, she was responsible for the translation of the major part of Oswald's remains (minus of course the head and arms) to the royal monastery of Bardney in Lindsey, the foundation of her husband and herself. The story is well known: Osthryth caused the relics to be brought to Bardney on a cart, but the brethren there refused to receive them because they hated Oswald as an alien who had imposed his rule upon their province.[51] It took a miracle to persuade the recalcitrant community to admit them. The bones were then taken from the tent which had been spread over them, and washed, the water used in the ceremony being carefully poured away in a corner of the sacristy. Finally they were enshrined in a casket placed within the church and covered with the king's gold and purple standard. The shrine itself, and dust from the pavement where the water used in the washing had been poured away, became the source of miracles.[52]

---

[49] See esp. Hoffmann, *Die heiligen Könige*, pp. 16-58, esp. pp. 46-56.
[50] Ibid. p. 23; Graus, *Volk, Herrscher und Heiliger*, pp. 416-20.
[51] And possibly because they did not then regard them as relics: Graus, *Volk, Herrscher und Heiliger*, p. 418; Wallace-Hadrill, *EGK*, p. 84; Folz, p. 52.
[52] *HE* III, 11.

With the exception of the highly unusual element of the initial rejection, all this bears a close resemblance to what we know of other important translations of the late seventh century: the tent, the washing, and the creation of a multiplicity of miracle-working sites are all features accompanying the enshrinements of, for example, Æthelthryth and Cuthbert in the 690s and Wilfrid in 709/10.[53] Like Oswiu's activities at Bamburgh, such ceremonies looked back to Gallic precedents. Undoubtedly the result of royal rather than ecclesiastical initiative, those at Bardney may have been the first of their kind in England.[54]

Oswald's translation to Bardney may be compared with another royal translation, that of his predecessor Edwin. At some date between 680 and 704 Edwin's remains were recovered from the battlefield at Hatfield Chase, where they had probably already attracted their share of secular votaries. They were translated to a shrine within the church of Whitby then ruled by the king's daughter Eanflæd and granddaughter Ælfflæd. The ceremony was the result of a series of visions in which an Anglian priest was instructed to go to a certain village in Lindsey and seek out a husbandman (*maritus*) named Teoful, who could tell him where the relics lay.[55] The story, which was ignored by Bede,[56] lacks the circumstantial detail of his account of Oswald's translation. Nevertheless, the similarities are highly suggestive. As with Oswald, the death site appears to have been neglected by the church, its memory retained only by local laymen of modest standing, until the cult of the warrior king was taken over and formalised by a great dynastic foundation.[57] Interestingly, too, Edwin's head had been separated from his body and buried or enshrined separately in the cathedral of York, a church with which Whitby had very close connexions at the time of the translation.[58]

These royal translations, the work of two sisters – daughters, nieces, and granddaughters respectively of Oswiu, Oswald and Edwin[59] – were almost

---

[53] *HE* IV, 19; *VCA* IV, 14-15; *VCP* chs. 40-2 (pp. 130-4, 284-94); *VW* ch. 66.

[54] For Gallic parallels see Thacker, 'Making of a local saint'.

[55] Colgrave, *Earliest Life of Greg.* chs. 18-19.

[56] There are good reasons for believing that he was acquainted with the Whitby Life and therefore with the traditions about Edwin: A. T. Thacker, 'The Social and Continental Background to Early Anglo-Saxon Hagiography' (unpublished D.Phil. thesis, University of Oxford 1976), pp. 56, 76-8.

[57] Thacker, 'Social and Continental Background', pp. 38-79, esp. pp. 48-56; S. E. Mosford, 'A Critical Edition of the *Vita Gregorii Magni* by an Anonymous Member of the Community of Whitby' (unpublished D.Phil. thesis, University of Oxford 1988); Hoffmann, *Die heiligen Könige*, pp. 23-6.

[58] *HE* II, 20. York, like Lindisfarne and perhaps for the same reasons, made little of its royal head. For a Welsh tradition that the head was taken to Anglesey see Wallace-Hadrill, *Comm*, p. 226.

[59] Above, p. 13. It is likely but not certain that Osthryth was, like Ælfflæd, the daughter of Oswiu's queen, Eanflæd.

certainly linked.[60] The cults which they promoted were similar not only in their legends and rituals but in their physical expression. Recent research at Whitby has drawn attention to its memorial stones, which include skeuomorphs of wooden crosses, an indication that one of the most potent symbols of Oswald's cult had an equal currency at the shrine of his predecessor.[61] Equally significant are the links which bound both saints to the area on either side of the Humber and which are illustrated by the large number of medieval dedications to Oswald in the East and West Ridings and the north midlands.[62] While, therefore, as I have argued elsewhere, there may have been a degree of emulation in the translations, they are perhaps most plausibly interpreted as two aspects of a single initiative, enhancing the claims of a chosen family to be the sanctified rulers of a united Northumbria, probably envisaged as including the disputed province of Lindsey as well as Bernicia and Deira.[63]

In their promotion of kingly warriors to sainthood, and in the associated rites and ceremonies, Oswiu, Eanflæd, and their daughters were breaking new ground. Under their forceful guidance ecclesiastical communities overcame their reluctance to sanctify such figures (though in Bardney's case not without a struggle). The chronology of these dynastic achievements is therefore highly significant. Though the conventional dating for both is imprecise – for Edwin between 680 and 704, for Oswald between 679 and 697[64] – in many ways a date at the beginning rather than the end of the range is most plausible. Osthryth became queen of Mercia before 679;[65] her union with Æthelred looks like a classic example of a superior kingship expressing its hegemony through the marriage of one of its princesses to the dependent ruler.[66] Her sponsorship of the cult of Oswald in Lindsey can be regarded as an appeal to Northumbrian sympathies within the province, a controversial

[60] For the view that the development of a kingly cult by the Mercians in Lindsey provided the stimulus for a rival cult by the Northumbrians in neighbouring Deira (or vice versa), see Thacker, 'Social and Continental Background', pp. 48-56; 'Kings, saints and monasteries', pp. 2-4.

[61] R. Cramp, 'A reconsideration of the monastic site of Whitby', in *AMI*, pp. 64-73, at pp. 68-9.

[62] Their numbers contrast sharply with the scarcity of dedications in ancient Bernicia. Cf. Cambridge and Binns, below, pp. 158-61, 268; Yorke, 'Lindsey: the lost kingdom found?', pp. 143-4.

[63] In this context it is interesting that the Bernician Oswiu was buried not (as we might expect) at Lindisfarne or Bamburgh, but at his daughter's house of Whitby, at first sight the mausoleum of the Deiran royal family: *HE* III, 24.

[64] Colgrave, *Earliest Life of Greg.*, pp. 47-8; Plummer II, 154-5.

[65] *HE* IV, 21; Plummer II, 242.

[66] I. N. Wood, *The Merovingian North Sea* (Alingsås 1983), pp. 15-16; idem, 'Frankish hegemony in England', in *The Age of Sutton Hoo* (Woodbridge 1992), pp. 235-41; idem, *The Merovingian Kingdoms, 450-751* (London 1994), pp. 176-7.

policy which may well have contributed to her assassination in 697.[67] Such a course of action is perhaps most likely to have been initiated when Osthryth's relations with Northumbria were at their closest, that is before the death of her brother Ecgfrith at Nechtansmere in 685.[68] If the promotion of Edwin's cult was a continuation of the same dynastic policy his enshrinement may well have taken place at much the same time.

Perhaps the most interesting aspect of the cults of Edwin and Oswald is not so much the similarity of the circumstances in which they were established as the differences in their subsequent development. Edwin languished in obscurity, whereas Oswald rapidly achieved spectacular success. It reminds us that there was nothing inevitable in Oswald's posthumous fame. Oswiu, Eanflæd, and their daughters invested as much in Edwin as his nephew. But by the time that Bede was writing the *Ecclesiastical History* Oswald had been transformed into the Northumbrian Constantine, while Edwin's cult (though not his role in promoting the Roman mission) had been forgotten or suppressed.[69]

The reasons for the contrast lay, it will be proposed, in the political turmoil into which Northumbria was plunged in the early eighth century, and in the crucial role which Bishop Wilfrid and his communities played in those events. Because the story is relatively complex it has to be examined in some detail.

It has long been noted that among the most important promoters of the cult of Oswald in its earlier phases were St Wilfrid and his community at Hexham.[70] More precisely, it may be observed that Bishop Acca, Bede's friend and diocesan and Wilfrid's successor at Hexham, was the direct source of much material about Oswald in the *Ecclesiastical History*, apart from the early stories focused on *Maserfelth* and Bardney.[71] The most striking element in Hexham tradition was the community's treatment of Heavenfield, some four miles from their monastery. The brethren initiated the custom of an annual pilgrimage to the battlefield on Oswald's death-day and dispensed miracle-working relics in the form of splinters of wood from the cross

---

[67] Cf. also Æthelred's abdication in 704 and retirement (significantly) to Bardney: *HE* V 24 (*s.a.* 704); Plummer II, pp. 154, 327.

[68] Ecgfrith's successor Aldfrith, though also Oswiu's son, was by a different wife. He had lived in exile in Ireland before his unexpected accession: Plummer II, pp. 263-4.

[69] Thacker, 'Social and Continental Background', pp. 56-7; below.

[70] E.g. D. P. Kirby, 'Bede's native sources in the *Historia Ecclesiastica*', *Bulletin of the John Rylands Library* 48 (1965-6), pp. 341-71, at p. 350; idem, 'Northumbria in the time of Wilfrid', in *Saint Wilfrid at Hexham*, ed. idem (Newcastle upon Tyne 1975), pp. 1-34, at pp. 26-8; P. Wormald, 'Bede and Benedict Biscop', in *Famulus Christi*, ed. G. Bonner (London 1976), pp. 141-69, at pp. 151, 166.

[71] Folz, p. 53; Kirby, 'Northumbria in time of Wilfrid', p. 26.

erected there. Bede expressly relates that because of the popularity of the pilgrimage the brethren had 'recently' (*nuper*) constructed a church on the site. Evidently then in his own day the church of Hexham was actively encouraging the cult.[72]

Hexham, or at least Bishop Acca as spokesman of the community, was also the source of stories in which it is first revealed that veneration for Oswald had spread throughout Britannia and beyond to Ireland and to 'the continental homelands of the English'. The monks were the self-conscious guardians of, so to speak, an 'imperial' cult, the posthumous counterpart of the living Oswald's hegemony over the English, British, Irish, and Picts.[73] Acca disclosed that when he accompanied Wilfrid on his second trip to Rome in 703/4, he participated in conversations in which Wilfrid and his host (and former pupil) Willibrord discussed the wonders which were performed by Oswald's relics in the kingdom of Frisia.[74] Likewise it was from Acca that Bede learned of a miracle performed by a relic of the king in Ireland before 690, and of the story of Oswald's intercession on behalf of the community which Wilfrid had founded at Selsey in Sussex.[75]

This last story is (as has long been recognised) a highly significant account of the inauguration of a cult. A recently converted Saxon boy had fallen sick of the plague; he received a vision in which SS Peter and Paul gave orders that the priest Eappa, who then ruled Selsey, was to be summoned and told that after receiving the viaticum he (the boy) would die but that the rest of the inhabitants of the monastery would be spared because of the intercession of King Oswald, whose anniversary it was. The boy transmitted commands from the two apostles that the brethren were to consult the books in which the deposition of the dead was recorded, to establish that it was Oswald's day. They were to offer masses in all their oratories in honour of the king and then assemble to receive communion and hold a feast. Eappa acted on the boy's words. He consulted the monastery's annals and found that Oswald had indeed been slain on that day. He ordered masses to be said, the brethren to receive communion, and the viaticum to be administered to the boy. Shortly afterwards the boy, but no one else, died of the plague and that confirmation of the vision ensured that Oswald's day (*dies natalicius*) was thereafter commemorated not only in the monastery of Selsey itself, but in many other places in Sussex. Oswald's obit, entered in the monastic calendar but hitherto ignored in the communal ritual, had been converted into a feast day and his cult implanted in Sussex without (as far as we know) the

---

[72] *HE* III, 2.

[73] *HE* II, 5; III, 6; A. T. Thacker, 'Bede and the Irish', in *Beda Venerabilis: Historian, Monk and Northumbrian*, ed. A. A. McDonald (forthcoming); Stancliffe, above, pp. 48-60.

[74] *HE* III, 13; *VW* ch. 50.

[75] *HE* IV, 14.

importation of a single relic.[76] All that was very definitely the work of churchmen.

Much hinges on the date of these events. Clearly they took place after Wilfrid's spell in Sussex in the 680s; but how long after? Eappa, though Wilfrid's companion in his Sussex mission, could easily have been alive and active in the early eighth century. The one thing that is clear is that the story came to Bede late: it is an addition to the *Ecclesiastical History*, not present in the early manuscripts of that work.[77] We may therefore conjecture that the observance of Oswald's cult in Sussex was itself relatively late, dating from, say, after 700 rather than from the conversion period.

In sum, it seems that after an early phase in which the cult had been primarily a secular and dynastic affair, Oswald was taken up by a great episcopal centre with a wide range of contacts. It was that development above all else which ensured that he was remembered so much more successfully than Edwin. The evidence suggests that the close link between Hexham and Oswald was relatively recent when Bede was writing his history, perhaps no earlier than the beginning of the eighth century. There is no indication that Wilfrid was much interested in Oswald for most of his career; after all he was at odds with the head of Oswald's dynasty almost continuously until a few years before his death.[78] Nor is there any sign that he was involved in the translation to Bardney; indeed his biographer Stephen expressly mentions that Queen Osthryth took her brother Ecgfrith's side against the bishop and refused to allow him shelter in Mercia in 681.[79] When in 686 the archbishop of Canterbury succeeded in establishing a few years' peace it was King Æthelred of Mercia who was singled out as Wilfrid's friend, not the Northumbrian royal sisters Osthryth and Ælfflæd.[80]

The crucial realignment which turned Wilfrid and the church of Hexham into zealous exponents of Oswald's cult is most likely to have been made in 705 after the death of King Aldfrith. Aldfrith left no adult heir to succeed him and for a short period a member of a different royal lineage was intruded into the kingship – the first break in the monopoly exercised by

---

[76] It is not entirely clear whether the original masses were offered for the repose of Oswald's soul or to obtain his intercession. The story's emphatic attribution to Oswald of the crucial power of effective intercession makes it clear that by then we are certainly dealing with a cult.

[77] Plummer I, pp. xciv-xcv; *HE*, pp. xl-xli.

[78] For Wilfrid's career see H. M. R. E. Mayr-Harting, *The Coming of Christianity to Anglo-Saxon England* (London 1972), pp. 129-47; D. H. Farmer, 'Saint Wilfrid', in *St Wilfrid at Hexham*, pp. 35-59. Kirby draws attention to the complexity of Wilfrid's relations with the Bernician royal family: 'Northumbria in time of Wilfrid', pp. 23-4.

[79] *VW* ch. 40.

[80] *VW* ch. 43.

Oswald's kindred since the death of Edwin.[81] It is quite clear that Wilfrid was involved in the coup and expected to benefit from it. According to Stephen he returned from exile to Ripon accompanied by Eadwulf's son and sent friendly messages to the new king. But for some reason Eadwulf rejected Wilfrid's advances and a regrouping took place. Eadwulf was expelled and Aldfrith's young son, the 'royal boy' Osred, succeeded him. Significantly, by then Osred had become, according to Stephen, Wilfrid's adopted son, *filius adoptivus*.[82]

The resolution of the turmoil came in the following year at the so-called synod of the Nidd. There assembled Wilfrid, Archbishop Berhtwald of Canterbury, Abbess Ælfflæd, and the young king with his bishops and advisers. The spokesman of the royal party was the *praefectus*, Berhtfrith, described by Stephen as second to the king and probably an Anglian equivalent of the Frankish mayor of the palace. Berhtfrith recommended a reconciliation with Wilfrid; his reasons are given by Stephen in a typically vivid and dramatic speech:

> 'When we were besieged in the city (*urbs*) called Bamburgh, and surrounded on all sides by a hostile force, we remained on the constricted site of the stony rock, and having taken counsel among ourselves, we vowed that if God granted our royal boy his father's kingdom we would fulfil the commands of the Apostolic See concerning Bishop Wilfrid. As soon as our vow was made the minds of our enemies were changed and they made haste to bind themselves to us by an oath of friendship. Then the gates of our confined refuge were opened, our enemies were put to flight, and we received the kingdom.'[83]

Berhtfrith's sentiments were echoed by Abbess Ælfflæd, the new king's aunt and perhaps at that time the leading ecclesiastical personage in Northumbria apart from Wilfrid himself. As a result Wilfrid received back Ripon and Hexham.

Stephen's account makes it clear that the citadel of Bamburgh was the physical and spiritual focus of Osred's party. It is tempting to suppose that in their time of trial the family and adherents of Aldfrith's son made their vow to Wilfrid before Oswald's imperishable arm, and that one of the fruits of the reconciliation was a fresh promoting of their dynastic cult. Quite possibly the annual pilgrimage to Heavenfield was then inaugurated or at least upgraded as a sign of the new concord between Bamburgh and Hexham; certainly it was after that date that the site was honoured with a church. Thenceforward, Hexham would be collecting the material that was to occupy such an important place in the *Ecclesiastical History* and spreading the cult among the many communities with which it had privileged contacts.

[81] Kirby, 'Northumbria in time of Wilfrid', esp. pp. 17- 21; *VW* ch. 59; *HE* V, 18.
[82] *VW* ch. 59.
[83] *VW* ch. 60 (my translation).

Clearly the link between Oswald and Hexham was still important in the 730s when Bede was writing his *History*. Oswald's royal line continued to hold the kingship with only a brief interruption until the death of Osred's brother Osric in 729. Thereafter it passed (according to Bede at Osric's express wish) to Ceolwulf, brother of Osric's predecessor and member of a different royal lineage.[84] Yet the dynastic issue was far from settled. We know that Aldfrith had at least one other son, Offa, to whom the church of Lindisfarne offered shelter as late as 750.[85] The loyalties of the churches which promoted Oswald's cult at that time are opaque; but doubtless they were crucial. The deposition of Acca, Oswald's most enthusiastic sponsor, has long been connected with the political upheaval of 731, when Ceolwulf was taken prisoner, forced into a monastery and subsequently restored. Acca is generally interpreted as a supporter of Ceolwulf, largely because of his close relations with Bede and the latter's dedication of the *History* to that king. But Acca's flight could just as easily be read as a consequence of a failed coup.[86] After all, he never returned to his see. When Ceolwulf, apparently voluntarily, resigned his kingship a second time, he withdrew not to Hexham but to Lindisfarne where he was remembered with affection.[87] Hexham's role and the implications of its ardent advocacy of Oswald remain ambiguous.

Something of the partisan feeling which clearly informed Stephen's account of those conflicts is evident in the *Historia Ecclesiastica*. Like Stephen, Bede was initially favourable to the young king Osred whom he hailed as a new Josiah.[88] Later, in the *Ecclesiastical History*, he quite failed to give any hint of the scandals which were to render Osred's name odious to St Boniface as a violator of virgins.[89] But although in the 730s Bede seems to have been following the line of his friend and diocesan Acca, it is important to remember that he had his own agenda. A very clear scheme informs the *Ecclesiastical History*, whose author is concerned to present the English as a chosen people achieving salvation under the guidance of the leaders of his own Northumbrian or, more specifically, Bernician *gens*.[90] The Bernician Oswald was assigned a prominent role within that scheme. The reuniter of the two Northumbrian *provinciae*, which had fallen apart after Edwin's death

---

[84] *HE* V, 22-4; Reginald, *VO* I, 21 (p. 360); Kirby, 'Northumbria in time of Wilfrid', pp. 20-1.

[85] Kirby, 'Northumbria in time of Wilfrid', p. 25.

[86] Ibid. pp. 24, 33; *HE*, p. 572; Plummer II, 330.

[87] *HE*, p. 572; Reginald, *VO* I, 21 (pp. 360-1); Plummer II, 340.

[88] Bede, *Vita Sancti Cuthberti metrica*, ed. W. Jaager, *Metrische Vita Sancti Cuthberti* (Palaestra 198; 1935), ch. 21 (lines 582-5).

[89] Boniface, *Sancti Bonifatii et Lulli Epistolae*, ed. M. Tangl (MGH, Epistolae Selectae 1; Berlin 1916), pp. 152-3.

[90] A. T. Thacker, 'Bede's ideal of reform', in *Ideal and Reality*, pp. 130-53.

in 633, he was also the ruler who reintroduced Christianity after the Roman mission had foundered. Oswald was the just king under whom, Bede believed, his native Northumbria had achieved its greatest temporal success. By the 730s indeed he could be cast in the role of the Northumbrian Constantine, whose victory at Heavenfield could be interpreted in the light of that even more momentous battle at the Milvian Bridge.[91] For Bede that was the day on which Christianity triumphed amongst the Northumbrian people, and he expressly says (contrary to what is implied in his own earlier narrative in book II) that 'no sign of the Christian faith, no church, no altar' was set up among the whole Bernician *gens* before Oswald erected his cross, that 'heavenly trophy' (*caeleste tropaeum*) or 'standard' (*vexillum*).[92] Here indeed is clear evidence of a reworking of the Oswald story in the interests of the ecclesiastical hierarchy in the early eighth century.[93]

Oswald then is undoubtedly presented as a sanctified ruler in the *Historia Ecclesiastica*.[94] It is not certain, however, that Bede had always regarded him in quite such an exalted light. He was, it seems, omitted from the original version of Bede's martyrology.[95] Even more significantly, in the *Chronica Maiora*, written in 725, Oswald and his protégé Aidan are not mentioned and instead Edwin and Paulinus are named as the progenitors of Northumbrian Christianity.[96] Bede was perhaps a late convert to Hexham's royal cult. Even in the *Historia Ecclesiastica* he shows himself wary of Oswald in one important respect: though it must have been tempting to do so, and indeed later ages did, he never attributes to the king the exalted status of martyr.[97] It may be that he was all too well aware of the ease with which the sainted warrior Oswald could be assimilated to his predecessors as a sacral embodiment of his people's luck, and that he sought to play down that aspect of the cult.

At all events, by the middle decades of the eighth century Oswald was established in Northumbria, and probably in Mercia and Lindsey as well, as the dominant English royal saint. There was nothing inevitable about this,

---

91 Wallace-Hadrill, *Comm*, pp. 88-9.

92 *HE* III, 2; Wallace-Hadrill, *Comm*, p. 89.

93 Cf. Stancliffe, above, pp. 50-1, 63 and n. 145.

94 Cf. Stancliffe, above, pp. 41, 61-4.

95 H. Quentin, *Les martyrologes historiques du moyen âge* (Paris 1908), p. 48; Folz, p. 59; Wormald, 'Bede and Biscop', p. 151.

96 Bede, *Opera Didaschalia*, ed. C. W. Jones (3 vols, Corpus Christianorum Series Latina 123A-123B; Turnhout 1975-8), II, pp. 241, 545.

97 Graus, *Volk, Herrscher und Heiliger*, p. 418; Wallace-Hadrill, *EGK*, p. 84. I am grateful to Victoria Gunn for drawing my attention to this point; for a full treatment see V. A. Gunn, 'Bede and the martyrdom of St Oswald', *Studies in Church History* 30, ed. D. Wood (Oxford 1993), pp. 57-66. See also Stancliffe, above, pp. 41-2.

and indeed but for the relatively late sponsorship of Bede and the Wilfridians he might never have emerged to such prominence. Nevertheless, the complex nature of the process was such that with the publication of the *Ecclesiastical History* Oswald's future was assured. Not only did he have Bede's incomparable advocacy, he also possessed an unusual number of major cult sites which transcended the boundaries of the English kingdoms: the uncorrupted arm at Bamburgh, the tomb chest at Bardney, the church and cross at Heavenfield, the battlefield at *Maserfelth*. No other English royal and dynastic cult could compete with that.

The fruit of those developments became apparent in the later eighth century, by which time Oswald's reputation was less closely bound up with contemporary political events. In Mercia, for example, King Offa adorned the shrine at Bardney with precious metals, gems and other ornaments, an action which Alcuin clearly approved as honouring the fount of English Christian kingship.[98] In Northumbria, when King Ælfwald was slain in 788 at Hadrian's Wall, a church was built on the site and dedicated to SS Cuthbert and Oswald.[99] It is one of the earliest known dedications to an English local saint – and again the moving force was the church at Hexham, to which the body of Ælfwald was taken and at which a cult of the murdered king developed. Hexham, it seems, had retained its interest in royal saints and above all in Oswald. Its manipulation of such an established cult was an important asset which could be deployed to the advantage of current rulers.

Other sources confirm that Oswald had emerged as a figure of more than regional importance by that time. His eminence is indicated, for example, by the exceptionally generous allowance of 272 lines meted out to him in Alcuin's poem on the saints of York, and by the entry for his feast day in the ninth-century Old English martyrology, which named the cult centres at Bamburgh, Lindisfarne, and Bardney, and concluded: 'his miracles were great on this side as well as beyond the sea.'[100] All this presumably reflects the tremendous prestige which Bede's and Hexham's endorsement had conferred upon the saint.

The Early Development of the Cult in Ireland and on the Continent
The martyrologist's reference to Oswald's miracles 'beyond the sea' is a reminder that from an early date the cult had been considered remarkable for the extent of its diffusion and in particular for its diffusion overseas. There is

---

[98] Alcuin, *BKS* lines 388-91 (p. 34); and cf. pp. xlv-xlvii.
[99] *HR* ch. 54 (Arnold II, 52); Kirby, 'Northumbria in time of Wilfrid', p. 25 .
[100] Alcuin, *BKS* lines 234-506 (pp. 24-44); G. Kotzor, *Das altenglische Martyrologium* (Bayerische Akademie Wissenschaften, philosophische-historische Klasse: Neue Folge 88; Munich 1981), pp. 171-2; *An Old English Martyrology*, ed. G. Herzfeld (Early English Text Society, old series 116; London 1900), p. 138.

clear evidence that from the late seventh century Oswald was venerated both in Ireland and on the continent.

One Irish community with especially good reasons to remember Oswald was, of course, Iona, where the young prince had spent time in exile and to which as a newly established ruler he sent for missionaries to convert his people. Nevertheless, although pride in the connexion is indicated by the passage in the *Life of Columba* which tells of the king's encouragement by the saint on the eve of the battle of Heavenfield, there is no evidence of a cult.[101] In fact, the best early evidence for Irish veneration of Oswald comes not from Iona but from Anglian-influenced milieux on the Irish mainland, to which the Northumbrian Willibrord brought a wonder-working relic of the king.[102] A splinter of wood from the stake upon which Oswald's head had been impaled, it was certainly in the saint's possession before he left for Frisia in 690 and presumably accompanied him on his departure from his native land in the 670s. Its existence is a further indication of the speed and zeal with which the Northumbrian kings capitalised on the items acquired in Oswiu's raid of 643.[103]

The milieu in which Willibrord moved in Ireland was that of the English *peregrini*,[104] dominated by the Anglian bishop Ecgberht who had left England in the 660s. Ecgberht's companions in the early stages of his pilgrimage included Æthelhun, a noble from a well connected Lindsey family and the brother of Æthelwine, bishop of Lindsey (*c*.680-?692), of Ealdwine, abbot of Partney, and of Æthelhild, abbess of a community near Bardney.[105] At least one of those relatives was involved in the propagation of Oswald's cult. Æthelhild, a confidant of Queen Osthryth, obtained dust from the pavement where water used in the washing of the saint's bones had been poured away, and preserved it at her monastery in a little casket.[106] Although Æthelhun himself died young, at the monastery of *Rath Melsigi* where he and Ecgberht were pursuing their studies, his brother Æthelwine also went to Ireland to study before returning to Lindsey as its bishop.[107] If Ecgberht maintained contact with the family, he may well have been stimulated into promoting Oswald's cult in his Irish community. Once again

---

[101] *VCol* I, 1, at 8a-9b (pp. 14-16).

[102] *HE* III, 13.

[103] Though if *Maserfelth* and the site of the display of the relics were in Lindsey it may have been obtained directly from thence: above.

[104] On *peregrini* and *peregrinatio* ('pilgrims', 'pilgrimage') see Stancliffe, above, p. 65 n. 151, and p. 82.

[105] *HE* III, 11, 27.

[106] *HE* III, 11.

[107] *HE* III, 27. On *Rath Melsigi*, see D. Ó Cróinín, 'Rath Melsigi, Willibrord and the earliest Echternach manuscripts', *Peritia* 3 (1984), pp. 17-49.

Lindsey's role appears to have been crucial.[108]

It was from that Irish and Anglian milieu that the cult seems to have moved over to the continent. When Willibrord was sent by Ecgberht to Frisia he took with him his devotion to Oswald. The calendar ascribed to him, presumably representing the observance of his monastery at Echternach, commemorates the king (*Oswaldi regis*) on August 5.[109] The entry, which is in the original hand, in no way differs from the later additions honouring Ecgfrith, Oswine, and Edwin on 20 May, 19 August, and 13 October, and it might be thought that it represents an obit rather than a feast day.[110] Nevertheless, the fact that Oswald is one of only two English saints to be included in a version of the Hieronymian martyrology produced at Echternach in the early eighth century[111] is sufficient to demonstrate his true status in Willibrord's monastery.[112] The cult was clearly well established when Wilfrid and Acca visited Willibrord on their way to Rome in 703/4, and the implication of Bede's account of that visit is that the relics were by then enshrined in some monument more substantial than a portable reliquary.[113]

---

[108] It is not clear how successful the Anglian *peregrini* were in diffusing the cult on the Irish mainland. Oswald's feast day (5 August) appears in the earliest Irish calendars, which stem from Tallaght and date from 828 x 833: *Martyrology of Tallaght*, ed. R. I. Best and H. J. Lawlor (HBS 68; London 1931, for 1929), p. 60 (*Osualdi regis*); *Martyrology of Oengus the Culdee* (HBS 29; London 1905), p. 174 ('holy Oswald whom we implore, the noble overking of the Saxons'); P. Ó Riain, 'The Tallaght martyrologies, redated', *Cambridge Medieval Celtic Studies* 20 (1990), pp. 21-38. In a recent paper, however, Ó Riain has argued that the Hieronymian martyrology which underlies these compilations came to Ireland from Northumbria via Iona. Almost certainly that explains why the calendars include various unlikely Anglo-Saxon names, and it may also account for the commemoration of Oswald: P. Ó Riain, *Anglo-Saxon Ireland* (H. M. Chadwick Memorial Lecture 3; Cambridge 1993).

[109] Paris, Bibliothèque Nationale, MS lat. 10837, fol. 38^r; *Calendar of St Willibrord*, ed. H. A. Wilson (HBS 55; London 1918), pp. 10, 36, plate VIII. For the dating of this manuscript see D. Ó Cróinín, 'Is the Augsburg Gospel codex a Northumbrian manuscript?', in *St Cuthbert*, pp. 189-201, at p. 195; N. Netzer, 'Willibrord's scriptorium at Echternach and its relationship to Ireland and Lindisfarne', in ibid., pp. 203-12 at p. 206.

[110] Paris, BN lat. 10837, fols. 36^v, 38^r, 39^r; Wilson, *Calendar of St Willibrord*, pp. xxii, 7, 10, 12, 30, 37-8, 41, plates V, VIII, X.

[111] It is bound up with the calendar in Paris BN lat. 10837, fols. 2^r-33^v. Oswald's entry reads simply *natalis Osualdi regis*: ibid. fol. 22^v.

[112] The calendar, of course, may well derive from a Northumbrian exemplar. Oswald was certainly commemorated at Jarrow by the mid 8th century: W. Böhne, 'Die älteste Lorscher Kalendar und seine Vorlagen', in *Die Reichsabtei Lorsche*, ed. F. Knopp (2 vols, Darmstadt 1973-7), II, pp. 171-220, esp. p. 186.

[113] *HE* III, 13.

At Echternach the cult of Oswald clearly had a close personal association with Willibrord, who came to be honoured with a special commemoration on the king's feast day (5 August).[114] It is, however, difficult to establish the nature of the relics installed there. According to a late tradition they included the head,[115] though it is as certain as anything can be in the history of relics that Lindisfarne never parted with that precious object.[116] Echternach's claim is probably no more than a confused recollection of the fact that Willibrord's original relics were in some way linked with the head. Though the bishop maintained close links with Lindisfarne,[117] it seems unlikely that he secured anything further from thence in view of the community's reserved treatment of Oswald.

The king's inclusion in Echternach's early and influential version of the Hieronymian martyrology ensured that knowledge of his feast would be widely disseminated. An early illustration of the monastery's role is to be found in the ninth-century martyrologies. Though his community had no special reason to be interested in Oswald apart from its relative proximity to Echternach, Wandelbert included the saint in the metrical martyrology which he compiled at the great Carolingian abbey of Prüm in 848.[118] Oswald also appears in what was to become the standard version of the martyrology, that of Usuard, active between c.850 and c.865; he is in fact the only English saint introduced by Usuard, whose entry is almost certainly borrowed from Wandelbert.[119] Equally crucial was the wide diffusion of Bede's *Historia Ecclesiastica* on the continent from the eighth century.[120] At Prüm, for example, Oswald is referred to as *rex pius Anglorum*, a description which goes beyond the Echternach entry and probably implies that Wandelbert drew upon Bede as well as the tradition of Echternach.[121]

Other material despatched from England during the eighth century which reinforced those main sources included Northumbrian calendars

---

[114] Paris BN lat. 10158, quoted in Wilson, *Calendar of Willibrord*, p. 36.

[115] Folz, p. 62, n. 66.

[116] Bailey, below, pp. 197-209.

[117] E.g. *VCA* IV, 16; *VCP* ch. 44.

[118] *Wandelberti Prumiensis Carmina*, ed. E. Dümmler (MGH, Poetae Latini Aevi Carolini 2; Berlin 1884), p. 591; Folz, pp. 60-2.

[119] *Le Martyrologe d'Usuard*, ed. J. Dubois (Subsidia Hagiographica 40; Brussels 1965), pp. 134-7, 278. Cf. Ó Riain-Raedel, below, p. 211. Although Oswald does not appear in the original version of Ado's martyrology, compiled c.855, he is included in the later family of manuscripts: *Le Martyrologe d'Adon*, ed. J. Dubois and G. Renaud (Paris 1984), pp. 249-50.

[120] *HE* pp. xxxix-lxx; D. Whitelock, *After Bede* (Jarrow Lecture 1960).

[121] J. Dubois, 'Le martyrologe metrique de Wandelbert', *AB* 79 (1961), pp. 257-93, esp. p. 272. Bede was also known to Usuard, as his entry on Oswald shows: *Mart. d'Usuard*, p. 278; Ó Riain-Raedel, below, pp. 210-11.

containing Oswald's feast day. Especially interesting is the transmission of a calendar produced by about 750 at Jarrow. Transcribed and augmented at Mainz in the late eighth century, it was copied again at Lorsch c.840.[122] Interestingly that calendar also included entries for Wilfrid, Ecgberht, and the two Hewalds, all saints to some degree involved in the Frisian mission.[123] The same commemorations, again reflecting an English or Frisian source, occur in other Carolingian calendars, most notably that in the Ambrosiana in Milan.[124] Oswald and Willibrord were also among the augmentations to Bede's martyrology made at Würzburg in the mid ninth century.[125]

All this is evidence that English and Frisian liturgical material combined to make knowledge of Oswald as a Christian saint comparatively widespread in Frisia and parts of Germany along the Rhine in the eighth and ninth centuries. It is not, however, proof of an active cult. At Lorsch, though Oswald's name was certainly included among the saints in the community's version of the martyrology and in its calendars, there is no evidence of liturgical commemoration in the early middle ages. In particular, no provision was made for a mass in his honour in the late-tenth-century sacramentary which is the earliest to survive from the abbey.[126]

Elsewhere in Germany evidence for the cult is even more ambiguous. It is interesting, for example, that it seems never to have been promoted by Boniface, whose great community of Fulda had no relics of Oswald though it certainly possessed some of Cuthbert and of Bede himself.[127] Even more significantly, a fragmentary calendar written in a mid-eighth-century Northumbrian hand, but preserved in the Regensburg area, contains no entry for the king, despite apparently sharing an origin with the calendar of Willibrord.[128] Indeed, the evidence of the calendars in general suggests that

122 Böhne, 'Die älteste Lorscher Kalendar', pp. 171-220; E. Munding, *Die Kalendarien von St Gallen* (Texte und Arbeiten, 36 (*Texte*), 37 (*Untersuchungen*); Beuron in Hohenzollern 1948-51), *U.* p. 86.

123 'Depositio domini Wilfridi et Egberti et Melliti episcoporum' (24 April); 'Nat[a]l[is] sanctorum martyrum Heowaldi et Heowaldi' (4 Oct.): Böhne, 'Die älteste Lorscher Kalendar', pp. 216, 219.

124 B. Bischoff, 'Das karolingischer Kalendar der Palimsesthandschrift Ambros. M. 12 sup.', in *Colligere Fragmenta: Festschrift Alban Dold zum 70 Geburtstag* (Beuron in Hohenzollern 1952), pp. 247-60.

125 Quentin, *Martyrologes*, pp. 20-3.

126 L. Einzenhofer, 'Das Lorscher Sacramentar im Cod. Vat. Pal. lat. 495', in *Die Reichsabtei Lorsch*, pp. 129-69.

127 *Hrabanis Mauri Carmina* (MGH, Poetae Latini 2), pp. 205–8. For the evidence of the Fuldan calendars see Ó Riain-Raedel, below, p. 211.

128 P. Siffrin, 'Das Walderdorffer Kalendarfragment saec. VIII und die Berliner Blatter eines Sakramentarium aus Regensburg', *Ephemerides Liturgicae* 47 (1933), pp. 201-24; *Codices Latini Antiquiores*, ed. E. A. Lowe (12 vols, Oxford 1934-71), VIII, no. 1052.

the highly limited commemoration implied by mere presence therein took off only in the tenth century. Oswald does not, for example, appear in the calendars of Trier, of Cologne and Essen, and of St Gall until that date.[129]

There is then little to flesh out Bede's assertion that already in his day 'the beams of Oswald's healing light' had spread as far afield as Germany.[130] Bede, however, had his own reasons for making such a claim. One of the most important themes of the last book of the *Ecclesiastical History* was the evangelising role of the *gens Anglorum* in bringing full catholic observance both to its spiritual parent, the community at Iona, and to the descendants of its physical progenitors, the continental Saxons. As Ecgberht was for Bede the crucial (Northumbrian) agent of that God-given mission, so the cult of Oswald, the Northumbrian Constantine, was for him its most appropriate spiritual expression. Bede may have been inclined to play up the significance of both.[131]

Besides Echternach itself the only continental centre which seems to have possessed a relic of the saint before the tenth century was the great Frankish monastery of Chelles. Identified by a tag dating from the late eighth century and bearing the legend *S[an]c[t]i Osuualdi regis*,[132] the relic belonged to a large collection (some 139) acquired during the abbacy of Gisela, sister of Charlemagne, the majority of which formed a single donation, perhaps made by Charles himself. Oswald's tag is among a group of about thirty written at the monastery.[133] Chelles had long had English affiliations; it had been richly endowed in the late 660s by Balthildis, English wife of the Merovingian King Clovis II, and it had attracted high-born Englishwomen even earlier, including, interestingly enough, the sister of Hild, first abbess of Whitby.[134]

129 P. Miesges, *Der Trierer Festkalendar: seine Entwicklung und seine Verwendung zu Urkundendatierung* (Trierisches Archiv 15; Trier 1915), pp. 9-11, 76; G. Zilliken, 'Der Kölner Festkalendar', *Bonner Jahrbucher* 119 (1910), pp. 88, 131; Munding, *Die Kalendarien von St Gallen*, T. pp. 65, 103; U. pp. 13, 33.

130 *HE* III, 13.

131 Cf. his remarkable failure to mention Boniface: Thacker, 'Bede and Irish'; W. Goffart, *The Narrators of Barbarian History* (Princeton 1988), pp. 249-53, esp. p. 252.

132 *Chartae Latinae Antiquiores*, ed. A. Bruckner and R. Marichal (in progress, 40 vols, Olten and Lausanne 1954-75, Dietikon-Zurich since 1975), XVIII, no. 669, xc.

133 J.-P. Laporte, *Le trésor des saints de Chelles (Bulletin de la Société Archéologique et Historique de Chelles*, nouvelle série, 8-9; Chelles 1988), pp. 115-60.

134 *HE* III, 8; IV, 23; R. Folz, 'Traditions hagiographiques et culte de Sainte Bathilde, reine des Francs', *Académie des Inscriptions et Belles-Lettres: Comptes Rendues* (Paris 1975), pp. 369-84, esp. 371-2; K. H. Krüger, *Königsgrabkirchen der Franken, Angelsachsen und Langobarden bis zur Mitte des 8 Jahrhunderts* (Münstersche Mittelalter-Schriften 4; Munich 1971), pp. 238-46.

Gisela herself was a friend and correspondent of Alcuin.[135] Given those links it is not wholly surprising that the monastery should have been the possessor of an Oswald relic from an early date. Nevertheless it does not appear to have been a particularly active centre of the cult; at nearby Jouarre, for example, an even larger collection of over 220 relic fragments, enshrined in three separate vessels, includes nothing relating to the king.[136] Indeed Oswald was never to become a significant saint in France.[137]

In sum, there is reason to believe that the cult of Oswald on the continent was restricted to a few centres with exceptionally strong Anglian connexions. Most probably it reflected private devotion of the *peregrini*. It should be noted, for example, that though Willibrord apparently encouraged devotion to Oswald in his monastery at Echternach, as bishop the cult which he sponsored above all others was (as we might expect) that of St Martin.[138] Remarkable though it was, the diffusion of Oswald's cult in the early period stemmed from unco-ordinated personal initiatives rather than a concerted attempt to disseminate veneration among the Frisians, the Germans and the Franks. The really startling continental developments must be ascribed to a later period.

The Cult in the Tenth and Earlier Eleventh Centuries

Although the cult undoubtedly survived in late Anglo-Saxon Northumbria, it is difficult to assess its vitality. The imperishable arm apparently remained at Bamburgh, at least until the 1050s (when it was allegedly stolen by the monks of Peterborough), but according to Reginald of Durham it was neglected.[139] On the other hand the head, which was said to have been placed in St Cuthbert's coffin and to have shared its travels,[140] probably became more celebrated. At Durham, where the Cuthbert Community had settled in 995, the mother church of Elvet was dedicated to Oswald by the late twelfth century, if not long before.[141] Even so, the scarcity of churches under the saint's patronage in ancient Bernicia is in marked contrast with, for example, the Deiran heartlands and suggests that the cult was not especially active there.[142]

[135] Alcuin, *Epistolae*, ed. E. Dümmler (MGH, Epistolae Karolini Aevi 4; Berlin 1895), pp. 40-2, 127, 132, 248-9, 292, 322-5, 354-60, 371-2.

[136] See A. Wilmart, *Analecta Reginensia: Extrait des manuscrits latins de la Reine Christine conservés au Vatican* (Studi e Testi 59; Vatican 1940), pp. 9-17.

[137] Folz, pp. 65-6.

[138] See for example his foundation of churches dedicated to the saint at Utrecht and Emmerich: H. L. de Groot, *Traces at Traiectum* (Utrecht 1992), pp. 15-17; H. Flintrop, *St Martinus Emmerich, Vorposten des Hochstiftes Utrecht* (Zutphen 1992).

[139] Tudor, below, p. 192; Reginald, *VO* II, 48 (pp. 374-5).

[140] *HDE* II, 6 (Arnold I, p. 57). Cf. Bailey and Tudor, below, pp. 197-9, 188-9.

[141] See Cambridge and Binns, below, pp. 148-54, 249.

[142] Binns, below, Fig. 8, pp. 268-9, and pp. 249, 255, 259-67.

The main centre of operations in the period seems in fact to have lain not in Oswald's native Northumbria but in Mercia. There the major event in the history of the cult was Æthelred and Æthelflæd's translation in 909 of the saint's remains from Bardney to the new minster which they had founded in Gloucester in the 890s.[143] Gloucester was a place of great importance to the Mercian rulers, and their new church, though small, was sumptuous, lavishly adorned with sculpture and ornament. Originally dedicated (like the early minster) to St Peter, it was soon enlarged by the addition of a square eastern crypt subdivided by columns, probably, as at Repton, to house the shrine of the saint and the tombs of the founders.[144] Oswald apparently had special significance for Æthelred and Æthelflæd; as David Rollason has suggested, the installation in their principal base of the bones of a royal saint with particularly close associations with past rulers of Mercia may have been a statement about their own ambitions in the dismembered kingdom.[145] In this context it may well be significant that the cult also appears in Chester, Æthelflæd's stronghold in the north-west midlands, where it was closely associated with the cult of St Werburg.[146] Since Werburg's remains were probably brought to the city by Æthelflæd herself, it is very likely that she also fostered there the cult of Oswald.[147]

That the cult enjoyed some success in its new home is indicated by Ælfric's conclusion to his vernacular Life of the saint: 'God there [i.e. in

143 ASC, 'A', 'D', s.a. 906; 'C' s.a. 909; D. W. Rollason, 'Lists of saints' resting-places in Anglo-Saxon England', ASE 7 (1978), pp. 61-93, at pp. 63, 87.

144 C. M. Heighway and R. Bryant, 'A reconstruction of the tenth-century church of St Oswald, Gloucester', in The Anglo-Saxon Church, ed. L. Butler and R. Morris (CBA, Research Report 60; London 1986), pp. 188-95, esp. pp. 191, 193-4; M. Hare, The Two Anglo-Saxon Minsters of Gloucester (Deerhurst Lecture 1992), pp. 2-11; M. Hare and C. M. Heighway, 'Introduction'; M. Hare, 'The documentary evidence for the early history of St Oswald's, Gloucester', both to appear in C. M. Heighway and R. M. Bryant, The Saxon Minster and Medieval Priory of St Oswald at Gloucester (forthcoming). I am very grateful to Michael Hare and Carolyn Heighway for allowing me to see these texts in advance of publication.

145 Rollason, Saints and Relics, p. 154. Note especially the remark of William of Malmesbury, quoted by Rollason, that Æthelred and Æthelflæd translated the relics 'because they had all Mercia under their power' (quod omnis Mertia eorum pareret imperio): Gesta Pontificum IV, 155, ed. N. E. S. A. Hamilton (RS, London 1870), p. 293.

146 By the 13th century the parish altar of the abbey church of St Werburgh (later established as a separate church) was dedicated to St Oswald: Chartulary of St Werburgh's Abbey, ed. J. Tait (Chetham Society, new series, 79, 82; Manchester 1920-23), pp. 117-19.

147 A. T. Thacker, 'Chester and Gloucester: early ecclesiastical organization in two Mercian boroughs', Northern History 18 (1982), pp. 199-211, at pp. 203-4; VCH Cheshire I, p. 252.

Gloucester] often showed many wonders through the holy man.'[148] Almost certainly it made an impact on the young Athelstan, who was being fostered at Æthelflæd's court at the time of the translation.[149] Athelstan's Mercian ties continued to be very important to him, even after his accession to the West Saxon kingship in 925, and, famously interested as he was in relics, he seems to have identified with Oswald's cult.[150] When his half-sister Edith was sent to Germany to marry the future Emperor Otto I, she was described as 'of the blessed line of Oswald' (*nata de stirpe beata Oswaldi regis*), an allusion which suggests that Athelstan made much of the saint and of his family's supposed descent from him.[151] That the king was also interested in the church which housed the saint's remains is suggested by a lost charter to which Michael Hare has recently drawn attention. Issued in the first year of Athelstan's reign, it grants privileges to the minster in fulfilment of 'a pact of paternal piety' made by the king to Ealdorman Æthelred.[152]

It was probably in Æthelflæd or Athelstan's time that the cult came to be associated with a number of important churches in the midlands and the north-west. Perhaps the most interesting is Winwick (Lancashire), whose dedication to Oswald is recorded in Domesday Book. Winwick, the focus of a large ancient parish comprising some eleven townships, formed the southern half of the hundred of Newton and included the royal estate centre

---

[148] *Aelfric's Lives of the Saints*, ed. W. Skeat (Early English Text Society, old series, 114; London 1900), no. 26 (p. 142).

[149] M. Wood, 'The making of King Athelstan's empire', in *Ideal and Reality*, pp. 250-72, at p. 259, n. 46; William of Malmesbury, *Gesta Regum* II, 133, ed. W. Stubbs (RS, 2 vols; London 1867-89), I, p. 145.

[150] For Athelstan and relics see S. Keynes, 'King Athelstan's books', in *Learning and Literature in Anglo-Saxon England*, ed. M. Lapidge and H. Gneuss (Cambridge 1985), pp. 143-201, at pp. 143-4; J. A. Robinson, *The Times of St Dunstan* (Oxford 1923), pp. 71-80; Rollason, *Saints and Relics*, pp. 159-63. There is no certain evidence that Athelstan had relics of Oswald among his personal collection or that he distributed any such to his favourite communities. Nevertheless, both Winchester's New Minster and Glastonbury, to which Athelstan is known to have given relics, later claimed to possess relics of Oswald, and in the case of Glastonbury at least later tradition attributed their presence to the king: *Liber Vitae: Register and Martyrology of Hyde Abbey*, ed. W. de Gray Birch (Hampshire Record Society, London and Winchester 1892), pp. lxv, 158-9, 162-3; William of Malmesbury, *De Antiquitate Glastonie Ecclesie*, ed. J. Scott, *The Early History of Glastonbury* (Woodbridge 1981), pp. 112-14, 139; I. G. Thomas, 'The Cult of Saints' Relics in Medieval England' (unpublished Ph.D. thesis, University of London 1975), p. 486.

[151] Hrotsvitha, *Gesta Ottonis*, lines 168-9 (p. 207); Hoffmann, *Die heiligen Könige*, p. 36; Ó Riain-Raedel, below, pp. 213-16.

[152] Hare, 'Documentary evidence'.

at Newton itself.[153] The parish's early importance is indicated by the enormous wealth of the medieval living and by the fact that it was still served by hereditary clerks in the early twelfth century. The church itself is sited in a large and crowded curvilinear churchyard, which in the late Saxon period was adorned with an enormous and iconographically unique stone cross.[154] All this is strong evidence that St Oswald's, Winwick, was an Anglo-Saxon minster.

It is possible, of course, that Winwick was a very ancient cult centre, dating from the days when south Lancashire was part of the kingdom of Northumbria. A recent discovery which might be held to favour that view is the large early Christian cemetery near the site of the church.[155] It is also significant that, like several other sites associated with the king, Winwick had a holy well.[156] But these features, though suggestive of antiquity, do not necessarily take us back to the pre-Viking period. Against such an early origin must be set the fact that the minster at Winwick seems bound up with the hundred of Newton, and that that hundred was (as its name implies) a relatively late, probably tenth-century, creation.[157]

Winwick, then, is important because it may well provide evidence for an obscure phase in Oswald's cult. There is a temptation in assessing dedications and sacred sites such as wells either to push back their origins to the very early pre-Viking period or to place them much later during the undoubted recrudescence of the cult under the Normans. Winwick is a site which will not fit easily into either of those contexts, and, along with Chester, seems rather to belong to the phase associated with the translation to Gloucester.

Another dedication which may also belong to this period is Malpas, a large ancient parish in south-west Cheshire.[158] Though the present church is probably of Norman origin, closely associated with the castle, it clearly succeeded a pre-Conquest foundation located at the earlier Saxon settlement of *Depenbech*. There is no known reason for the new Norman lord, Robert FitzHugh, to have been devoted to Oswald, and it is therefore more than possible that the dedication may be related to Æthelflæd's promotion of the cult at Chester.[159] Perhaps too Oswestry in neighbouring Shropshire was of a similar date. Although there is no evidence for a church dedicated to St

---

153 D. Freke and A. T. Thacker, 'Excavations at Winwick, Cheshire, in 1980: Part 2. The inhumation cemetery at Southworth Hall Farm, Winwick', *Journal of Chester Archaeological Society* 70 (1990, for 1987-8), pp. 31-8, at pp. 34-6.

154 Freke and Thacker, 'Excavations at Winwick', p. 34; Bailey, *VAS*, pp. 159-61.

155 Freke and Thacker, 'Excavations at Winwick', pp. 31-6.

156 Hope, *Legendary Lore*, pp. 84-5; above, n. 42.

157 Freke and Thacker, 'Excavations at Winwick', p. 35.

158 A. T. Thacker, 'Anglo-Saxon Cheshire', in VCH *Cheshire* I, pp. 266-7.

159 J. McN. Dodgson, *Place-Names of Cheshire* (English Place-Name Society, 5 vols, Cambridge 1970-81), IV, pp. 38-40.

Oswald on the site earlier than the late eleventh century, the extensive parish was almost certainly inherited from an Anglo-Saxon minster serving the great estate of Maesbury.[160] Oswestry itself is first mentioned as the location of a newly constructed Norman castle. While it is possible that the church was moved there at that time, the luxuriance of the local legends relating to Oswald suggest that it may well have been a focus of the cult for considerably longer.[161] That development may well have been the product of a tenth-century reorganisation of the Shropshire minsters.[162]

By the mid tenth century the renewed interest in Oswald had resulted in fresh and important transmissions of the cult to the continent. Not only was it reinforced in Germany by Edith's marriage to Otto, with the result that it was diffused much more widely in calendars from the Rhineland,[163] but it was also apparently fostered in Switzerland by Gregory, the English abbot of Einsiedeln (960/4-996).[164] Gregory, a reformer under whom the monastic scriptorium flourished, was almost certainly responsible for the presence in the abbey's library of a tenth-century version of Oswald's acts, excerpted from the *Historia Ecclesiastica*,[165] and for the inclusion of the saint in the abbey's calendars.[166] From Einsiedeln knowledge of the cult seems to have spread to other major centres; Oswald was, for example, included in

---

[160] Gelling, 'Early hist. of W. Mercia', as n. 19 above, pp. 188-9; *Ctl. Shrewsbury* I, pp. 6, 33; R. W. Eyton, *Antiquities of Shropshire* (12 vols, London 1854-60), X, pp. 319, 335.

[161] Stancliffe, above, p. 88; Rollason and Tudor, below, pp. 170, 190-1.

[162] For the probability that the hundreds were the product of 10th-century reorganisation see D. Cox, 'County government in the early middle ages', in VCH *Shropshire* II, p. 6. It is, of course, possible that the sites at Oswestry were originally associated with a Celtic saint and only later ascribed to Oswald. An example of such transference is to be found at Cerne Abbas (Dorset), where there is a well which was associated by Goscelin and William of Malmesbury with St Augustine, but in an alternative tradition was linked with St Paston. I owe this point to Dr Yorke.

[163] Above, pp. 116-17; below, Ó Riain-Raedel, pp. 210-16.

[164] *Dictionnaire d'histoire et de géographie ecclésiastiques*, ed. A. Baudrillart *et al.* (in progress, 24 vols, Paris 1912-), XV, cols 95-7; K. Heller, *Kloster Einsiedeln in Ottonischen Schwaben* (Forschungen zur oberrheinischen Landesgeschichte, 13; Freiburg im Breisgau 1964), pp. 35-6, 49-50, 55-6, 105.

[165] A. Bruckner, *Scriptoria Medii Aevi Helvetica* (14 vols, Geneva 1935-78), V, pp. 15-41, 181-2; Heller, *Kloster Einsiedeln*, pp. 52-61; G. Meier, *Catalogus Codicum Manu Scriptorum qui Bibliotheca Monasterii Einsidlensis Servantur*, I (Einsiedeln 1899), p. 226 (MS 256, pp. 348-64); M. L. W. Laistner and H. H. King, *A Handlist of Bede Manuscripts* (Ithaca 1943), p. 105.

[166] Munding, *Die Kalendarien von St Gallen*, U. p. 86; Meier, *Catalogus*, pp. 288, 292, 320 (MSS 319, 321, 356); Bruckner, *Scriptoria* V, pp. 183-4; Heller, *Kloster Einsiedeln*, pp. 56-7.

calendars from St Gall by the late tenth or early eleventh century.[167]

During the tenth-century Benedictine reform Oswald's standing in England was assured. He appears in all but one of the surviving pre-Conquest calendars[168] and was frequently invoked in the litanies.[169] That this implied a widespread liturgical cult is apparent from the existence in eleventh-century England of two different sets of mass propers for the feast,[170] one in an apparently unique version from Wells,[171] the other quite widely diffused and represented in a missal from New Minster[172] and in service books belonging to Robert of Jumièges[173] and Wulfstan of Worcester.[174] The main reason for that popularity was undoubtedly the reformers' interest in royal martyr cults, a preoccupation connected with the murder of the young King Edward in 978.[175] Ramsey, Worcester and other centres particularly associated with Archbishop Oswald took a leading role in the revival of such cults, including those of Edmund of East Anglia, the young Kentish princes Æthelred and Æthelberht, and the Mercian princes Wystan and Kenelm.[176] By the late

[167] Munding, *Die Kalendarien von St Gallen, T.* pp. 65, 103; *U.* p. 13.

[168] *English Kalendars Before 1100*, ed. F. Wormald (HBS 72; London 1934), pp. 9, 23, 37, 65, 79, 93, 107, 121, 135, 149, 163, 177, 191, 205, 219, 233, 247, 261; I. Atkins, 'An investigation of two Anglo-Saxon calendars', *Archaeologia* 78 (1928), pp. 219-54, at p. 248; Paris, Bibliothèque Nationale, MS lat. 7239, fol. 7ʳ. The exception, curiously, is the Glastonbury calendar in the Leofric missal. Cf. n. 150 above.

[169] *Anglo-Saxon Litanies of the Saints*, ed. M. Lapidge (HBS 106; London 1991), pp. 94, 116, 123, 126, 133, 143, 158, 163, 183, 188, 196, 205, 236, 251, 280, 284.

[170] I am very grateful to Dr Alicia Correâ for help with the liturgical material. It should be noted that Oswald does not occur in another important class of liturgical material, the benedictionals: *Corpus Benedictionum Pontificalium*, ed. E. Moeller (4 vols, Corpus Christianorum Series Latina 162, 162 A-C; Turnhout 1971-9).

[171] BL, Cotton MS Vitellius A XVIII, fol. 123ʳ; *The Leofric Missal*, ed. F. E. Warren (Oxford 1883), pp. 306-7 (no preface). On this and the other missals see H. Gneuss, 'Liturgical books in Anglo-Saxon England', in *Learning and Literature*, pp. 91-141, esp. A1, A5, A10, G1.

[172] *The Missal of New Minster*, ed. D. H. Turner (HBS 93; London 1962), pp. viii-ix, 135. The propers are the same as those in the missal of Robert of Jumièges, except for the preface.

[173] *Missal of Robert of Jumièges*, ed. H. A. Wilson (HBS 11; London 1896), pp. xxviii, 195.

[174] *Portiforium of St Wulfstan*, ed. A. Hughes (2 vols, HBS 89-90; London 1958-60), no. 1892 (collect only).

[175] D. W. Rollason, 'The cult of murdered royal saints in Anglo-Saxon England', *ASE* 11 (1983), pp. 1-22.

[176] A. T. Thacker, 'Saint making and relic collecting by Oswald and his communities', in *Saint Oswald of Worcester: His Life and Influence*, ed. N. Brooks (forthcoming).

tenth century Oswald was included among their number; he is usually associated with them in the litanies and is expressly styled 'king and martyr' in late tenth- and early eleventh-century calendars in use at or emanating from Canterbury, Winchester, and Worcester.[177] An important factor underlying Oswald's inclusion in the group was the increasing formalisation of saintly categories in the litanies, where those invoked were placed in a rigid sequence of apostles, martyrs, confessors, and virgins.[178] The fact that Oswald could scarcely have been accommodated other than among the martyrs must have influenced contemporary perceptions of his status.

The liturgical material is supplemented by Ælfric's vernacular Life, probably written in the 990s.[179] Ælfric's work was based upon extracts taken from the *Historia Ecclesiastica* together with an episode from Bede's prose *Life of Cuthbert*, condensed and rearranged in the final, Old English, text.[180] Like his other saints' Lives, and unlike the catholic homilies, it was intended primarily as a demonstration of reformed monastic piety and had only a limited circulation. It cannot therefore be adduced as proof of the popularity of Oswald's cult in the late tenth century.[181] What it does demonstrate is the saint's high standing in reformed circles and the fact that his martyrial status required neither discussion nor proof. Although Ælfric, who followed Bede very closely, did not explicitly refer to Oswald as a martyr, he probably regarded the matter as self-evident. In the compilation which Professor Lapidge considers a later copy of Ælfric's 'hagiographical commonplace book', the Bedan extracts relating to the saint are introduced as the 'Passion of St Oswald, king of the English' (*Passio sancti Oswaldi Anglorum regis*).[182] Similarly, in the principal surviving manuscript of Ælfric's *Lives*, which dates from the early eleventh century, the saint is designated 'king and martyr' in the heading to the text.[183]

---

[177] E.g. *Eng. Kal. Before 1100*, pp. 65, 121, 135, 233.

[178] *Anglo-Saxon Litanies*, pp. 1-61, esp. pp. 25-33; E. Bishop, *Liturgica Historica* (Oxford 1918), pp. 137-64.

[179] *Aelfric's Lives*, no. 26 (pp. 125-43).

[180] *Wulfstan's Life of St Æthelwold*, ed. M. Lapidge and M. Winterbottom (Oxford 1991), pp. cxlviii-cxlix. The Cuthbert story, alluded to at the end of Ælfric's *Life* (p. 142), forms ch. 4 of *VCP*.

[181] I am grateful to Dr Joyce Hill for help with Ælfric's *Lives of the Saints*.

[182] BL, Cotton Julius E VII, fol. 153[r]; N. R. Ker, *Catalogue of Manuscripts Containing Anglo-Saxon* (Oxford 1957), pp. 206-10, esp. p. 209. Cf. the heading 'Passion of Oswald, king and martyr' in a twelfth-century version of the text: Cambridge, University Library, Ii. 1. 33, fol. 161[r]; Ker, op. cit. pp. 23-7, esp. p. 25.

[183] *Wulfstan's Life*, pp. cxlviii-cxlix; Paris, Bibliothèque Nationale, MS lat. 5362, fols 68[v]-70[v], esp. fol. 68[v]. I am grateful to Professor Lapidge for the loan of a microfilm of this manuscript.

Oswald's prestige remained high in late Anglo-Saxon England, high enough indeed for his cult to have been further diffused abroad. He was among those saints whose cult was established in Scandinavia as a result of English missionary activity there in the tenth and eleventh centuries; he is, for example, commemorated in the Nidaros ordinary, a customary compiled in the mid twelfth century and subsequently adopted throughout Norway.[184] By 1058, moreover, a continental *Vita* had also been written, by Drogo, a young monk from Saint-Winnoc at Bergues in Flanders.[185] Founded as a secular community by Count Baldwin II in 900 and reformed from St Bertin in the 1020s, the community possessed relics (*reliquiae*) of the saint, and was clearly an active centre of the cult, for in addition to the Life Drogo also went on to produce two sermons.[186] Drogo's knowledge of Oswald, however, appears to have been limited. His *Life* is simply a compilation of extracts culled from Bede's *Historia Ecclesiastica*, occasionally interspersed with conventional linking passages of the author's own devising.[187] It has no independent historical value and is interesting only for its unequivocal designation of Oswald as a martyr.[188] How the cult was transmitted to Bergues remains a mystery.[189] It has been suggested that relics of St Oswald were brought thither by Judith, wife successively of the West Saxon kings Æthelwulf (died 858) and Æthelbald (died 860) before she became first countess of Flanders. More probably, however, they are to be associated with Otgiva, wife of Count Baldwin IV (died 1036) and a descendant of the count-abbots of Echternach. She is known to have been a lover of relics and was in a position to obtain them from Echternach had she so wished.[190] While the process may have been encouraged in a general way by Oswald's enhanced prestige among the English reformers, there is little to suggest that

184 *Ordo Nidrosensis Ecclesiae*, ed. L. Gjerløw (Oslo 1968), pp. 124-5, 377. I am grateful to Dr Alicia Correâ for help with this material. The English missions to Scandinavia and the liturgical texts which accompanied them were the subject of an important re-evaluation by Dr Correâ and Dr Leslie Abrams at the ISAS 1993 conference.

185 *Acta Sancti Oswaldi*, ed. J. B. Solerio et al., *AASS, Augusti* II (Antwerp 1735), pp. 94-103; N. Huyghebaert, 'Un moine hagiographe: Droge de Bergues', *Sacris Erudiri* 20 (1971), pp. 191-256.

186 *Acta Oswaldi*, p. 94. On Bergues see N. Huyghebaert, 'Les deux translations du roi Saint Oswald à Bergues-Saint-Winoc', *Revue Bénédictine* 86 (1976), pp. 83-93, esp. 89. The sermons are unpublished: *BHL*, nos. 6363-4; *AASS, Aug.* II, pp. 93, 103. A Latin office for the feast day, formerly attributed to Drogo, is now considered to date from the mid twelfth century: Clemoes, pp. 6-7; Folz, p. 71.

187 The more interesting are translated by Clemoes, p. 6. Cf. Folz, pp. 52-3.

188 E.g. *Acta Oswaldi*, para. 2 (p. 94), and esp. para. 25 (p. 99): *illius martyrium, quod pro fide sua suaeque gentis salute suscepit.*

189 Cf. Ó Riain-Raedel, below, pp. 217-20.

190 Huyghebaert, 'Les deux translations', pp. 91-2.

they made a significant contribution, despite their close contacts with Flanders. Drogo exhibits no knowledge of post-Bedan developments of the cult, and in particular of the translation to Gloucester; that and the fact that the relics were subject to no *adventio* or *translatio*, and were almost certainly not corporeal, points to Echternach rather than England as their source.

The extraordinary success of Oswald's cult is largely the product of its complex early history. A dynastically promoted devotion to a royal warrior hero with a strong appeal to pagan traditionalists received (eventually) the full endorsement of the church. The practical support of the Wilfridians, with their wide network of contacts, and the eloquence and skill of Bede in the *Historia Ecclesiastica* were undoubtedly crucial. They were not, however, of themselves sufficient; the unique dispersal of the corporeal remains was equally indispensable. Even so, the cult achieved its remarkable expansion in the early middle ages only by stages and we may detect several turning points. Clearly Oswald's emergence as the premier royal saint of Mercia as well as Northumbria was vital, for by that means the cult attracted the attention of Athelstan and received thereby a fresh impetus on the continent. Oswald's adoption in the tenth-century reformed liturgy in England was also highly significant. By the mid eleventh century the ground work had been laid for the even more extravagant developments of the later medieval cult.

Acknowledgements
I am grateful to Dr Barbara Yorke for reading and commenting on an earlier draft of this paper and to Dr Stancliffe for much helpful editorial advice.

Archaeology and the Cult of St Oswald in Pre-Conquest Northumbria

ERIC CAMBRIDGE

I

Introduction

The evidence for those of the numerous dedications to St Oswald in the north of England which can be traced back to before the Reformation has been collected by Alison Binns and is presented elsewhere in this volume; the purpose of the present paper is to venture into all but uncharted waters by attempting to consider how many of those dedications (whether or not their medieval ancestry is demonstrable) may date to before the Norman Conquest. Where possible, it will attempt to place them within the four centuries or so which separate Oswald's death from the Norman invasion, and to consider why Oswald came to be chosen as the dedicatee. Given that there are few Oswald dedications indeed which can be demonstrated to be early by documentary evidence, it must be stressed at the outset that this paper cannot pretend to supply conclusive answers to questions of this kind; rather, it attempts to outline a general historical and archaeological framework within which they may be appropriately considered. Of course, future detailed studies of particular sites, which are so urgently needed, may often require the interpretations tentatively advanced here to be revised; but at least enough may have been said to establish that there is an archaeological dimension which deserves to be considered in such analyses. Only the fifty-nine dedications recorded in the north of the country, that is, those anciently in northern Mercia and Northumbria, will be examined; for it is surely here, in the territory of Oswald's native land and where all of the most ancient centres of his cult lie, that the earliest dedications are most likely to be encountered.

The only explicit documentation of a dedication to Oswald in pre-Viking Northumbria concerns the site of *Scythlescester*, where a church commemorating the site of the murder of king Ælfwald of Northumbria in 788 was dedicated to Saints Oswald and Cuthbert.[1] The importance of this chance reference lies in its implication that the practice of dedicating churches to

---

[1] *HR, s.a.* 788. On the pre-Conquest annalistic material incorporated into the *Historia Regum*, see P. Hunter Blair, 'Some observations on the *Historia Regum* attributed to Symeon of Durham' in *Celt and Saxon: Studies in the Early British Border*, ed. N. K. Chadwick (Cambridge 1963), pp. 63-118, at pp. 86-99, 117. On *Scythlescester*, see further Binns, below, p. 255.

indigenous saints was established by the late eighth century in Northumbria.[2]

The evidence of place-names in the form Oswaldkirk and Kirkoswald, which incorporate the element *Oswald* as a specific, provides another potential means of dating the church dedications which they presuppose, albeit an indirect and considerably less precise one. Four such names are recorded: Oswaldkirk in the North Riding of Yorkshire; Kirkoswald in Cumberland; and the two Kirkoswalds in Ayrshire. The form of the generic element indicates a derivation from Old Norse *kirkja*, a church. The two English examples must therefore have been coined between the arrival of Viking settlers in the regions in which they are situated and their first mention in documentary records. This gives *termini* of between *c*.900 and 1162 for the Cumberland Kirkoswald and *c*.876 and 1086 for Oswaldkirk;[3] a pre-Conquest date for the formulation of the latter at least is thus highly probable. What is more, the distinction between the period in which such names came into existence in their current form, and the time of the dedication to Oswald of the churches to which they bear witness, must be kept clearly in mind. Both these names leave open the possibility that the Oswald dedication, if not also the practice of distinguishing those places as 'Oswald's church', might have been older (perhaps considerably so) and, as will be explained below, there are other grounds for suspecting this to be so.[4] The date of formulation of the place-name and the date of the original dedication of the church are likely to have diverged even more markedly in the case of the two Scottish Kirkoswalds, both of them in Ayrshire. The class of *kirk*-compound names to which these belong continued to be coined in this area of south-west Scotland until late in the middle ages.[5] The possibility that the Oswald dedications implied by these names merely reflect the individual devotional preferences of, say, twelfth-century settlers, cannot therefore be ruled out on purely onomastic grounds (and indeed, the presence

[2] At first sight the joint dedication looks like an early example of that pairing of Cuthbert and Oswald which became popular in Durham iconography from the late 12th century (Bailey, below, p. 195); such an interpretation would, however, probably be anachronistic given the Lindisfarne community's apparent indifference (or even antipathy) to Oswald's cult at this period (see below, p. 158; and Thacker above, pp. 101-2). The intention here may rather have been to promote the cult of a new royal martyr by associating him with the two most important indigenous Northumbrian cults.

[3] G. Fellows[-]Jensen, *Scandinavian Settlement Names in Yorkshire* (Copenhagen 1972), pp. 134, 246; Kirkoswald is first recorded in 1167: G. Fellows-Jensen, *Scandinavian Settlement Names in the North-West* (Copenhagen 1985), p. 200.

[4] For Kirkoswald in Cumberland, see below, p. 147, and for Oswaldkirk, pp. 143-4.

[5] D. Brooke, 'Kirk-compound place-names of Galloway and Carrick', *Transactions of the Dumfriesshire and Galloway Natural History and Antiquarian Society*, 3rd series 58 (1983), pp. 56-71.

of a dedication to this saint as far north as Cathcart, just south of Glasgow, is perhaps best explained as belonging to such a chronological stratum). Nevertheless, from an historical perspective, the likeliest context in this part of Britain for the dedication of churches to such a quintessentially Northumbrian saint arguably lies much further back, during the period of Northumbrian occupation. In the southern parts of the area this had begun well before the establishment of a Northumbrian bishopric at Whithorn c.730, while the most plausible explanation for the presence of the two churches dedicated to Oswald further north in Carrick is that their dedications originated in a period beginning some time before the Northumbrian conquest of Kyle (the area immediately to the north) in 750, and ending with the eventual loss of both regions to the kingdom of Strathclyde, perhaps during the later ninth century.[6]

Meagre though the harvest of the documentary, onomastic, and historical sources may seem, even a sceptic will be forced to concede that some churches had been dedicated to Oswald well before the Norman Conquest, and at least one in the pre-Viking period. And given that the Northumbrians had a more obvious motive for promoting Oswald's commemoration in this way than their Viking successors, it seems not unlikely that there were other dedications to the saint of comparable antiquity. It is therefore at least possible that some of the dedications to Oswald recorded only at a much later period might have originated centuries earlier. The most immediate obstacle when it comes to trying to determine which are early, and which not, is that Oswald's cult remained popular throughout the middle ages, so that other Oswald dedications might equally well reflect later medieval rather than Anglo-Saxon piety. One possible way round this problem is to consider whether there are any distinctive archaeological characteristics associated with the sites of Oswald dedications and their immediate environs which might point to a possible period of origin for the dedication, and whether such characteristics might change over time, thus enabling the dedications to be placed in an approximate chronological sequence.

Inference from such inherently ambiguous evidence is obviously a procedure fraught with difficulties. For example, some ecclesiastical sites

6   For the north shores of the Solway, see D. Brooke, 'The Northumbrian settlements in Galloway and Carrick: an historical assessment', *Proceedings of the Society of Antiquaries of Scotland* 121 (1991), pp. 295-327, at pp. 300-1. Eadberht's conquest of Kyle is recorded in the annals added to Bede's *Ecclesiastical History* (*HE*, pp. 574-5). Strathclyde had probably advanced as far south as the northern parts of English Cumbria by the early 10th century (R. N. Bailey and R. J. Cramp, *Corpus of Anglo-Saxon Stone Sculpture in England*, vol. II, *Cumberland, Westmorland and Lancashire North-of-the-Sands* (Oxford 1988) (hereafter cited as *Corpus* II), p. 6); this suggests that the loss of Anglian control in parts of south-west Scotland would have been earlier.

with early archaeological features may nevertheless contain churches which only came to be dedicated to Oswald centuries later, and there can be no knowing how often this might have occurred. Other churches dedicated to Oswald may have shed their original archaeological context by moving their site, while others again may subsequently have been rededicated to another saint, so rendering their previous Oswald associations undetectable. Later loss and destruction of archaeological evidence (and perhaps also the failure to recognise the potential significance of what does survive) presumably also means that fewer sites retain identifiable evidence of an early context today than was once the case. The presence of archaeological indications at a site suggestive of a pre-Conquest context thus need not imply that the dedication to Oswald of a church there is early, nor their absence that it might not be.

Bearing all these caveats in mind, four criteria have been selected to provide as comprehensive a basis for comparison as possible: the presence or absence of Anglian (that is, pre-Viking) sculpture; the presence or absence of Viking-age sculpture; the degree of proximity to sites which have produced Anglian sculpture; and the degree of proximity to roads of Roman origin. The results have been summarised in the Appendix (pp. 162-3). Before considering the possible implications, two of these criteria, and the hazards of interpreting them, need further explanation.

First, the evidence of stone sculpture has been included, as this is the most widely distributed type of artefact surviving from the early middle ages. Its possible implications for the function of the sites at which it occurs is controversial; but it is almost always found in ecclesiastical contexts, which at least raises the possibility that churches at sites where it is present might have been in existence comparatively early. Carvings of the pre-Viking period are more common in the north of England and the adjacent parts of southern Scotland and the north midlands than in any of the regions further south; yet it remains a comparatively unusual phenomenon even in these areas. Though it is not always possible to distinguish carvings of this period from those of the Viking age (dubious examples being indicated with question marks and linked by a horizontal line in the Appendix), this can be done with confidence in the majority of cases. The point is of importance because the distribution of sculpture datable to the Viking age differs significantly from that of the earlier material; while most of the sites which have produced pre-Viking carvings have also produced Viking-age stones (though there are significant exceptions), there are perhaps as many sites again which have *only* produced Viking-age carvings.

Second, though it is generally recognised that there are significant relationships between early ecclesiastical sites and Roman roads,[7] the evidence for the latter raises problems of its own. By no means all roads

---

[7]   Morris, *Churches*, p. 113, fig. 25.

which have been claimed as Roman are accepted as such by more cautious scholarship; and even if they are, some parts of their courses remain more or less inferential. Sometimes the equivalent medieval routes deviated partly or wholly from their Roman predecessors, as, for example, Morris's detailed survey of Ermine Street north of Lincoln clearly shows.[8] While many Roman roads clearly continued in use into the early middle ages, not all did, so some instances of juxtaposition with church sites may be fortuitous; on the other hand, those which continued in use throughout the medieval period and into modern times might give rise to juxtapositions which, even if not accidental, derive only from the circumstances of a much later period. What is more, even if proximity is defined fairly strictly, as here (within three miles), the likelihood of fortuitousness increases appreciably in circumstances such as proximity to major route centres approached by several roads (such as York or Chester), or where roads run through pronounced valleys; in either case, churches erected at any date could hardly have avoided being near the line of a Roman road. Indeed, it is abundantly clear from existing case studies that many instances of proximity need carry no implication of an early medieval origin.[9] Clearly, then, this criterion is a crude and potentially misleading instrument, and much detailed fieldwork both on the routes themselves and on their relationship to settlement morphology would be required before the possible significance of juxtapositions between churches and roads of Roman origin can even begin to be properly evaluated; nevertheless, such evidence has been included as it may be potentially significant in combination with other factors. Instances which appear *prima facie* to be dubious are indicated by brackets in the Appendix.

Do any significant correlations at all emerge from the data presented in the Appendix?[10] First, it is doubtful whether any *general* importance should be attached to the number of sites with Oswald dedications at which pre-Conquest sculpture has been found.[11] A sceptic might justifiably argue that, in a random sample of this size taken in the north of England, a few examples of church sites with Anglian material, and rather more with only Viking-age sculpture, would be precisely what one would expect. And even if the number of sites within three miles of a road of Roman origin, that is, somewhere between one-third and perhaps as many as a half of the total, seems unexpectedly high given that there is no obvious *prima facie* reason to

8   Op. cit., fig. 64.

9   Op. cit., figs. 26, 64.

10   In the following notes, the minimum figure is given first, followed by the maximum possible (in brackets). All instances where there is reason to doubt either the quality or relevance of the evidence are included in the bracketed figures.

11   Anglian sculpture occurs at 4 (8) sites, Viking-age sculpture at 10 (13) sites with Oswald dedications in the north.

expect any significant correlation between the two, the problems of interpretation outlined above make it hazardous to assess whether or in what way this phenomenon is significant.[12]

By far the most striking correlation is the number of Oswald dedications – somewhere between one quarter and one third – which are *adjacent* to a site which has produced Anglian sculpture.[13] Again, the juxtapositions may well be fortuitous in a number of cases: for example, by casual migration of early carvings to adjacent sites, or by the dedication of later churches near early sites (or the rededication of ancient ones) to Oswald. But it has already been noted that sites at which this material occurs are comparatively uncommon, and as there is again no obvious *prima facie* reason why Oswald dedications should be juxtaposed with them in this way, the degree of correlation does appear to be significantly high. What is more, at least half of the Oswald sites at which Viking-age sculpture has been found are also close to sites which have produced Anglian material; and most of them are also near to roads of Roman origin.

It seems, then, that some potentially significant combinations of characteristics do begin to emerge when the archaeological contexts of Oswald dedications are examined. The likelihood that this is not wholly fortuitous is appreciably strengthened when the evidence of regional variation is taken into account. Thus the degree of correlation between Oswald dedications and sites with any of the above material characteristics is markedly low in Lincolnshire, particularly when the sole example of a site with Viking-age sculpture (Crowle) should probably be placed in the early Anglo-Saxon *regio* of *Hæthfeld* (Hatfield), a distinct territory lying on the borders of Northumbria, Mercia, and Lindsey, rather than in the kingdom of Lindsey proper.[14] Though Anglian-period sculpture is markedly less frequent here than further north, this is not true of Viking-age material nor of Roman roads, so the lack of correlation may be significant, perhaps lending some support to the suggestion that most of the Lincolnshire dedications are not early but rather reflect the refoundation of Bardney Abbey in the late eleventh century.[15] Conversely, this variation gives one some confidence in supposing that the notably high degree of correlation in some regions (Yorkshire, Cumberland and Westmorland, and perhaps also Cheshire) may indicate that appreciable numbers of early Oswald dedications with distinctive archaeological profiles may survive there.

[12] Roman roads run within three miles of 17 (30) sites with Oswald dedications in the north.

[13] Sites with Anglian sculpture lie within five miles of 17 (19) sites with Oswald dedications in the north.

[14] M. S. Parker, 'The province of Hatfield', *Northern History* 28 (1992), pp. 42-69, at pp. 48-9, 60, map. 6 on p. 61.

[15] Butler, 'Dedications', p. 45.

If it is accepted that there may be significant trends in the material evidence associated with the sites of churches dedicated to Oswald, the next problem is to explain what these apparent patterns might mean. This question is probably best tackled only after reviewing in detail a number of particular sites where there is evidence (not invariably confined to the archaeological evidence) to indicate the date and context in which the Oswald dedication, if early, might have arisen.

II
Cult Centres

It will be as well to begin with Bamburgh (Fig. 8, no. 7, on p. 268), for its association with Oswald is demonstrably early; according to Bede, this was the place at which major relics of St Oswald, his arms and hands, were enshrined within a generation of his death, having been retrieved by Oswald's brother and successor, Oswiu, and placed in a church dedicated to St Peter.[16] This church must therefore have been in existence before Oswiu's death in 670. Yet there is another (considerably later) tradition that there were two churches in Bamburgh, dedicated respectively to St Oswald and St Aidan, but with no mention by this time of a church of St Peter. The evidence is principally contained in a group of twelfth-century and later charters granted in favour of the priory of Nostell in Yorkshire, which in consequence became the proprietor of the parish church of Bamburgh and established a small dependent monastery or cell there. How are these apparent discrepancies between the number of churches in early medieval Bamburgh, and the saints to whom they were dedicated, to be explained?

One major difficulty in understanding the charter evidence must be faced at the outset, for it seems that there are two distinct versions, the first recording the grant of only one church without specifying its dedication,[17] while the second (attested only in charters of confirmation) records the grant of the two churches of St Oswald and St Aidan as noted above.[18] One

16 *HE* III, 6, 12.
17 The formula 'ecclesiam de Baenburch' (alternatively 'ecclesiam suam de Bamburgh') first occurs in a grant of Henry I dated c.1119 (BL MS Vespasian E. XIX, fol. 8 (E. Bateson, *A History of Northumberland*, I, *The Parish of Bamburgh with the Chapelry of Belford* (Newcastle upon Tyne and London 1893), p. 74, note 1; *Regesta Regum Anglo-Normannorum, 1066-1154*, Vol. II, *1100-35* (ed. C. Johnson and H. A. Cronne; Oxford 1956), no. 1217; *EYC*, II, no. 1424)). It is followed by: a mandate of Henry II to Bishop Hugh of Le Puiset of Durham (Vespasian E. XIX, fol. 6 (*EYC*, II, no. 1456)); and a notification by the former to the latter concerning the royal clerk Hugh Murdac (Vespasian E. XIX, fol. 7 (*EYC*, II, no. 1457)), which is in turn confirmed by Le Puiset (Vespasian E. XIX, fol. 7); three further royal documents of the reign of King John (Vespasian E. XIX, fol. 8) also refer to the church in these terms.
18 The formula 'ecclesias sancti Osualdi et [sancti] Aidani de Bamburg' sicut Algarus

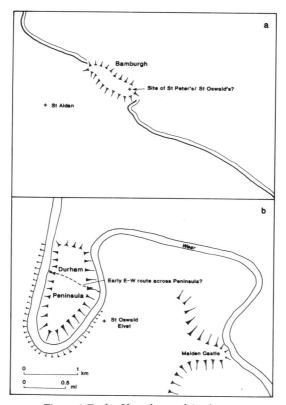

Figure 4: Early Churches and Settlements

commentator has sought to account for the second version as merely an attempt to amplify the terms of the original grant,[19] but while this may be on the right lines, the discrepancies seem too substantial as they stand to be wholly explained in this way. Alternatively, the traditions might be reconciled by supposing that there were originally two separate grants of two different churches, though evidence for only one now survives (in the first version), and that their dedications came to be specified in subsequent confirmations in order to distinguish the two. But if that were the case, it would be difficult to explain why that first version, mentioning only one

presbiter unquam eas melius tenuit' first occurs in a general confirmation of Henry I dated to between 1121 and 1127 (Vespasian E. XIX, fol. 150 (*EYC*, II, no. 1428)). It is followed by: a general confirmation of Henry II (adding 'cum capellis' (*EYC*, III, p. 135)); a Le Puiset confirmation of c.1160 (also mentioning Hugh Murdac) (Vespasian E. XIX, fol. 118); and by later royal confirmations of Richard I, John, and Henry III (respectively Vespasian E. XIX, fols. 4, 5, and 8).

19 Bateson, *Bamburgh*, p. 74.

church without giving its dedication, persisted alongside the other for so long. One may even wonder whether there was in fact only one church involved all the way through (though there may have been two grants of it in different terms), and the references to two churches only arose later, as a result of confusion.[20]

The evidence of the Nostell charters alone thus provides an insecure basis from which to infer the presence of two churches dedicated to St Oswald and St Aidan in twelfth-century Bamburgh. That there was a church dedicated to St Aidan there at least seems reasonably probable on other grounds, however. The present-day parish church is situated about one-third of a mile west of the castle rock, at the opposite end of the modern village (Fig. 4a). Though largely of thirteenth-century and later date, its earliest extant fabric is Romanesque, and enough of this survives to indicate that already in the twelfth century the church was an elaborate cruciform structure.[21] As the church is dedicated to St Aidan, it seems reasonable *prima facie* to identify it with the one mentioned in the twelfth-century charters, and this presumption must be considerably strengthened by the consideration that this dedication – perhaps surprisingly – was apparently unique in England until modern times.[22] What is more, its rarity strongly suggests that the church was dedicated to that saint for a particular reason. The probable explanation is provided by Bede's account of Aidan's death as he was leaning against the buttress of a church in a royal estate centre (*uilla regia*), in which he also had a residence, not far from the fortress (*urbs*) of Bamburgh.[23] The buttress miraculously survived two fires and was preserved as a relic in the rebuilt church.[24] It is difficult not to believe that the existence of this early cult site accounts for the unusual later medieval dedication. While it is always possible that the latter reflects no more than the piety of later generations familiar with Bede's account, the apparent general unpopularity of Aidan's

20 Confusion could have arisen if that church had (or had acquired) a double dedication, which could then easily have been misinterpreted as referring to two different buildings. As none of the documents is known to survive in the original, it is unclear whether confusion might have arisen at the hands of a twelfth-century forger or of the later medieval copyist of the Nostell cartulary, which is our only surviving source for their texts. A dedication to Oswald might even have been added by the monks of Nostell, given their obvious interest in the saint (see Rollason below, pp. 173-4); for the likelihood that the dedication to Aidan is early, see below.

21 Bateson, *Bamburgh*, p. 104.

22 Arnold-Forster, II, p. 235. The rarity of the dedication may be an indication of how successfully the Cuthbert Community eclipsed the cult of Aidan by promoting that of Cuthbert.

23 'Erat in uilla regia non longe ab urbe... In hac enim habens ecclesiam et cubiculum...' (*HE* III, 17).

24 *HE* III, 17.

cult in the later middle ages, and the incentive to favour a dedication to Oswald rather than Aidan once the church had passed to the priory of Nostell, combine to make this explanation unlikely.[25]

Despite the considerable difficulties of interpreting the charter evidence, it may be that the former existence of a church of St Oswald at Bamburgh cannot be entirely rejected, since one containing relics of Oswald is mentioned in Reginald of Durham's Life of the saint and, as will be explained elsewhere, this text does seem to incorporate genuine traditions about Bamburgh in the late pre-Conquest period.[26] If so, then it seems likely that, as Bateson long ago surmised, the church which had become identified with St Oswald by that time was identical to (or at any rate a successor of) the seventh-century church of St Peter.[27] The assimilation of the dedicatee of a church to the saint whose relic it had long housed is a phenomenon which can be paralleled elsewhere, at Repton in Derbyshire, for example; if such an explanation holds good at Bamburgh, assimilation had evidently still not taken place at the end of the eighth century.[28] Assuming that St Peter's is indeed to be identified with the later St Oswald's, where was it located? According to Bede and to the annals in the *Historia Regum* St Peter's lay within the *urbs* of Bamburgh, that is, presumably, the defensible area on the rocky outcrop now occupied by the twelfth-century and later royal castle,[29] and Bateson may well also be right in supposing that the twelfth-century

---

[25] See above, note 20. Professor Bullough seems to have considered the above possibility, though later he doubts the antiquity of the dedication to Aidan. His grounds for considering this site to have been monastic in the 7th century are not clear, however: see D. Bullough, 'The missions to the English and Picts and their heritage', in *Die Iren und Europa*, ed. H. Löwe (2 vols.; Stuttgart 1982), I, pp. 80-98, at pp. 86-7, note 20.

[26] The evidence is discussed below by Bailey (pp. 198-9) and Tudor (p. 189).

[27] Bateson, *Bamburgh*, p. 74.

[28] For the phenomenon in general, see W. Levison, 'Medieval church dedications in England: some problems', *Transactions of the Architectural and Archaeological Societies of Durham and Northumberland* 10 (1946), pp. 55-79, at p. 78. The existence at Repton of structures presumably associated with the monastery documented from the late 7th century (for which see *Felix's Life of St Guthlac*, ed. and trans. B. Colgrave (Cambridge 1956), pp. 178-9), but in any case dating from well before the interment of the remains of the present dedicatee there in 849, has been demonstrated by archaeological and structural analysis: see H. M. Taylor, 'St Wystan's church, Repton, Derbyshire. A reconstruction essay', *Archaeological Journal* 144 (1987), pp. 205-45, at pp. 211, 243-4. The church of St Peter at Bamburgh is referred to by Alcuin, *BKS*, lines 304-7.

[29] *HE* III, 6, 12. (It is clear from the circumstantial details of Bede's account of Penda's attempt to raze the *urbs* by fire in *HE* III, 16 that he thought of it as confined to the rock.) *HR s.a.* 774; cf. J. Campbell, 'Bede's words for places', in *Names, Words and Graves*, ed. P. H. Sawyer (Leeds 1979), pp. 34-51, at pp. 35, 39.

castle chapel on the south-eastern extremity of the rock perpetuates its site.[30] In turn, this evidence suggests that the interpretation of the Nostell charters as indicating grants of two different churches cannot be dismissed out of hand either. Indeed, given the long struggle of the Nostell monks to gain effective control of the revenues of St Aidan's, is it possible that their earliest foothold in Bamburgh was in fact within the castle?[31]

What does seem reasonably clear from the foregoing discussion is that there are grounds for assuming continuity of site as regards the present-day parish church and Aidan's church and residence on the one hand, and (though its precise location on the rock remains in some doubt) the Romanesque castle chapel and the church of St Peter's/St Oswald's on the other. The nature of the topographical relationship between these two sites (Fig. 4a) has been obscured to some extent by a misunderstanding of what Bede has to say about Aidan's church and residence. In particular, the *uilla regia* at which Aidan died seems sometimes to have been interpreted as distinct from Bamburgh itself,[32] whereas the topographical evidence presented above suggests rather that the two formed part of the same estate, and therefore that Bede thought of the *uilla regia* as a polyfocal settlement comprising both the *urbs* and Aidan's church and residence (and conceivably other components not mentioned).[33] Bede's account makes it clear that one of the functions of Aidan's residence was to serve as a base from which to carry out preaching tours in the surrounding area. If the contention that the later parish church perpetuated its site is correct, these two facts together

---

[30] Bateson, *Bamburgh*, pp. 57, 74. A fragment of pre-Viking sculpture from the castle site, convincingly interpreted by Cramp as the arm of a chair, may have been associated with St Peter's, though its context is not certainly ecclesiastical (R. Cramp, *Corpus of Anglo-Saxon Stone Sculpture in England,* vol. I, *County Durham and Northumberland* (Oxford 1984) (hereafter cited as *Corpus* I), 162-3, fig. 18, ills. 812-17).

[31] Bateson, *Bamburgh*, pp. 75-83.

[32] Colgrave (*HE*, p. 263) seems to take the passage in this sense, as do Campbell (Campbell, 'Bede's words', 46), and L. Alcock, *Bede, Eddius, and the Forts of the North Britons* (Jarrow Lecture 1988; Jarrow 1989), p. 11.

[33] These might have included the 'uiculis in uicinia urbis' demolished by Penda to provide fuel for his attempt to set fire to the *urbs* (*HE* III, 16). Aidan's buildings might have counted as a *uiculus* for these purposes, since the church at which he died, together with its *uicus*, were burnt by Penda in the course of a later attack on Bamburgh during the episcopate of Aidan's successor (*HE* III, 17), and since there are contexts in Bede's writings in which it is certain that *uicus* and *uiculus* are being used interchangeably (Campbell, 'Bede's words', p. 43). Alternatively Bede may mean that this satellite settlement near the *urbs* was itself capable of being described as a *uilla regia*, though this seems unlikely as recorded occurrences of the term *uilla regia* generally refer to the principal settlement of an estate (Campbell, 'Bede's words', pp. 46-8).

suggest that the pastoral needs of the surrounding area have always been served from this church. In contrast, there are no grounds for supposing that they were ever exercised from the church of St Peter/St Oswald; from its location and its early function as the place in which a major dynastic relic was housed, this must presumably be envisaged as the palace chapel of the Bernician royal fortress, later perpetuated as a shrine church after the political importance of the site declined. It appears, then, that we may have here an early and comparatively well documented example of a church at an episcopal residence, near to yet distinct from the secular focus of a great royal estate, and remaining (as had been intended from the start) the centre of pastoral care for the area. Initially occupied periodically by the bishop of Lindisfarne in person (or perhaps by one of his priests in his absence), it may in time have come to have a permanently resident staff, and to have been provided with endowments of its own.[34]

Evidence for the date at which other early cult sites associated with Oswald came to possess churches dedicated to him is uncertain. It can be assumed that Bardney in Lincolnshire (Fig. 8, no. 68, on p. 268), like Bamburgh, must have had another dedication at the outset, because it was obviously already in existence when Oswald's relics were installed there. There is no evidence on the point, but it is conceivable that the twelfth-century and later dedication of the refounded abbey to saints Peter, Paul, and Oswald perpetuates a memory of the primary dedication combined with a commemoration of Oswald, whose relics had been housed in the church between the late seventh and early tenth centuries.[35] The evidence regarding Oswald's death-site at *Maserfelth* is even more tenuous given the controversy as to its location, though Stancliffe has made a plausible case for identifying it with Oswestry in Shropshire (Fig. 9, no. 53, on p. 270). The

[34] If Bede's statement in *HE* III, 17 that Aidan '...owned nothing except his own church and small adjacent fields' ('...nil propriae possessionis excepta ecclesia sua et adiacentibus agellis habens') is correctly interpreted as referring not to his church at Bamburgh but rather to his monastery on Lindisfarne (see Stancliffe above, p. 65), the implication is that, in the beginning at least, not even the church and accommodation at Bamburgh and at other royal vills were owned by the bishop, but rather were provided by the king for his use. The possible modes of development of such episcopal churches in royal centres are briefly considered by P. H. Sawyer, 'The royal tun in pre-Conquest England', in *Ideal and Reality*, pp. 273-99, at pp. 277-8.

[35] See Thacker (above, pp. 104-5) and Binns (below, p. 253). St Oswald's Gloucester had apparently originally been dedicated to St Peter at its foundation *c*.900 (see M. Hare, *The Two Anglo-Saxon Minsters at Gloucester* (Deerhurst Lecture 1992; Deerhurst 1993), p. 6). The dedication must have changed to St Oswald after the translation there of his relics in 909 and before the later 11th century, by which time Oswald seems to have been well established as the patron saint: see Binns, p. 250.

church there was known by the early twelfth century simply as 'the church of St Oswald' in a way which implies that its dedication to the saint was already well established, and therefore it can probably be assigned to at least the late pre-Conquest period.[36] Finally, the church at Heavenfield in Northumberland (Fig. 8, no. 8) might have been dedicated to Oswald from the period of its construction in the early eighth century since it was specially built to honour a site associated with the saint. The only direct documentation of the dedication is much later, however, so such an interpretation must remain hypothetical.[37] There is thus at least no evidence from the other early cult sites to contradict the sequence suggested by the evidence relating to Bamburgh (that is, that the dedication to Oswald only came about comparatively late in the pre-Conquest period), though a dedication to Oswald may be more likely to be early in cases where the church was purpose built to honour his cult than where one was already in existence before the Oswald association arose.

III

Monastic Sites

Though the church of Lythe,[38] in the North Riding of Yorkshire (Fig. 8, no. 26), boasts a large collection of Viking-age sculpture, the only earlier carving from the site is probably architectural in character. This has been identified and interpreted by James Lang as a gable-finial from a stone church; its nearest analogues, at Lastingham, Yorkshire, and Heysham, Lancashire, lie firmly in pre-Viking contexts, and the former is also documented as a monastic site.[39] What is more, given the tendency for early stone churches in

36   See Stancliffe, above, pp. 84-96. Her interpretation of the Welsh name for Oswestry, *Croesoswald*, implies that a cross commemorating the saint predated the church (ibid., pp. 88-91). See also Binns below, p. 258.

37   See Binns, below, p. 255.

38   The grant of this church to Nostell Priory in the twelfth century may suggest that its dedication to Oswald is ancient: see below, Rollason, p. 173, n. 44, and Binns, p. 263.

39   I am most grateful to James Lang for supplying information about this carving, and for drawing to my attention a second stone at Lythe which (to judge from the lack of taper and the fact that carving occurs only on one face) may also have been architectural in function (presumably an impost): see W. G. Collingwood, 'Anglian and Anglo-Danish sculpture in the East Riding, with addenda to the North Riding', *Yorkshire Archaeological Journal* 21 (1911), pp. 254-302, at p. 288, fig. k on p. 289. The form of the interlace suggests that this piece must be considerably later than the late 7th century, however. For the Lastingham finial, see J. T. Lang, *Corpus of Anglo-Saxon Stone Sculpture in England*, vol. III, *York and Eastern Yorkshire* (Oxford 1991) (hereafter cited as *Corpus III*), pp. 171-2, ills. 610-13; and for that at Heysham, R. D. Andrews, 'St Patrick's Chapel, Heysham, Lancashire', *Bulletin of the CBA Churches Committee* 8 (1978), p. 2.

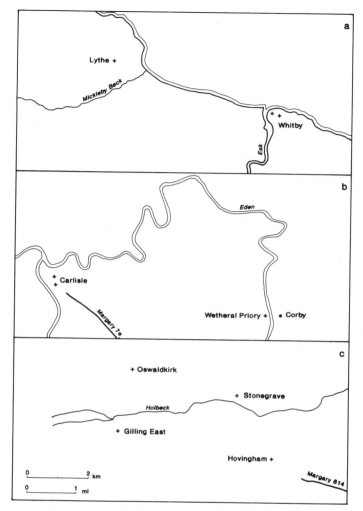

Figure 5: Oswald Dedications and Early Settlements, I

Northumbria to be associated with monastic sites,[40] the presence of such a carving at the site would strengthen the case for a monastic association. The proximity of Lythe to Whitby, which lies only four miles south-east, and has itself produced pre-Viking sculpture in quantity, suggests an association with the latter (Fig. 5a); if this speculation is right, Lythe may be seen as falling within a context of royal patronage, for Whitby is probably to be identified with *Streanaeshalch*, the monastery which contained the dynastic mausoleum

[40]   E. Cambridge, 'The early church in County Durham: a reassessment', *Journal of the British Archaeological Association* 137 (1984), pp. 65-85, at pp. 66-71.

of the Deiran ruling family.[41] It therefore raises the possibility that the community whose principal church housed the relics of Edwin and the tombs of several prominent royal descendants also had associated with it a church dedicated to the other great Northumbrian royal saint, Edwin's nephew, Oswald.[42]

The place-name Lythe is Norse in origin and so (like Whitby itself) the earlier name of the site may have been completely different.[43] If the association with Whitby suggested above is correct, however, the site should perhaps be considered as a candidate for the location of *Osingadun*, the place at which St Cuthbert had a premonition of the death of one of the Whitby brethren while feasting the day before dedicating a church there for Abbess Ælfflæd.[44] This site has not been convincingly identified hitherto. As I have pointed out elsewhere, the internal evidence of the story, in which the messenger sent by the abbess to Whitby to verify Cuthbert's vision made the return journey before the dedication ceremony on the day following the feast, implies that *Osingadun* was located fairly close to Whitby;[45] this makes Colgrave's suggestion of Kirkdale (thirty miles south-west over difficult terrain) unlikely.[46] I have also argued that the vocabulary used to describe the church suggests that it was intended to house monks (and thus perhaps was meant to form the principal male focus of the double monastery). This would be consistent with the implication of the presence of an early stone church suggested by the carved fragment. What is more, the potential significance of the Lythe carving increases in the light of the fact that it is the only site at all close to Whitby which has produced pre-Viking sculpture of any kind. The above interpretation is, it must be frankly admitted, highly speculative. Nevertheless, it involves one intriguing implication, and that is that the surviving carved fragment is actually from the church dedicated by Cuthbert.

[41] For the difficulties, see Butler, 'Dedications', n. 11, pp. 49-50. While Hunter Blair perhaps too easily dismissed the possibility of an identification with Strensall, his discussion of Bede's interpretation of the name (as *sinus fari*, 'bay of light') still points to a coastal location (P. Hunter Blair, 'Whitby as a centre of learning in the seventh century', in *Learning and Literature in Anglo-Saxon England. Studies Presented to Peter Clemoes*, ed. M. Lapidge and H. Gneuss (Cambridge 1985), pp. 3-32, at pp. 9-12). For the archaeology, see R. Cramp. 'A reconsideration of the monastic site of Whitby', in *AMI*, pp. 64-73.

[42] Oswald's Deiran blood may have been one factor underlying his choice as dedicatee (*HE* III, 6); but surely more pertinent is the fact that Oswiu, his brother and successor, who was clearly instrumental in establishing his cult at Bamburgh (see above, p. 134), was himself buried at Whitby (*HE* III, 24).

[43] Fellowes[-]Jensen, *Scandinavian Settlement Names in Yorkshire*, p. 100.

[44] *VCA* IV, 10 (pp. 126-9); *VCP*, ch. 34 (pp. 260-5).

[45] Cambridge, 'Early church', p. 74.

[46] B. Colgrave (ed. and trans.), *The Earliest Life of Gregory the Great* (Cambridge 1968), p. 41.

What remains, alas, unknowable, is the identity of the saint to whom he dedicated it; but the possibility that the Oswald dedication might go back as far as c.686 cannot be ruled out.[47]

In addition to Lythe, Filey in the East Riding of Yorkshire (Fig. 8, no. 31) and Wetheral in Cumberland (Fig. 8, no. 10) are further examples of the small group of sites at which dedications to Oswald and finds of indisputably pre-Viking sculpture occur together. Wetheral lies four and a half miles east of Carlisle, which is well documented as an important monastic centre (Fig. 5b). Though the precise location of the chapel dedicated to Oswald, which is mentioned in a thirteenth-century source, is not known, it seems to have been near the site of the later medieval priory. What is more, as Carlisle seems to have been a double monastery in origin,[48] it is tempting to compare the possible relationship between it and Wetheral with that proposed above for Whitby and Lythe.

The church of Filey lies three miles north-east of that at Hunmanby, which has produced sculpture of Viking-age date and perhaps also a pre-Viking piece;[49] though no early documentation survives for either site, indirect evidence of the pre-Conquest importance of Hunmanby is provided by the extensive parish which was formerly dependent on it. What is more, before that parish became fragmented later in the middle ages, the parish of Filey directly adjoined that of Hunmanby, and it may be that the two sites had once been associated.[50] By analogy with the sites already mentioned it is tempting to suppose that the Oswald dedication might be early, perhaps originally associated with the adjacent early ecclesiastical centre at Hunmanby. As with Lythe and Whitby, the comparative rarity in eastern Yorkshire both of pre-Viking sculpture and of churches dedicated to Oswald must be particularly emphasised; this suggests that the juxtaposition of these two categories of evidence here is unlikely to be coincidental.[51]

Unlike the sites considered so far, there is no pre-Viking sculpture at Oswaldkirk in the North Riding of Yorkshire (Fig. 8, no. 30), where the surviving stone carving dates only from the Viking period.[52] Nevertheless, there are some grounds for supposing that it may belong in a similar context,

---

[47]   A recent suggestion that the whole *Osingadun* episode was originally set near Carlisle (S. Hollis, *Anglo-Saxon Women and the Church: Sharing a Common Fate* (Woodbridge 1992), p. 202, n. 112, cf. p. 203, n. 116) ignores the other possible interpretations of the phrase 'in parrochia eius' in *VCA* IV, 10 (discussed in Cambridge, 'Early church', p. 84, n. 62).

[48]   *Corpus* II, p. 84, note 1.

[49]   For Hunmanby, see *Corpus* III, pp. 148-9, ills. 500, 502; for Filey, ibid., p. 130, ill. 450.

[50]   Morris, *Churches*, figs. 32, 27, 29.

[51]   *Corpus* III, fig. 3; Fig. 8.

[52]   *Corpus* III, 197-8, ills. 741-4.

for its parish lies immediately adjacent to that of Stonegrave, the church of which lies just over two miles south-east. Stonegrave is documented as a *monasterium* by a chance reference in a papal adjudication of an ownership dispute in the mid eighth century;[53] pre-Viking sculpture has also been found there. Admittedly, this may be of less significance than the case of Filey/Hunmanby considered above, for carving of pre-Viking date is comparatively common in this area of Yorkshire, and is also present at Gilling, the parish immediately adjacent to the south, though the major centre in the area is presumably Hovingham (Fig. 5c).[54] Nevertheless, the archaeological context may well suggest that a church dedicated to Oswald and associated with a documented adjacent Anglian ecclesiastical centre was in existence in the pre-Viking period, that is, before its existence was registered either archaeologically or onomastically.[55]

IV
Episcopal Residences

Tempting though it may be to attempt to interpret the remaining evidence for sites with potentially early dedications to Oswald as monastic dependencies along the lines argued above, this would certainly be unwise, for in at least one case there are grounds for supposing that another kind of ecclesiastical function may be involved. The evidence relates to the church of Guiseley in the West Riding of Yorkshire (Fig. 8, no. 35).

For an unknown period anterior to the late tenth century Guiseley had formed a component of a large estate centred on Otley, the archaeological evidence from which marks it out as the most important pre-Viking ecclesiastical centre in Wharfedale.[56] By the 970s the Otley estate had come under the control of the archbishops of York, for a memorandum of that time records that during the episcopate of Archbishop Oswald (972-92)

---

[53] Printed in A. W. Haddan and W. Stubbs, *Councils and Ecclesiastical Documents Relating to Great Britain and Ireland* (3 vols; Oxford 1869-78), III, 394-6.

[54] For Stonegrave, see *Corpus* III, pp. 216-17, ills. 824-5, 827-8; for Gilling, ibid., p. 133, ill. 440; for Hovingham, ibid., pp. 145-8, ills. 484, 490-9.

[55] Conceivably Collingham, the only other Yorkshire Oswald dedication which has produced pre-Viking (as well as Viking-age) sculpture (W. G. Collingwood, 'Anglian and Anglo-Danish sculpture in the West Riding, with addenda to the North and East Ridings and York, and a general review of the Early Christian monuments of Yorkshire', *Yorkshire Archaeological Journal* 23 (1915), pp. 129-299, at pp. 155-61), should also be thought of in a monastic context. But it differs from the others in showing no discernible sign of being associated with any other adjacent sites.

[56] Collingwood, 'West Riding', pp. 224-31. Some possible implications of the sculpture for the function of the site are discussed in I. N. Wood, 'Anglo-Saxon Otley: an archiepiscopal estate and its crosses in a Northumbrian context', *Northern History* 23 (1987), pp. 20-37, at pp. 30-6.

several of its components, including Guiseley, were alienated from the see. Guiseley itself was recovered by the archbishops between c.1020 and 1086.[57] The surviving sculpture from the site may be dated stylistically to the late ninth or earlier tenth century,[58] though whether or not it was produced under archiepiscopal patronage remains uncertain. At any rate, the available evidence does not enable one to determine whether there was an ecclesiastical site of any kind at Guiseley as early as the pre-Viking period, nor whether archiepiscopal ownership of the settlement stretched back that far.

Nevertheless, the possibility that the ecclesiastical site at Guiseley might have originated in a pre-Viking context should not be ruled out. Addingham, some ten miles further north-west up Wharfedale, and on the same Roman road which passes just over a mile north of Guiseley, was probably an archiepiscopal residence in the late ninth century; at any rate, this appears to be the likeliest explanation of why it was chosen as a refuge by Archbishop Wulfhere following his flight from York after the Viking assault in 867.[59] Addingham itself is not dedicated to Oswald, but twelve miles down the valley from Guiseley, approximately equidistant between it and York, lies Collingham, another Oswald dedication which may be of early date, and a site which has produced Viking-age and also pre-Viking sculpture.[60] Richard Bailey has drawn attention to the possible role of the Roman roads as a determinant of the stylistic relationships of Viking-age monuments in the Wharfe valley and adjacent areas;[61] the above evidence may provide a possible pre-Viking context for the importance of such routes, and the ecclesiastical settlements connected by them. Even if the possibility that Guiseley might have originated in this way is accepted, however, this is very far from proving that its dedication to Oswald is of comparable antiquity. But it may be worth advancing the speculation that the Oswald dedications at Guiseley and Collingham should be seen as components in a sequence of archiepiscopal possessions stretching westwards along one of the main routes from York across the Pennines, and one which must have been of fundamental importance to the episcopal administration of southern Cumbria and northern Lancashire which, it may be assumed, were already in the pre-Viking period (as certainly later) within the see of York.[62]

---

[57] For a summary of the documentary evidence relating to Guiseley, see Wood, 'Otley', pp. 20-3.

[58] Collingwood, 'West Riding', pp. 179-81.

[59] Wood, 'Otley', p. 23.

[60] See above, n. 55.

[61] Bailey, VAS, pp. 189-90, fig. 52.

[62] I have drawn attention elsewhere to a comparable north-south sequence of sites associated with the bishops of Lindisfarne (E. Cambridge, 'Why did the community of St Cuthbert settle at Chester-le-Street?', in St Cuthbert, pp. 367-86, at pp. 380-5); it is possible that such a context may also help to explain some of

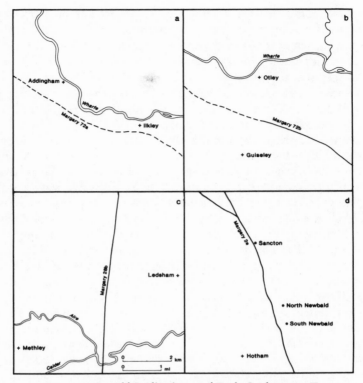

Figure 6: Oswald Dedications and Early Settlements, II

One further aspect of the siting of Guiseley calls for comment. This is its situation adjacent to, yet distinct from, the major early ecclesiastical centre of Otley, which lies two and a half miles to the north, on the other side of the Roman road (Fig. 6b). It has been noted above that, by the later pre-Conquest period, Guiseley had come to form a component of the Otley estate, though the antiquity of the territorial association between the two remains uncertain. Their juxtaposition is, nevertheless, comparable to that of Addingham and Ilkley (Fig. 6a). As has been seen, there is some evidence to suggest that the former may have been a pre-Viking episcopal residence; as at Guiseley, Viking-age sculpture has been recovered from the site.[63] In contrast, Ilkley, like Otley, preserves a large collection of Anglian

---

the Oswald dedications in the High Pennines (notably Thornton in Craven, which lies on the line of a Roman road), and perhaps also some of those in Cumberland and Westmorland.

[63] Bailey, *VAS*, pp. 170, 189, fig. 40 on p. 162.

sculpture,[64] suggesting that it was second only to the latter as an early ecclesiastical centre in Wharfedale.

V

Other Early Ecclesiastical Centres

Although there is evidence to suggest that other churches dedicated to Oswald may well belong in a pre-Viking ecclesiastical context of some kind, there seems to be no possibility of determining their function more precisely. In view of its place-name, the most important of these is probably Kirkoswald in Cumberland (Fig. 8, no. 11). A mile to the south-east lies the site of Addingham (now submerged beneath the river Eden).[65] To judge by its sculptural remains, that site must have been the major Anglian ecclesiastical centre of the middle Eden valley.[66] At Kirkoswald itself there is sculpture which may also be pre-Viking in date, though a later date cannot be ruled out.[67] As with its Yorkshire counterpart at Oswaldkirk, the possibility therefore arises that the dedication of the church may be appreciably older than the date of formation of the place-name in the tenth century or later.

In other instances the absence of any early material context at the site of an Oswald dedication perhaps makes the possibility of a pre-Viking context weaker; nevertheless, the proximity of the church of Dean in Cumberland (Fig. 8, no. 12) to the major pre-Viking centre of Brigham may be significant,[68] as might the possible relationship between Methley (Fig. 8, no. 40) and the important pre-Viking church of Ledsham in the West Riding of Yorkshire (Fig. 6c).[69] Finally, it is conceivable that the phenomenon extends beyond Northumbria into parts of northern Mercia, where the scarcity of pre-Viking sculpture makes the juxtapositions all the more striking. For example, in Cheshire, the church at Brereton (Fig. 8, no. 51) may stand in a comparable situation with respect to Sandbach, which has produced major pre-Viking sculpture; so might Bidston (Fig. 8, no. 46), which lies one and a quarter miles north-east of Overchurch where such carving has also been

---

[64] Collingwood, 'West Riding', pp. 185-97.

[65] C. J. Gordon, 'A submerged church in the River Eden', *Transactions of the Cumberland and Westmorland Antiquarian and Archaeological Society*, 2nd series 14 (1914), pp. 328-36, fig. facing p. 328.

[66] *Corpus* II, pp. 46-8; not to be confused with Addingham, Yorkshire (see p. 145, above).

[67] *Corpus* II, p. 125.

[68] *Corpus* II, pp. 74-5; for the extent of the large medieval parish, see A. Winchester, 'Medieval Cockermouth', *Transactions of the Cumberland and Westmorland Antiquarian and Archaeological Society*, 2nd series 86 (1986), pp. 109-28, at pp. 122-5, fig. 4.

[69] H. M. and J. Taylor, *Anglo-Saxon Architecture* (2 vols, Cambridge 1965), I, pp. 378-84.

found.[70] In some cases there may also be significant relationships to the Roman road network (see Appendix).

VI
Royal Centres

The final category of potentially early dedications to Oswald which remains to be considered consists of those whose most significant relationship appears to be not with an ecclesiastical centre, but rather with an adjacent secular settlement.

The dedication of the church of Elvet in Durham City (Fig. 8, no. 9) to St Oswald was first recorded in the late twelfth century, and the earliest extant fabric dates from that same period;[71] but if one can assume that the pre-Conquest carving found reused in the church tower anciently belonged here, it points to a significantly earlier stratum in the site's ecclesiastical use. This cross-shaft has been variously dated to between the late ninth and early eleventh centuries. Advocates of the later date stress the similarity of some of its motifs to those on carvings found at the cathedral site itself, which are usually assumed to date from after the Cuthbert Community's arrival there in 995.[72] These motifs are, however, also found on carvings elsewhere in the region which are usually dated to the late ninth or early tenth centuries, at Tynemouth and Aycliffe for example.[73] The date of the St Oswald's cross thus depends on the possibility of making a fine distinction between the first currency of the motifs c.900 and their apparent revival at Durham in the early eleventh century. For present purposes, only two features of this controversy are significant. One is that the earlier possibility is one factor among others pointing to the existence of an ecclesiastical presence at Elvet before the arrival of the Community of St Cuthbert on the Durham peninsula in 995; the second is that, whatever its date, this carving clearly belongs in a Viking-age rather than a pre-Viking context.

[70] On the other hand, Brereton seems to have been dependent on Astbury in the later pre-Conquest period at least (see Binns below, p. 246); on Sandbach, see J. D. Bu'lock, *Pre-Conquest Cheshire 383-1066* (Chester 1972), pp. 45-8. On Over-church, see op. cit., pp. 48-9; a possible pre-Conquest association between Overchurch and Bidston has been postulated by Bu'lock on other grounds (op. cit., p. 80).

[71] N. Pevsner et al., *The Buildings of England, County Durham* (2nd edn.; Harmondsworth 1983), p. 223.

[72] Summarised in *Corpus* I, p. 32; see also pp. 66-7, ills. 189-92. For a cautionary note on the latter assumption, see R. N. Bailey, 'The chronology of Viking-Age sculpture in Northumbria', in *Anglo-Saxon and Viking-Age Sculpture*, ed. J. Lang (BAR, Brit. ser., 49; Oxford 1978), pp. 173-203, at pp. 173-4.

[73] *Corpus* I, ill. 1266 (Tynemouth 4A), ill. 28 (Aycliffe 1D) (cf. ill. 189); Bailey, *VAS*, pp. 194-5.

More specific in its chronological implications than the uncertain evidence of the sculptural finds is the place-name Elvet, for it is generally accepted that this is to be identified with the *Aelfet ee* at which, according to one of the versions of the *Anglo-Saxon Chronicle*, Pehtwine was consecrated bishop of Whithorn in 762.[74] If this identification is correct it implies that a settlement of some importance was present in or near Elvet long before the surviving sculpture (whatever date is preferred for it) was carved. The possible topographical reference of the place-name is ambivalent, however. The meaning of the specific element *Aelfet* ('swan') is clear enough; but the generic element *ee* is more ambiguous, for it may represent either Old English *ea* ('stream') or *eg* ('island').[75] The present location of Elvet on the eastern bank of the loop of the river Wear may seem to make the former the more likely interpretation, as its topography is not very obviously insular (Fig. 4b). Other considerations, however, suggest that we should be wary of accepting that the *prima facie* interpretation is necessarily the correct one; and that it may be misleading to assume that the ancient reference of the name was so restricted, for besides meaning island in the modern sense *eg* was also used to refer to peninsulas, whether defined by water or simply a hill projecting from flatter land.[76]

Two recent discussions of place-names incorporating the generic *eg* are particularly relevant to our understanding both of the possible original reference of the name *Aelfet ee* and of its significance as a settlement. The first is the suggestion that the original topographical reference of the name Lindsey (Old English *Lindes-eg*), which came to be applied to an entire Anglo-Saxon kingdom (Fig. 2, p. 14), was to the prominently elevated upper parts of the city of Lincoln rather than to a low-lying island near the river below.[77] The second is provided by an early form of the place-name now familiar to us as Hexham, which occurs in early sources as *(H)agustaldesei*. Of particular significance as regards the original meaning of *Aelfet ee* is the fact that, in this case, there are enough early attestations to enable it to be determined that the element represented by *ei* (alternatively *ae*, *iae*) in the early forms is more likely to be the generic *eg* than *ea*.[78] The Anglo-Saxon

---

[74] *ASC*, 'E', *s.a. 762*.

[75] These two elements are ultimately connected and sometimes confused: see A. H. Smith, *English Place-Name Elements*, I (English Place-Name Society 25; Cambridge 1958), p. 147; for Elvet see E. Ekwall, *The Concise Oxford Dictionary of English Place-Names* (4th ed; Oxford 1960), p. 166 (*sub* 'Elvet Hall'). I am grateful to Victor Watts for pointing out to me that the recorded forms of the name do not enable the form of the generic to be determined on linguistic grounds.

[76] M. Gelling, *Place-Names in the Landscape* (London 1984), p. 36.

[77] B. Yorke, 'Lindsey: the lost kingdom found?' in *Pre-Viking Lindsey*, ed. A. Vince (Lincoln 1993), pp. 141-150, at p. 143, quoting a suggestion by Mrs M. Gelling.

[78] For the early forms, see *VW* 22, 44, 51, 60, 62, 65 (pp. 44, 90, 106, 132, 134, 140).

monastery at Hexham (the site of which is certainly perpetuated by the existing abbey church) was situated on a pronounced bluff clearly visible from across the Tyne valley. What is more, it has been suggested that the first element of this name implies that the settlement was held by a person of high status before the monastery was founded there.[79] These examples thus not only provide parallels for the application of the generic element *eg* to prominent peninsular sites, but also raise the intriguing possibility that such sites were favoured locations for early centres of secular power.

In the light of this comparative evidence, the possibility that *Aelfet ee* might originally have referred to the Durham peninsula itself needs to be considered. The name Durham is late Old English in origin (*dun holm*, 'hill island'), the element *holmr* being of Old Norse derivation.[80] The fact that this later name describes the peninsula as an island may be significant here, for it raises the possibility that it perpetuated the topographical reference of the generic element of a more ancient name which it in part supplanted. In other words, it implies, like the comparative evidence adduced above, that the peninsula could appropriately have been described by the generic *eg*, and hence that *Aelfet ee* might originally have been coined with reference to it.[81] Of course, the peninsula is not the only available candidate which might be described as an *eg* in this sense – the hill east of present-day Elvet known as Maiden Castle should not be ruled out, for example – but it does appear to be the most obvious one in the area.

The physical separation of the peninsula from the ecclesiastical site at Elvet (Fig. 4b) may seem to raise a difficulty with the above interpretation, for it is not immediately apparent how a name which originally referred to the peninsula should have come to refer to an area on the opposite side of the river, nor why the latter should have perpetuated the early name after it had been abandoned with respect to its original point of reference. In practice it is not difficult to envisage how this might have come about, as the phenomenon of extending the original terms of reference of a place-name to the surrounding territory can be paralleled in other Anglo-Saxon contexts. Again Bamburgh supplies a local parallel: the name which had in origin applied to the fortress on the rock was used for the parish church one third of a mile distant by the twelfth century, and probably long before (Fig. 4a). Similarly, a recent analysis of Selsey in Sussex (Old English *Sealæs-eg* 'seal island') has demonstrated that the name referred to an extensive adjacent territory from an early period and was not restricted to the coastal peninsular

---

[79] I am grateful to Victor Watts for the information on the generic.
See, for example, Ekwall, *Place-Names*, p. 237 (*sub* 'Hestercombe'). I am most grateful to Tom Corfe for allowing me to see his unpublished work on this topic.

[80] Ekwall, *Place-Names*, p. 154.

[81] Smith (loc. cit.) points out that *holmr* is used as the equivalent of *eg* in the areas of Scandinavian settlement.

site itself.[82]

If the above suggestion is right, how, then, did the name Elvet later come to be restricted to the suburbs east of the peninsula? This usage may be explicable as a relict use of the old name. The obvious context for this would have been a time when settlement was disrupted on the peninsula itself but continued on the eastern bank of the river thanks to the persistence of an ecclesiastical centre in that area. This would also explain why the *eg* element of the name subsequently dropped out of use. The likeliest period for the renaming of the peninsula in the late Saxon period must surely be the arrival of the Cuthbert Community there *c.*995. If this interpretation is right, the fact that a renaming took place at all would also suggest that (in contrast to sites such as Bamburgh) there had been major discontinuity in the occupation of the peninsula itself, a circumstance which might be explained by supposing that the site became much more marginal in the Viking period, when it lay near the border with the Viking kingdom of York, than it had been previously, when it lay mid-way between the Bernician and Deiran centres of power.

The above hypothesis also implies that the ecclesiastical site at Elvet is likely to have originated appreciably earlier than its archaeological context alone would indicate. Again, comparative evidence suggests that there is nothing unlikely about this. A site where there are grounds for supposing that the associated archaeological evidence appears significantly later than the likely period of origin has already been encountered at Oswaldkirk; another, more local example, at Coniscliffe, is discussed below. A further point is that recent work on the relationship between early ecclesiastical sites and their secular counterparts suggests that a degree of separation is precisely what one would expect.[83] If the recent proposal to identify the *urbs regis* called *Inbroninis* mentioned in Stephen's *Life of Wilfrid* with the rock of Beblowe (now the site of the castle) on Lindisfarne is correct, a comparable disjunction of secular and ecclesiastical centres would have applied to Lindisfarne itself, at least in the seventh century; and, as we have already seen, Bamburgh is another local example of similar date.[84] It seems likely therefore that the

---

[82] For the phenomenon in general, see Campbell, 'Bede's words', pp. 45-6; for Bamburgh, see above, pp. 137-9; for Selsey (a former royal vill given to found a monastery), see G. R. J. Jones, 'Broninis', *Bulletin of the Board of Celtic Studies* 37 (1990), pp. 125-32, at pp. 127-8. If his identification of *Inbroninis* with Lindisfarne is correct, its generic element *ynys* ('island') may provide a British parallel to the use of Old English *eg* proposed above, for he argues that the name referred to the extensive mainland territory dependent on Lindisfarne and not just to the island itself (art. cit., p. 131).

[83] For the phenomenon in general, see J. Blair, 'Minster churches in the landscape', in *Anglo-Saxon Settlements*, ed. D. Hooke (Oxford 1988), pp. 35-58, at pp. 40-8.

[84] Jones, 'Broninis', pp. 129-30; see above, pp. 137-9.

early ecclesiastical settlement at *Aelfet ee* would have been adjacent to the secular focus but would not have been sited actually within it. None of this, of course, proves that the present-day church of Elvet perpetuates the site of an eighth-century predecessor, but it does mean that this location should not be considered at all anomalous in terms of what is known about how such early settlements were laid out. It may therefore be misleading to treat the site at Elvet in isolation and as antecedent to the establishment of any settlement on the peninsula, as previous discussions have tended to do;[85] recent research suggests rather that the two locations would more likely have been complementary in function and chronologically contemporaneous rather than successive.

If the above interpretation of the place-name *Aelfet ee* is accepted, the implications for the status of the proposed early settlement on the peninsula which it originally designated remain to be considered. It has already been noted that the consecration of a bishop at this place suggests a settlement of high status; the comparative evidence of the kinds of site designated by the element *eg* appears to point in the same direction. Other considerations may hint at the former presence of a royal centre on the Durham peninsula. The active support of the earl of Northumbria in establishing the Cuthbert Community on the peninsula may itself hint that it had been inherited (like Bamburgh itself) by the earls as successors of the Northumbrian kings. What is more, its proximity to the likely course of the eastern of the two Roman roads running through the Tyne-Tees area perhaps suggests that its location may have been important in the pre-Viking period, when north-south communications must have been essential to the viability of the Northumbrian kingdom.[86]

Neither of the preceding considerations is at all conclusive when taken in isolation; when seen in the light of an important piece of comparative evidence, however, they may lend support to the contention that the church of Elvet was associated with a pre-Viking royal centre. This relates to High Coniscliffe, on the north bank of the Tees, the traditional dedicatee of which is another Northumbrian sainted king, Edwin. It must be admitted that there seems to be no direct medieval documentation of this dedication; but its rarity perhaps argues in favour of its authenticity.[87] As the place-name itself

---

[85] For example, H. Gee, 'City of Durham: general history of the city' in VCH, *Durham*, III, pp. 1-52, at pp. 6-7.

[86] Compare the relationship of Coniscliffe to Dere Street (discussed below, p. 153).

[87] Arnold-Forster, III, 360. For the possibility that the place-name Edwinstowe (Nottinghamshire) reflects a (perhaps early) dedication to Edwin, see Butler, 'Dedications', pp. 47-8. The subsequent unpopularity of Edwin's cult may have resulted in other early dedications being supplanted elsewhere, so that the contrast with the number of Oswald dedications may have been somewhat less pronounced in the pre-Viking period.

suggests, the church was probably situated on a royal estate,[88] and this may receive further indirect support from a record of the murder there in 778 of a Northumbrian *ealdorman* on the orders of King Æthelred of Northumbria.[89] Further, the site is only a mile east of Dere Street, and proximity to Roman roads has already been noted as a characteristic of (among others) early royal centres. What makes this evidence particularly significant for present purposes is that the early royal associations of the site are independently documented. Furthermore, the unusual choice of dedicatee presumably reflects the site's royal status; it also seems most likely to have arisen in a pre-Viking context, for it is possible to envisage that a later Anglo-Saxon king of Northumbria might have wished to dedicate a church on one of his estates to a sainted royal predecessor, but difficult to see why any later lord would have been motivated to commemorate an increasingly obscure saint.[90] The archaeological implications of the comparison with Coniscliffe are also important; for, despite the circumstantial evidence that its church dates from the pre-Viking period, the existing fabric contains no features datable to the pre-Conquest period, while none of the stone sculptures from the site is earlier than the Viking period.[91] This suggests that the similar archaeological profile of Elvet by no means argues against its having being an important place in the pre-Viking period; on the contrary, the lack of pre-Viking material remains of this kind may be precisely what one should expect from churches serving such royal estate centres.[92]

The preceding evidence thus offers some support for the hypothesis outlined above: that is, the existence of a pre-Viking royal centre, probably on the Durham peninsula, served by its associated ecclesiastical settlement nearby at Elvet, and both originally known as *Aelfet ee*. The significance of

[88] It is a Scandinavianised version of Old English *Ciningesclif*, 'the king's cliff' (Ekwall, *Place-Names*, p. 120). For the likelihood that it is to be identified with *Ædwinesclif*, the setting of a royal murder in 761 (*ASC*, 'E', *s.a.* 761), see W. Pearson, 'Edwin, Coniscliffe and the quest for Hela and "Thorns"', *Durham Archaeological Journal* 7 (1991), pp. 113-21, at pp. 113-14.

[89] *ASC*, 'E', *s.a.* 778. For other examples of murder carried out at royal vills see Sawyer, 'Royal tun' (as n. 34), at p. 276.

[90] Particularly if Coniscliffe, on the north bank of the Tees, was regarded as part of Deira, to whose ruling dynasty Edwin belonged and where (at Whitby) his relics were enshrined (see above, pp. 141-2, and Thacker, above, p. 105).

[91] For the church, see P. F. Ryder, 'St Edwin's church, High Coniscliffe', *Durham Archaeological Journal* 5 (1989), pp. 55-65. Might the extraordinarily long and narrow proportions of the nave (art. cit., fig. 1, p. 56) conceivably have been to some extent determined by a timber predecessor? For the sculpture, see *Corpus I*, pp. 59-61, ills. 152-5, 157-9 (with Ryder's correction, art. cit., p. 64, n. 11).

[92] I have suggested elsewhere that these features typify non-monastic churches serving estate centres (Cambridge, 'Early church', p. 81). St Aidan's at Bamburgh also appears to conform to this pattern.

the dedication of Elvet church to St Oswald, particularly in view of its rarity north of Tees at any period of the middle ages, therefore needs to be assessed in the light of it. If the possibility that the dedication is early can be accepted, there are two ways in which it might have come about. The first is that, as at Coniscliffe, the dedication is a direct consequence of the presence nearby of a royal centre, reflecting an interest on the part of the Northumbrian kings in promoting the cult of their sainted ancestor. The second (which does not necessarily exclude the first) depends upon the topographical analogy between Durham/Elvet and sites such as Bamburgh, as analysed above (Fig. 4); this may imply that the church of Elvet originated in an episcopal residence adjacent to a royal centre.[93] If so, this need not have been for the benefit of the bishops of Lindisfarne, particularly if, as I have argued elsewhere, the latter may already have had a residence nearby at Chester-le-Street long before that site became the resting-place of Cuthbert's relics in 883;[94] what is more, the church of Elvet is conspicuous by its absence from the extensive and comparatively well documented pre-Conquest possessions of the Cuthbert Community. The bishops of Hexham would also have needed similar provision at the principal royal centres within their diocese, of which, if the above speculation is right, *Aelfet ee*/Durham would have been one. Moreover, Durham lies at the first point at which the eastern of the two principal north-south Roman roads traversing the county is easily accessible from Dere Street, the obvious route south from Hexham.[95] If the suggestion of a Hexham rather than a Lindisfarne link is right, the Oswald dedication would become more easily comprehensible given the active promotion of Oswald's cult on the part of the Hexham community.[96]

Another Oswald dedication which may be explicable in terms of an association with a possible pre-Viking royal centre is the church of Hotham (Fig. 8, no. 39) in the East Riding of Yorkshire. It must at once be admitted that nothing in the fabric of the church itself gives any indication of a pre-Conquest origin; the argument depends rather on its archaeological context. Three miles north-east of Hotham, on the other side of the Roman road from Lincoln to York, lies Sancton, the most extensive of the Deiran

---

[93] The street leading from the Durham peninsula to the ford giving access to the east bank of the river and St Oswald's church may thus be a significant early surviving feature of the settlement plan. Might its later medieval name, Kingsgate, preserve a memory of its early function in linking the royal and ecclesiastical settlements? It seems to have formed the principal east-west route across the peninsula (Fig. 4b) before its displacement northwards by the construction of the two bridges in the 12th century.

[94] Cambridge, 'Chester-le-Street', pp. 379-86.

[95] Cambridge, 'Chester-le-Street', fig. 33, p. 381.

[96] See Thacker, above, pp. 107-11.

cremation cemeteries (Fig. 6d), and five miles north lies Goodmanham, site of the pagan sanctuary mentioned in a famous episode in Bede's *Ecclesiastical History*.[97] In the light of these associations, Higham has recently postulated an early palace site within Sancton parish, pointing to a field-name which incorporates the element *cyning* in support of its early royal associations, and suggesting that it may have been succeeded by a later royal residence nearby at Newbald (Old English *niwe bold*, 'new building' or 'new palace'), one and a half miles east of Hotham on the other side of the Roman road.[98] The rarity of dedications to Oswald in this area of Yorkshire in contrast to their apparent frequency in others (Fig. 8) may lend some support to the hypothesis that the one at Hotham originated in association with an adjacent pre-Viking royal centre. A second site in the same county for which an early royal context may be tentatively suggested is Flamborough (Fig. 8, no. 32). Here the coastal peninsular site is not unlike Bamburgh's, and the possibility that the Danes' Dyke (the great linear earthwork which defends the peninsula on its landward side) is early Anglian in date suggests that its occupation sequence might also have been similar, originating as a pre-Christian stronghold and continuing as an important centre into the post-conversion period.[99] Finally, as regards Whittingehame in East Lothian (Fig. 8, no. 6), two preliminary observations may be made, though more work is urgently needed to establish the antiquity both of its dedication and of the present-day location of the church. First, the place-name in *-ingaham* may indicate an early phase in the Anglian settlement of the region.[100] Second, the site's location, a mile and a half south-east of the major late Iron-age and sub-Roman fortress of Traprain Law, may be significant: their relative location is reminiscent of that of Yeavering Bell on the one hand, and

---

[97] *HE* II, 13.

[98] N. J. Higham, *The Kingdom of Northumbria AD 350-1100* (Stroud 1993), p. 81. (For the name, see Ekwall, *Place-Names*, p. 339.) The complex intermingling of adjacent parts of the parishes of Hotham and North and South Newbald, an arrangement which was apparently established as early as 963, not only attests the antiquity of their relationship, but may also suggest that they had anciently been part of a single territory: see M. H. Long and M. F. Pickles, 'Newbald', in *Yorkshire Boundaries*, ed. H. E. J. Le Patourel, M. H. Long, and M. F. Pickles (Leeds 1993), pp. 135-41, at p. 136, and fig. 49 on p. 138.

[99] The first element in the place-name is a personal name of Scandinavian origin (Ekwall, *Place-Names*, p. 181); conceivably, however, the generic might have been formulated earlier, like that of Bamburgh. For the possible date of the Danes' Dyke, see J. R. Watkin, 'The archaeology of Anglian east Yorkshire – a review of some published evidence and proposals for future research', *East Riding Archaeology* 7 (1983), pp. 25-39, at p. 33, and for early Anglian settlement within it, p. 31.

[100] W. F. H. Nicolaisen, *Scottish Place-Names, their Study and Significance* (London 1976), pp. 20, 72.

the potentially early ecclesiastical site of Kirknewton on the other. Close to these two lies the early Anglo-Saxon palace site at Yeavering itself;[101] so, if this comparison has any validity it implies the existence of another, possibly royal, site in the immediate vicinity of Whittingehame and Traprain; at least one other neighbouring and independently documented royal site, at Dunbar, would presumably also have been in existence contemporaneously, suggesting a major focus of Northumbrian royal power in this area of Lothian.

The above group of sites, together with analogous settlements like Coniscliffe and Bamburgh, suggests that there is a significant correlation between dedications to Oswald and early royal centres. The Oswald sites themselves may be explained either as royal chapels or (perhaps more likely in view of the evidence for their subsidiary locations) in terms of nearby episcopal residences. They may therefore not differ as much as might at first appear from episcopal residences adjacent to ecclesiastical centres, as already postulated for sites such as Guiseley.

VII

Conclusions

It must be stressed that the preceding survey of the variety of contexts in which dedications to Oswald might have originated in pre-Viking Northumbria has of necessity been put forward only very tentatively; clearly much more detailed work on both the history (including the later medieval history) and the archaeology of individual sites is required before the degree of probability that any dedication to Oswald really does belong in so early a context, and if so, in what sort of context, can be properly assessed. Nevertheless, there seems to be at least enough *prima facie* evidence to suggest that a number may well have arisen in that period. Though it is undoubtedly hazardous to go further at present, several more general observations may be made.

The range of possible functional contexts suggested for sites at which potentially early Oswald dedications occur should not be allowed to obscure the one feature they appear to have in common to a striking degree, and that is their tendency to be dependent in some way on other adjacent places of higher status; only rarely can a case be made for an early dedication to Oswald being at a high-status site itself. In ecclesiastical complexes at least this may in part reflect a preference for dedicating the principal church to a universal saint, restricting indigenous dedicatees to subsidiary contexts. More fundamentally, however, it presumably reflects one of the basic characteristics of the structure of early medieval settlement, in which the principal focus is surrounded by a series of dependent settlements, one of which happens to have become fossilised as a result of its ecclesiastical associations.

101 B. Hope-Taylor, *Yeavering: An Anglo-British Centre of Early Northumbria* (London 1977), fig. 2.

In favour of this interpretation is the way in which the feature seems to be common to dedications associated with high-status secular centres as well as ecclesiastical ones. On the other hand, one should perhaps be wary of too readily assuming that all examples of dependent and focal settlements are instances of the *same* phenomenon; there may also be significant differences. For example, possible instances of episcopal residences near to royal centres, as suggested at Bamburgh and Durham (Fig. 4), appear to be significantly closer to each other than those associated with major ecclesiastical centres, as postulated at Guiseley (Fig. 6b); other sites, such as Whitby and Lythe, or Carlisle and Wetheral, for which a monastic context has been suggested, seem to be significantly further apart again (Fig. 5a). Whether such differences are to be explained in functional or chronological terms (or both) raises questions about the morphology of early medieval settlement which cannot be entered into here; but the potential significance of this evidence for addressing such questions should at least be apparent.[102]

One general feature of the dedications identified above as possibly pre-Viking remains to be considered, and that is the significance of their overall distribution, which appears not to be confined to Northumbria, but extends into northern Mercia. Of course, from the beginning Oswald's had not been an exclusively Northumbrian cult, receiving Mercian royal patronage from as early as c.700.[103] Given that at least one (Bardney) if not two (*Maserfelth*/Oswestry) major centres of the saint's cult lay within Mercian territory, it should not be surprising if this were reflected in early dedications to the saint to some extent. It is notable, however, that Bardney, though the best attested early site outside of Northumbria, seems to have generated no identifiably early dedications in its region; perhaps the anti-Northumbrian sentiments which led to the initial rejection of Oswald's relics by the monks of Bardney died hard in Lindsey. In contrast, a case can be made for some of those in north-western Mercia being early, such as Brereton and Bidston in Cheshire (Fig. 8, nos. 51, 46), and Winwick in south Lancashire (Fig. 8, no. 45).[104] This perhaps lends support to Stancliffe's suggestion that Oswald's death-site lay in that same region, and may have had

---

[102] The way in which several complexes appear to straddle the Roman roads to which they are adjacent, the subsidiary element lying on the opposite side to the principal one, may also be a diagnostic early feature (for example, Guiseley and Otley (Fig. 6b), Hotham and Sancton/Newbald (Fig. 6d), and perhaps also Methley and Ledsham (Fig. 6c)); it is not, of course, restricted to sites containing Oswald dedications.

[103] Æthelred of Mercia retired to the monastery of Bardney in 704 (*HE* V, 24); his queen, Osthryth, had earlier translated relics of Oswald there (see Thacker above, pp. 104-5). For Offa's bequests to Bardney in the later eighth century, see Alcuin, *BKS*, lines 388ff.

[104] See above, pp. 147-8, and Appendix, p. 162.

a continuous existence as a cult-centre in the early middle ages.[105]

Within Northumbria itself, there are marked contrasts in the distribution of Oswald dedications. They are rare north of the Tees at any period (Fig. 8, nos. 6-9), the few examples being certainly or probably early in date; whereas they appear to be significantly more common south of the Tees and west of the Pennines, not only in the later middle ages but also, if the preceding analysis is correct, in the pre-Viking period (Fig. 8). Despite the considerable uncertainty which accompanies any attempt to define the geographical extent of the pre-Viking Northumbrian dioceses, it may be worth speculating that these contrasts are in some way to be associated with differing attitudes on the part of the various sees, at any rate so far as their core territories are concerned. To judge by the promotion of the battle site of Heavenfield, Hexham was an active supporter of Oswald's cult, at any rate from the early eighth century, while the dedications at *Scythlescester* and (if the arguments set out above are accepted) that of Elvet are almost certainly also to be associated with that diocese.[106] The number of potentially early dedications south of the Tees suggests that the cult was also vigorously promoted within the diocese of York, both in its core territory east of the Pennines in Deira, and in areas west of the Pennines which probably also came under its control.[107] From this perspective, the almost total absence of Oswald dedications in the diocese of Lindisfarne becomes all the more striking. It is tempting to conclude that there was a positive antipathy to Oswald dedications at Lindisfarne, despite the presence of major corporeal relics at both Bamburgh and Lindisfarne itself. The attitude of the Lindisfarne community towards its relic seems to have been remarkably ambivalent.[108] How might this state of affairs be explained? Possibly the espousal of Oswald's cult by Hexham presented an unwelcome (and perhaps all too successful) challenge to Lindisfarne as a centre of his cult. From this point of view, the alternative promotion of Cuthbert's cult after the elevation of his relics in 698 had the distinct advantage of being exclusively under Lindisfarne's control. It may not be coincidental that the distribution of potentially early Cuthbert dedications is to some extent complementary to that of the Oswald ones, for, though by no means confined to the area north of the Tees, they are notably more common there.

There may also have been political overtones in the promotion of Oswald's cult in parts of pre-Viking Northumbria. If Alcuin's poem on the bishops, kings and saints of York is any guide to the way in which Oswald

[105] See Stancliffe, above, pp. 84-96.
[106] See Thacker, above, pp. 107-8, 113, and Binns, below, pp. 255, 249.
[107] See above, p. 145 and n. 62. Oswald's popularity in these regions may in part reflect the failure of widely popular saints' cults to establish themselves either at York itself or within its diocese.
[108] See Thacker, above, pp. 101-2, 104, and Bailey, below, p. 198.

was perceived at York by the later eighth century, the saint had clearly acquired something of the status of a Christian founding father of the Northumbrian nation. In the light of Godman's observations on the increasing political status of the archbishops of York in the later eighth century, as royal power was eroded by dynastic conflict,[109] their patronage may well have been an important factor behind the number of probable pre-Viking Oswald dedications in southern and western Northumbria. Circumstantial evidence has been adduced in support of archiepiscopal involvement in the case of Guiseley; others may have arisen in similar circumstances.[110]

The distribution of sites with potentially early dedications to Oswald within Deira may itself be significant, for these are confined to two areas: the Deiran heartland east of Dere Street, in which lie Lythe, Oswaldkirk, Filey, Flamborough and Hotham (Fig. 8, nos. 26, 30-2 and 39); and Elmet, containing Guiseley, Collingham and Methley (Fig. 8, nos. 35, 37 and 40). Whether a further contrast should be drawn, on the basis of the foregoing analysis, between the apparently royal and monastic associations of the eastern sites and the possible archiepiscopal ones of those in Elmet, it is difficult to decide, though in view of the landed interests of later archbishops in the latter area it may not be wholly inappropriate to do so. What does seem clear is the contrast between the southern and eastern distribution of all the potentially early sites on the one hand and the more northerly and westerly distribution of pre-Reformation dedications to Oswald in Yorkshire as a whole on the other (Fig. 8). However this apparent shift is to be explained, it seems unlikely to be fortuitous, which suggests that the identification of the early sites may not be altogether wide of the mark.

Besides going some way towards explaining the disparity between the small number of dedications to Oswald within the diocese of Lindisfarne and those elsewhere, the increasing popularity of the saint in episcopal circles other than Lindisfarne may also supply a clue to their chronological sequence. If the apparent indifference to Oswald on the part of the Lindisfarne community and its bishops was indeed a consequence of the desire to promote Cuthbert's cult from 698 onwards, their attitude before that momentous event, in the half-century or so after Oswald's death, need not have been so negative. Indeed, the possibility that Cuthbert might himself have dedicated a church to Oswald has been raised in connection with Lythe, and if the possible dedication at Wetheral is rightly interpreted

[109] Alcuin, *BKS*, pp. lix-lx.
[110] The correlation between episcopal estates and early dedications to St Chad in the north-west midlands to which Alan Thacker has recently drawn attention forms an instructive parallel, particularly as in at least one instance (Tushingham) the dedication to Chad apparently occurs in a subsidiary context: see VCH *Cheshire*, I, pp. 266, 271.

as dependent on the important monastery at Carlisle, which appears to have been under Lindisfarne's control (at least during Cuthbert's lifetime), it may also be best explained as originating in a later seventh-century context. Slight though the evidence is, it suggests that the earliest Oswald dedications tended to be associated either with royal centres (such as Hotham or Elvet) or with major monasteries (such as Whitby or Carlisle). Their rarity in the diocese of Lindisfarne may, however, suggest that they only became more common in Northumbria as a whole from the eighth century onwards, and that this fashion failed to take root (or was actively discouraged) in that diocese, due to the vigorous promotion of Cuthbert's cult there after 698. The more general spread of Oswald dedications elsewhere in Northumbria might then be seen as a later, eighth- to ninth-century, phenomenon, the consequence of the more universalised view of the saint's status as reflected in the verses of Alcuin. It must be stressed that Cuthbert also figures prominently in Alcuin's poem, so there is no attempt to present the cults as rivals, at least in York circles. The dedication to Oswald and Cuthbert jointly at *Scythlescester* at much the same time Alcuin was writing may reflect a comparable outlook. So may the way in which churches dedicated to Oswald in south-west Scotland tend to occur beside others dedicated to Cuthbert.[111] It has already been noted that the most plausible historical context for the establishment of the Oswald dedications in this region is an early one.[112] Of course, even if this is correct, there can be no certainty that the Cuthbert dedications are contemporaneous with those to Oswald. Nevertheless, in a region in which dedications to native Northumbrian saints were probably always uncommon, such strikingly similar distribution patterns seem unlikely to be coincidental, and might belong in a similar conceptual and chronological context.[113] And here, in the farthest outposts of Northumbrian rule, the political (indeed, propagandist) overtones are surely unmistakable; nor should the possibility that such a message was also intended by similar juxtapositions elsewhere in

[111] Daphne Brooke has drawn attention to the juxtaposition of the Oswald dedication implied by the name Kirkoswald of Turnberry (Fig. 8, no. 2) with the Cuthbert dedication in the adjacent parish of Maybole (Brooke, 'Northumbrian settlements' (as n. 6), pp. 310-11). A similar situation arises with Kirkoswald, alias Balmaknele (Fig. 8, no. 3), and Ballantrae; the first element of the ancient name of the latter, *Kirkcudbright-Innertig*, fossilises its Cuthbert dedication, and though the site of the former is uncertain, it was clearly within Ballantrae parish. A further example may occur in the southern part of this region, where the Oswald dedication at Kelton (and, if the place-name is correctly interpreted, that at Kirkcarswell: Fig. 8, nos. 4-5) is near to Kirkcudbright, the specific of which again fossilises a dedication to Cuthbert.

[112] See above, p. 130.

[113] This also suggests that the attitude of the bishops of Whithorn resembled that of York and Hexham, and not that of Lindisfarne.

Northumbria be ruled out.[114] It seems that, by the late eighth century, Oswald (whether in conjunction with Cuthbert or alone) was being widely promoted by the Northumbrian establishment, both ecclesiastical and secular, the patriotic overtones of his cult being succinctly captured in Alcuin's characterisation: 'vir virtute potens, patriae tutator, amator'.[115]

Acknowledgements

I am particularly indebted to Richard Bailey for reading and commenting on several drafts of this paper, and to the following for their help and advice on particular points: Daphne Brooke; Tom Corfe; Derek Craig; Rosemary Cramp; Jane Cunningham; Margaret Gelling; Martin Snape; Clare Stancliffe; and Victor Watts.

Explanatory Note for Following Appendix

Oswald dedication numbers are as for Figs. 8-9, pp. 268-71. Roman road numbers after I. D. Margary, *Roman Roads in Britain* (2nd edn; London 1967), except for the one near to Burneside, Westmorland, for which see J. S. and J. A. Andrews, 'A Roman road from Kendal to Ambleside. A field survey. Part I : Kendal to Broadgate', *Transactions of the Cumberland and Westmorland Antiquarian and Archaeological Society* 91 (1991), pp. 49-57. Brackets indicate significant uncertainty about date of road or line of route.

Abbreviations and symbols used

ANG, Anglian; VA, Viking-age; *, presence; *?, evidence uncertain; *?——*?, date uncertain as between Anglian and Viking-age.

[114] The occurrence of Oswald and Cuthbert dedications near to one another in areas where neither is common, such as Warton (Fig. 8, no. 44) and St Cuthbert at Over Kellet in north Lancashire, or Filey (Fig. 8, no. 31) and St Cuthbert at Burton Fleming (both perhaps to be associated with a major centre at Hunmanby, see above, p. 143) in eastern Yorkshire, are reminiscent of the south-west Scottish examples.

[115] 'A man of mighty virtue, guardian and lover of the fatherland' (Alcuin, *BKS*, line 267).

APPENDIX
Oswald Dedications and Archaeological Features

Oswald Dedication	Sculpture ANG VA	Anglian Sculpture within 5 miles	Roman Road within 3 miles
CHESHIRE			
47. Backford		Chester	(670/701)
46. Bidston		Overchurch	
51. Brereton		Sandbach	
48. Chester	*?		(6a/7a)
50. Lower Peover			(700)
52. Malpas			6a
49. Worleston			(700)
CUMBERLAND / WESTMORLAND			
12. Dean (Cu)		Brigham	(75)
11. Kirkoswald (Cu)	*?———*?	Addingham	
10. Wetheral (Cu)	*	Carlisle	7e/85b
14. Burneside (We)		Kendal	()
13. Grasmere (We)			
15. Ravenstonedale (We)		Kirkby Stephen	
DERBYSHIRE			
55. Ashbourne			
DURHAM			
9. Elvet	*		(80a)
LANCASHIRE			
44. Warton		Halton	
45. Winwick	*		70a
LINCOLNSHIRE			
65. Althorpe			
68. Bardney Abbey			
69. Blankney			
63. Crowle	*		
71. Howell			
64. Luddington			
66. Rand			(27/272)
67. Strubby			
70. Walcot			

Oswald Dedication	Sculpture ANG VA	Anglian Sculpture within 5 miles	Roman Road within 3 miles
NORTHUMBERLAND			
7. Bamburgh	*?———*?		
8. St Oswald in Lee	*?		8c/86
NOTTINGHAMSHIRE			
62. Broughton Sulney			5f/58a
61. Burton Joyce			
59. East Stoke			5f
SHROPSHIRE			
54. Hinstock			19
53. Oswestry			
YORKSHIRE			
18. Arncliffe			(731)
19. Askrigg			73/730
20. Castle Bolton		West Witton	
37. Collingham	* *		72b
24. East Harlsey			80
28. Farnham			(720b)
31. Filey	*	Hunmanby	(816)
32. Flamborough			810/811
38. Fulford	*	York	(28c)
35. Guiseley	*	Otley	72b
21. Hauxwell	*		
17. Horton in Ribblesdale			
39. Hotham			2e
43. Kirk Sandall			
36. Leathley		Otley	72b
26. Lythe	* *	Whitby	
40. Methley	*?	Ledsham	28b
25. Newton in Cleveland			
30. Oswaldkirk	*	Gilling East, Stonegrave	
29. Sowerby			80
33. Thornton in Craven			72a
16. Thornton in Lonsdale			
22. Thornton Steward	*		
23. West Rounton			80
27. Winksley cum Grantley		Ripon	
42. Wragby		Crofton	

163

St Oswald in Post-Conquest England

DAVID ROLLASON

I

In 1496, only a generation before the English Reformation, the abbot of Fountains, Marmaduke Huby, wrote to the general chapter of the Cistercian order, to which Fountains belonged, concerning St Oswald, king and martyr. Noting the merits and miracles of the saint and the fact that many remains and relics of his holy body were preserved in diverse monasteries of this kingdom, he regretted that the Cistercian order alone among the faithful of all types failed to celebrate Oswald's feast day with praises and devotion, although, he went on, Cistercian houses possessed many relics of Oswald and longed deeply to observe his feast properly. The abbot requested the general chapter to permit the monasteries of the province of York to honour Oswald with services of twelve lections, two masses and a proper collect.[1] The letter is eloquent testimony to the popularity and vitality of the cult of Oswald at the very end of the middle ages, showing that the Cistercians, who had not in their early days been enthusiasts for the cult of saints,[2] were now being drawn by Oswald's popularity and importance to treat him as a major saint.

The abbot of Fountains's observations about that popularity and importance seem entirely justified by the evidence at our disposal. Oswald was very widely commemorated in the church calendars of post-Conquest England and his feast appears, for example, in the Sarum Missal, the York Missal, the Hereford Missal, the Aberdeen Breviary, and in calendars from Abbotsbury, Abingdon, Barking, Bath, Canterbury, Chertsey, Chester, Croyland, Deeping Priory, Dunster, Ely, Evesham, Exeter, Gloucester, Llanthony, Malmesbury, Muchelney, Reading, Romsey, St Albans, Southwark, Tewkesbury, Wells, Westminster, Winchcombe, and Winchester, as well as in a twelfth-century Welsh calendar and in the medieval calendars of Durham. The importance of Oswald's feast at Durham is attested also by the survival in Cambridge, Trinity College, MS O.3.55 of prayers for St Oswald, the sequence 'Regis Oswaldi inclita' with music, and the office for the feast of St Oswald with music. The same office is found in manuscripts from

---

1   *Letters from the English Abbots to the Chapter at Cîteaux 1442-1521*, ed. C. H. Talbot (Camden Fourth Series 4; London 1967), no. 94 (pp. 189-90); cf. no. 89 (pp. 181-2); cited by R. B. Dobson, *Durham Priory 1400-1450* (Cambridge 1973), p. 21 n. 2. On Marmaduke Huby's construction of a chapel of St Oswald at Winksley cum Grantley (Yorkshire West Riding), a very late example of a dedication to the saint, see Binns, below, p. 266.

2   I. G. Thomas, 'The Cult of Saints' Relics in Medieval England' (unpublished Ph.D. thesis, University of London, 1974), pp. 273-9. I am very grateful to the author for permission to use his work.

Coldingham, Peterborough, and Canterbury diocese.[3] Entries for him were also to be found in martyrologies, notably in compilations from the eastern counties and from the south-west.[4] Frequently in the calendars his feast was graded as of particular importance, and evidence that the feast was indeed still one of vitality at the end of the middle ages is provided by Cambridge, Trinity College, MS R.7.5, a copy probably from northern England of Bede's *Ecclesiastical History of the English People*, in which a sixteenth-century hand has written notes of nine lessons for St Oswald taken out of the text of the *History*.[5]

St Oswald also found a place in English hagiographical writings and compilations of the middle ages.[6] Durham Cathedral Priory produced two Lives of him. Of these the best known was written in the 1160s by the Durham hagiographer Reginald.[7] The other is preserved in three twelfth-century Durham manuscripts of Bede's *Life of St Cuthbert*: Durham, Cathedral Library, MS A.IV.35, Oxford, Bodleian Libary, MS Laud Misc. 491, and Cambridge, Trinity College, MS O.3.55.[8] The Life consists of a series of

3   M. R. James, *The Western Manuscripts in the Library of Trinity College, Cambridge* (4 vols; Cambridge 1900-4), no. 1227 (III, 241-3), who dates the manuscript to the early twelfth century; and S. Rankin in *Cambridge Music Manuscripts, 900-1700*, ed. I. Fenlon (Cambridge 1982), pp. 33-5, who dates it, probably correctly, to the second half of the twelfth century and lists the other manuscripts referred to.

4   R. Stanton, *A Menology of England and Wales* (London 1887), p. 382; and *English Benedictine Kalendars after AD 1100*, ed. F. Wormald (2 vols.; HBS 77, 88, London 1938-46).

5   James, *Western Manuscripts*, no. 743 (II, 219-22).

6   The Lives of Oswald have never been fully studied or related to one another as a group, apart from the work of the Bollandists who provided brief notes on them (*AASS*, August II, p. 93), and the work of Dr Tudor on the Life by Reginald of Durham (below, pp. 178-94). What follows must therefore be regarded as preliminary and provisional.

7   See Tudor, below, pp. 178-82.

8   For the attribution of these manuscripts to Durham, see *Medieval Libraries of Great Britain: A List of Surviving Books*, ed. N. R. Ker, *Supplement to the Second Edition*, ed. A. G. Watson (London 1987), pp. 18, 21, and 32. See also H. O. Coxe, *Laudian Manuscripts*, with corrections by R. W. Hunt (Bodleian Library Quarto Catalogues II; Oxford repr. 1973), cols. 352-3, where Laud Misc. 491 is dated to the end of the twelfth century. Two other manuscripts of Bede's *Life of St Cuthbert*, which are probably to be associated with Durham, also contained the Life: Oxford, Bodleian Library, MS Digby 175, of the late eleventh or early twelfth century; and London, BL Additional MS 35110, of the late twelfth. See *Two Lives*, pp. 21-2, 26, 31-3; *Catalogi Codicum Manuscriptorum Bibliothecae Bodleianae pars nona, Codices a viro clarissimo Kenelm Digby anno 1634 donatos complectentes*, ed. W. D. Macray (Oxford 1883), no. 175 (p. 187); and *Catalogue of Additions to the Manuscripts in the British Museum in the Years 1894-1899* (London 1901), no. 35110.

accounts taken from Bede's *Ecclesiastical History*, to a large extent verbatim, and describing principally the victory of Heavenfield, the cure of Bothelm, the foundation of Lindisfarne, the incorruption of Oswald's arm, the cures of the traveller's horse and the paralytic girl, the efficacy of earth from the place of Oswald's death against fire, the reception of his relics at Bardney and miracles performed there, and the miracle worked through him at Selsey.[9] The last of these may be a subsequent addition to the original Life since it is preceded in Durham A.IV.35 by a rubric announcing the end of Oswald's Life and Miracles. Following the account of the miracle of Selsey, the manuscript has a further miracle apparently of more recent date, concerning the fate of a thief who stole from St Oswald's church at Farnham in the West Riding of Yorkshire. Trinity O.3.55 and Laud Misc. 491 have this too, together with another concerned with Gloucester and detailing the punishment of a woman who worked on St Oswald's feast day.[10] The date of the manuscripts suggests that this Life was composed in the late eleventh or early twelfth century. The material relating to Gloucester must have been written in or after the time of Thomas, archbishop of York (1108/9-14), who is mentioned as having supervised a translation of Oswald's relics at Gloucester.

Other churches also had Lives of the saint. The fourteenth-century collection of saints' Lives preserved in Dublin, Trinity College, MS 172 (B.2.7), a manuscript which may possibly have come from Northampton, contains a Life of Oswald composed of extracts from Bede's *Ecclesiastical History* as in Cambridge, Trinity College, MS O.3.55, and Oxford, Bodleian Library, MS Laud Misc. 491;[11] and there is a similar compilation in the

---

9   *HE* III, 1-3, 6, and 8-14. The Life is entitled: 'Hic describuntur uita et miracula gloriosissimi et sanctissimi regis Oswaldi sicut in libro ecclesiastico gentis Anglorum continetur'. It begins 'Successores Eadwini regis Anglorum in apostasiam corruentes'; the *explicit* rubric in Durham A.IV.35 is preceded by 'fidelis eius famuli Oswaldi regis gloriam predicabat'; the Selsey account ends 'Oswaldi natalicius dies missarum celebratione uenerari ad laudem...amen'; the Farnham miracle begins 'Multimoda patrum antiquorum attestatione didicimus' and ends 'satisfactionis purgaret penitencia'; and the Gloucester account begins 'Est in prouincia Merciorum regia ciuitas' and ends 'Eius precibus et meritis mereamur peccatis emundari et perpetua cum illo beatitudine diteri. Amen'. It does not appear to correspond to any of the Lives listed in *BHL*, nos. 6361-72.

10   See below, p. 169.

11   M. L. Colker, *Trinity College Library, Dublin; Descriptive Catalogue of the Medieval and Renaissance Manuscripts* (2 vols; Aldershot 1991), I, pp. 310, 313; cf. T. K. Abbott, *Catalogue of the Manuscripts in the Library of Trinity College Dublin* (London 1900), no. 172, and P. Grosjean, 'Catalogus codicum hagiographicorum latinorum bibliothecarum Dubliniensium', *AB* 46 (1928), pp. 81-148 at p. 87. The Life, which occupies pp. 243-52 of the manuscript, is entitled 'Vita et passio beatissimi regis Oswaldi martyris a paganis interfectis'. It begins 'Interfecto in pugna nobilissimo rege' and ends 'per annos octo laboriosissime tenuit, regnante...

fourteenth-century English collection now preserved in the library at Gotha in Germany as Gotha, Forschungsbibliothek, MS I.81 (fols. 25^v-29^r).[12] An abbreviated version of Reginald's Life was included in the great fourteenth-century collection of English saints' Lives made by John of Tynemouth and subsequently printed as *Nova Legenda Anglie*.[13] The late fourteenth-century catalogue of Peterborough preserved in Peterborough, Cathedral Library, MS 15, fols. 1^r-19^v, mentions a Life of St Oswald in verse in one manuscript and some verses on St Oswald in another. Neither appears to be extant.[14] Finally, Reginald reports the existence in his time of Old English verses on St Oswald at York and of rude miracle accounts at Bardney, but these cannot now be traced.[15]

---

[12] Amen'. I should like to thank Dr Bernard Meehan for his help with this.
P. Grosjean, 'De codice hagiographico Gothano', *AB* 48 (1940), pp. 90-103 and 177-204, at p. 92. This is entitled 'Vita et miracula sancti Oswaldi regis Nordanhymbrorum'. The prologue begins: 'Quoniam uita et miracula Deo dilecti regis et martyris Oswaldi in sequentibus describenda sunt', and ends 'miracula sequentia presentis libelli uenerabili Beda describente declarabunt'. The Life begins 'Interfecto in pugna nobilissimo rege Eadwino anno Verbi incarnati sexcentesimo tricesimo tercio', and ends 'hoc se fecisse publice protestatus est.' This Life, which seems to correspond to *BHL* no. 6367 and is also preserved in fragmentary form in Society of Bollandists, Collectanea Bollandiana, MS 127 (Grosjean, art. cit.), is a compilation of material from Bede, concluding with the miracle at Selsey.

[13] *Nova Legenda Anglie: As Collected by John of Tynemouth, John Capgrave, and Others, and First Printed, with New Lives, by Wynkyn de Worde a.d. m d xui*, ed. C. Horstmann (2 vols; Oxford 1901), II, pp. 261-7.

[14] M. R. James, *Lists of Manuscripts formerly in Peterborough Abbey Library* (Transactions of the Bibliographical Society, Supplements 5; Oxford 1926), pp. 42 and 45. On the catalogue, see N. R. Ker and A. J. Piper, *Medieval Manuscripts in British Libraries*, IV, *Paisley-York* (Oxford 1992), p. 168. T. D. Hardy, *Descriptive Catalogue of Materials Relating to the History of Great Britain and Ireland to the End of the Reign of Henry VII* (3 vols.; RS, 1862-71), I, 614 (no. 1212) mentions a Life in a manuscript which he refers to as 'Ecc. Petroburg. D.2.4'. This began imperfectly 'hodie multi de ipso', and finished identically with the Life in Trinity Dublin 172 'et per annos viginti octo laboriosissime tenuit, regnante...' Horstmann is presumably following Hardy in referring to a Life extant at Peterborough (*Nova Legenda*, II, p. 261, n. 1). There appears, however, to be no such Life in the presently known medieval manuscripts of Peterborough Cathedral, nor does the shelf-mark bear any relationship to their shelf-marks. Hardy may have been mistaken (he was evidently confused since he catalogued this Life alongside Lives of St Oswald of Worcester), or he may have been referring to a modern transcript which has not been subsequently identified.

[15] Reginald, *VO* II, 45 and 50 (pp. 372, 378-9); cf. Tudor, below, pp. 187, 189. A Middle English Life describing, for example, how Oswald preserved his chastity by the application of cold water may represent the sort of tradition to which

All this was matched – as the abbot of Fountains claimed – by an impressive array of Oswald's relics in medieval England. Durham had the finest collection which included not only the head, but also, according to the late fourteenth-century relic-list of the cathedral priory, the martyr's banner, a portion of his mail-shirt, some of the cross which he had erected at Heavenfield, his ivory horn and his ivory sceptre, and a rib enclosed in the chest of a silver gilt image of him.[16] According to the early twelfth-century Durham writer Symeon, there was also the undecayed right hand and arm which had often been seen, Symeon tells us, by 'Swartebrand, a monk of our church of Durham, a venerable white-haired man of great honesty who died recently';[17] but the hand and arm do not appear in the relic-lists of Durham and Symeon may possibly have meant that Swartebrand had seen them at Peterborough. The monks of that church claimed to have obtained the undecayed right arm from Bamburgh – by theft, according to Reginald of Durham.[18] At all events, the twelfth-century Peterborough chronicler Hugh Candidus made much of it as one of the principal items in Peterborough's relic-collection:

> There is preserved here a relic precious above all gold, the right arm of St Oswald king and martyr, intact with both flesh and skin, according to the vow of benediction of St Aidan the bishop. I myself have inspected it with my own eyes, kissed it, handled it, and washed it, when it was shown to Bishop Alexander of Lincoln, to the whole convent and to many other clerics and laymen...in the four hundred and eighty-seventh year from the martyr's death.[19]

The Augustinian canons of St Oswald's, Gloucester, claimed to possess the body of the martyr as it had been translated to their church from Bardney in 909.[20] In fact a passage which is common to both Reginald of Durham's Life of Oswald and the version of the twelfth-century Durham Life in Trinity O.3.55 and Laud Misc. 491 only assigned to them his left arm and some of his

---

Reginald was referring. See C. Horstmann, 'Die Evangelien-Geschichten der Homilien- sammlung des MS Vernon', *Archiv für das Studium der neueren Sprachen* 57 (1977), pp. 241-316, at pp. 289-90.

[16] *Extracts from the Account Rolls of the Abbey of Durham*, II, ed. J. T. Fowler (SS 100; Durham 1899), pp. 425-39.

[17] *HDE* I, 2 (pp. 20-1). For a new edition and translation of this work, see Symeon of Durham, *Libellus de Exordio atque Procursu istius, hoc est Dunelmensis, Ecclesie*, ed. and trans. D. Rollason (Oxford forthcoming).

[18] Reginald, *VO* II, 48 (pp. 374-5).

[19] *The Chronicle of Hugh Candidus*, ed. W. T. Mellows (Oxford 1949), p. 52. See also pp. 70 and 105-7 and, for the date, see pp. xvi-xvii, n. 1.

[20] *ASC* 'C', *s.a.* 909; *Willelmi Malmesbiriensis Monachi De Gestis Pontificum Anglorum Libri Quinque*, IV, 155; ed. N. E. S. A. Hamilton (RS, 1870), p. 293. See VCH *Gloucestershire*, II, pp. 84-7, IV, pp. 289-90.

hair, but it did acknowledge that there was a flourishing cult at Gloucester and described the translation of his relics there by Archbishop Thomas of York (1108/9-14). Trinity O.3.55 also related a miracle account of a woman at Gloucester whose sickle stuck fast to her hand when she refused to abstain from work on Oswald's feast day.[21] According to Reginald, three bones of the saint nevertheless remained at Bardney,[22] and the thirteenth-century list of saints' resting-places bound up with the Breviate of Domesday went so far as to assign the whole of Oswald's relics to that church, although it admitted that dispute was possible:

> St Oswald was placed at Bardney, although it is said that he is at Nostell. But the monks of Peterborough say that they have his hands intact.[23]

As this text suggests, the Augustinian priory of Nostell near Pontefract was thought to possess relics of Oswald, for a pilgrimage was still apparently being made to them when Henry VIII's commissioners visited the church in 1536.[24] The abbot of Fountains's letter shows that Cistercian monasteries also possessed relics, and in addition we find Oswald relics in many of the relic-lists of other English churches.[25] Hyde Abbey in Winchester claimed a tooth. St Paul's, London, listed in its relic-list an arm and a finger, and, although it is not certain whether these were relics of Oswald the archbishop or Oswald king and martyr, the latter seem the most likely since, according to Hugh Candidus, water used in washing the arm of St Oswald at Peterborough had cured many at St Paul's where an altar had been dedicated to the martyr.[26] Unspecified relics of the martyr were apparently to be found at Bath, Glastonbury,[27] Reading, St Albans, Salisbury, Christ Church (Hampshire), Tynemouth, and York. There were inevitably doubts and

---

[21] Reginald, *VO* I, 44 (pp. 369-70); Trinity O.3.55, fols. 65^v-66^r; and Laud Misc. 491, fol. 173.

[22] Reginald, *VO* I, 43 (pp. 368-9).

[23] 'Saint Oswald fu posez en Bardeneie, or dit lom kil est enostle. Mes li Moigne de Burc dient kil ont les mains entiers.' Lawrence Butler, 'Two twelfth-century lists of saints' resting-places', *AB* 105 (1987), pp. 87-103, at pp. 87-93; cf. D. W. Rollason, 'Lists of saints' resting-places in Anglo-Saxon England', *ASE* 7 (1982), pp. 61-93, at p. 69.

[24] *Letters and Papers Foreign and Domestic of the Reign of Henry VIII* (21 vols; London 1862-1908), X (ed. J. Gairdner), p. 138 (no. 364), cited by Thomas, 'Cult of Relics', p. 442.

[25] Thomas, loc. cit.

[26] W. Sparrow Simpson, 'Two inventories of the cathedral church of St Paul, London', *Archaeologia* 50 (1887), pp. 439-524, at pp. 469 and 471; and *Chron. Hugh Candidus*, ed. Mellows, p. 108.

[27] *The Chronicle of Glastonbury Abbey: An Edition, Translation and Study of John of Glastonbury's Cronica siue Antiquitates Glastoniensis Ecclesie*, ed. J. P. Carley (2nd edn; Woodbridge 1985), ch. 5 (p. 18 and n. 25, pp. 274-5).

conflicting claims about where the relics really were – on which subject William of Malmesbury had some despairing remarks to make – but the existence of such controversy is itself an indication of how highly the relics were valued.[28]

Nor was devotion to Oswald restricted to the greater churches and monasteries. Over sixty parish churches and chapels in England are thought to have been dedicated to him in the middle ages, chiefly in the north, with some twenty-seven in Yorkshire, eight in Lincolnshire, six in Cumberland and Westmorland, two in Lancashire, and six or seven in Cheshire, but also with a certain number in the midlands and south, in Derbyshire, Nottinghamshire, Shropshire, Gloucestershire, Oxfordshire, and Kent.[29]

As regards holy wells, dedications to Oswald were not as numerous as those, for example, to St Helen, but in addition to the well on the river bank below St Oswald's Church in Durham, there was a St Oswald's well at Woodhead near Winwick in Lancashire. There is no indication as to the age of this but, according to the nineteenth-century antiquary R. C. Hope, it was 'substantially walled inside, and two or three deeply-worn steps lead to the water.'[30] Rather more is known about another St Oswald's well at Oswestry in Shropshire, because the twelfth-century hagiographer Reginald of Durham identified this as the place where Oswald was killed by Penda. In this connection he tells a strange tale. Before Oswald's brother Oswiu arrived to retrieve the martyr's arms and head which had been impaled on stakes by the pagan King Penda, a great bird of the crow family, previously unseen in those parts, had taken the right arm into a neighbouring ash tree. On Oswiu's appearance, however, the bird dropped the arm on to a stone from which there at once appeared a spring which cushioned the arm's fall.[31] The historian Erich Hoffmann has seen in the references here to an ash tree and a large bird of the crow family, possibly a raven, evidence for the survival of quasi-pagan traditions about Oswald, for both the ash tree and the raven were sacred to the Germanic pagan god Woden.[32] Be that as it may, it seems certain that the story is evidence for popular veneration of Oswald at Oswestry in the late twelfth century. Reginald says that the tree was called St Oswald's Tree and had curative properties, as also did the spring. The spring is referred to as the Fount of St Oswald in a thirteenth-century document,

28   *Willelmi Malmesbiriensis De Gestis Pontificum*, IV, 180; ed. Hamilton, pp. 317-18; and *Willelmi Malmesbiriensis Monachi De Gestis Regum Anglorum Libri Quinque*, I, 49; ed. W. Stubbs (2 vols, RS, 1887-9), I, pp. 52-4.

29   See Binns below, pp. 245-71.

30   R. C. Hope, *The Legendary Lore of the Holy Wells of England, including Rivers, Lakes, Fountains, and Springs* (London 1893), pp. 84-5.

31   Reginald, *VO* I, 12-19 (pp. 350-9).

32   E. Hoffmann, *Die heiligen Könige bei den Angelsachsen und den skandinavischen Völkern: Königsheiler und Königshaus* (Neumünster 1975), pp. 31-8.

and it was apparently still curing local people in the early nineteenth century. Over the site of the martyrdom, the local inhabitants had by Reginald's time built a 'white church'.[33]

One of the miracle accounts in the earlier Durham Life referred to above provides evidence for a popular cult of the saint at Farnham, presumably the place of that name in Yorkshire which has a church dedicated to St Oswald.[34] Many cures are said to have happened there. A miracle story is related in which a stranger in clerical habit came to Farnham when the priest and the caretaker of the church were away. He took the key to the church from the priest's house, let himself into the church, and stole everything inside the church and on the altar. As he was making his escape, however, he went blind and, after spending the day in distress and confusion, he was met by the priest himself who was thus able to recover the stolen goods thanks, it was thought, to the intercession of St Oswald.

II

Why then did Oswald enjoy such popularity in post-Conquest England? Why was his cult a success where those of his fellow Northumbrian royal saints Edwin and Oswine were not? The evidence suggests that the momentum of pre-Conquest cults of Anglo-Saxon saints was increased by the Norman Conquest and the accompanying developments in the English church. This was not the view of the great monastic historian David Knowles who wrote that 'the Norman abbots, it seems, frequently outraged the feelings of their monks by their disrespectful attitude towards the Old English saints.'[35] More recently, however, it has been convincingly shown by Susan Ridyard that, on the contrary, the continental churchmen who dominated the English church in the late eleventh and early twelfth centuries were only too anxious to develop and exploit the traditions and cults of Anglo-Saxon saints. Thus at Ely, Peterborough, Bury St Edmunds, and many other churches including Durham itself in 1104, we see sumptuous translations of the relics of Anglo-Saxon saints into the vast new Norman churches of the post-Conquest period.[36]

There were of course dislocations in the course of the Conquest and its aftermath, and the case of the abbey of Peterborough illustrates both this and the positive attitude of Norman abbots towards Anglo-Saxon saints and their relics. The abbey was embroiled in political and military affairs, for its abbot

[33] Hope, *Legendary Lore*, pp. 143-5.
[34] Trinity O.3.55, fols. 65[r-v]; Binns, below, p. 261.
[35] D. Knowles, *The Monastic Order in England* (Cambridge 1966), pp. 118-19.
[36] S. Ridyard, 'Condigna veneratio: post-conquest attitudes to the saints of the Anglo-Saxons', in *Proceedings of the Battle Conference 1986*, ed. R. Allen Brown (Anglo-Norman Studies 9; Woodbridge 1987), pp. 179-206; and D. Rollason, *Saints and Relics in Anglo-Saxon England* (Oxford 1989), pp. 215-39.

Leofric had died with the English army in 1066 and his successor Brand (1066-9) was an uncle of the English rebel Hereward the Wake. After his premature death, a Norman warrior-abbot called Turold was imposed on the abbey. While he was absent with his knights, Hereward the Wake and his Danish allies attacked Peterborough, fired and looted the abbey, and abducted the prior and some of the monks – and also some relics including the arm of St Oswald – and held them captive at Ely. The prior, however, was a match for his captors. Secretly obtaining a hammer and tools, he waited for them to fall into drunken revelry, broke open the chest containing the relics and concealed them, including the arm of St Oswald, in the straw of his bed, and later arranged for them to be sent for safe keeping to Ramsey. The prior was clearly a resourceful man, but the real interest of the story lies in its sequel. When the monks of Ramsey unscrupulously declined to return the relics, which they wished to keep for their own church, it was the Norman abbot of Peterborough, Turold, who secured their return, threatening that otherwise he would burn their church down.[37]

If Anglo-Saxon saints' cults were promoted rather than inhibited by the Norman Conquest, there were also particular reasons why the cult of St Oswald should have flourished. First amongst these was the considerable celebrity Oswald enjoyed in the pre-Conquest period. He was assigned a prominent position by Bede, and there are clear indications of an important pre-Conquest cult devoted to him at Bardney, then Gloucester, Bamburgh, to some extent at Lindisfarne, and also perhaps at ancient churches such as Winwick.[38] Moreover, the feast of St Oswald appears in almost all English calendars of the eleventh century and earlier, indicating as widespread a liturgical cult as in the post-Conquest period.[39]

The importance of the saint's prominence in Bede's work can only have been increased by the renewed interest in that writer's *Ecclesiastical History of the English People* in late eleventh- and twelfth-century England. Many manuscripts of the work survive from that period, and we are told that influential figures such as Aldwin, the monk who refounded Bede's Jarrow in the late eleventh century, and William of St Calais, the second post-Conquest bishop of Durham, were inspired by reading it.[40] Interest in Bede would naturally have increased the veneration of Oswald as one of his principal heroes.

In addition to all this, however, the cult of Oswald benefited from the support of powerful and influential churches. We have looked already at the importance of the arm of St Oswald at the abbey of Peterborough. We need

37 Rollason, op. cit., pp. 221-2, and *Chron. Hugh Candidus*, ed. Mellows, pp. 76-83.
38 See above, pp. 100-7, 120-2, 134-9; on Winwick, see also below, p. 173.
39 See Thacker, above, p. 124 and n. 168.
40 R. H. C. Davis, 'Bede after Bede', in *Studies in Medieval History for R. Allen Brown*, ed. C. Harper-Bill, C. J. Holdsworth and J. L. Nelson (Woodbridge 1989), pp. 103-16; *HDE* III, 21 and IV, 2 (pp. 108, 120).

now to turn to the church of Augustinian canons at Nostell near Pontefract in Yorkshire. The early history of this church is obscure, but it appears that around the year 1100 a group of hermits was granted permission to settle there. They rapidly attracted benefactions from local potentates such as the de Lacy family, from donors elsewhere in England, and from the king himself, and by 1119 they were describing themselves as 'regular canons'. In 1122 King Henry I's chaplain and confessor visited the north with the king and was so impressed by what he found at Nostell that he joined the community and became its prior. Nostell therefore enjoyed patronage at the highest level, and together with the active support of Archbishop Thurstan of York, it became a wealthy and influential house with numerous churches under its dominion.[41] It was also very closely connected with the cult of St Oswald. As we have seen, it seems to have claimed possession of relics of the martyr which were the object of a pilgrimage as late as the sixteenth century.[42] Nothing is known of how these relics were acquired. It is possible that they were somehow connected with the origins of the community, for already in a confirmation of its land in 1120-2 the woods which it owned are referred to as the 'woods of St Oswald', indicating that the community already had a close interest in the saint.[43] Moreover, in the early twelfth century it received a gift of the church of St Oswald at Winwick in Makerfield (Lancashire), the site (as we noted above) of a well of St Oswald and a church which may well have been an early centre of his cult, since already in Domesday Book it appears as the church of St Oswald.[44] In addition, King Henry I granted Nostell the reversion of the church of Bamburgh; this was the place where Oswald's arms had been preserved and where traditions of a close association with the saint were still prominent, to judge from the story told by Reginald of how the head was taken from Lindisfarne to Bamburgh and then removed thence to be placed in the coffin of St Cuthbert.[45] This can only have increased Nostell's interest in Oswald, especially as the church of Bamburgh was a very wealthy one and must have

[41] See Binns, below, p. 264.

[42] See above, n. 24.

[43] *EYC*, III, 128 (no. 1425).

[44] Ibid., III, 132 (no. 1428); Domesday Book, fol. 269b (i.e. fol. 269^v, col. b), on which see VCH *Lancashire*, I, p. 280; Thacker, above, p. 121. (The pre-Conquest sculpture at Winwick, once thought to represent Oswald, is now thought to show the death of Isaiah; see Bailey, *VAS*, pp. 159-60 and, for the earlier view, VCH *Lancashire*, I, pp. 262-3.) Lythe, in the North Riding of Yorkshire, which was also granted to Nostell in the twelfth century, may possibly have had an ancient association with Oswald (see Cambridge, above, pp. 140-3), though the direct evidence for the Oswald dedication is late medieval (see below, Binns, p. 263).

[45] *EYC*, III, p. 128 (no. 1424); and Reginald, *VO* I, 13, II, 47, 49 (pp. 351, 373-4, 375-8). See Cambridge, above, pp. 134-8, and Bailey, below, pp. 197-9.

ranked highly among Nostell's possessions.[46] Nor was the canons' interest in Oswald restricted to property. By another grant of Henry I, they received the right to hold a fair at Nostell during the two days before St Oswald's feast.[47]

It is not easy to interpret the evidence provided by the case of Nostell. It may be that, as Donald Nicholl suggested, the community was 'borne aloft on the surge of devotion to St Oswald' caused by the discovery of his head at Durham in 1104.[48] But the community's role in the development of Oswald's cult may have been more positive, using its considerable resources to revive, amplify, and focus on itself traditions associated with the ancient sites of Winwick and Bamburgh. It is notable in this connection that the archbishop of York, Thurstan, was a moving force in the development of Nostell. By the early twelfth century, the archbishops of York were also in control of St Oswald's, Gloucester, where Thurstan seems to have been responsible for rebuilding the church and his successor Henry Murdac (1147-53) for reconstituting the community as Augustinian canons. It is possible therefore that Thurstan himself was behind the exploitation of the cult of Oswald to enhance the fame and prestige of both Nostell and St Oswald's, Gloucester.[49]

Much more clearly documented is the case of the cathedral of Durham, where, as we have seen, interest in the cult of St Oswald was especially strong. The monks of Durham had a particular view of the importance of the saint to them which their early twelfth-century historian Symeon spelled out at the beginning of his history:

> This venerable church derived its status and its divine religion from the fervent faith in Christ of the former glorious king of the Northumbrians and estimable martyr Oswald. In praise of God and under his perpetual guardianship it preserves those relics of devout veneration, the undecayed body of the most saintly father Cuthbert and the venerable head of that same king and martyr Oswald, both lodged in a single shrine. Although for various reasons this church no longer stands in the place where Oswald founded it, nevertheless by virtue of the constancy of its faith, the dignity and authority of its episcopal throne, and the status of the dwelling-place of monks established there by the king himself and by Bishop Aidan, it is still the very same church founded by God's command.[50]

In short, the monks regarded Oswald as quite simply the founder – with Bishop Aidan – of their church. Now, the Durham historical tradition was

---

[46] Its income in 1292 was £230, although this was probably reduced as a result of Scottish raids in 1297; see D. Knowles and R. N. Hadcock, *Medieval Religious Houses in England and Wales* (London 1971), p. 145, and references therein.

[47] *EYC*, III, p. 139 (no. 1433).

[48] D. Nicholl, *Thurstan Archbishop of York (1114-1140)* (York 1964), pp. 131-4.

[49] Ibid., pp. 123-37.

[50] *HDE* I, 1 (pp. 17-18).

that the community of Lindisfarne had in 875 fled with the body of St Cuthbert, the head of St Oswald, and the relics of St Aidan and others first to Chester-le-Street and then to Durham in 995.[51] The church of Durham in the post-Conquest period was very anxious to present itself as the direct successor by these means of the church of Lindisfarne, even though in fact the introduction of Benedictine monks from Jarrow to Durham in 1083 and the consequent expulsion of the former community of clerks at Durham had created an almost complete discontinuity in its history.[52] This accounts for the importance to them of Oswald as well as of their other early saints Aidan and Cuthbert. Oswald's role as founder was not only described in Symeon's writing, but also represented in images and words in the late medieval painted glass of the cathedral which had under an image of St Oswald the inscription: 'St Oswald, founder of this church and of the episcopal see and the community of monks which were formerly on Lindisfarne but which are now in Durham.'[53]

The same purpose was served by associating Oswald as closely as possible with Cuthbert, the church's principal saint and a late seventh-century bishop of Lindisfarne. As we have seen, Symeon does this at the beginning of his history, and he emphasises it towards the end in a passage describing the flight of the Durham community to Lindisfarne for fear of the wrath of William the Conqueror. According to this an old man was sent back to spy out the land and he had a vision as follows:

'I was taken to Durham', he said, 'and there it seemed to me that I was standing in the church, when I saw two men of the highest authority who stood before the altar and looked towards the east. One of them was a middle-aged man, whose solemn episcopal vestments, venerable appearance, and dignified features showed him to be a very reverend bishop. The other, who stood on his right and was clad in a robe of reddish colour, had a long face, a very wispy beard, a noble stature, and the appearance of a very handsome young man. ...The young man pointed to me and in a quiet voice called me by name, asking me whether I knew the identity of that episcopal personage. When I replied that I did not know, he said: "He is your lord, that is the holy bishop Cuthbert." At once I threw myself at his feet, begging him to come to the aid of his church in its adversity. Shortly afterwards they both bowed their heads to the altar, and then together they set off first at a slow pace and then more quickly. When they had reached the door the young man went out first and proceeded a little way ahead of the bishop, who stood on the doorstep. The bishop looked round and called to me as I was following at a distance. "Tell me, Earnanus," he said, "do you know who

[51] *HDE* I, 1 – III, 5 (pp. 1-84).

[52] The question is discussed primarily in connection with St Cuthbert in Rollason, *Saints and Relics*, pp. 197-202, and A. J. Piper, 'The first generations of Durham monks and the cult of St Cuthbert', in *St Cuthbert*, pp. 437-46.

[53] *The Rites of Durham*, ed. J. T. Fowler (SS 107, 1903), p. 138.

that young man is?" "I do not know, my lord," I replied. "This," he said, "is St Oswald."[54]

This association between Cuthbert and Oswald – and also Aidan – was made in the manuscripts of Bede's *Life of St Cuthbert* from (or probably to be associated with) Durham.[55] As Alan Piper has noted, these follow the Life of Cuthbert and the Life of Oswald with a Life of Aidan composed, like that of Oswald, chiefly of passages drawn from the *Ecclesiastical History*. Durham, MS A.IV.35 even has its edges decorated with paintings of St Oswald, St Cuthbert and St Aidan.[56]

The association between Oswald and Cuthbert found tangible symbolism in the cult of relics at Durham. Already in the Old English poem on the site of Durham, written probably in the second half of the eleventh century, Oswald's pure head is set alongside St Cuthbert's body.[57] But this idea reached its clearest expression in the translation of 1104. There in the very coffin of Cuthbert was found along with other relics the head of St Oswald – severed from its body by the sword of Penda with a sweeping lateral stroke, as Reginald of Durham was careful to note in what can only be described as a forensic report on the skull. This relic alone was replaced with St Cuthbert in the coffin. The relics of other saints formerly in the coffin were enshrined separately.[58] Thus the bishop and the king were intimately linked – in Symeon's words, 'lodged in a single shrine'.[59]

This association was represented on the seal of Durham Cathedral Priory which had originally consisted of an obverse only bearing a cross and the inscription 'Seal of St Cuthbert the Bishop', but which had added to it around the year 1200 a reverse showing the head of what was meant to be a king but was in fact the head of the pagan god Jupiter with the inscription 'head of St Oswald the king'.[60]

---

54 *HDE* III, 16 (pp. 102-3).
55 See above, pp. 165-6.
56 Piper, 'First Durham monks', p. 443; *Two Lives*, pp. 21-2, 26, 31, 32-3. Although Colgrave (ibid., p. 33) tentatively suggested that these paintings were fourteenth-century, their date has never been authoritatively established.
57 Ed. Arnold, I, pp. 221-2. For the date, see H. S. Offler, 'The date of Durham (*Carmen de Situ Dunelmi*)', *Journal of English and Germanic Philology* 61 (1962), pp. 591-4. For the most recent discussion of this poem, see D. Howlett, 'The shape and meaning of the Old English poem "Durham"', in *Anglo-Norman Durham*, ed. D. Rollason, M. Harvey and M. Prestwich (Woodbridge 1994), pp. 485-95.
58 Ed. Arnold, I, pp. 247-61, translated in *Relics*, pp. 99-107; and Reginald, *VO* II, 51 (pp. 379-81); see Tudor, below, pp. 187-8.
59 See above, n. 50.
60 *Catalogue of the Seals in the Treasury of the Dean and Chapter of Durham*, ed. C. H. Hunter Blair (1911-21), p. 251, and see Bailey, below, p. 195. For the suggestion

The same association was found also in the iconography of the cathedral's decoration. The surviving twelfth-century paintings in the Galilee Chapel almost certainly show St Oswald on the left and St Cuthbert on the right flanking an altar of St Mary,[61] and the same juxtaposition was found in the later middle ages on the Neville screen. According to the *Rites of Durham*, 'right over the ... high altar were artificially placed in very fine alabaster the picture of Our Lady standing in the midst, and the picture of St Cuthbert on the one side and the picture of St Oswald on the other, being all richly gilded'.[62]

The association between the two saints was made explicit also in the development of images of St Cuthbert represented as carrying the head of St Oswald.[63] In the south aisle of the choir was a window showing on one side St Oswald with his sceptre in his hand and on the other St Cuthbert with St Oswald's head in his hand, and there were other representations of St Cuthbert with the king's head in the chapel of the Nine Altars, in the Galilee, and elsewhere in the cathedral – including probably a representation in stone on the central tower.[64] The head of St Oswald had become in effect an attribute of St Cuthbert. A symbol of the association between the two saints was also taken outside the cathedral when, in the annual processions on Ascension Day, Whit Sunday and Trinity Sunday, a silver gilt image of St Oswald was carried through Durham in company with the banner of St Cuthbert and, for good measure, the shrine of St Bede.[65]

Durham clearly had particular reason to promote and develop the cult of St Oswald for its associations with the past which Durham wished to claim as its own, and for the association which could be developed between it and St Cuthbert. In general, however, the cult of Oswald is testimony to the potential of the cults of long dead saints to play an important role in the churches of post-Conquest England, a potential clearly evident on the very eve of the protestant Reformation in Marmaduke Huby's enthusiasm for Oswald's cult.[66]

---

that the obverse may have pre-dated 1083, see Piper, 'First Durham monks', pp. 443-4.

[61] *Relics*, pp. 528-30; and see now D. Park, 'The wall-paintings in the Galilee Chapel', *Friends of Durham Cathedral, 57th Annual Report* (Durham 1990), pp. 21-34.

[62] *Rites of Durham*, ed. Fowler, p. 7.

[63] See, for example, Pl. 19.

[64] Ibid., pp. 47-8, 49, 110, 116, 117, 118, and 119, and A. I. Doyle, C. W. Gibby, and J. H. S. Wild, 'Further corrections to Dr Pevsner's *Durham*', *Transactions of the Architectural and Archaeological Society of Durham and Northumberland*, new series, 1 (1968), pp. 107-8, at p. 107. See above, p. 8.

[65] *Rites of Durham*, p. 105; cf. above, p. 168.

[66] See above, p. 164.

Reginald's Life of St Oswald

VICTORIA TUDOR

Reginald of Durham or Coldingham was the most prominent hagiographer produced by the monastery of Durham in the twelfth century. He appears to have been of English descent and his career as a monk of St Cuthbert's Community began before 1154. During the 1160s and 1170s he seems to have spent a great deal of time at Finchale, near Durham, where he cared for the elderly hermit, Godric, to whom he may have been related, and then, after the old man's death, recorded the miracles that occurred at his tomb. A fourteenth-century source connects Reginald with Durham's Scottish dependency at Coldingham and he may have spent the last part of his life there, in the years after 1188. In addition to his literary skills, there are indications that he had some knowledge of medicine.[1]

Reginald's reputation is based chiefly on two works. The first is an account of the life and miracles of his contemporary, St Godric, written in the 1160s and 1170s, if not slightly later,[2] the second a collection of miracles of St Cuthbert composed at approximately the same period.[3] These works are characterised by their length, a lack of organisation and a style which frequently lapses into verbosity. Thanks to the provision of generous quantities of incidental detail in these compositions, however, Reginald succeeds in evoking twelfth-century conditions to a remarkable degree. The *Life of St Oswald* is a secondary work by the same author.[4] It is shorter than the pieces on Godric and Cuthbert and while possessing few of the virtues of these two works demonstrates all the faults. It was probably never finished and is thoroughly unsatisfactory in a great many ways. It is not entirely lacking in a value and interest of its own, nevertheless, not least because of the light it sheds on the cult of the saint in the twelfth century.

1   For Reginald, see V. Tudor, 'Reginald of Durham and St Godric of Finchale: a study of a twelfth-century hagiographer and his major subject' (unpublished Ph.D. thesis, University of Reading, 1979), pp. 58-78.

2   The *Libellus de Vita et Miraculis S. Godrici, Heremitae de Finchale* was edited by Joseph Stevenson as SS 20 (London 1845). For this work, see Tudor, 'Reginald', pp. 79-87.

3   The *Libellus de Admirandis Beati Cuthberti Virtutibus* was published by the elder James Raine as SS 1 (London 1835). For a discussion of this miracle collection, see V. Tudor, 'The cult of St Cuthbert in the twelfth century: the evidence of Reginald of Durham', in *St Cuthbert*, pp. 447-67, at pp. 448-50.

4   A further minor work, a Life of St Ebba, the patron saint of Durham's cell of Coldingham, has been associated with Reginald. While there may be some connection, the work in its present form is not by him, however. For the Life, see Tudor, 'Reginald', pp. 97-102.

Reginald's *Life of St Oswald* is preserved in two manuscripts, a fourteenth-century one now in the Bodleian Library in Oxford, MS Fairfax 6, and a sixteenth-century copy of it now in the British Library, London, MS Harley 4843.[5] Unfortunately the only printed edition, that published by Thomas Arnold more than a century ago, has many disadvantages. The most serious is the fact that it is incomplete: thirty-six out of a total of sixty-eight chapters, that is, more than half of the Life in the Oxford manuscript, were omitted. However, Arnold also included a list of chapter headings drawn from the later London manuscript,[6] albeit without acknowledging the fact and with the addition of chapter numbers not found in the original. This does at least provide a useful guide to the material he chose not to include in his edition. We can tell that the bulk of the unprinted material relates to Oswald himself but is derived for the most part from Bede, while the remainder is not concerned with the king at all. It would appear that Arnold printed the most valuable sections of Reginald's Life and provided a reliable guide to the chapters left unprinted. Arnold also supplied his text with chapter and book numbers, which Reginald's original seems to have lacked, but which accurately reflect the writer's arrangement of his material. His edition, therefore, if far from ideal, is at least tolerable.[7]

The Life begins with an introductory letter, addressed by 'his Reginald' to Henry, the former subprior of Durham. If the recipient of the letter was the same individual as Henry, the Durham subprior, to whom the author refers elsewhere,[8] he was 'natione Teutonicus', that is, a German. He may therefore have been influenced in some way by the continental cult of the saint before coming to Durham. The letter is couched in the author's most florid style and in it Reginald declares, following the usual hagiographical convention, that he writes at Henry's insistence. The former subprior had received the first of a series of important appointments on St Oswald's feast day and, as a result, seems to have expressed an interest in the king's

---

5   Tudor, 'Reginald', pp. 354-5. For the dates of the Bodleian MS and BL Harley MS 4843, see *Two Lives*, pp. 23, 28-9.

6   This is not found in the Oxford MS. It is printed in Arnold, I, pp. 330-7, and this published version will hereafter be referred to as 'List'.

7   One should, however, be aware that Arnold's transcription appears to have been careless and unintelligent. For example, Arnold, I, p. 328 reads 'nos' (lines 19, 21) when the sense demands 'vos', and on p. 354 Arnold prints 'Oswyn' and 'Oswin' when the sense demands, and the original reads, 'Oswiu'. (I am grateful to Dr Martin Kauffman for help on this point.) Footnotes, in addition, are not always accurate. In note (a) on p. 326, for example, the editor declares that Reginald, in his introductory letter, alludes to his being the second Durham monk of that name. A more careful reading of the author's words reveals this not to be the case.

8   *Lib. Cuth.* 51, p. 107.

ancestry. Responding to his friend's curiosity Reginald has read various historical works and composed a brief account of Oswald's genealogy, which he has placed at the beginning of his text.[9]

In addition to the letter, the Life in Arnold's edition consists of sixty-eight chapters numbered consecutively but divided into three books. The first, made up of forty-four chapters, is the longest and most substantial of the three. It contains most of Reginald's information about the life of Oswald, describing, in addition to his ancestry, such aspects of his career as his exile and conversion, the baptism of his father-in-law, his victory at Heavenfield, the area under his authority and his death. A certain amount of space is also devoted to the history of his relics, that is, his head, body and two arms. Almost half of the chapters in book I seem, however, to contain nothing of significance on the saint at all. They, and even parts of the chapters devoted to Oswald, discuss members of Oswald's family and, less significantly, individuals linked more tenuously to the king. Among the relatives of Oswald introduced by Reginald are his father, Æthelfrith,[10] his son, Oethelwald, his uncle, Edwin, and his immediate predecessors, Eanfrith and Osric.[11] Space is also allotted to the eighth-century King Ceolwulf, however, merely on the grounds that he and Oswald shared a common ancestor.[12] Reginald, as we shall see, had less material for his work, especially information relating to the lifetime of his subject, than he might have liked.[13] The inclusion of this superfluous matter was no doubt a way of padding the work out and it may have been suggested to him by his friend's interest in Oswald's forebears.

[9]   Reginald, *VO, Epistola*, pp. 326-30. For the value of this letter in explaining the origin of the Life, see below, p. 183, and for Henry the former subprior, his career and his friendship with Reginald, see Tudor, 'Reginald', pp. 63, 77 and note 3. Reginald's letter may also have had a secondary purpose, that of promoting Henry's election to the priorate. The enigmatic first four lines of the letter can be interpreted as meaning that Reginald hoped Henry would one day be subprior without the prefix; cf. p. 329, lines 19 ff., which I take to express the same idea. The language of the letter is, in addition, not merely ornate, but also veiled, suggesting that some at least of what Reginald had to say would not be acceptable to all of his readers.

[10]   For example Reginald, *VO* I, 23 ('List', p. 332); I, 24, loc. cit., reading 'Ethelfridi' for the 'Alfridi' of the text; I, 25-9.

[11]   For example, Reginald, *VO* I, 4-7; I, 20; I, 28-30 and 32-4.

[12]   Reginald, *VO* I, 21, pp. 360-1; I, 22 ('List', p. 332). It is noticeable that the additional figures Reginald chose to include in book I were all members of royal families. There is very little information on ecclesiastics, for example Bishop Aidan (see Reginald, *VO* I, 5 ('List', p. 330)).

[13]   For the main reason for this, see below, pp. 184-5.

The author's original intention may have been to write no more than a single book, as there are indications that the second book of the Life is an entity separate from that which precedes it and is, as such, an afterthought.[14] Reginald's book II is significantly shorter than book I, consisting of merely twelve chapters. The book is devoted to the king himself – his relatives and others do not intrude – but material relating to Oswald's head or arms, that is, to his relics, is found in most of the chapters, rather than information about the king's life. The last lines of the book have a final ring to them,[15] so, as he wrote them, Reginald may have believed yet again that he was bringing his work to a close.

The contents of the third book present such a striking contrast to those of the two earlier sections of the work that one is led to question whether Reginald was responsible for the last part of the Life at all. The twelve chapters in this section consist of material drawn from Bede's main discussion of the saint,[16] with only two omissions.[17] The inclusion of this Bedan material, which does not appear in books I and II, must either represent a major change of heart on Reginald's part or constitute a later addition by a different individual. Neither of the manuscripts containing the Life dates from the twelfth century, so there is no possibility of saying which of these explanations is correct. Whatever took place, however, someone presumably came to feel that, irrespective of the value of Reginald's information, no account of Oswald was complete without Bede's material on the subject.[18]

There are various reasons for supposing that the Life as we have it is merely a draft rather than the completed work. Book I is an incoherent mass of undigested information. It begins sensibly enough, with a discussion of the

---

[14] In the heading to Reginald's VO II, 45 (p. 371), book II is referred to as 'sequens opus' ('the following work') and in the course of the chapter (p. 372) Reginald speaks of decanting a miracle story into 'vas aliud' ('another vessel').

[15] Reginald, VO II, 56, p. 385.

[16] Reginald, VO III, 57-68 ('List', pp. 336-7); p. 385, note (a). Cf. HE III, 2-3, pp. 214-20; III, 6, p. 230; III, 9-13, pp. 240-54; IV, 14, pp. 376-80. It is not possible to state which chapter of Bede's History Reginald used for his chapter 57. Perhaps it was HE III, 1, pp. 212-14.

[17] The accounts of Oswald's conversion and victory at Heavenfield (HE III, 1), together with the baptism of his future father-in-law Cynegils (HE III, 7), do not appear in Reginald's book III, probably because they had been discussed in book I: see VO I, 2, 6, and 35 for the saint's conversion and victory; and chapters 3 and 38 for the baptism of Cynegils. Oswald's conversion and victory at Heavenfield may figure in VO III, 57 ('List', p. 336), however.

[18] It is interesting to note that, in the 14th century, readings from Reginald's Life for use in the refectory at Durham on St Oswald's day began with the first chapter of his book III. (See the note on fol. 155ᵛ of Bodleian MS Fairfax 6.)

king's ancestry,[19] but even the events of his life do not all conform to a chronological pattern. Material on the living Oswald is not separated from information relating to his relics, while matter devoted to his family and others mingles indiscriminately with both. Book I is repetitious, in addition. The baptism of King Cynegils and the descent of Oswald's father, for example, are both described twice.[20] Furthermore, the ornate chapter which introduces the second section of the work gives a similar unfinished air to book II.[21] While some at least of this chapter may well be nothing more than polished fiction,[22] a passage towards the end claims to describe the arrangement of material at the beginning of the book.[23] The first chapters, as organised at present, do not correspond to the plan which is set out there.

What sources did the author draw on when compiling his Life? Inevitably a foundation derived from Bede's *Ecclesiastical History* underlies the whole of Reginald's work and has left its mark, in one form or another, on virtually every chapter. Setting the hagiographer's information on Oswald himself to one side for the moment, it is no surprise to find that most of his material about the king's relatives seems to have been drawn directly from Bede,[24] while other sources were employed to a far smaller degree. These minor sources were mainly works connected with Durham. The *De Primo Saxonum Adventu*, a twelfth-century Durham composition devoted to the kings of Anglo-Saxon England, was useful for royal genealogy.[25] One of the chapters which discuss King Ceolwulf of Northumbria is made up largely of quotations from the *Historia Dunelmensis Ecclesiae* attributed to Symeon,[26] but it also contains two quotations from the *Historia Regum*,[27] and a few

---

[19] Reginald, *VO* I, 1, pp. 338-40; I, 2, pp. 340-1.

[20] Reginald, *VO* I, 3, pp. 342-3; I, 38 ('List', p. 333) (the baptism of Cynegils); I, 1, pp. 338-40; I, 26, pp. 362-3 (the ancestors of Æthelfrith).

[21] Reginald, *VO* II, 45, pp. 371-3.

[22] Reginald's information about the circumstances in which book II was written (*VO* II, 45, pp. 371-2) seems to bear very little relation to anything to be found at present in the Life.

[23] Reginald, *VO* II, 45, p. 372.

[24] E.g., on Æthelfrith, cf. Reginald, *VO* I, 23-5 ('List', p. 332) with *HE* I, 34 and II, 2; on Oethelwald, cf. *VO* I, 4, 7, and 20 with *HE* III, 14, 23, 24; on Eanfrith and Osric, cf. *VO* I, 6, 32-4 with *HE* III, 1 and 9.

[25] Reginald, *VO* I, 1, pp. 338-40. Cf. *De Primo Saxonum Adventu*, Arnold, II, p. 374. Reginald, *VO* I, 1, p. 338, line 18, 'Anno nimirum ab incarnatione...', to p. 339, line 7, '...Scor et Steotheri' is virtually a direct quotation. For the *De Primo Saxonum Adventu*, see H. S. Offler, *Medieval Historians of Durham* (Inaugural Lecture, Durham 1958), pp. 11-12.

[26] Reginald, *VO* I, 21, pp. 360-1. Cf. *HDE* I, 13; II, 1, 5; Arnold, I, pp. 40, 47, 50-2.

[27] The reference to the old name of Norham comes from *HR* 89 (Arnold, II, p. 101), and the last seven lines of Reginald's chapter 21 come largely from the same source (*HR* 89; Arnold, II, p. 102).

lines remembered from the *Historia de Sancto Cuthberto*.[28] Two works unconnected with Durham seem also to have furnished information. The contribution of Henry of Huntingdon's *Historia Anglorum* may have included further material associated with Ceolwulf,[29] while, perhaps more surprisingly, Reginald allowed himself to be led astray by the *Historia Regum Britanniae* of Geoffrey of Monmouth.[30]

There are no problems regarding the date of Reginald's Life. In book II he refers to 1165 as the year in which he is writing;[31] presumably book I was composed shortly before this date. Depending on the individual responsible, book III could have been added not long afterwards or at some subsequent period.

Why was the Life composed? As we have seen, Reginald claimed in his letter that he wrote on the orders of his friend, Henry, the former subprior.[32] At the beginning of book II he tells us that he applied himself to this additional composition at the command of a certain Brother H. and writes to satisfy an obligation to a friend.[33] It is possible therefore that Henry had some role to play in the production of book I, and perhaps also of book II.[34] Another factor was of much greater significance, however: Oswald was one of the pre-eminent saints of the church of Durham. The author of the *History*

---

[28] Reginald, *VO* I, 21, p. 361, lines 18-21, 'ecclesiam quandam olim... ad Northam... transtulit.' Cf. *Historia de Sancto Cuthberto*, 9; Arnold, I, p. 201. On this work, see Craster, 'Patrimony'.

[29] Reginald, *VO* I, 4-7 ('List', p. 330); see p. 343, note (b); *VO* I, 22-5 ('List', p. 332); see p. 361, note (a). It is hard to say precisely what material Reginald borrowed from Henry of Huntingdon here, but cf. *Henrici Huntendunensis Historia Anglorum* (hereafter *Hist. Angl.*) III, 34; IV, 16; ed. T. Arnold (RS 74, 1879), pp. 91, 118.

[30] Reginald's *VO* I, 9 uses material from this work. Cf. the *Historia Regum Britanniae of Geoffrey of Monmouth*, 193-4, 197, 201-4, 206; ed. N. Wright and others (Cambridge 1984-), I, pp. 138-9, 141, 144-6. Reginald's curious use of the term Armonica/Armonia (*VO* I, 9 and 12), which on one occasion he explains as meaning the greater part of Wales, may perhaps have been inspired by some misunderstanding to which Geoffrey of Monmouth contributed. Similar forms occur in one extant manuscript of the *History of the Kings of Britain* (op. cit., p. 136, note 2; p. 145, note 3), though they refer to Brittany.

[31] Reginald, *VO* II, 55, p. 382.

[32] See p. 179, above.

[33] Reginald, *VO* II, 45, p. 372. It does not seem possible to identify the miracle which, according to this passage, Brother H. wished to see in the second part of the work.

[34] It was a commonplace of hagiography that the author had been commanded to write by some important figure (see B. Ward, *Miracles and the Medieval Mind: Theory, Record and Event, 1000-1215* (revised edition, Aldershot 1987), p. 30); but the circumstantial details that Reginald supplies when describing the inception of book I at least sound convincing.

ascribed to Symeon regarded him as one of the founders of his church,[35] and his head alone, among numerous other relics, was restored to Cuthbert's coffin after its formal opening in 1104.[36] At the same time stories relating to St Oswald were obviously in circulation,[37] and, in terms of written resources, the church of Durham appears to have possessed very little beyond the information to be found in Bede.[38] Reginald's Life was no doubt intended to equip his church with a more substantial account of one of its founders than was provided by the Anglo-Saxon historian and to set down material relating to the saint that had emerged since the *Ecclesiastical History* was composed.

Turning now to Oswald himself, what does Reginald have to say about him in books I and II[39] and how much of this information is derived from Bede? It must be stated immediately that Reginald makes absolutely no attempt in these books to incorporate Bede's well-known account of King Oswald,[40] either in full or in an abbreviated form, into his text. The author makes his aim quite plain in the heading to his first chapter. He is concerned with Oswald's ancestry, his life and manner of living, his death and the burial of his relics.[41] Elsewhere he also states that he has not wished to include miracles that have been committed to writing before.[42] In practice he had great difficulty fleshing out the skeleton he had chosen, with the result that he was forced to introduce Oswald's relatives and other, more peripheral, characters into his work. It is clear, nevertheless, that his aim was not the same as Bede's, that is, to describe Oswald's place in the great story of the genesis and development of the English church.[43] Reginald was interested in producing an account of the king as an individual in his own right, and he had obviously taken the decision to avoid using Bede's material on Oswald as far as possible.

35 *HDE* I, 1; Arnold, I, pp. 17-18. See Rollason, above, pp. 174-5.
36 *Capitula de Miraculis et Translationibus Sancti Cuthberti*, 7: Arnold, I, p. 255; Reginald, *Lib. Cuth.* 42, p. 89. Cf. Rollason, above, p. 176.
37 See below, pp. 187-8, 190-3; Rollason, above, p. 166.
38 At the time that Reginald was writing the monastery owned (apart from Bede's *Ecclesiastical History*) at least one manuscript containing a Life of St Oswald. The Life in it was derived for the most part from Bede, however. See Rollason above, pp. 165-6.
39 Book III, as we have seen, may have been a later addition and was certainly not part of Reginald's original plan for the work.
40 *HE* III, 1-3, 6-7, 9-13, and IV, 14.
41 Reginald, *VO* I, 1, p. 338.
42 Reginald, *VO* I, 43, p. 368. He was unable to keep to this intention. Cf. below, p. 193.
43 *HE*, p. xxx.

Thus, although, as was pointed out above, a Bedan substructure underlies everything that the author writes about the king, the direct use that he makes of the *Ecclesiastical History* is limited. Based directly on Bede are Reginald's description of Oswald's exile in *Scotia* and his accession,[44] his victory at Heavenfield and the death of Cadwallon,[45] the baptism of Cynegils,[46] the extent of Oswald's kingdom and, perhaps, the year added to his reign.[47] It would appear that out of a total of fifty-six chapters in the first two books of Reginald's Life only seven contain a significant element derived from Bede. To judge from the limited material available to us, furthermore, none of these 'significant elements' is of great length, and even here Reginald preferred to extract odd points, to paraphrase or to expand rather than use the wording of the original.[48]

If the author was reluctant to make much direct use of Bede, he did employ material from this source in another way. A number of chapters in the work contain Reginald's own reflections on various aspects of Oswald's life and the starting point for these is provided by details found wholly or in part in Bede. One such passage seeks to excuse the king's pagan origins and enables Reginald to compare Oswald with Abraham, Moses and Lot.[49] Inserted into a chapter devoted to the site of the saint's death is an account, almost certainly the work of Reginald, of the thoughts that passed through the king's mind as Penda confronted him.[50] There are, in addition, four chapters of figures and calculations associated with the dates of Oswald's

---

[44] Reginald, *VO* I, 2, pp. 341-2; I, 31 ('List', p. 333). Cf. *HE* III, 1 and 6.

[45] Reginald, *VO* I, 6 ('List', p. 330), reading 'Oswaldus' for 'Osdus'; I, 35 ('List', p. 333). Cf. *HE* III, 1, 2, p. 214.

[46] Reginald, *VO* I, 3, pp. 342-3; I, 38 ('List', p. 333). Cf. *HE* III, 7.

[47] Reginald, *VO* I, 36 ('List', p. 333). Cf. *HE* III, 1, 6, 9. Arnold claims (*VO*, p. 364, note (a)) that Reginald's I, 37 ('List', p. 333) is also derived from Bede but I have not been able to find a passage in the *Ecclesiastical History* that corresponds to it.

[48] It is probably to his taste for expanding on the basis of Bede's facts that we should attribute Reginald's ideas about the beliefs of Oswald's mother, Acha: see *VO* I, 2, which portrays her as a Christian at the time of Oswald's exile or even before; cf. *VO* II, 56 (p. 385). There is no evidence, however, that she was ever converted to Christianity. Again, Reginald may be inventing when he twice makes Oswald's father, Æthelfrith, responsible for the death of Ælle, his own father-in-law (*VO* I, 26, 27); I know of no other source which makes such a claim.

[49] Reginald, *VO* I, 8, pp. 344-5.

[50] Reginald, *VO* I, 14, pp. 352-3. Cf. *HE* III, 9. Reginald declares here that, just before his death, Oswald had forced Penda to flee into Wales and, feeling secure, had sent his army away (p. 352; cf. ibid., I, 12, p. 350). This sounds eminently plausible but I know of no other source which mentions it, and it may well represent another example of Reginald using his imagination.

life.[51] The symbolism of some of the numbers is explained and it is obvious that, whatever gifts Reginald possessed, he had no head for figures.[52]

In contrast to his use of Bede, Reginald had no qualms about quoting from other works. His description of the vision of St Columba which Oswald experienced just before his battle with Cadwallon is taken almost verbatim from Adomnán's Life of the Irish saint.[53] Henry of Huntingdon's *Historia Anglorum* is also followed closely for a brief account of Oswald's death.[54]

Just under a half of the chapters devoted to Oswald in Reginald's first two books contain narratives and descriptions which are derived from no obvious literary source. What is this material unique to Reginald and what does it contribute to our knowledge of the saint and his cult? In two of these chapters the author tries, perhaps surprisingly, to amplify the body of received information relating to the king himself. The first recounts a hitherto unknown incident in the king's life. It describes the prosperity of England under Oswald's rule and how this was threatened by an outbreak of plague. The king himself fell ill but when close to death experienced a vision. He was told that his prayers had released all English people from the scourge of plague and that martyrdom awaited him. As a result of the vision Oswald reformed his manner of living. Reginald declares that he translated this story from English into Latin and that he found it in a very old source, the nature of which he leaves unspecified.[55]

It is doubtful if any credence can be given to this story. It contains no concrete details; indeed there is nothing here which could not be drawn from the hagiographer's repertoire of commonplaces.[56] Oswald, in addition, rules not Northumbria but the anachronistic 'land of the English', while there seems no evidence to support the contention that the saint's reign witnessed an attack of plague. It would appear therefore that the narrative is at best a

---

51 Reginald, *VO* I, 39, 40, II, 55-6; pp. 364-6, 382-5. To quote but one example of Reginald's debt to Bede here: material on Augustine's mission on p. 364 is taken from *HE* V, 24, p. 562.

52 His greatest howler occurs in *VO* II, 55 (pp. 382-3) where, after an elaborate calculation, he declares 675 (twelve years too early), to be the date of Cuthbert's death. Likewise inspired by details in Bede is *VO* I, 19, while the author was also responsible for *VO* II, 52 and 54 ('List', p. 335), where the allegorical significance of two of Oswald's relics is explained.

53 Reginald, *VO* I, 42, p. 367. Cf. *VCol* I, 1, pp. 14-16.

54 Reginald, *VO* I, 3, p. 343. Cf. *Hist. Angl.* III, 39 (RS 74, p. 95).

55 Reginald, *VO* I, 10, pp. 346-9.

56 Robert Folz has suggested that this account merely applies to the king himself the story of the miracle which occurred at the monastery of Selsey (Folz, p. 55; cf. *HE* IV, 14, pp. 376-80), though in that the recipient of the vision dies, unlike Oswald in Reginald's narrative.

relatively late story of unknown origin or at worst pure invention.[57]

Not much more confidence is inspired by a second chapter relating to the king, which claims to describe his physical appearance. According to this Oswald was tall, with fair hair and shining blue-grey eyes. His face was long, his mouth and beard small. He possessed long limbs and broad shoulders. The king, Reginald adds, was bold and warlike but also compassionate. The writer's source for this description is strikingly similar to that for the plague story. This account was conveyed to Reginald by a certain Robert, from the hospital in York, who declared he had found it written in verse in an old English book.[58]

It is noteworthy that this description contains few convincing details and, as Robert Folz has pointed out, reflects an idealised portrait of the twelfth-century knight.[59] More damning is the debt that it owes to another physical description composed by Reginald, that of the hermit, Godric of Finchale. Godric likewise had a long face and shining blue-grey eyes, while the breadth of his shoulders was similarly taken to be a sign of strength.[60] All these factors would tend to suggest that the account of Oswald's appearance is again pure fiction. The reference to Robert from the hospital in York carries more conviction,[61] but may well merely indicate an attempt by Reginald to make his fictional description acceptable by attaching to it the name of a historical character.

The remaining chapters of new material relate to the saint's relics. These can at least claim, in varying degrees, to convey authentic traditions associated with the saint's cult in the twelfth century, if not always historical fact.

In Durham interest centred on the king's head which was found in Cuthbert's coffin at the time of the 1104 translation of his body.[62] Reginald

---

[57] The suspicion attached to this account must be extended to the chapter which follows (*VO* I, 11, p. 349), the natural sequel to the plague story. It describes the consequences of Oswald's moral reformation for his wife and is the only source known to supply her name, *Kyneburga*. King Penda of Mercia had a daughter of this name (*Cyniburga*, Cyneburh: *HE* III, 21) and it is conceivable that Reginald borrowed the name from her.

[58] Reginald, *VO* II, 50, pp. 378-9.

[59] Folz, p. 54.

[60] *Lib. God.* (op. cit. in n. 2) 100, p. 212: 'facie... producta' (*VO* II, 50, p. 378: 'facie producta'); 'oculis glaucis et... radiantibus' (*VO*: 'glaucis oculis radiantibus'); 'Humeri vero lata spissitudine se distenderant, quae fortitudinis indicio esse consuevit' (*VO*: 'In humeris vero illius plenitudo eminebat, condensae spissitudinis, quae, ut aiunt, indicium solet esse fortitudinis...').

[61] At the time that Reginald was writing there were probably two hospitals in York (see VCH *Yorkshire*, III, pp. 336, 346) and of these St Leonard's (formerly St Peter's) may have had a certain Robert as master (ibid., p. 343).

[62] *Cap. de mir.* (op. cit. in n. 36) 7: Arnold, I, p. 255; Reginald, *Lib. Cuth.* 42, p. 89.

includes a description of this relic in his Life. It was of a reddish-brown colour that resembled gold and, although large, less heavy than a person holding it would have anticipated. This feature, together with the sweet odour that emanated from it, suggests that it had been embalmed, presumably before its original burial. The head possessed a full set of teeth, while the wound that had killed the king was still visible on one side.[63] Reginald could not have seen this relic in person as it had been sealed up in Cuthbert's coffin in 1104,[64] but his description must be derived from some record made at that time. There seems no reason to doubt its essential accuracy and it deserves to be recognised as one of the reports deriving from the investigation of Cuthbert's coffin carried out in that year.[65]

Two further chapters, although widely separated in the Life, obviously form part of a single tradition relating to the head. In the first Reginald describes how a miraculous light drew attention to the grave in the churchyard on Lindisfarne where the head had been buried. Aware of this, Oswald's relatives transferred the head to the royal city of Bamburgh, where it remained for a lengthy period.[66] A later chapter explains how, many years after Oswald's death, St Cuthbert appeared to an elderly servant of his, who was dutiful in the care of his incorrupt body. The saint complained indignantly of the removal of Oswald's head from his monastery of Lindisfarne and ordered his servant to fetch it. By means of a ruse the man carried off the head and brought it to Cuthbert's tomb. At this point, as the elders of the church were in the habit of relating, the tomb opened noisily and then, once the head had been placed inside, closed again of its own accord.[67]

It is interesting to compare these narratives with some comments of Reginald's which suggest a difference of opinion in local circles about this particular relic. In the last chapter of book II the author declares that he cannot agree with those who believe Oswald's head remained on Lindisfarne from the time of its burial until the departure of Cuthbert's body about 875. It would have been too attractive to relic thieves. He prefers to accept the narrative he has already recounted but he is at pains to state that this story does not in any way conflict with the evidence of the *History of the Church of Durham*. This, he points out, merely lists the relics which left the island with Cuthbert's body; the circumstances in which they first joined it are not

---

63 Reginald, *VO* II, 51, pp. 379-81.
64 *Cap. de mir.* 7: Arnold, I, p. 255; Reginald, *Lib. Cuth.* 42, p. 89.
65 *Cap. de mir.* 7: Arnold, I, pp. 247-61; Reginald, *Lib. Cuth.* 40-3, pp. 84-90. Reginald's account of the head is followed, as was mentioned above, by a chapter in which he explains its allegorical significance (*VO* II, 52 ('List', p. 335)).
66 Reginald, *VO* I, 13, p. 351; cf. *HE* III, 12, p. 252.
67 Reginald, *VO* II, 49, pp. 375-8.

specified.[68]

Despite Reginald's protestations there is almost certainly no truth behind this story.[69] The account of the theft of the head from Bamburgh came from Reginald's friend, Ailred, abbot of Rievaulx,[70] so he can be held responsible for the entire story. The servant of St Cuthbert who carried out the theft bears a striking resemblance, furthermore, to Ailred's great-grandfather, Alfred, son of Westou. This worthy was devoted to Cuthbert, collected the relics of other saints and brought them to Durham and was associated with miraculous stories connected with Cuthbert's coffin like that with which Ailred's story ends.[71] Alfred, however, died during the pontificate of Bishop Æthelwine of Durham (1056-71)[72] and thus could not have brought Oswald's head back to Lindisfarne before 875. The most likely explanation for this story is that it represents a tradition that had grown up in Ailred's family and was probably designed to increase the prestige of his great-grandfather. Reginald, who wrote about Alfred elsewhere[73] and cannot have been ignorant of the identity of Cuthbert's servant, must have included this story out of respect for his friend and indeed it may have circulated independently of the *Life of St Oswald*.

Only one chapter in Reginald's work is devoted to Oswald's body. This begins with a summary of Bede's account of the reception of the body at the monastery of Bardney and refers to two stone crosses which were placed one at each end of the saint's tomb. With the passage of time the guardians of the body became slothful and careless. Gradually most of the bones were dispersed, both within England and abroad, through the agency, Reginald seems rather surprisingly to suggest, of the Vikings. Only three small bones remained but, despite their small size, the water in which they had been washed was extremely efficacious against fevers.[74]

The seventh-century monastery of Bardney seems to have been destroyed in the 860s and in 909 the king's body was transferred to a new church dedicated to him in Gloucester. The new Benedictine house of Bardney was

68   Reginald, *VO* II, 56, pp. 384-5: cf. *HDE* II, 6; Arnold, I, p. 57.
69   For an alternative view, see Bailey, below, pp. 197-9.
70   Reginald, *VO* II, 49, p. 378. In the text Reginald merely describes his source as 'the lord of Rievaulx'; but the years of Ailred's abbacy at Rievaulx (1147-67) fit well with the date of Reginald's *Life of St Oswald*, c.1165, and he was a close friend of Reginald, contributing in various ways to the author's other works: see Tudor, 'Reginald', pp. 76 and note 4, 80, 87-8.
71   For Alfred, see *HDE* III, 7, and Reginald, *Lib. Cuth.* 16 and 26.
72   *HDE* III, 7; Arnold, I, p. 87.
73   See n. 71 above.
74   Reginald, *VO* I, 43, pp. 368-9; cf. *HE* III, 11, p. 246.

not founded until the reign of William the Conqueror.[75] It seems highly unlikely that authentic traditions or relics could have survived from the earlier house, but the post-Conquest monastery may well have seen fit to equip itself with a history and some relics of its saint of more doubtful origin. Reginald may be repeating here some official Bardney account of the contemporary cult and its history.[76]

Material relating to Oswald's right arm is supplied in greater measure. Six chapters, which almost form a continuous narrative,[77] are devoted to Oswestry in Shropshire and describe Oswald's death, which Reginald obviously believed took place there, and traditions associated with his relics, especially his right arm. Reginald describes in some detail the location of Oswestry, which he always refers to as 'Maserfeld', and mentions the 'white church', dedicated to Oswald, which stood there.[78] Nearby were to be found Oswald's well or spring and a huge ash tree, also named after the saint. These were located close to the place where the king's head and arms remained fixed to stakes for a year after his death, and wood from these stakes was still preserved in the locality.[79] Reginald goes on to describe the vision in which Oswald's brother, Oswiu, was commanded to retrieve these relics.[80] The right arm, however, had been carried off by a great bird to an ancient ash tree. The arm, which enjoyed the gift of incorruption thanks to Aidan's prophecy, conferred on the tree a renewed freshness and vigour, which it never subsequently lost. The bird let its booty fall, however, and where the arm struck the ground, the spring burst forth.[81] Oswiu carried the relics away with him, but the tree and the spring still demonstrated the saint's miraculous power even in Reginald's time. No one damaged the tree with impunity, while the sick received healing from its shade or by touching or even tasting its leaves. Water from the spring similarly had healing properties, releasing the possessed from their affliction and curing all manner

---

[75]   VCH *Lincolnshire*, II, p. 97; VCH *Gloucestershire*, II, p. 84. Cf. *The Anglo-Saxon Chronicle*, ed. D. Dumville and S. Keynes (Cambridge 1986-), IV (MS B), p. 49, s.a. 909; Thacker, above, p. 120; Binns, below, p. 253.

[76]   The monasteries of Durham and Bardney are known to have entered into a prayer agreement which indicates contact between them and may date from this period (*Liber Vitae Ecclesiae Dunelmensis*, ed. J. Stevenson (SS 13, London 1841), p. 136). Cf. Rollason, above, p. 169.

[77]   Reginald, *VO* I, 12, p. 350; I, 14-18, pp. 352-8.

[78]   Reginald, *VO* I, 12 and 14, pp. 350, 352-3; cf. *VO* I, 3. On the question of *Maserfelth*'s identification with Oswestry, see Stancliffe, above, pp. 84-96.

[79]   Reginald, *VO* I, 12 and 17-18, pp. 350, 355-8. Cf. *HE* III, 12.

[80]   Reginald, *VO* I, 15, p. 354.

[81]   Reginald, *VO* I, 17-18, pp. 355-8; cf. *HE* III, 6, p. 230. See also Rollason, above, pp. 170-1.

of ailments.[82]

There is no doubt that some at least of the information contained in these chapters is reliable. The site of Oswestry is described more or less accurately;[83] and the 'white church', together with the estates dependent on it, were in the possession of the abbey of Shrewsbury, as Reginald states.[84] The description of the supernatural powers vested in the tree and spring may also be grounded in genuine local beliefs: these natural features are unlikely to have attained a measure of celebrity unless they were credited with exceptional properties. Even the bird, the most fanciful element in Reginald's narrative, may well reflect popular belief rather than the author's imagination, as it was necessary to explain the existence of the apparently ageless tree and the spring. A quite striking measure of agreement exists between Reginald's evidence and that of the sixteenth-century traveller, John Leland, who visited Oswestry almost four hundred years later. Leland noted the church formerly known as 'the White Minster' and St Oswald's well in the fields outside the town. He had even heard the story of the 'eagle' which carried off the king's arm.[85] It is possible, of course, that local people had been influenced in some way by information contained within Reginald's Life, perhaps through the agency of the monks of Shrewsbury Abbey. (After all, they probably represent the most likely route by which this information on Oswestry reached Durham.) It is equally reasonable to suppose that both Reginald and Leland were drawing on the same local tradition, and this is probably the more likely explanation, given that we can quite easily account for the least credible elements in the story.[86] Thus at Oswestry the cult seems to have become entangled with older, more primitive beliefs and to have adopted a rather colourful form.[87]

Further material on the king's arms is provided by two consecutive chapters in book II. The first contains a garbled version of Bede's information on this subject.[88] According to Reginald, Queen Bebba, from whom the

[82] Reginald, *VO* I, 17-18, pp. 357-8.
[83] Reginald, *VO* I, 12 and 14. Chapter 14 includes an interesting account of Offa's Dyke (p. 353).
[84] See *Ctl. Shrewsbury*, I, p. 135.
[85] *The Itinerary of John Leland*, ed. L. Toulmin Smith (5 vols.; London 1907-10; reprinted 1964), III, pp. 74-5.
[86] This is not to suggest that Reginald did not make his own additions to the information that he had received about Oswestry. As was said above (p. 185), the account of Oswald's thoughts as he faced Penda is almost certainly by Reginald as are other descriptive passages (*VO* I, 17, pp. 356-7: St Oswald's ash tree; I, 18, p. 358: the emergence of the spring). The accounts of Oswiu's vision and the heavenly being who spoke to him (*VO* I, 15-16) are probably the products of Reginald's imagination: the narrative does not require them.
[87] See Thacker above, pp. 102-3; Jansen below, pp. 234-5.

royal city of Bamburgh derived its name, claimed the king's arms and enclosed them in a silver reliquary in the church of St Peter in the 'city' (*civitas*). There they remained for some time, the object of the greatest veneration. Both arms enjoyed the gift of incorruption and had retained not only their bones but also their flesh, nerves and blood vessels. The next chapter speaks of the decay of Bamburgh in more recent times. Just as it had exchanged its former glory for rustic isolation, so too the relics of Oswald had come to be neglected. A monk of Peterborough who was visiting the area noted this state of affairs and at length carried off the right arm and returned with it to his church. This act benefited both saint and church, as Oswald became the object of increased veneration, while the church of Peterborough received increased benefactions from the faithful.[89]

It is hardly necessary to point out that Bede had claimed the gift of incorruption for the king's right arm alone and that Bebba, who may have been the first wife of King Æthelfrith,[90] is most unlikely to have been associated with Oswald's relics in any way. In the second of the two chapters Reginald is at pains to excuse the theft of the arm and this indulgent attitude suggests that this material may well have originated in Peterborough itself.[91] In the twelfth century the monks of that house certainly believed themselves to be in possession of the king's right arm.[92] In this case Reginald's material may represent some Peterborough tradition recounting the history of their relic. Quite possibly the detailed (but unprinted) description of the right arm contained in a third chapter in book II was derived from the same source as these two narratives.[93]

[88] Reginald, *VO* II, 47, pp. 373-4. Cf. *HE* III, 6 and 12; Thacker, above, pp. 100-1.
[89] Reginald, *VO* II, 48, pp. 374-5. Cf. Rollason above, pp. 168, 171-2.
[90] *HE*, p. 231, note 3.
[91] At one point Reginald refers to the earlier name of Peterborough which he gives as 'Middilhame' (*VO* II, 48, p. 374). This is of course a mistake, Peterborough being known earlier as 'Medeshamstede' (E. Ekwall, *The Concise Oxford Dictionary of English Place-Names* (4th edn; Oxford 1960), p. 364), and tends to cast doubt on the idea of a Peterborough provenance for this material. Reginald may have believed, however, that the element 'Mede' carried the meaning 'middle' (cf. Bishop Middleham, not far from Durham). In any case this comment was probably an insertion made by Reginald into material derived essentially from Peterborough.
[92] See *The Chronicle of Hugh Candidus*, ed. W. T. Mellows (London 1949), pp. 52, 70 (where the thief who brought the arm from Bamburgh is named as 'Winegot'), 83, 105, 106-7; Rollason, above, p. 168.
[93] Reginald, *VO* II, 53 ('List', p. 335). This description is followed by Reginald's account of the allegorical significance of the arm (*VO* II, 54 ('List', p. 335)). Durham and Peterborough shared a prayer agreement which may date from this period (above, n. 76) and would denote communication between the two houses. Despite Arnold's statement (*VO*, p. 381, note (a)), there seems no evidence to

Finally, an incident involving Oswald's left arm and lesser relics is described at the end of book I.[94] The setting is the city of Gloucester where the church of St Oswald was richly endowed, and, thanks to the innumerable miracles performed by the saint, held in very high esteem.[95] The church possessed the saint's left arm together with some of his hair, which had arrived there long before, and Reginald's account describes a miracle which occurred when these relics were transferred to a new reliquary by Archbishop Thomas II of York (1108/9-14). Those present, Reginald declares, experienced an inexpressibly delightful fragrance which made them forget earthly cares and pleasures, as though inebriated with heavenly joys. Somewhat disconcertingly Reginald writes in this chapter as though present at the ceremony, but in fact he almost certainly borrowed its contents – copying presumably word for word – from some miracles associated with an earlier Life of the saint.[96] This account may well be an accurate record of what was believed to have taken place.

What does this information, much of which may be oral rather than literary in origin, tell us of Oswald's cult in this period? Reginald's evidence shows that the saint was not lacking in attention and veneration at a number of different centres. It is noticeable, however, that much of this information is historical in character, that is, it recounts events that led to the veneration of Oswald in a particular locality, rather than providing evidence for the contemporary cult. Reginald expresses an interest in recently-performed miracles on two occasions,[97] but the story of the events that occurred in Gloucester is the only example that he provides and by the time he was writing it was probably at least fifty years old. The absence of contemporary miracles is striking and the reason for it is perhaps to be sought in the nature of Oswald's cult as it developed at Durham. Both the account of the royal head and Ailred's narrative bear witness to the subordination of the cult of

---

suggest that Durham ever claimed an arm of the saint. Admittedly, *HDE* I, 2, declares that the Durham monk Swartebrand had often seen it (Rollason, above, p. 168), but he does not explain where and it is not mentioned in the monastery's relic lists. (For these, see *Relics*, pp. 113-14; *Extracts from the Account Rolls of the Abbey of Durham*, ed. J. T. Fowler (3 vols; SS 99, 100, 103, Durham 1898-1900), II, pp. 425-40; *Historiae Dunelmensis Scriptores Tres*, ed. J. Raine (SS 9; London 1839), Appendix, no. 331, pp. ccccxxvi-xxx.)

[94] Reginald, *VO* I, 44, pp. 369-70. Rollason, above, p. 169.

[95] See Thacker, above, p. 120. Reginald makes no mention of the church possessing the body of the saint.

[96] For this short Life of Oswald, based largely on Bede, see Rollason, above, pp. 165-6. It is highly unlikely that Reginald was in Gloucester between 1108 and 1114 and therefore he almost certainly copied his account of the translation miracle from this short Life.

[97] Reginald, *VO* I, 43, p. 368; II, 45, p. 372.

Oswald there to that of Cuthbert, a subordination which found expression in the iconography of the two saints.[98] In his *Life of St Oswald* Reginald certainly wished to bring honour to the king and martyr, but not too much honour. He may well have felt that, while it was useful for his church to possess additional material about one of its major saints, nothing – and especially not the evidence of continued, active involvement in human affairs provided by contemporary miracles – should be allowed to threaten, even to the smallest degree, the overwhelming predominance of Cuthbert. Whatever happened elsewhere, at Durham Priory the cult of St Oswald, overshadowed as it was by that of Cuthbert, would never be more than a stunted growth.

[98] See Rollason above, p. 177; Pl. 19.

St Oswald's Heads

RICHARD N. BAILEY

I

When the Lysons brothers published their Cumberland volume of *Magna Britannia* in 1816 they remarked upon the paucity of medieval glass in the county. Some of it had disappeared comparatively recently and, as an example, they illustrated a figure from a window at Edenhall showing a bishop, with pastoral staff and mitre, carrying a crowned and bearded human head in his left hand (Fig. 7).[1] This particular window was probably of fourteenth-century date and we now recognise its iconography as that of St Cuthbert carrying the severed head of King Oswald. There are numerous examples of analogous figural arrangements known from the late medieval period. Durham Priory seals of the fourteenth and fifteenth centuries, for instance, carry several depictions whilst the *Rites of Durham* of 1593 lists frequent occurrences among the now lost medieval glass of the cathedral.[2] Still surviving in the feretory at Durham are the battered remnants of a fourteenth-century statue of this type and Henry VII's Chapel in Westminster Abbey houses a similar effigy dating to the sixteenth century. Nineteenth-century glass in the great hall of Durham Castle and the 1880s reredos of Newcastle Cathedral provide further, more recent, examples of the same theme.

What is visually expressed here is a union of two Northumbrian saints, who, though not living at the same period, had been yoked together in order to justify the spiritual authority of the priory church at Durham which sheltered their mortal remains. Twelfth- and thirteenth-century sources are quite clear on this issue. A Durham Priory seal introduced under Prior Bertram (died 1213), for example, carries on one face a cross and the legend *sigillum cudberhti praesulis sci* ('seal of Bishop Cuthbert, saint') whilst the reverse uses an antique gem of Jupiter Serapis and labels it *caput sancti oswaldi regis* ('head of St Oswald, king').[3] A century earlier, between 1104 and 1107,

---

[1] D. and S. Lysons, *Magna Britannia*, IV, *Cumberland* (London 1816), p. cxcii.

[2] W. Greenwell and C. Hunter Blair, 'Durham seals', *Archaeologia Aeliana*, 3rd series, 15 (1918), pp. 115-204, at pp. 167-71. *Rites of Durham*, ed. J. T. Fowler (SS 107, 1903), pp. 109-22; extracts of the relevant material are printed in J. Raine, *St Cuthbert, with an Account of the State in which his Remains were found upon the Opening of his Tomb in Durham Cathedral, in the year 1827* (Durham 1828), pp. 169-72.

[3] Greenwell and Hunter Blair, 'Durham seals', no. 3427. For date see A. J. Piper, 'The first generation of Durham monks and the cult of St Cuthbert', in *St Cuthbert*, pp. 437-46, at p. 444.

Figure 7: St Cuthbert Holding Oswald's Head. Engraving of stained glass formerly in St Cuthbert's church, Edenhall, Cumberland.

Symeon of Durham had made the same point in the opening words of the first chapter of his *Historia Dunelmensis Ecclesiae*:

> From the most fervent faith in Christ of Oswald, glorious former king of the Northumbrians and precious martyr, this holy church, which, in praise of God and his perpetual protection, keeps lodged in a single container those relics of sacred veneration, the incorrupt body of the most holy father Cuthbert and the venerable head of that king and martyr, takes the origin of its position and sacred religion ...[4]

My concern here is with the earlier of these two saints whose relics were so central to Durham's ecclesiastical history. Specifically I wish to focus on the orthodox belief that St Cuthbert's shrine at the east end of the cathedral still contains the head of St Oswald, who died in the battle of *Maserfelth* in 642.

[4]   *HDE* I, 1 (pp. 17-18). For another pairing of these saints in protection of Durham, see the story of Gillomichael in *HDE* III, 16. A church jointly dedicated to the saints is recorded in *HR*, *s.a.* 788 (p. 52); this very early linking probably reflects the impact of Hexham and its Oswald interests, for which see Thacker, above, p. 113 (and cf. pp. 107-11), and Cambridge, above, pp. 128-9.

II

The documentary and archaeological evidence for the history of this Durham head relic is intriguingly complex. Bede tells us that, after the battle, Oswald's body was dismembered and the head placed on a stake. In the following year it was recovered by Oswiu and interred in a 'burial place (*cymiterio*) at the church of Lindisfarne'.[5] Bede himself then shows no further interest in the head, choosing to focus instead on the enshrinement of the incorrupt right arm at Bamburgh, the problems encountered by Osthryth and Æthelred when they tried to introduce other relics of St Oswald to Bardney in Lincolnshire, and miracles associated with the cross erected at Heavenfield and with the stake on which the head had been impaled.[6] We have to wait for Symeon's *Historia Dunelmensis Ecclesiae* to provide the next part of the conventional narrative. He claims, on the basis of written authority (*ut in veteribus libris invenitur*), that when the Cuthbert Community fled Lindisfarne *c.*875 under the threat of Viking disruption, they took with them in St Cuthbert's reliquary-coffin 'the head of Oswald which had formerly been buried in the cemetery of that same church ...'.[7] The head thus joined St Cuthbert's body in that peripatetic phase of the Community's life which eventually brought it, after a lengthy sojourn at Chester-le-Street, to Durham *c.*995.

Symeon's account of the post-Bedan history of the relic is thus clear and seemingly authoritative. It may even be true. Yet his version of events is not the only one to survive among medieval Durham sources, and there are two variant narratives which are particularly relevant to our concerns here. The first relies upon a statement in the *Historia de Sancto Cuthberto*, a document descending from a tenth-century archetype which is, however, supported by a list of saints' resting places which may go back a century earlier.[8] These two sources, which are also picked up later by Reginald of Durham, suggest that, far from leaving Lindisfarne under Viking threat *c.*875, the Community had already moved to Norham during the period of Bishop Ecgred (830-46) and had taken Cuthbert's body with them.[9] This may well be a more accurate record than that preserved by Symeon, for it is easy to see why it should be suppressed in favour of a version which more closely linked the Benedictine monks of Durham with the island home of their Anglo-Saxon

5   *HE* III, 13 (p. 252). Cf. Thacker above, pp. 101-2.
6   *HE* III, 2, 9-13; IV, 14 (pp. 214-18, 242-54, 377-80).
7   *HDE* II, 6 (p. 57).
8   *Historia de S. Cuth.* §9, ed. Arnold I, p. 201; D. W. Rollason, 'Lists of saints' resting places in Anglo-Saxon England', *ASE* 7 (1978), pp. 61-93, at pp. 64, 68. For a discussion of the Norham episode see Craster, 'Patrimony', pp. 187-8.
9   Reginald's treatment can be found in *VO* I, 21, p. 361. For the date, see Craster, 'Patrimony', pp. 177-8.

predecessors. Yet, if we accept the Norham episode and assume that Symeon and others were correct in believing that Oswald's head was in Durham by the early twelfth century, when was it removed from the island? Was it translated in Ecgred's time to Norham or collected from Lindisfarne when the monks finally left the area in the ninth century? Was it even abandoned on the island until a much later period?

To complicate matters further we have yet another possibility presented by the second variant on Symeon's story. This comes to us in the *Vita Sancti Oswaldi* written by Reginald of Durham *c.*1165, which refers in three separate chapters to the removal of Oswald's head from Lindisfarne to Bamburgh and its eventual re-acquisition by the Cuthbert Community.[10] Now, there are certainly various fabulous elements permeating Reginald's account and, consequently, there are undoubted attractions in subscribing to Plummer's dismissal of the whole story as 'foolish and legendary'.[11] Yet, whilst one can see how a 'Bamburgh connection' might have evolved by confusion with the history of the arm-relic,[12] it is *just* possible that Reginald has caught a piece of genuine information, because the royal dynasty does seem to have developed rather more enthusiasm for the Oswald cult than appears to be evidenced at Lindisfarne; witness, for example, the curious fact that no miracles were recorded in connection with the head during the period before the early ninth century when the Cuthbert Community apparently had the skull in its care. Reginald's story therefore deserves more attention than it has hitherto received.

As we examine Reginald's account, however, we are faced with difficult chronological issues. It is noticeable that, in his narrative sections, Reginald is totally vague about the dates of the removal of the head from Lindisfarne and its re-acquisition by the Community. He describes the removal as being the work of unspecified 'relatives' of Oswald (chapter 13) and of 'the successors of Oswiu' (chapter 49), whilst the precise location of Cuthbert's shrine when the skull was returned is left intriguingly uncertain; on the basis of the text, it could have been at Lindisfarne, Norham, Chester-le-Street, or Durham. Only in his final summary in chapter 56, where he faces up to the need to reconcile his account with the orthodox tradition of Symeon, does he set the whole Bamburgh episode in the period before the *c.*875 exodus from Lindisfarne. But if we were to depend solely on chapters 13 and 49 then a rather startling possibility emerges. For the return of the relic Reginald acknowledges his source as being Ailred of Rievaulx. What is so interesting about this fact is that the methodology involved in spiriting the head away from Bamburgh, and the description of the elderly servant involved, both echo narratives

---

10   Reginald, *VO* I, 13, II, 47-9, 51, pp. 351, 373-81, 384-5. Cf. Tudor, above, p. 188.
11   Plummer II, p. 157.
12   For a summary history of this relic, see Plummer II, pp. 157-8.

about Ailred's ancestor, Alfred of Westou, who was famously responsible for gathering the remains of many northern saints into the new ecclesiastical centre of Durham in the early years of the eleventh century.[13] On the basis of chapters 13 and 49 it is at least arguable that Oswald's head only joined the Cuthbert shrine during its Durham phase, just as Bede's bones did,[14] and that what has survived in Reginald is a record of a Westou exploit whose context, in the final chronological summary, has been deliberately manipulated so as not to contradict the dominant Durham tradition which laid so much emphasis on the inseparable nature of Cuthbert and Oswald throughout the Community's history.

Whilst recognising that much of the above discussion has become dangerously speculative, we are nevertheless presented with at least four sequences of location for the head relic between its initial burial on Lindisfarne and its discovery in Durham in 1104. Firstly, on Symeon's evidence, it was transported with the Cuthbert relics from the island c.875, and was presumably at Chester-le-Street before the Community's final move to Durham in the late tenth century. Secondly, on the basis of other Durham sources, it was removed from Lindisfarne before 875 to Norham; it is still not clear whether it was subsequently returned to the island and then joined the general exodus of c.875 or was picked up at Norham en route to Chester-le-Street and Durham. Thirdly, on the basis of Reginald's chronological summary, it spent part of the period before c.875 at Bamburgh, before joining the Cuthbert relics in the wanderings after c.875. Finally (on the basis of other chapters in Reginald), there is the possibility that the head was taken from Lindisfarne before c.875 and only returned to the Community through the intervention of Alfred of Westou in the early eleventh century. To complicate the issue yet further we ought perhaps to acknowledge that elements of these four routes may have been combined. Symeon's narrative provides us with the orthodox path but it will be clear that this head relic may have had a more mobile history in the pre-Norman period than appears even in his record.

Whatever the precise sequence of its pre-Conquest locations, all available sources share the conviction that Oswald's head had reached Durham before (indeed some time before) the great translation of St Cuthbert's relics into the new Norman cathedral in 1104. We have already seen that Symeon, writing between 1104 and 1107, was firmly convinced of this fact and a late Anglo-Saxon poetic encomium on Durham, which he quotes, provides a record of the same belief which may date back to the 1050s.[15]

13   For Westou see *HDE* III, 7 (pp. 88-9).
14   Loc. cit.
15   See above, note 4. For the text of the poem, see Arnold I, pp. 221-2, and for its date see H. S. Offler, 'The date of Durham (*Carmen de Situ Dunelmi*)', *Journal of*

Two accounts have survived of the 1104 translation. The earliest, dating probably to c.1123, is the anonymous *Historia Translationum Sancti Cuthberti*, whilst the second was written by Reginald of Durham in the period 1165-74 as *Libellus de Admirandis Beati Cuthberti Virtutibus.*[16] Both mention Oswald's head and claim that it alone was replaced in the reliquary-coffin alongside Cuthbert in the new shrine.[17] An early twelfth-century relic list from Durham Priory, compiled between 1104 and c.1150, makes the same point; only Oswald's head is there located as being 'in the shrine with the body of St Cuthbert' (*in scrinio cum corpore sancti Cuthberti*).[18] How it was possible in 1104 to distinguish that particular head from others which may then have been available in the Durham relic collection is an issue to which we return below.

We have no evidence for subsequent sightings of the skull through the late medieval and early modern periods. The scanty records of the destruction of the Cuthbert shrine by Henry VIII's commissioners, in particular, make no mention of this specific relic.[19] When Canon Raine opened the Cuthbert tomb in 1827, however, he recognised what he thought to be Oswald's skull 'in a somewhat imperfect state', asserting that it was 'evidently' under the lid of the innermost of the three coffins in which he found St Cuthbert's body enclosed.[20] Raine's mind was obsessed with the question of Cuthbert's incorruptibility and, arguably as a result, he displayed curiously little interest in this particular discovery.[21] By contrast, when the tomb was re-opened by Canon Greenwell in 1899 for a more leisurely examination, the discovery of an 'Oswald' skull attracted much more attention.[22] The four (perhaps six) fragments remaining were photographed

---

English and Germanic Philology 61 (1962), pp. 591-4.

16 *Historia Translationum* ch. 7, ed. Arnold I, pp. 229-61, at pp. 247-61; for Reginald's text see *Reginaldi Monachi Dunelmensis Libellus*, ed. J. Raine (SS 1, 1835), pp. 84-90. For translations of both sources see *Relics*, pp. 99-112. For the dates and contexts of these works, see: B. Colgrave, 'The post-Bedan miracles and translations of St Cuthbert', in *The Early Cultures of North-West Europe*, ed. C. Fox and B. Dickins (Cambridge 1950), pp. 307-32, at p. 331; W. M. Aird, 'The making of a medieval miracle collection', *Northern History* 28 (1992), pp. 1-24; *Relics*, p. 56; V. Tudor, 'The cult of St Cuthbert in the twelfth century: the evidence of Reginald of Durham', in *St Cuthbert*, pp. 447-67, at p. 449.

17 *Historia Translationum* ch. 7, §8, ed. Arnold I, p. 255; Reginald, *Libellus*, p. 89.

18 *Relics*, p. 113.

19 *Relics*, pp. 79-89; Raine, *St Cuthbert*, pp. 173-80.

20 Raine, *St Cuthbert*, p. 187.

21 For Raine's motive for this investigation see R. N. Bailey, 'St Cuthbert's relics: some neglected evidence', in *St Cuthbert*, pp. 231-46, at pp. 231-4.

22 J. T. Fowler, 'On an examination of the grave of St Cuthbert in Durham cathedral church, in March 1899', *Archaeologia* 57 (1900), pp. 11-28, at pp. 15, 24-6; S. Plummer, 'St Cuthbert', *The Northumberland and Durham Medical Journal*

and drawn; the photographs failed but the drawings (Pl. 9) were promptly published, along with a detailed anatomical commentary, by Dr Selby Plummer.[23] These fragments were then subsequently discussed in lively exchanges in the *Durham Advertiser* between Selby Plummer and Father William Brown on the authenticity of the Cuthbert remains; Selby Plummer indeed saw this 'Oswald' skull as a key element in the case for arguing that the skeleton found by Raine had actually been that of Cuthbert.[24]

Durham's claim to possess the head of Oswald has therefore a long history behind it. There are, as we have seen, confusions in the story of the relic's early transmission but these could charitably be explained as the inevitable results of such a long-standing title to guardianship. It might consequently be argued that no real problem exists. The difficulty, however, is that there are at least four other candidates for the title of 'St Oswald's head'.

III

All of these claimants are continental. There is, in fact, potentially a much larger number of them but it is possible to sift out a considerable quantity by discarding items where the 'Oswald relic' is either vaguely listed as 'from the body of St Oswald' (*de corpore Sancti Oswaldi*) or is implausibly claimed to consist of the whole body.[25] Some other references to possession of a head relic may actually be of the 'contact type' recorded by Bede in connection with St Willibrord where the object was part of the stake on which the head had been fixed.[26] Yet, even after a fairly ruthless weeding, there remain four heads to set alongside the one now enclosed within Cuthbert's tomb at Durham. They are:

(a) *Zug and Schaffhausen, Switzerland.*[27]

A portion of what is claimed to be Oswald's skull is now set in a tall silver reliquary of mid-eighteenth-century date at Zug. This relic seems to have come from Schaffhausen in 1502, after an earlier attempt to acquire a similar piece had failed in 1485. The head is recorded at Schaffhausen *c.*1300 and some of the skull still remained there after the gift to Zug though no fragments of this original now survive. It has been argued that the

---

23 (1899), pp. 231-45.
    S. Plummer, loc. cit.

24 The letters are usefully published in W. Brown, 'St Cuthbert's remains', *Ushaw Magazine* 19 (1909), pp. 25-39, especially pp. 32-4.

25 For the continental relics, see: Plummer II, pp. 157-61; Folz, pp. 62-5; Baker, 'Zug'; E. P. Baker, 'The cult of St Oswald in northern Italy', *Archaeologia* 94 (1951), pp. 167-94; N. Huyghebaert, 'Les deux translations du roi Saint Oswald à Bergues-Saint-Winoc', *Revue Bénédictine* 86 (1976), pp. 83-93; Clemoes.

26 *HE* III, 13 (p. 254).

27 Baker, 'Zug'.

Schaffhausen relic probably travelled there via Weingarten in Swabia which was visited by Judith in 1094; she had been in a position to acquire relics of Oswald and may have taken them with her to the continent after the death of her first husband, Tostig, in 1066.[28]

(b) *Hildesheim, Germany.*[29]

A composite reliquary, parts of which date to the twelfth century, has recently been opened and fully examined (Pl. 10). Inside, wrapped in textiles from a 1779 restoration, was a skull which lacked lower jaw and had been further damaged at the point where the nose meets the upper jaw. An inscription running round the outside beneath the cupola identifies the skull as that of Oswald: 'the pious King Oswald gave himself and his possessions to Christ, and to the executioner his head which is preserved in this gold'.[30] The earliest reference to this piece at Hildesheim dates to 1286.

(c) *Utrecht, Holland, Rijksmuseum, Het Catharijneconvent.*[31]

A substantial proportion of the top of a skull survives with the remains of a late fifteenth- or early sixteenth-century inscription identifying it as belonging to Oswald (Pl. 11). A recent paper has argued that this relic once belonged to the church at Zeddam, a foundation recorded in 1571 as carrying an Oswald dedication (though other evidence suggests that the Oswald link goes back at least another century). The relic may have been brought to Zeddam in the late fifteenth or early sixteenth century.

(d) *Relic lists from Echternach, Luxembourg.*

These include Oswald's head among that monastery's possessions though nothing now survives from the site.[32] As this is one of Willibrord's foundations and the saint is recorded as possessing Oswald relics, this claim should not perhaps be dismissed lightly, though it is possible that it was of the 'contact' type.[33]

---

[28] On Judith, see Ó Riain-Raedel, below, pp. 220-2.

[29] Brandt, *Kirchenkunst*, pp. 135-60; V. H. Elbern and H. Reuther, *Der Hildesheimer Domschatz* (Hildesheim 1969), no. 23; J. Geddes, 'The twelfth-century metalwork at Durham Cathedral', in *Medieval Art and Architecture at Durham Cathedral*, ed. N. Coldstream and P. Draper (British Archaeological Association Conference Transactions, 3, London 1980), pp. 140-8, at pp. 143-4.

[30] For the context of this head-reliquary, see Ó Riain-Raedel, below, pp. 223-4.

[31] R. R. A. van Gruting, 'Lotgevallen van relieken van H. Oswald en H. Eusebius uit het bezit van Apostolisch-Vicaris Sasbout Vosmeer', *Bijdragen en Mededelingen van de Vereniging Gelre* 83 (1992), pp. 51-83. I am grateful to Professor Noel Osselton for help in the translation of this paper.

[32] Folz, p. 62 and references; Baker, 'Zug', p. 1.

[33] *HE* III, 13 (p. 254). See Thacker above, pp. 115-16.

Lacking further information on Echternach's relic, we can only concentrate on the first three items. Of these it might be argued that the Zug/Schaffhausen fragment had somehow been cut from a genuine Oswald head whose main components lie elsewhere. There is, however, no possibility whatsoever that the Hildesheim, Utrecht, and Durham heads can all be reassembled to form a single skull. At least two of them must be forgeries. But which? The rest of this paper attempts to test the authenticity of the Durham fragments which have, it should be emphasised, the longest recorded history of all the rival claimants.

IV

It will be obvious that any investigation of the Durham head relic cannot hope to be conclusive but, as we have seen, the enquiry can draw upon a variety and quantity of evidence which is not usually available in such cases. The pursuit of this relic is best divided into two halves. After the 1104 translation, despite the messiness of the evidence, the descent is clear; before that it is a good deal more shadowy.

If we are to accept the Durham fragments as genuinely those of Oswald then we have to make certain assumptions about their pre-1104 history. We must first suppose that after his death and the ritual exposure of his head, Oswald's skull was sufficiently recognisable for it to be recovered and brought to Lindisfarne. That *a* skull reached Lindisfarne which was believed to be that of Oswald is not in doubt, given Bede's evidence, and I see little cause to question the fact that Oswald's remains could have been correctly identified given the special and exemplary nature of their post-mortem exhibition. We must next assume that the resting place in the cemetery at Lindisfarne was sufficiently well known to allow the recovery of the head either for transfer to Bamburgh (if we accept Reginald's version of events) or for the exodus from Lindisfarne and/or Norham recorded in other Durham traditions. Again I see little need for doubts on this score. The Cuthbert Community may have been very late converts to the cult of St Oswald, but the king had been a major figure in Aidan's mission centred on Lindisfarne, and his remains consequently ought to have been accorded some distinctive marker on the island.

The last assumption relating to the pre-1104 history of this relic involves the belief that, in all the potential confusion of the Community's wanderings and the numerous openings of the coffin-reliquary after c.875, Oswald's head remained sufficiently distinctive not to become muddled with other similar types of relic in the Lindisfarne, Chester-le-Street and Durham collections. We know that there were at least two other skulls in these assemblages with which Oswald's head *might* have become confused. There was, first of all, Aidan. Symeon records that, according to his documentary sources, 'bones' (*ossium*) of Aidan were placed in Cuthbert's reliquary-coffin when the

Community fled Lindisfarne.[34] It is, again, simply as 'bones' (*ossa*) that Aidan's relics are listed in the earliest of the Durham inventories, which dates to between 1104 and *c*.1150,[35] but by the time we reach Richard de Segbruk's list of 1383, Aidan's remains are catalogued as including his head (*caput sci Aydani*) which was set in a jewel-covered reliquary.[36] It is therefore at least theoretically possible that his skull shared Cuthbert's wanderings in the same reliquary-coffin as Oswald's head – and that the two might have exchanged identities en route.

Ceolwulf offers a second candidate for confusion, though with a weaker case than can be mustered for Aidan. According to both the *Historia de Sancto Cuthberto* and Symeon (and later echoed in Reginald) Ceolwulf's body was translated to Norham during Ecgred's episcopate.[37] Symeon makes no mention of the inclusion of this relic among the material taken during the flight from Lindisfarne but records that his head was removed to Durham many years later.[38] It is therefore no surprise to find it listed as *caput Ceolwulfi* in both the early twelfth-century relic list and de Segbruk's inventory.[39] Consequently, whilst it is just possible that the Ceolwulf skull shared Cuthbert's wanderings, what evidence we have suggests that it is more likely that it arrived in Durham during the first half of the eleventh century, probably during the period when Alfred of Westou was assembling a great variety of early Northumbrian relics into the new cathedral.[40] Given that Bede's remains, gathered at this same late period, finished up in Cuthbert's coffin, even an eleventh-century acquisition of Ceolwulf's skull would not, however, rule out the possibility of its confusion with Oswald's head before the 1104 translation.[41]

Two other known Durham head relics need not, fortunately, detain us further. Both the head of Boisil and of one of the eleven thousand virgins (*caput ... unius virginis xj milium virginum*) appear in de Segbruk's 1383 list but their known history does not seem to bring them into contact with

---

34 *HDE* II, 6 (p. 57).

35 *Relics*, p. 113.

36 *Extracts from the Account Rolls of the Abbey of Durham*, II, ed. J. T. Fowler (SS 100, 1898), p. 433. Aidan's head does not appear in the early 14th-century list of Durham relics in York Minster MS XVI.I.12 (printed in *Historiae Dunelmensis Scriptores Tres*, ed. J. Raine (SS 9, 1839), pp. cccxxvi-ccccxxx).

37 *Historia de S. Cuth.* §9 (Arnold I, p. 201); Symeon, *HDE* II, 1 and 5 (Arnold I, pp. 47, 52-3); Reginald, *VO* I, 21 (Arnold I, p. 361).

38 For the flight, see *HDE* II, 6 (p. 57); for the removal to Durham, *HDE* II, 1 (p. 47). Reginald is equally vague as to the date of the translation of the head to Durham; see Reginald, *VO* I, 21, p. 361.

39 *Relics*, p. 113; *Account Rolls*, p. 433.

40 For Westou see *HDE* III, 7 (pp. 87-9).

41 *Relics*, p. 102.

Oswald's skull.[42] Even without these two, however, we still face the question: how could Oswald's head be distinguished from Aidan's (and perhaps Ceolwulf's) so that it could be convincingly identified in 1104 and, alone, given the honour of reinterment alongside the body of Cuthbert?

One explanation might be that they, or their containers, were all labelled, as was the earlier material collected by St Wilfrid.[43] The need for some such kind of distinctive marking is surely implied by the teeming contents of the post-Conquest relic lists. We do not, however, have to rely upon this supposition alone because Reginald gives a description of the skull which, if true, would clearly obviate any possibility whatsoever of confusion with other Durham head relics. In his *Vita Sancti Oswaldi* he gives a lengthy account of the saint's head, which carried a deep cut in its crown:

> There appears yawning the opening of a certain aperture, from a side blow, which the enemy's sword inflicted in the battle wherein he fell, and which lies open quite three fingers depth in the crown of the sacred head. For the crown of the head was so cut away by the devouring sword that it looks as though the hole in question had been sliced open by the stroke of a very sharp razor or by a headsman's slash. Still the stroke of the shattering sword seems not to have inflicted any other injury except that opening, which through separation of part of the skull is so conspicuous, unless perchance some little notch appears visible anywhere else in the whole sacred head.[44]

If Reginald's description is accurate then any likelihood of confusion with Aidan and Ceolwulf can be ruled out since the latter two saints died peaceful deaths. So the question arises as to whether Reginald can be trusted, given that he was writing some sixty years after the 1104 translation on which his description must be based. In his account of the 1104 ceremony in the *Libellus* he quite explicitly acknowledges dependence on oral sources for his information – a statement which might now seem to throw doubts upon the accuracy of his record. Yet we should remember that it is Reginald, and not his anonymous predecessor, who accurately records that the Cuthbert shrine was made of oak and was decorated; his account of the repairs to the reliquary also carries conviction.[45] He may therefore similarly be recording

---

[42] *Account Rolls*, p. 433. Symeon describes the recovery of Boisil's relics from Melrose by Alfred of Westou and their placement in a separate shrine; see *HDE* III, 7 (p. 88). The early 12th-century list merely catalogues *corpus ... sancti boisili*; see *Relics*, p. 113. This early list does not include relics of the virgins. Other Durham head relics were clearly only fragmentary, being listed as, for example, *de capite sancti Benedicti* and *de osse capitis Sci Petri*.

[43] *VW* ch. 33 (p. 66); for the bag in which Oswald's head was kept, see Reginald, *VO* III, 51 (p. 381).

[44] *VO* II, 51 (pp. 380-1); translation based on that by Father Brown (as above, n. 24).

[45] For a translation (by E. G. Pace) of Reginald's account of the events of 1104, see *Relics*, pp. 107-22.

perfectly genuine information about Oswald's skull, which had been passed on to him by his informants. His comments on the colour, lightness, and dentistry of the relic certainly give the impression of being derived from eye-witnesses (as do the details of the bag in which the head was placed) and, as we will see, his description of the skull wound receives strong support from later discoveries. We can, I believe, trust him here.

In summary, the case for Durham's possession of a genuine head relic of St Oswald in 1104 clearly relies upon a series of assumptions. None, in my view, strains credulity too far. I now turn to the post-1104 history where the trail is much clearer, despite, ironically, the confusion sown by Raine's (no doubt, well-intentioned) attempts to make the track even better defined.

Raine's description of the opening of Cuthbert's tomb in 1827 records his finding of three skulls.[46] Two, he thought, lay outside the inner coffin, one being that of a child and the other that of an adult. The third skull which he 'presumed' was that of Oswald 'evidently' lay under the lid of the third, inner, reliquary-coffin. He made no comment on this skull apart from noting that it was in a 'somewhat imperfect state'.

It is quite clear from his account that his identification of the skull depended on its position *within* the innermost of the three coffins discovered; on the basis of the two accounts of the 1104 translation he reasonably argued that this could only be the skull of Oswald. Unfortunately we must be wary of accepting Raine's record without some scepticism. Descriptions by others of the 1827 opening, which I have published elsewhere, show a high degree of chaos attending the hurried excavation and also hint at the general unlikelihood of Raine being able to distinguish precise positioning of finds in relation to the three coffins.[47] In addition, we have the evidence of the sub-dean, Darnell, who, within days of the discovery, was telling a rather different story to the one reported later by Raine: 'at the lower part of the chest or coffin were laid several detached bones, two full-grown skulls, and the cranium of a child'.[48] Whilst agreeing with Raine on the number of skulls, therefore, Darnell's account gives no hint that they could be assigned to different coffins. Nearly half a century later another eyewitness of the 1827 opening, Joseph Taylor, also remembered *all three* skulls as being in the same coffin, claiming that two of them were children's whilst the third was that of an adult set 'midway down' the coffin.[49]

[46] Raine, *St Cuthbert*, pp. 136-7.
[47] Bailey, 'St Cuthbert's relics', pp. 231-6.
[48] Newspaper cutting from *Durham Advertiser*, dated 26 May 1827, pasted in Durham Cathedral Additional MS 148; Raine's annotation attributes the article to Darnell.
[49] Taylor died in 1875; his recollections can be found in a newspaper cutting pasted into the Newcastle Central Library copy of J. Lingard, *Remarks on the St Cuthbert of the Rev. James Raine* (Newcastle 1828). See also Bailey, 'St Cuthbert's relics', p.

It is, of course, a well known archaeological truth that the perceptions of onlookers are not always as well-informed as those of an excavation director, and we might therefore be tempted to reject Darnell and Taylor in favour of Raine's seemingly more authoritative report. Yet there is further evidence, this time from Raine himself, to suggest that his final account tidied up the record of what was found so as better to match what, in retrospect, he might have expected to discover. This evidence comes from a watercolour among the cathedral's manuscripts, which was apparently intended for use in Raine's *St Cuthbert*, published in 1828 (Pl. 8).[50] It never appeared in print but shows Cuthbert's body as Raine believed it to be on discovery. Towards Cuthbert's feet are *three* skulls, a lay-out which better matches the recollections of Darnell and Taylor than it does the published report of Raine. The painting has been annotated by Raine but there is no comment on the skulls, whose position is so clearly at odds with his final description. It follows from all this that Raine's attempts to identify an Oswald head among his finds on the basis of its position must be rejected.[51] Reluctantly, we must set his testimony aside.

Much more useful is the evidence of the 1899 excavation. Amongst the material removed and examined then were four fragments of a skull, together with two additional pieces of a lower jaw and a much-mutilated upper jaw which probably belonged with them (Pl. 9).[52] The largest fragment consisted of the posterior portion of the frontal bone together with an adjacent portion of the right and left parietal bones; this exhibited a large cut half an inch in front of the coronal suture. Dr Selby Plummer's very competent anatomical analysis concluded that this cut was the result of an injury inflicted with a weapon.[53]

That this was a weapon cut does not seem to be in doubt. What is more, material in the University of Newcastle's Medical School collection suggests that the particular form of cut exhibited by this skull – one with sharp edges through both tables of the skull, but with ragged terminations at both ends – is of a type which was almost certainly inflicted at the time of death; skulls at a later post-mortem stage, even those which have been kept under damp conditions, usually either shatter or break along the sutures if subjected to a

---

233.

50 Durham Cathedral Additional MS 149; see Bailey, 'St Cuthbert's relics', p. 234. Raine's suggestion that the other skulls and bones found in 1827 represented the contents of other reliquaries deposited in the grave by Henry VIII's commissioners seems reasonable.

51 A similar conclusion, based on the internal evidence of Raine's own book, had been reached by Lingard, *Remarks*, pp. 45-6.

52 S. Plummer (art. cit. in note 22).

53 Art. cit., p. 243.

cutting blow.[54] What this observation implies is that the skull examined by Selby Plummer is unlikely to have been given a forged battle-injury long after death, nor can the cut be the result of partition for relic-giving at a later date. This is the head of a man who had met a violent death.

Selby Plummer naturally drew attention to the account of Oswald's skull provided by Reginald of Durham and argued that the remains which he had examined were identical to those described by Reginald. There may be certain discrepancies, as Father Brown observed,[55] but they do not undermine the essential conviction of Plummer's case. Reginald does therefore seem to have captured a genuine piece of information about the contents of the tomb after the 1104 translation: a skull carrying a battle-wound *was* included and, in the twelfth century at least, this head was believed to be that of Oswald.

We are left, of course, with a minor puzzle. How did Raine miss this vital piece of evidence which would more strongly have supported his arguments than the ones which he advanced on the basis of the position of the skull? Two explanations are possible. The first is that he was essentially concerned with the figure of St Cuthbert and everything else was secondary in his hurried excavation. Secondly, if Selby Plummer's 'Oswald' skull was (as is likely) the one described by Raine as being in 'somewhat imperfect condition', then, in the absence of a leisurely professional medical examination, he may well have missed the crucial evidence of a weapon cut on one of the fragments. Whatever the cause, Raine's lack of comment should not detract from the significance of Selby Plummer's observations.

V

It is time to summarise. Was the skull examined by Selby Plummer that of Oswald? The answer, I believe, should be a guarded 'yes'. There is a very attractive equation to be made between the head with its wound as described by Plummer and the skull identified as that of Oswald reported by Reginald. Beyond Reginald and the 1104 translation, our survey has shown that we are into difficult territory for authentication. In the swirl of conflicting evidence, however, we would do well to remember two facts. The first is that Durham has a longer recorded claim to possession of this relic than any of its competitors. And the second is that the Cuthbert Community was a group which, more than any of its contemporaries, constantly (and, as time went on, increasingly) evoked its splendid past and revered the physical remains of its earlier glories. If Oswald's head were to survive anywhere, then it was most likely so to do within this antiquarianising Community and among its successors in the priory at Durham.

[54] I gratefully record my thanks to Professor Simon Miller for his advice on this material.

[55] Brown (art. cit. in note 24), pp. 32-4.

When Cuthbert's remains and the accompanying skeletal material were re-interred after the excavation of 1899, the lid of the new coffin carried two incised symbols. One was the cross of St Cuthbert; the other was a crown to indicate the presence of St Oswald. The use of both symbols was, I would argue, fully justified.

Edith, Judith, Matilda: the Role of Royal Ladies in the Propagation of the Continental Cult

DAGMAR Ó RIAIN-RAEDEL

The documents testifying to the presence of a cult of St Oswald on the continent span approximately eight hundred years. While apparently confined to German-speaking countries, with the notable exception of Flanders, the centres of the cult vary over the centuries. Thus, in the period under discussion here, the cult is to be found in Saxony in the tenth century, in Weingarten near Lake Constance in the eleventh, and at Regensburg in the twelfth. While there would have been some interaction between these various centres, it seems that the impetus for the cult mostly came afresh from England. Furthermore, in each of these cases an upsurge of interest in Oswald may well have been linked to the arrival in Germany, in order to marry a German noble, of a royal lady with English connections.

The spread of the cult within the period from the tenth to the twelfth centuries must also be placed within the general framework of Oswald's early popularity on the continent. My paper fills the space between the end of the early diffusion of the cult by Willibrord and his companions, which forms the subject of Alan Thacker's article, and the reception of Oswald legends into German vernacular literature, which is discussed by Annemiek Jansen. This latter development may well have arisen as a more or less direct result of an upsurge in interest in the saint at Regensburg in the twelfth century, as I shall be explaining towards the end of my paper. However, to begin with, let me document briefly what appear to be traces of Northumbrian influence on the diffusion of the cult in the period after its introduction at Echternach, where its presence in the early eighth century is already attested by no less an authority than Bede.[1]

A western regional diffusion of the cult by the ninth century appears to be implied by Wandelbert of Prüm's metrical martyrology. This carries an entry on the saint, on Oswald's feast day of 5 August, qualified by the phrase *rex pius Anglorum*. As Dom J. Dubois has pointed out, the Echternach manuscript of the Hieronymian martyrology, which does not localise the saint, cannot have been Wandelbert's only source.[2] Accordingly, it is

---

1   *HE* III, 13. For a survey of entries on Oswald in calendars and martyrologies, see Folz, pp. 60-2. On the possible connections of the head relic of Oswald at Utrecht and Zeddam with Echternach, see R. R. A. van Gruting, 'Lotgevallen van relieken van H. Oswald en H. Eusebius uit het bezit van Apostolisch-Vicaris Sasbout Vosmeer', *Bijdragen en Mededelingen van de Vereniging Gelre* 83 (1992), pp. 51-83; cf. Bailey, above, p. 202.

2   J. Dubois, *Le Martyrologe d'Usuard. Texte et Commentaire* (Brussels 1965), pp. 58,

reasonable to suppose that a copy of Bede's *Historia Ecclesiastica* must also have been in circulation then in the region of the river Mosel, at such monastic centres as Prüm, Trier or Echternach. This need occasion no surprise because from this general area we also possess a calendar, written *c*.840, which, according to its editor, Winfried Böhne, can be traced back to Lorsch, Mainz and eventually to Jarrow itself.[3] It would appear that by then works of Northumbrian provenance may have been circulating freely on the continent. And, by way of confirmation, the martyrology of Usuard, which was completed about 865 and which was followed by that of Ado of Vienne (died 874), actually specifies Bede's work as the source of its entry: 'Eodem die, sancti Osvaldi regis Anglorum, cuius actus commemorat venerabilis Beda in gestis eiusdem gentis'.[4]

The occurrence of liturgical documents bearing on Oswald further east on the continent is less well attested. The presence at Fulda of a copy of the *Historia Ecclesiastica*, written in a late eighth-century Northumbrian hand, does not seem to have sparked off any major diffusion of the cult.[5] The notice of his death is, however, entered in two calendars from Fulda itself, one now in St Gall, the other in Bamberg, both of which are of tenth-century origin.[6] Fulda may also have had some influence on the inclusion of Oswald's day in the calendar of Borghorst,[7] but, in this case, it cannot be overlooked that quite a few members of the Saxon royal house are also included in the text. Since their names belong to the period before the foundation of Borghorst in 968, their inclusion, together with that of Oswald, could also reflect an interest of the founding nuns, who were recruited from the Ottonian abbey of Essen.[8] The benefactors of this abbey, as we shall now see, were connected familially with both the continental Saxon and the Anglo-Saxon royal houses.

278-9. For a recent opinion on the Northumbrian provenance of the Echternach martyrology, see P. Ó Riain, *Anglo-Saxon Ireland: the Evidence of the Martyrology of Tallaght* (H. M. Chadwick Memorial Lectures 3, Cambridge 1992), pp. 1-2.

3   W. Böhne, 'Das älteste Lorscher Kalendar', in *Die Reichsabtei Lorsch. Festschrift zum Gedenken an ihre Stiftung 764* (Darmstadt 1977), pp. 171-221. See Thacker, above, pp. 116-17.

4   'On the same day, that of St Oswald king of the English, whose deeds the Venerable Bede records in his history of that same people.' Dubois, *Le Martyrologe*, p. 278. On these liturgical documents see Folz, pp. 60-2.

5   *HE*, p. xlii.

6   G. Althoff, *Das Necrolog von Borghorst* (Münster 1987), pp. 107, 121.

7   Althoff, ibid.; B. Bischoff, 'Eine Sammelhandschrift Walafrid Strabos', in his *Mittelalterliche Studien* (3 vols., Stuttgart 1966-81), II, pp. 42-3.

8   A late 10th-century calendar, in contrast to two earlier ones, also included the feast day. This was possibly due to the influence of Abbess Matilda, grand-daughter of Queen Edith; see K. Leyser, 'Die Ottonen und Wessex', *Frühmittelalterliche Studien* 17(1983), pp. 73-97, at p. 78. Althoff, *Das Necrolog*, p. 107.

Edith

As already stated, the presence of Oswald's cult at Borghorst in the tenth century may well have been due to circumstances quite unconnected with the putative influence of Bede, of Fulda, or of Echternach. When the son of Henry I of Saxony, Otto (later to be called 'the Great'), married Edith (Eadgyth), daughter of Edward the Elder of Wessex and half-sister of Athelstan in 929/930, the event was deemed worthy of notice by most historians of the period. It is, however, the *Gesta Ottonis*, written by Hrotsvitha of Gandersheim *c*.965 at the behest of Abbess Gerberga, niece of Otto, that concerns us here. Hrotsvitha included in her work passages not only on Otto, but also on his son Liudolf, his younger brother Henry, and his second wife, Adelheid.[9] As might be expected of a female writer, queens received special attention from Hrotsvitha, who in this case mostly expressed her interest through superlatives.[10] As has been pointed out by R. McKitterick, an important aspect of Hrotsvitha's work is the manner in which it presents the women of the Liudolfing house as transmitters of information about their families and as preservers of tradition.[11] There was also, however, a critical political dimension to the work, which could not have been more timely.[12] Both Leyser and Corbet have stressed the difficulties encountered by Henry and his son Otto in establishing their authority over Saxony.[13] It is clear, however, that the arrangement of marriages with daughters of foreign noble families was regarded as an acceptable means of addressing these difficulties. And in Otto's case, very special care seems to have been taken with the choice of a bride. Two daughters of Edward of Wessex were sent for consideration, but, we are told, Otto spontaneously chose Edith.[14] Edward's other daughter, Ælfgifu, seems

9   *Gesta Ottonis*, pp. 201-28.
10   Hrotsvitha's style and intention have been studied closely by P. Corbet, *Les saints ottoniens. Sainteté dynastique, sainteté royale et sainteté féminine autour de l'an mil* (Beihefte der Francia 15, Sigmaringen 1986), pp. 111-14.
11   R. McKitterick, 'Ottonian intellectual culture in the tenth century and the role of Theophanu', *Early Medieval Europe* 2 (1993), pp. 53-74, at p. 68. E. van Houts, 'Women and the writing of history in the early middle ages: the case of Abbess Matilda of Essen and Aethelweard', *Early Medieval Europe* 1 (1992), pp. 53-68.
12   K. Hauck, 'Geblütsheiligkeit', in B. Bischoff and S. Brechter, *Liber Floridus* (St Ottilien 1950), pp. 187-240. Hrotsvitha's interest in and knowledge of genealogies was based on the daily practice of *memoria* at Gandersheim. On this, see G. Althoff, 'Beobachtung zum liuldolfingisch-ottonischen Gedenkwesen', in *Memoria. Der geschichtliche Zeugniswert des liturgischen Gedenkens im Mittelalter*, ed. K. Schmid and J. Wollasch (Munich 1984), pp. 649-65, at p. 662.
13   Leyser, 'Die Ottonen', pp. 77-80, 82-5, 95-6; P. Corbet speaks of 'la sainteté comme forme d'illustration du pouvoir', op. cit., p. 114.
14   Henry seems to have favoured Otto as successor, against the wishes of his wife,

then to have been betrothed to the king of Burgundy.[15]

All of this is recorded by Hrotsvitha. Moreover, while her eulogy of the new house of Saxon kings showed their right to rule to have derived both from 'Geblütsheiligkeit' or sanctity of ancestors and from the virtuous lives of its members, it also laid special stress on the contribution of the female line to these factors, including that of Edith, Otto's Anglo-Saxon bride.[16] Edith's mother, for example, is presented as of far superior pedigree to that of her half-brother, Athelstan;[17] and, clearly with a view to underlining even more forcibly the ancient and sainted royal authority derived by Otto from his marriage, Hrotsvitha also wrote of Edith that she was 'natam de stirpe beata / Oswaldi regis, laudem cuius canit orbis,/ se quia subdiderat morti pro

---

Matilda, who favoured her younger son, Henry. This led to strife within the family; see Leyser, 'Die Ottonen', pp. 79-80, 86. On Edith's position see D. A. Bullough, 'The continental background of the reform', in *Tenth-Century Studies. Essays in Commemoration of the Millennium of the Council of Winchester and Regularis Concordia*, ed. D. Parsons (Chichester 1975), pp. 20-36, notes 210-17, at pp. 34-5.

15 Leyser, 'Die Ottonen', pp. 86-7.

16 The female members of the family who were the subject of hagiographical treatment in this crucial period form the topic of P. Corbet's book: *Les saints ottoniens*. The preoccupation with the Saxon queens is not surprising considering that a large percentage of the religious houses in the kingdom were *Familienklöster*, as in the case of Hrotsvitha's abbey. While the posthumous reputations of Otto's mother Matilda, who merited two Lives, and of his second wife, Adelheid, were quite longlived, this does not seem to have been the case with Edith. This may be due to Edith's early death, sixteen years after her wedding, and to the early prominence of her successor, Adelheid. There is some evidence, however, of a cult of Edith. The twelfth-century Bavarian recensions of the Martyrology of Hermann the Lame of Reichenau have the following entry at July 8: 'Apud Parthenopolim civitatem Saxonie sancte Enid reginae, uxoris quondam primi Ottonis'. Magdeburg (Parthenopolis) is quite rightly given as the place of her burial; her anniversary, however, appears as Jan 26 in the Necrology of Borghorst: see J. McCulloh, 'Herman the Lame's Martyrology', *AB* 104 (1986), pp. 349-70. For a study of the political implications of the two *vitae* of Matilda, see G. Althoff, 'Causa scribendi und Darstellungsabsicht: Die Lebensbeschreibungen der Königin Mathilde und andere Beispiele', in *Litterae Medii Aevi*, ed. M. Borgolte and H. Spilling (Sigmaringen 1988), pp. 117-33.

17 *Gesta Ottonis*, lines 79-83 (p. 207): 'Fratre suo regni sceptrum gestante paterni;/ Quem peperit regi consors non inclita regni,/ Istius egregiae genitrix clarissima domnae,/ Altera sed generis mulier satis inferioris.' Athelstan's mother, whose name, Ecgwynn (?), is recorded only in post-Conquest sources, may have been a concubine. Edith's mother was either Ælfflæd, daughter of ealdorman Æthelhelm, or Eadgifu, daughter of ealdorman Sigehelm. For this see E. B. Fryde, D. E. Greenway, S. Porter, I. Roy, *Handbook of British Chronology* (3rd edn London 1986), pp. 24-5; and P. Corbet, *Les saints ottoniens*, p. 112, n. 7.

nomine Christi'.[18] The question is: what grounds can Hrotsvitha have had for embellishing Edith's descent with the claim of a relationship between her and Oswald? In the words of Charles Plummer: 'That this is not genealogically correct only makes the testimony the more striking'.[19]

Oswald's wife, whose name is given in the twelfth-century *Vita S. Oswaldi* by Reginald of Durham as Kyneburga, is said by Bede to have been the daughter of Cynegils, king of the West Saxons.[20] Their son, Oethelwald, seems not to have been able to exercise independent or lasting royal power. So, in terms of kingship, Oswald's direct line appears to have died out.[21] On the other hand, the evidence of the West Saxon royal genealogies, which were compiled in a variety of forms in the ninth century, combined with some key passages in Bede's *Historia Ecclesiastica*, arguably could have lent some tenuous substance to a claim of a relationship between Edith's family and that of Oswald, in the form of *Ansippung* or 'kinning'.[22] Manipulation of the Anglo-Saxon royal record in Oswald's case may also be implied by certain king lists, such as those which appear in the *Liber Vitae* of Durham, where Oswald's name, which is given precedence over those of Oswiu and his sons, is second in place to that of King Edwin of Deira. Another possible example of manipulation of Oswald's record is provided by the king list compiled at New Minster, Winchester, a foundation and burial place of the West Saxon kings. Here, Oswald's father-in-law, Cynegils, is given pride of place.[23] While the evidence is totally circumstantial, it could be that when King Athelstan's name was entered in the *Liber Vitae* of Durham, probably

[18]   *Gesta Ottonis*, lines 95-7 (page 207): 'born of the blessed lineage of King Oswald, whose praise the world sings, because he yielded himself to death for the sake of Christ's name'.

[19]   Plummer, II, p. 160. E. van Houts, 'Women', p. 57, sees no reason to doubt Hrotsvitha's statement that Edith was a descendant of Oswald 'despite the fact that no other evidence is available to corroborate it'.

[20]   *HE* III, 7, pp. 232-3 and n. 3; Tudor, above, p. 187, n. 57.

[21]   B. Yorke, *Kings and Kingdoms of Early Anglo-Saxon England* (London 1990), pp. 78-9.

[22]   On the West Saxon genealogies, see D. N. Dumville, 'Kingship, genealogies and regnal lists', in *Early Medieval Kingship*, ed. P. H. Sawyer and I. N. Wood (Leeds 1977), pp. 72-104, at pp. 77-81; and idem, 'The West Saxon genealogical regnal list and the chronology of early Wessex', *Peritia* 4 (1985), pp. 21-66. See also L. Simpson, 'The King Alfred/St Cuthbert episode in the *Historia de S. Cuthberto*', in *St Cuthbert*, pp. 397-411, esp. pp. 403-4.

[23]   J. Gerchow, *Die Gedenküberlieferung der Angelsachsen* (Arbeiten zur Frühmittelalterforschung vol. 20; Berlin/New York 1988): *Liber Vitae Dunelmensis* (BL Cotton MS Domitian A.VII), ibid, pp. 109-54; 304-20. *Liber Vitae* of Newminster/Hyde Abbey (BL Stowe MS 994), ibid, pp. 155-85; 320-26. The opening entry of the West Saxon king list shows signs of having been influenced by Bede: 'Cynegils rex q[u]i a s[an]c[t]o Byrino baptizat[us] est': Gerchow, p. 320.

during his visit to the St Cuthbert Community at Chester-le-Street in 934, there was already in existence a belief in the supposed connection of his family with that of Oswald.[24] Certainly Athelstan's family had developed an interest in the saint, because by then Oswald's relics had been translated from Bardney to St Peter's Gloucester by Æthelflæd, Athelstan's paternal aunt, wife of Æthelred of Mercia.[25] Could it not be, therefore, that Hrotsvitha's claim simply echoes a tradition brought to Saxony at the time of Edith's marriage to Otto? That royal marriages gave rise to the reception of such traditions is hardly open to question. Moreover, it is worth emphasising in this instance that Athelstan is himself credited with having maintained a lively interest in saints and in the diffusion of their cults.

A great collector of relics, Athelstan is also known to have distributed them generously.[26] That Edith benefited from such largesse on the occasion of her marriage to Otto can hardly be doubted. The cult of St Maurice, leader of the Theban legion, whose standard was among the relics brought to Athelstan by a mission originating in Flanders, arguably provides proof of this. The cathedral church at Magdeburg, the main foundation of Otto of Saxony and of his wife Edith, is also dedicated to St Maurice.[27] We may surely infer, therefore, that the relics used at Magdeburg came with Edith as a gift to Otto from Athelstan.

The exchange of such gifts is also exemplified in regard to manuscripts. The so-called Gandersheim Gospels, for instance, which were written at Metz c.860, appear then to have been taken to England. Here, they received an entry commemorating Queen Eadgifu and King Athelstan before ending up, by the eleventh century, on the continent in the monastery from which they now derive their name.[28] Another, more pertinent case, this time by way of witness to the movement of manuscripts in the opposite direction, is provided by another gospel-book, British Library, Cotton MS Tiberius A.II.

[24] Gerchow, *Die Gedenküberlieferung*, pp. 121-2, discusses the visit to Chester-le-Street; see also S. Keynes, 'King Athelstan's books', in *Learning and Literature in Anglo-Saxon England*, ed. M. Lapidge and H. Gneuss (Cambridge 1985), pp. 143-201, at pp. 170-1, n. 135.

[25] Thacker, above, pp. 120-1.

[26] Keynes, 'King Athelstan's books', pp. 143-4.

[27] Leyser, 'Die Ottonen', p. 84.

[28] The manuscript is Coburg, Landesbibliothek 1. It is not certain whether Eadgifu should be identified with the step-mother or with the half-sister of Athelstan. On the manuscript, see Keynes, 'King Athelstan's books', pp. 189-93. About the same time, there possibly arrived at this abbey the so-called Gandersheim casket of late eighth-century origin. However, as its runic inscriptions have yet to be deciphered, it is not known whether this casket also served as a reliquary; see L. Webster and J. Backhouse, *The Making of England. Anglo-Saxon Art and Culture AD 600-900* (London 1991), pp. 177-9.

This was perhaps written at Lobbes *c.*900, and carries the inscription, in an Anglo-Saxon hand, of *Odda Rex* and *Mihthild Mater Regis*. The commemoration indicates that this manuscript may have been given by Otto, son of Matilda, to Athelstan on the occasion of his marriage to Edith.[29]

As we have seen, the lack of direct evidence for the presence of Oswald's cult at Athelstan's court by no means precludes the possibility of West Saxon interest in its promotion. Indeed, quite apart from the implications of the evidence provided by Hrotsvitha of Gandersheim, a vested interest in Oswald would have greatly assisted Athelstan in the furtherance of his authority over the Northumbrian kingdom, where the conversion of the Danes had been secured only during his lifetime.[30] As the first southern king of this region, Athelstan's efforts to impose his authority could only have benefited from a claim to a relationship with a historical king and martyr of the calibre of Oswald. Further, the suggestion of illegitimacy in his own background would no doubt have made this course of action all the more imperative.

In sum, therefore, possibly inspired by his visit to Chester-le-Street, Athelstan is very likely to have cultivated Oswald's memory actively as a useful means of promoting his own interest. Moreover, through the mediation of his half-sister Edith, his example may well have been followed in Saxony. Here, too, Hrotsvitha of Gandersheim's *Gesta Ottonis* suggests an awareness of the potential of the king-saint as a means of promoting political ambition. The subsequent diffusion of Oswald's cult in the eastern parts of the empire was no doubt largely due to the interest in the saint, which was thus stimulated among the religious communities connected familially with the Saxon royal house.[31]

Judith

After an interval of about a century the cult of St Oswald again made an appearance on the continent. Now, however, while it is also attested in Germany, its centre has shifted westwards, to Flanders, where similar patterns can be detected in its progress: these include patronage by the nobility, and the possible involvement of a lady of noble origin with English

[29] Keynes, 'King Athelstan's books', pp. 147-53. On the cultural background of these gifts, see McKitterick, *Early Medieval Europe* 2, pp. 57-9.

[30] D. Dumville, *Wessex and England from Alfred to Edgar* (Woodbridge 1992), pp. 147-51. D. Dumville also draws attention elsewhere to the fact that on the occasion of the annexation of Northumbria, manuscripts from its monasteries travelled south and found their way into Wessex: see D. Dumville, *Liturgy and the Ecclesiastical History of Late Anglo-Saxon England* (Woodbridge 1992), pp. 105-7.

[31] On the literary and liturgical connections between Anglo-Saxon England and such abbeys, see J. Campbell, *Essays in Anglo-Saxon History* (London 1986), pp. 194-6.

connections. The lady in question, Judith (c.1027-1094), was the stepdaughter of Baldwin IV of Flanders, and her first marriage was to Tostig (died 1066), earl of Northumbria and brother of King Harold. Subsequently she married Welf IV, duke of Bavaria (died 1101). Oswald's cult, accompanied by relics, is thought to have reached southern Germany as an immediate consequence of this arrangement. Also, Judith's connections with the court of Flanders are thought to have had a direct bearing on the arrival of Oswald's cult in northern France.

Close contacts had existed for centuries between England and Flanders, and, in theory, the cult could have spread there at any time.[32] However, the composition about 1050 of a Life of Oswald by Drogo (died 1084), monk of Bergues-Saint-Winnoc, marks an upsurge of interest in the saint.[33] The Life is drawn mostly from Bede, and Drogo claimed that he had only added what Bede might have said himself, given more space and time.[34] Yet, while his source is immediately identifiable, some doubt still remains as to how it became accessible. It is clear from internal evidence that the *Vita* was not written at Bergues itself; and, since Bergues had been colonised by monks of St Bertin in 1022, it is tempting to assume that Drogo composed his Life of Oswald while in temporary residence at that great monastery.[35] However, N. Huyghebaert, in his extensive survey of the career of Drogo and of the cult of Oswald at Bergues, decided against this possibility on the grounds that there is no liturgical evidence whatsoever at St Bertin of the presence there of the saint's cult.[36] Consequently, Huyghebaert is inclined to date the presence at Bergues of the saint's relics, which presumably influenced the decision to have a Life composed by Drogo in the first place, to the time prior to the colonisation of 1022. Could it be that earlier connections of benefactors of Bergues with the monastery of Echternach had resulted in the arrival there of relics? Drogo does not refer in Oswald's case to the presence at Bergues of

[32] These connections are discussed by J. Campbell, *Essays*, pp. 191-207. Included is the marriage of Alfred's daughter Ælfthryth to Baldwin II of Flanders, ibid, p. 197.

[33] On Bergues (Groenberg) and the cult there of St Winnoc, see C. de Croocq, 'Saint Winoc. Abbé de Wormhout, patron de Bergues (vers 640-717)', *Annales du comité flamand de France* (1944), pp. 1-191.

[34] The Life (*BHL* 6362) is edited by the Bollandists: *AASS Aug*. II (Paris 1867), pp. 83-103. Two sermons on the miracles associated with Oswald (*BHL* 6363) have yet to be edited. Drogo refers to his source in his prologue, ibid., p. 94.

[35] On the relations between England and St Bertin, see Campbell, *Essays*, pp. 203-4; Keynes, 'King Athelstan's books', p. 161; D. Dumville, *Wessex and England*, p. 160.

[36] N. Huyghebaert, 'Un moine hagiographe: Drogon de Bergues', *Sacris Erudiri* 20 (1971), pp. 191-256; idem, 'Les deux translations du roi saint Oswald à Bergues-Saint-Winoc', *Revue Bénédictine* 86 (1976), pp. 83-93, at pp. 88-90.

corporeal relics, which are specifically mentioned by him elsewhere in relation to the other saints of the abbey, Winnoc and Lewinna. It could be, therefore, as Huyghebaert has suggested, that a relic in the form of a fragment of the wood on which Oswald's head had allegedly been impaled was kept at Bergues. Such a fragment is known, for instance, to have been venerated by Willibrord.[37]

There could also be another reason, however, for the presence at Bergues of Oswald's relics. The historical records show that the abbey's main benefactors, the counts of Flanders, traditionally enjoyed close contacts with England.[38] Two possible occasions which could have given rise to the transference of some Oswald relics from England to Bergues have been discussed and subsequently rejected by N. Huyghebaert.

The first possibility concerns an earlier Judith, daughter of Charles the Bald and mother of Baldwin II of Flanders, founder of the abbey, who had previously been wife successively to Æthelwulf (839-55) and to Æthelbald (855-60) of Wessex. Huyghebaert, not aware of a possible West Saxon interest in Oswald, as witnessed above, dismissed the possibility that Oswald's relics could have reached Bergues through the good offices of the mother of the abbey's founder.

A second set of suggestions regarding a possible connection between the presence of Oswald's cult in Flanders and West Saxon influence, this time focusing on the role of an intermediary called Balger, is likewise rejected by Huyghebaert. One difficulty is knowing how to assess the reliability of the account in the *Catalogus Reverendorum Abbatum Monasterii S. Winoci*, composed at the end of the sixteenth century by the then prior of Bergues, Pierre de Walloncapelle. The text mentions two translations of Oswald's relics at Bergues, the first of which, in 1038, is described in the following words:

> In the year 1038 the bodies of St Oswald, king and martyr of the English, and of St Idaberg, virgin, were translated hither to us from England by Balger, a monk of this monastery, thanks to his close friendship with St Edward, king of the English.

A similar wording is used by the author in dating a second, historically authenticated, translation of these saints to the year 1221;[39] and Huyghebaert believes that de Walloncapelle's account of the 1038 translation derived from a confusion with the translation of St Lewinna in 1058. It is in this context that Drogo refers to his own fellow monk Balger who was 'known to the

---

[37] Idem, 'Un moine hagiographe', pp. 90-2. Thacker, above, pp. 114-16, 126-7.

[38] Huyghebaert, 'Les deux translations', p. 91. Dumville, *Wessex and England*, p. 160.

[39] I quote the passage from Huyghebaert, 'Les deux translations', pp. 84-5; the edition of the source, A. Pruvost, *Chronique et cartulaire de l'abbaye de Bergues-Saint-Winoc* (I, Bruges 1875), p. 89 and p. 208, was not accessible to me.

king, queen, and to several leading men of the country', i.e. England, presumably the same monk as is mentioned by de Walloncapelle.[40] Huyghebaert further points out that, *pace* de Walloncapelle's claim, Edward could not be called king of England until 1042. However, it is possible that Pierre de Walloncapelle's passage presumes the memory of an earlier translation, albeit in garbled form, and it is to this possibility that we will now turn.

The famous embassy sent by Hugh, duke of the Franks, to King Athelstan in 926 had been led by Count Adelolf of Boulogne, brother of Arnulf of Flanders and lay-abbot of St Bertin.[41] A son of Ealswith, King Alfred's daughter, Adelolf was eminently qualified for the task of negotiating the terms of a marriage between Athelstan's half-sister Eadhild and Duke Hugh. Further, whatever the exact terms may have been, the occasion is known to have been marked by an exchange of relics, apparently at the monastery of Abingdon. J. A. Robinson has shown, for instance, that the monks at Abingdon later claimed possession of some relics presented by Duke Hugh.[42] Could it be that Athelstan had responded in kind by presenting Adelolf with, among others, relics of Oswald? It may be a very tenuous link that connects Abingdon with St Bertin and so Bergues. But we should at least allow for the possibility that, having been kept at St Bertin since Athelstan's time, Oswald's relics were then translated to Bergues probably shortly before Drogo composed the saint's Life c.1050. Indeed, there can have been no more suitable occasion for the transfer of these relics, presumably among others, than the arrival at Bergues in 1022 of a colony of monks from St Bertin. It is possible, then, that Balger, the eleventh-century monk of Bergues mentioned by de Walloncapelle and Drogo, became interested in St Oswald through his close links with England, and inspired his fellow monks at Bergues to accord an active cult to their relics of St Oswald.[43] Pierre de Walloncapelle's version of events is clearly quite

---

[40] Drogo of Bergues, *Historia translationis S. Lewinnae*, MGH *Scriptores* 15, pp. 782-9, at p. 783; see also Huyghebaert, 'Les deux translations', pp. 87-8.

[41] J. A. Robinson, *The Times of St Dunstan* (Oxford 1923), pp. 79-80; D. W. Rollason, 'Relic-cults as an instrument of royal policy c.900-c.1050', *ASE* 15 (1986), pp. 91-103, at p. 93.

[42] Robinson, op. cit., p. 80. See also Thacker, above, p. 121, n.150.

[43] Alternative possibilities are that Balger himself might have initiated the transfer of Oswald relics from St Bertin to Bergues; or that Balger might himself have obtained relics of St Oswald in England, and been responsible for transmitting them to Bergues. Might he have been able to procure them from Abingdon, scene of the 926 relic exchange? It is worth noting that the only *Baldgarus* noted by Gerchow in the Anglo-Saxon necrological tradition is found in the chapter-book of Abingdon: ed. J. Gerchow, *Die Gedenküberlieferung*, p. 336.

inaccurate in its detail. This is not to say, however, that it does not contain a grain of historical truth.

Before ever Judith of Flanders moved to Northumbria about the middle of the eleventh century, therefore, she could have been aware of Oswald's cult. According to Symeon of Durham, the monks of Lindisfarne had placed St Oswald's head (formerly buried in their cemetery), in the reliquary-coffin holding St Cuthbert's body when they abandoned their monastery in 875; and subsequently the relics of the two saints shared the same itinerary.[44] Thus, by the time of Judith's marriage to Tostig, which lasted from c.1051 to 1064/5, the relics had already reached their final resting place at Durham. The remains of Oswine, king of Deira after Oswald, had likewise reached Durham, where Judith is known to have procured part of them.[45] The queen's devotion to St Cuthbert is similarly attested by Symeon of Durham.[46] Despite the lack of direct evidence in Oswald's case, therefore, it must seem very likely that Judith's proven interest in relics extended also to him.

Certainly, the king's relics figure prominently among the treasures donated to the monastery of Weingarten near Lake Constance by Judith's second husband, Welf IV. Despite being very closely connected with the imperial city of Regensburg, which was their main seat, the Welfs had selected Weingarten as their burial place and Judith herself is known to have endowed the monastery lavishly.[47] Her endowment mostly took the form of manuscripts, and of those commissioned by her for the library at Weingarten, and still extant, three gospel books are of particular interest. One of them, now Pierpont Morgan Library MS 709, depicts a famous crucifixion scene; in this, the figure embracing the base of the cross, a rough-hewn tree, is thought to represent Judith herself.[48] However, while

---

44 Plummer, II, 157. Athelstan probably saw Oswald's relics during his sojourn at Chester-le-Street.

45 Plummer, II, 164.

46 *HDE* III, 11: Arnold I, pp. 94-5.

47 A twelfth-century Weingarten manuscript, at the end of 'De Inventione et Translatione Sanguinis Domine', relates of Judith: 'Domina vero Iuditha fletibus uberrimis lacrimosa obtulit pallam auro purissimo intextam, maspas habentem dispositas per loca aurifrigias; scrinea eburnea, auro et argento circumornata; cruces aureas cum reliquiis sanctorum, gemmis optimis plene ornatas; calices aureos, thuribula et candelabra aurea, plenaria plurima, arcellam fabrefactam, plenam reliquiis sancti Oswaldi; postremo quidem in timore Domini sacrosanctum Christi cruorem adolevit et obtulit quasi incensum in odorem sanctitatis; quo libamine hunc locum beavit. His patratis, Welfo dux, valedicens omnibus, ad Terram [Sanctam] profecturus discedit', MGH *Scriptores* 15, p. 923. See also Baker, 'Zug', p. 106.

48 Fol.1^v. See E. Temple, *Anglo-Saxon Manuscripts 999-1066* (London 1976), no. 93, pp. 108-11 and plate 289.

this manuscript may have originated in the first half of the eleventh century, the crucifixion scene, if it does depict Judith, must be a later addition: the earliest it could date from is 1051, the year of her marriage to Tostig. J. O'Reilly, taking her cue from the identifications of the wood of the cross made in the liturgical ceremonies on Good Friday, comments 'that the *lignum vitae* in Judith's miniature conveys with metaphysical wit the divine plan of salvation and the relationship of the redeeming Cross with the Tree of Death (the *lignum scientiae*) and the paradisal and eschatological Tree of Life'. I would like to suggest that there is also a possible link here with Bede's portrayal of Oswald setting up a cross and praying to God to help his army in battle. Amalarius of Metz's citation of Bede's testimony in this instance formed part of the *adoratio crucis* ceremony copied at Canterbury, c.975.[49] Splinters of the cross allegedly set up by Oswald came to be regarded as relics almost immediately after the king's death. Moreover, relics in this form seem likewise to have become objects of veneration at such abbeys as Bergues on the continent, a development no doubt facilitated by the fact that the cult of the Holy Cross itself was already well established. King Athelstan's collection of relics, for instance, included a particle of the Holy Cross.[50]

However the question of Judith's involvement may finally be resolved, Oswald's cult at Weingarten is certainly well attested in the period after her death. Thus, after being kept for some time in a chapel dedicated to St Leonard, the Northumbrian king's relics are known to have been moved nearer the burial vault of the founders themselves in 1182. Later still, the saint's cult was to be eclipsed to a certain degree by veneration of a relic of the Holy Blood, which had been presented to Judith's step-father by the Emperor Henry III.[51] In the meantime, however, as E. P. Baker has shown,

---

[49] I want to thank Dr Jennifer O'Reilly for providing me with this reference; see also J. O'Reilly, 'The rough-hewn cross in Anglo-Saxon art', in *Ireland and Insular Art A.D. 500-1200*, ed. M. Ryan (Royal Irish Academy, Dublin 1987), pp. 153-8, at pp. 156-7.

[50] On the distribution of the texts of Amalarius within England see Dumville, *Liturgy and the Ecclesiastical History*, pp. 135-6. The *adoratio crucis* is also represented in the inscriptions of a portable altar (Musée de Cluny, Paris, cl.II.459), which, since it shows affinities to her manuscripts, may have been part of the treasures presented by Judith to Weingarten: E. Okasha and J. O'Reilly, 'An Anglo-Saxon portable altar: inscription and iconography', *Journal of the Warburg and Courtauld Institutes* 47 (1984), pp. 32-51. K. H. Göller and J. Ritzke-Rutherford have drawn attention to the possibility that the cult of the Holy Cross may have aided the spread of Oswald's cult: 'St Oswald in Regensburg. A reconsideration', *Bavarica Anglica*, vol. I: *A Cross-Cultural Miscellany presented to Tom Fletcher* (Frankfurt am Main 1979), pp. 98-118, at pp. 100-1.

[51] Baker, 'Zug', p. 106; H. Schnell, *Weingarten* (Kunstführer Nr. 528, Munich and Zurich 1950), pp. 8-10.

Weingarten was instrumental in the diffusion of Oswald's cult in south-west Germany and Switzerland, where veneration was largely confined to the dioceses of Chur and Constance within the metropolitan province of Mainz. Other local dedications, as listed by R. Folz, can similarly be linked to Welf land-holdings.[52] A lively local traffic in Oswald's relics must have accompanied the expansion of the cult in the area in question. However, the earliest direct testimony to this kind of activity is dated to the end of the twelfth century.[53]

In sum, therefore, of the saints whose cults Judith appears to have brought with her from Northumbria, Oswald certainly flourished most of all. Just as the Saxons had done before them, the Welfs showed a keen awareness of the political benefits which might accrue to them from the promotion of the king's cult by adopting him as their patron saint. His connection with kingship lent a special aura to his devotees, which was enhanced by the other royal saints commemorated regularly with him. Oswald's credentials eminently qualified him for inclusion in the category of sainted ancestors, by then so prevalent in continental royal houses. Indeed, he is found in such exalted company as that of a sainted emperor, Charlemagne, besides that of less well known continental kings, such as Sigismund of Burgundy.[54]

Oswald's popularity may also be explained by reference to the fact that his biography lent itself to interpretation in a way particularly suited to the times in question. As E. P. Baker has argued, the emergence of warrior saints may well have been an important contributory factor to the growth of Oswald's cult.[55] And in this respect, it is surely significant that the name of Oswald has sometimes been added to apparently prior dedications to St Martin, as appears to have happened at Bergues, for instance, and again at Weingarten.[56]

---

[52] Folz, pp. 67-70.

[53] The roll-call of relics, some of which were collected by the church at Zug, the centre of Oswald's cult in Switzerland, is very interesting, but outside the scope of this paper. Reference is made to Oswald's head as a relic at Schaffhausen and part of his arm is said to have been procured from Peterborough. Baker, 'Zug', pp. 103-23.

[54] Folz, p. 67, n. 83. On the English royal saints, see Campbell, *Essays*, pp. 192-3. Concerning the whole phenomenon of sainted ancestors, see Hauck, 'Geblütsheiligkeit'.

[55] Baker, 'Zug', p. 107, note 4.

[56] The dedication to St Martin already existed at St Bertin: C. de Croocq, 'Saint Winoc', pp. 51, 64, 76. On Weingarten, see Folz, p. 69.

Matilda

As a warrior saint celebrated for his warfare against the heathen, Oswald would have acquired great symbolic relevance by the time kings and nobles were embarking on the second crusade at Regensburg in 1147. Moreover, among the pilgrims on this occasion was another Welf, Henry the Lion. In 1168 he was to marry Matilda, daughter of Henry II of England; and this arranged marriage marked the beginning of a new English–Welf alliance.[57]

Twelfth-century Regensburg was not only the principal seat of the Welfs, it was also the location of a bishopric and of a number of extremely powerful and productive abbeys. As such it was well placed to serve as a centre for the dissemination of Oswald's cult. As Welf power expanded, so also devotion to Oswald seems to have spread. Thus it was probably after Henry the Lion extended his hegemony in the north-east of Germany about the middle of the twelfth century that one of the most important surviving witnesses to the cult arrived there, the famous St Oswald head-reliquary of the cathedral at Hildesheim (Pl. 12). Although an Oswald relic was at Hildesheim in 1061,[58] it seems likely that the cult was reintroduced by Henry and his English wife, and that it was they who brought the reliquary to Hildesheim. This assumption is supported by the fact that beneath the octagonal dome, with its supposed particle of Oswald's head, there are eight panels depicting kings, nearly all of English origin (Pls 10, 12). Their names, Ædwardus, Elfredus, Ædelwoldus, Canutus, Ædelbertus and Edmundus, which are accompanied by those of Oswaldus and Sigemundus (of Burgundy), bear unmistakable witness to an ultimately English provenance for the reliquary, which is also indicated by details of the workmanship.[59] If it can be further inferred from the names on the reliquary that Henry's English wife, Matilda, counted these kings amongst her saintly forebears, then her ambitions in this regard may be said to have greatly exceeded those of her predecessor, Edith, some three centuries before. It should not be overlooked, however, that Matilda found herself in the very place where her illustrious compatriot had previously lived. Indeed, the presence of the apparently English reliquary at Hildesheim is scarcely an accident. On the contrary, its presentation to the cathedral may well have represented something of a political statement on Matilda's part, an act of solidarity with her earlier role model. Furthermore, commemoration

---

[57] On Henry the Lion, see K. Jordan, *Heinrich der Löwe* (Munich 1979).

[58] Brandt, *Kirchenkunst*, p. 135.

[59] C. M. Fandrey, *Das Oswald-Reliquiar im Hildesheimer Domschatz* (Göppinger Akademische Beiträge no. 125, Göppingen 1987); but for another view, see above, p. 5, n. 6. The presence of the reliquary at Hildesheim is attested from the beginning of the fifteenth century. The inscription underneath the head is given by Clemoes, p. 9, as: REX PIVS OSWALDVS SESE DEDIT ET SVA CHRISTO LICTORIQVE CAPVT QVOD IN AVRO CONDITVR ISTO.

on the reliquary of so many sainted royal ancestors could also have been used with another political purpose in mind: to further the status of the Welfs in their claims to authority over Saxony.

The potential usefulness of liturgical objects as a means of furthering political ambition was fully appreciated by the Welfs. Thus, following the example of other important rulers before them, Henry and Matilda had arranged to have parts of their illustrious genealogies entered in a specially commissioned liturgical manuscript. Accompanying the genealogy on Henry's side is a cloak adorned by the sign of the cross, a symbol justified by his pilgrimage to Palestine in 1172. Elsewhere his descent is traced, in several illuminations, back as far as his grandfather, the Emperor Lothar. Matilda, for her part, is accompanied by a portrait of her father, Henry II, and of her grandmother, REGINA MATHILDA, grand-daughter of William the Conqueror and at one time childless wife of the last Salian emperor, Henry V.[60]

The reliquary apart, no further attestations of Oswald's cult are recorded in Saxony. This is in marked contrast to Regensburg itself where various strands of devotion to the sainted king seem to have converged. Here Henry the Lion's political ambitions found expression, among other ways, in more secular literary manifestations. Thus, following the epoch-making ceremony of the canonisation of Charlemagne in 1165, instigated by Frederick Barbarossa, a German version of the *Chanson de Roland* was composed by the Regensburg cleric Conrad. Interestingly, according to its epilogue, the source for the translation of the *Chanson* was procured from England at the behest of the Duchess Matilda. Moreover the theme of this work, the fighting and forcible conversion of Saracen Spain by Charlemagne, lent itself to reinterpretation in terms of Henry's glorious crusade against the pagan territories of eastern Germany and of the Orient. Other texts appear to have been composed for the same purpose, a case in point being *König Rother*, likewise of Regensburg provenance, which reveals many similarities to the *Chanson*, and which could also be reinterpreted to the glory of the Welfs. An example of the *Spielmannsepos* or minstrel poetry, *König Rother* may be dated to c.1160-1170 on the basis of its allusions to political contemporary events in general, and to the fortunes of the Welfs in particular. The *Brautentführung* or elopement theme present in *König Rother* appears to have influenced the composition of the German poem on Oswald, which is discussed in

---

[60] K. Bertau, *Deutsche Literatur im europäischen Mittelalter im europäischen Mittelalter* (2 vols, Munich 1972-3), vol. I: *800-1197*, pp. 459-60. For an illustration of the page containing the genealogy see ibid., II, pl. 64. This manuscript and others were written at the monastery of Helmarshausen on the Weser. The lead slab in the altar of the cathedral at Brunswick, which became the main seat of the couple, displays a similar inscription, including a reference to Matilda as FILIA HENRICI SECVNDI REGIS ANGLORVM FILII MATHILDIS IMPERATRICIS ROMANORVM; Bertau I, p. 460.

Annemiek Jansen's paper. This is but one, however, of many motifs shared by *König Rother* with the Munich *Oswald*.[61]

Certain parallels between the German poem and the *Life of St Oswald* composed by Reginald of Durham in 1165, which are listed by Annemiek Jansen, suggest that the Regensburg writer of the Munich *Oswald* could have been drawing on this work. However, we must also take account of the role possibly played by the enigmatic addressee of the introductory letter of Reginald's Life, who is named Henricus. Could he have been identical with *Henricus*, subprior of Durham, *natione Teutonicus*? Victoria Tudor takes the view that this German, who is otherwise unknown, could have furnished Reginald with details of the Oswald legend current on the continent.[62] In view of the fact that the themes shared by the texts are also otherwise attested in works produced in Regensburg, Tudor's view must be allowed to carry weight. As it happens, no trace has been discovered at Regensburg of a copy of Reginald's Life of the saint. However, there is evidence to show that extracts were made locally from Bede's account of Oswald, and also that a copy was procured there of Drogo's Life of the saint. Furthermore, these two texts were considered important enough to be included in the great legendaries which began to be pieced together at Regensburg around the 1160s.

Oswald and the Irish Monastery at Regensburg

Strange as it may seem, Oswald's admission to continental legendaries may well have been due initially to a community of Irish Benedictine monks which had become established in Regensburg *c.*1080. The mother house of a number of other *Schottenklöster* or Irish monasteries, at Würzburg, Nürnberg, Erfurt and Vienna, to mention only the more important, this foundation had a very active scriptorium from about the middle of the twelfth century onwards.[63] Its known production included liturgical manuscripts, and

---

[61] On all these literary works see ibid., I, pp. 460-78. The connections with Regensburg are stressed by K. Reich, 'Das mittelhochdeutsche Rotherepos und seine Beziehungen zu Bayern und Regensburg', *Zeitschrift für bayerische Landesgeschichte* 1 (1928), pp. 403-15; H. Menhardt, 'Regensburg ein Mittelpunkt der deutschen Epik des 12. Jahrhunderts', *Zeitschrift für deutsches Altertum und Literatur* 89 (1958), pp. 271-4; J. Dünninger, 'St Oswald und Regensburg', in: *Gedächtnisschrift für A. Hämel* (Würzburg 1953), pp. 17-26; K. H. Göller, 'König Oswald von Northumbrien: von der *Historia Ecclesiastica* bis zur Regensburger Stadtsage', in *Festschrift für Karl Schneider*, ed. E. S. Dick and K. R. Jankowsky (Amsterdam and Philadelphia 1982), pp. 305-23. For A. Jansen's paper see below, pp. 230-40, esp. pp. 230-1.

[62] See V. Tudor's article, above, p. 179.

[63] For recent histories of the *Schottenklöster* see L. Hammermeyer, 'Die irischen Benediktiner "Schottenklöster" in Deutschland und ihr institutioneller Zusammenschluss vom 12.-16. Jahrhundert', *Studien und Mitteilungen zur*

historiographical and hagiographical works. Moreover, while keeping in close contact with their Irish homeland, the Regensburg monks also maintained good relations with neighbouring monasteries.[64] It is in this capacity that they appear to have contributed to the compilation of the most substantial legendary of all, the so-called *Magnum Legendarium Austriacum*. Despite the Austrian provenance of its surviving manuscripts, it has been argued that the exemplar of this great legendary was compiled at Regensburg from about 1160 onwards, as a co-operative monastic venture. Furthermore, the presence of a number of Irish Lives in the legendary implies active involvement in the compilation by the local Irish monastery, which was dedicated to St James.[65] As we shall see, the presence of Oswald's Life in the collection may well be due to this involvement.

An early interest in Oswald on the part of the compilers of the *Magnum Legendarium Austriacum* is variously attested. In three manuscripts, including the oldest surviving one at Heiligenkreuz near Vienna, Oswald's Life is drawn from that compiled by Drogo of Bergues.[66] This sets Oswald apart from other English saints in the legendary, whose lives almost invariably consist of extracts from Bede.[67] In fact, this is also true of Oswald himself in a collection predating the manuscripts of the great Austrian legendary,

Geschichte des Benediktiner-Ordens und seiner Zweige 87 (1976), pp. 249-338; P. Breatnach, *Die Regensburger Schottenlegende: Libellus de Fundacione Ecclesie Consecrati Petri* (Munich 1977).

[64] The contacts of the Irish community with German monasteries are reflected in *Gebetsverbrüderungen* or prayer fraternities, entered in a necrology commenced at St James in 1150. This document also contains the obits of Irish benefactors: D. Ó Riain-Raedel, 'Irish kings and bishops in the memoria of the German Schottenklöster', in *Irland und Europa*, ed. P. Ní Chatháin and M. Richter (Stuttgart 1984), pp. 390-404; eadem, 'Das Nekrolog der irischen Schottenklöster. Edition der Handschrift Vat. lat. 10100 mit einer Untersuchung der hagiographischen und liturgischen Handschriften der Schottenklöster', *Beiträge zur Geschichte des Bistums Regensburg* 26 (1992), pp. 1-119.

[65] On the *Magnum Legendarium Austriacum* see A. Poncelet, 'De Magno Legendario Austriaco', *AB* 17 (1898), pp. 24-216. The 580 *vitae* are divided according to the calendar into four volumes. The full legendary is nowhere extant. However, its contents can be pieced together from the disparate surviving volumes. On the Irish Lives see L. Bieler, *Four Latin Lives of St Patrick* (Scriptores Latini Hiberniae 8, Dublin 1971), pp. 13-21, 233-4. The pivotal role played by the various Regensburg monasteries will be discussed in my forthcoming edition of the Irish saints' Lives in the legendary.

[66] Heiligenkreuz (Ord Cist) MS 13, fols 78v-80r; Lilienfeld (Ord Cist) MS 60, fols 115v–118r; Melk (Ord Ben) MS 6 (nunc: 101), fols 180v-184v.

[67] This includes the Lives of S. Albani mart., S. Cuthberti ep., S. Willifridi ep. Eboracensis et mart., S. Augustini Anglorum ep., S. Ediltrudis virg. et reginae, SS. duorum Ewaldorum; S. Aidani ep. Lindisfarnensis and Obitus Bedae presb. (Epistula Cuthberti).

known as the *Legendarium Windbergense*. This was compiled at the Premonstratensian house at Windberg, near Regensburg, in the second half of the twelfth century, probably between 1150 and 1160. As Poncelet has shown, both this collection and the Austrian legendary relied on the same or very similar sources, each adding further Lives from independent sources.[68]

Be this as it may, extracts from Bede on Oswald turn up in two other manuscript witnesses besides the *Legendarium Windbergense*. One of these is Munich Universitätsbibliothek 2° Cod. ms. 312, a manuscript which was at one time at the Benedictine monastery of Biburg. This preserves Oswald's Life in a form nearly identical to that of the Windberg manuscript. In this case, however, there are some unequivocal pointers to Irish involvement in the compilation of the manuscript. Thus, in the first part of the manuscript, which contains a collection of sermons, special attention is paid to St James, patron of the Irish at Regensburg. Here also, evincing the same interest, is found a copy of the *Translatio Iacobi Maioris*; and, most significantly, a list of saints' Lives of mainly Irish interest is also added to this part of the manuscript, in a later hand. Included in the list are such notable saints as Patrick and Kevin, who are accompanied by continental saints with Irish connections, such as Gall and Pirmin. What is particularly pertinent for us is that the list also refers to the Life of *Oswaldus rex*, which is further distinguished at its place in the manuscript by a large historiated initial (Pl. 17).[69] Purely on the evidence of its emphasis on St James and of its list of mainly Irish saints, the Munich manuscript can hardly have been written in a scriptorium other than that of the Irish monastery at Regensburg. It also appears from the contents of the list that its compiler must have had a particular interest in Oswald: an interest presumably shared by the whole Irish community at Regensburg. The existence of this interest may also

---

[68] The six volumes of the Windberg legendary are now Munich Staatsbibliothek clm 22240-22245. For a description see Poncelet, art. cit., pp. 97-122. Since they already appear in a library catalogue of 1165, a date of compilation shortly prior to this seems likely. The excerpts from Bede comprise: *HE* II, 9; II, 20, III, 1-3; III, 5-7, finishing in the middle of the sentence and omitting the last paragraph; III, 8-13; IV, 14, omitting the first paragraph. Oswald's Life appears in volume clm 22242, ranging from 1 July to 15 August, as item no. 31, fols 114ᵛ-121ʳ.

[69] The importance of this volume for Irish studies has been recognised since the early seventeenth century, when a copy of its *Vita tertia Sti Patricii* was made by the Irish Jesuit Stephen White. Bieler, *Four Latin Lives*, pp. 14-15. Oswald's Life is at fols. 101ᵛ-123ᵛ. The other Lives are: Otmar, Hieronymus, Alexius, Augustinus, Martialis. For a description of the manuscript, see N. Daniel, G. Schott and P. Zahn, *Die lateinischen mittelalterlichen Handschriften der Universitätsbibliothek München. Die Handschriften aus der Folioreihe*, part II (Wiesbaden 1979), pp. 55-7. A large initial at the beginning of Oswald's Life is also found in the Windberg manuscript.

underlie the survival at Regensburg of a twelfth-century fragment of a very similar Oswald dossier. While there is nothing to connect this fragment with the *Schottenkloster*, its text of the Life contains more or less the same excerpts as the other manuscript. However, unlike the Munich manuscript, the Regensburg Life of Oswald is distinguished by its strict omission of all extraneous matter present in Bede's account of Oswald.[70] If there was interdependence between the manuscripts, therefore, then the Regensburg fragment must have been copied from the *Schottenkloster* Life.

Oswald's obvious importance to the Irish community at Regensburg may have arisen from the part played in his life by St Aidan of Lindisfarne. In the sometimes hostile or envious foreign surroundings of their monastery at Regensburg, the Irish monks sought justification for the protection of their privileges and immunities in the glorious historical role of their people in converting others to the true faith. Thus, the foundation chronicle of the *Schottenkloster*, entitled *Libellus de Fundacione Ecclesie Consecrati Petri*, devoted a paragraph to the role played by St Aidan in the conversion of heathen Northumbria. Its account was based on an existing text, also written at Regensburg, the *Vita Mariani*. What is particularly interesting about the *Libellus*'s treatment of Aidan is its claim that he was buried 'cum honore et reverencia debita in civitate Windonia'.[71] According to Bede, Aidan had been buried at Lindisfarne.[72] Even if his relics may have shared the subsequent travels of those of Cuthbert and Oswald, it surely comes as a surprise to hear that he is supposed to have been buried at Winchester. Could it be that account has been taken here of Welf connections, through marriage, with southern England? The Welf connection may also help to explain the *Schottenkloster* interest in Oswald. The Welfs were in fact benefactors of the Irish monasteries in Germany: thus, the *Schottenkloster* of St Nicholas, a daughter house of the Regensburg community at Memmingen, was founded by Duke Welf VI c.1180.[73]

Yet another possible explanation of *Schottenkloster* interest in Oswald lies, curiously enough, in the monastery's ongoing dependence for its well-being on lay benefactions. All documents written at St James from the 1150s onwards stress the role of lay benefactors and the pressing need of generosity towards the *pauperes*, another word for monks. This is one of the central themes, for instance, of the *Visio Tnugdali*, composed in St James c.1150,

---

[70] Curschmann, *MODSE*, pp. 192-3, gives a description of the text; see also K. H. Göller, 'König Oswald' (as n. 60), p. 308.

[71] 'With honour and due reverence in the city of Winchester': Breatnach, *Die Regensburger Schottenlegende*, pp. 143-4. The *Vita Mariani* is edited in *AASS Feb.* II (1658), pp. 361-72.

[72] *HE* III, 17. Plummer II, p. 167, notes the claim of the abbey of Glastonbury to relics of Aidan.

[73] Breatnach, *Libellus*, pp. 65-71, 275-310.

which claims that only noblemen who entered a monastery, or otherwise contributed generously towards its upkeep, might be encountered in heaven's joyful fields.[74] Here, the generosity displayed by Oswald during his Easter meal with Aidan, when he divided his silver dish among the *pauperes*,[75] would have served as an excellent paradigm of the importance attached by the monks to their lay benefactors. And that Oswald in fact served as a role-model for benefactors is clear from the relevant illustration in the early thirteenth-century Berthold Missal from Weingarten (Pl. 13).[76]

To sum up, then, the figure of Oswald *rex et martyrus* clearly lent itself to a wide range of adaptations. Repeatedly, his cult appears to have attracted the attention of groups well placed genealogically to use his memory to their own advantage. In this way, for instance, his cult came to be fostered by such German noble houses as those of the Saxons and Welfs, who, through their marital connections with English ladies of royal birth, could more or less legitimately use the saint's legend as a means of promoting their own political aims. Similarly, the house of Wessex itself may have 'adopted' Oswald in its own political interest. Later, through his transformation into the hero of a *Spielmannsepos*, Oswald the warrior-saint became a patron of crusaders. This appears to have occurred at Regensburg, where he also captured the imagination of Irish Benedictine monks, possibly first attracted to him by his connections with Aidan of Lindisfarne. In any case, his proven generosity to the poor also made him an excellent champion of monks dependent on largesse. Finally, while it lies outside the scope of the present article, this latter trait of his character, together with the fact that his feast day coincided with the harvest season, transformed Oswald into a saint widely venerated by the lower groups of society. Of Oswald it can be truthfully said, that his was a multifaceted cult.

---

[74] Ó Riain-Raedel, 'Das Nekrolog', p. 29. The *Visio Tnugdali* has been edited by A. Wagner, *Visio Tnugdali. Lateinisch und Altdeutsch* (Erlangen 1882).
[75] *HE* III, 6. Cf. Stancliffe, above, p. 65 and n. 151.
[76] Cf. Stancliffe and Cambridge, above, p. 5.

The Development of the St Oswald Legends on the Continent

ANNEMIEK JANSEN

This paper will attempt to show how the legends concerning St Oswald, the Northumbrian king who became honoured as a martyr, developed on the continent. Oswald became a very popular saint there, as may be gathered from the fact that his cult flourished in the Low Countries, Germany, Austria, Switzerland, parts of eastern Europe, northern Italy, and Scandinavia, including Iceland. Oswald's life was first described by the Venerable Bede in his *Ecclesiastical History of the English People*. From Bede's account Oswald emerges as a devout and most charitable king, who was very eager to convert his subjects to the Christian faith. According to Bede, Oswald married the daughter of Cynegils, king of the West Saxons, while standing godfather to Cynegils at the latter's baptism. Bede also tells of Oswald's battles: he defeated the savage Cadwallon, king of the Britons, after having prayed with his whole army by a wooden cross he had set up, and in 642 he was killed in a battle against Penda, the heathen king of Mercia.[1]

Oswald's cult started early, not only in England, but also on the continent.[2] Wherever the cult flourished texts were produced which, in their turn, supported the cult. Those produced on the continent are of two kinds. On the one hand, there is a group of texts meant for liturgical and monastic purposes, such as offices and homilies, and the Latin Life of Oswald written c.1050 by Drogo, a monk of St Winnoc's Abbey at Bergues in Flanders. Drogo also wrote two sermons, one on the subject of Oswald's charity, the other on Oswald's care for the spiritual well-being of his subjects.[3] These liturgical and monastic texts were all based on Bede. On the other hand, there is a group of texts which constitutes the distinctively continental Oswald tradition. This tradition started to develop more than a century after Drogo wrote his Life of Oswald. Oswald underwent a change. The historical king became a hero of romance, and it was in this new capacity that he made a successful career on the continent as a popular saint.

The birthplace of this literary tradition was probably the Bavarian city of Regensburg, where, presumably in the second half of the twelfth century, the original versions were written of five epic poems which are commonly known by the term *Spielmannsepik* ('minstrel's tale'). This term suggests that they were written by minstrels, but this is by no means certain. These five

---

1   *HE* III, 1-3, 6-7, 9.
2   *HE* III, 2, 9-13; Thacker, above, pp. 97-119.
3   The Life of Oswald by Drogo is in *AASS* August, vol. II, pp. 94-103. The sermons are unpublished. See Clemoes, pp. 6-7.

Middle High German poems, which are neither heroic legend nor courtly romance, are all built on the same theme: the gaining of a bride. They are, by name: *König Rother*; *Herzog Ernst*; *Orendel*; *Salman und Morolf*; and *Oswald*. It is the last of these which concerns us here.[4] This poem, which is also known as the Munich *Oswald* (or *Münchener Oswald*) consists, in its present form, of 3,550 lines, and it probably developed over a long period of time. Michael Curschmann, its editor, assumes that both the author and the audience belonged to court circles. This hypothesis is supported by a fact which he points out, namely, that the cult of Oswald in twelfth-century Germany was mainly instigated by the high nobility.[5] The following description of the contents of the poem will show what became of Oswald on the continent.

Oswald, the young, mighty, and very pious king of England, wants to marry. He is, however, unsuccessful in his attempts to find a bride who is his equal; but in a dream an angel appears to him, telling him to sail to a certain pagan country, to convert the people there to the Christian faith and to marry their king's daughter. Oswald, quite at a loss what to do, deliberates with his advisers on the matter. While they are thus occupied a pilgrim arrives, who says that he knows a beautiful princess, who is the daughter of the king of a pagan country. She is secretly a Christian, but her father, Aron, is a heathen, a savage man who kills everyone courting his daughter, for he wants to marry her himself, should his wife die. Therefore the pilgrim dissuades Oswald from going straightaway, but advises him to send his raven as a messenger to King Aron. This raven had been reared at Oswald's court, and is now suddenly able to speak. After its feathers have been adorned with gold the bird sets out on its journey, with a letter and a gold ring for the princess. After an adventurous journey it reaches King Aron's castle, but as soon as it has conveyed its message to the king it is captured and is to be put to death the next day. The king's daughter threatens to marry a minstrel if her father refuses to release the raven, at which the king puts the bird at her disposal. The princess gives the raven a letter and a ring for Oswald, saying that its master should call for her next year with seventy-two ships, a large army, a quantity of food and drink that will last them eight years, a gold deer and, what is very important, the raven itself. On the homeward journey the raven, flying across the sea, is caught in a storm and loses the letter and the ring. It flies back to the shore and alights on a rock, where it finds a hermit to whom it tells what has happened. The hermit prays to God for help; soon a fish comes swimming along, which gives back both the letter and the ring, and the raven resumes its journey.

As soon as the ships are finished and ready, Oswald has thousands of gold crosses made; each of his men has to wear one. They put out to sea, and

---

4   Ed. Baesecke, *MO*; ed. Curschmann, *MO*. Cf. Ó Riain-Raedel, above, pp. 224-5.
5   Curschmann, *MODSE*, pp. 78, 177f., 180.

after a year and twelve weeks they reach King Aron's country. When Oswald wants to send his raven as a messenger to King Aron, he discovers that the bird has been left behind. God, hearing Oswald's fervent prayer for help, sends an angel to England, and the angel induces the raven, after much persuasion, to fly to Oswald, whom it reaches after four days. Oswald sends the raven to the princess, who gives the following instructions: during the night Oswald is to come to the castle with a hundred men. He is to pitch a tent in front of the castle, and he and the other occupants of his tent are to pose as goldsmiths. Together with a hundred men and twelve knights who had been goldsmiths Oswald settles in front of the castle; its inmates are wakened by the loud hammering of the goldsmiths, and the king's daughter persuades her father to commission rings and other jewels, and a crown for himself. He assents. However, after a year and twelve weeks Oswald and his company are still there without having met the king's daughter. One night Oswald has a dream in which it is revealed to him how he may gain his bride. He acts upon it, ordering the goldsmiths to make two gold claws, a pair of gold antlers, and a gold cover. With these he adorns the deer, intending to lure Aron away from the castle, in the hope that he will leave the door unlocked, giving Oswald an opportunity to enter the castle. Aron, eager to catch the deer, leaves the castle, but the doorkeeper bolts the door on the outside. The princess, standing on the battlements with her mother and her ladies-in-waiting, knows that her father is gone, and she and three of the maids disguise themselves as knights and hurry downstairs, where they find the door bolted on the outside. They pray to the Christian God, and instantly the door opens. They hurry to Oswald's tent; Oswald gathers his men, and they all board the ships and put out to sea.

As soon as Aron discovers what has happened he sounds his magic horn, summoning all his men. In their pirate ships they pursue Oswald and his army. To give Oswald an advantage over his pursuers God sends a dense fog and wind to confuse the pagans, but he sends sunshine to Oswald, giving the latter an opportunity to reach the shore of an island before he is overtaken by his enemies. Oswald and Aron join battle; Aron is defeated, and now Oswald demands that Aron should receive baptism. When the latter refuses Oswald raises all Aron's soldiers from the dead, thus giving a proof of God's power, but as soon as the soldiers are alive again Aron wants to start another battle. However, his soldiers refuse, for they were in hell while they were dead, and now they believe only in Jesus Christ. Aron, persisting in his unbelief, demands another miracle: he wants a particular rock to yield water. This feat is also performed, and now Aron is willing to receive baptism. From now on he will be called Zentinus. His soldiers are baptized too, after which they soon die again and are led to heaven by angels. Oswald returns to England with his bride and his men. As soon as he is home again he celebrates his wedding, to which he also invites many poor people. Christ himself is among them, disguised as a pilgrim. He wants to put Oswald's charity to the test, asking him for bread, meat, money, a gold vessel, a towel adorned with gold and silver, and eventually for Oswald's kingdom and his wife.[6] Oswald gives him everything and then expresses a wish to leave, intending to live by begging from now on. But Christ says that the king has stood the test and gives him back everything. He tells Oswald that he and his wife will die within two years. They should live in chastity, taming their carnal lust by jumping into a tub of cold water placed by the bed. After two years they indeed die, and are led to heaven by angels.

Far removed as the Munich *Oswald* may seem from Bede's account of Oswald's life, there are still various similarities. The main characteristics of the historical Oswald – his eagerness to convert people to the Christian faith, his reliance on God's help when confronting his enemies, his charity towards the poor, and his piety – are retained in the Munich *Oswald*. In the German poem Oswald marries the daughter of a pagan king who is converted to Christianity and baptized, and this is exactly what, according to Bede, the historical Oswald did. In the Munich *Oswald*, however, Oswald's zeal for the Christian faith is put in a wider context. The Anglo-Saxon king, who still had to fight paganism in his own country, has changed into a crusader. He is the personification of the Christian world and has to go abroad, by divine command, to bring Christianity to that part of the world which is still shrouded in the darkness of pagan beliefs. It would seem that Oswald's role as a converter of pagans is not only derived from the missionary activities of the historical king in his native country, but is also reminiscent of the proselytism of such continental monarchs as Charlemagne and King Olaf of Norway. Bede was not the only source for the Munich *Oswald*. We shall not investigate here all the possible sources, which must have been many and various, but it should be noted that there are a number of similarities between the Munich *Oswald* and the Latin *Life of St Oswald* written by Reginald of Durham in 1165.[7]

Reginald's work is based on Bede, but he adds many elements which he had from oral tradition, as he himself says. We find the following parallels between Reginald's work and the Munich *Oswald*: 1. Oswald wants his future bride to be his equal in all respects.[8] 2. Oswald insists that his future

---

[6] Oswald's charity is put to the test in consequence of a vow he makes when he is pursued by the pagans: when praying to God for help he promises that henceforward he will yield anything, even his head, to anybody asking him for it for the sake of God.

[7] Much of Reginald's *Life of St Oswald* has been printed in Reginald, *VO*, on which see Tudor, above, pp. 178-94.

[8] Reginald, *VO* I, 3; Baesecke, *MO* lines 51-8, 158.

father-in-law should receive baptism.[9] 3. The time of Oswald's death is predicted to him: in Reginald's work by angels, in a vision Oswald has when he is suffering from the plague, and in the Munich *Oswald* by Christ, who is present at Oswald's wedding disguised as a pilgrim.[10] 4. Oswald and his wife live in chastity. In the Munich *Oswald* they are exhorted to this way of life by Christ himself; in Reginald's *Life* Oswald adopts a life of chastity as a result of the vision he had during his illness.[11] 5. A rock is made to yield water. In Reginald's work this rock is near the place where Oswald is killed: a large raven-like bird seizes Oswald's right arm and drops it on the rock, at which a spring rises from the rock. In the Munich *Oswald* the king, with God's help, makes a rock yield water at the request of his pagan opponent, Aron.[12] 6. A multitude of people wants to receive baptism. In the Munich *Oswald* Aron's whole army is baptized; in Reginald's *Life* all Oswald's subjects want to be baptized after Oswald has had a vision in which St Columba appeared to him.[13]

On the basis of these similarities some scholars, including Curschmann, believe that Reginald's *Life of St Oswald* may have been one of the sources for the Munich *Oswald*.[14] According to others, however, these similarities are wholly coincidental.[15] In this matter nothing can be said with any certainty. There is no denying, however, that Reginald's work represents the first stage of Oswald's transformation from a historical into a legendary figure, and may thus have started a development which was completed on the continent. Whereas Bede's approach is that of the historian, Reginald's *Life of St Oswald* bears all the characteristics of a saint's legend: there, angels and visions play an important role in Oswald's life, in that they determine the actions which lead him to holiness. Bede saw a relationship between Oswald's Christian virtues and the extension of his kingdom.[16] So does Reginald, but he also tells how during Oswald's reign his subjects became more and more prosperous; poverty was almost unknown then in England because during that period the

9 Reginald, loc. cit.; Baesecke, *MO* lines 2946, 3091-6.
10 Reginald, *VO* I, 10; Baesecke, *MO* line 3500.
11 Reginald, *VO* I, 10-11; Baesecke, *MO* line 3499.
12 Reginald, *VO* I, 18; cf. the description of the bird in *VO* I, 17: 'Eratque ales ipsa, ut putabatur, corvini generis; sed pro grandibus rostro et unguibus aquilarum similitudini conformis fuisse videbatur.' ('For that bird was, it was thought, of the corvine family; but in virtue of its beak and huge talons it seemed rather to resemble an eagle.') Baesecke, *MO* lines 3075-87.
13 Reginald, *VO* I, 42; Baesecke, *MO* lines 3121-30.
14 Curschmann, *MODSE*, pp. 79, 175. Cf. also Tudor, above, p. 179, and Ó Riain-Raedel, above, p. 225.
15 See, for example, S. Schultze, *Die Entwicklung der deutschen Oswaldlegende* (dissertation, Halle 1888), pp. 33ff.
16 *HE* III, 6.

earth was extremely fertile, yielding abundant crops. Reginald's statement lends the figure of Oswald an almost mythical quality, by suggesting that his reign was a kind of golden age.[17]

Although the possibility that Reginald's *Life of St Oswald* may have been one of the sources for the Munich *Oswald* need not be ruled out, it is probably unsafe to hypothesise any relationship beyond the most general sort between the raven-like bird which steals Oswald's arm on the battlefield in Reginald's work, and the raven which, as Oswald's faithful companion, plays such a prominent role in the Munich *Oswald*, and which thereby became part and parcel of the continental Oswald tradition.

We will return to the raven shortly. First, however, something ought to be said about the further development of the Oswald tradition on the continent. This is complex, but three main branches can be distinguished: the Munich Oswald ('Münchener Oswald') branch; the Vienna Oswald ('Wiener Oswald') branch; and, thirdly, the Oswald Life in *Der Heiligen Leben*, a collection of saints' Lives.[18] It should be noted that terms such as Munich Oswald and Vienna Oswald denote the present location of important manuscripts of these texts,[19] not the place of origin of the variants of the Oswald story. The first and the third of these main branches of the Oswald tradition themselves contain variants. We will discuss the three branches in turn.

We begin with the Munich Oswald. This branch is represented not only by the poem of that name, but also by three prose versions of the poem, one of which is known – again, from the location of the manuscript – as the Budapest *Oswald*.[20] Although the poem and these prose texts all differ from each other in certain respects, they have so much in common that they are regarded as forming one, distinct, branch of the tradition.

A second branch consists of the Vienna *Oswald*, a poem of 1465 lines. This dates from the fourteenth century and was written in the Silesian dialect, probably on the occasion of the foundation of St Oswald's church at Krummendorf, the only church dedicated to Oswald in Silesia.[21] Although

---

[17] *VO* I, 10 (p. 346).

[18] In this paper we have preferred the anglicised version of place-names where these are in common English use. We have used italics to denote the titles of specific texts (Munich *Oswald*, Budapest *Oswald*); and roman to denote the main branches of the Oswald tradition (Munich Oswald, Vienna Oswald). Absolute consistency is impossible to achieve with the Vienna Oswald, since this is simultaneously both a text and a branch of the Oswald tradition.

[19] For these see Curschmann, *MODSE*, pp. 2-3.

[20] Ed. A. Vizkelety, 'Der Budapester Oswald', *Beiträge zur Geschichte der deutschen Sprache und Literatur* 86 (1964), pp. 107-88.

[21] Krummendorf belonged to a district, the capital of which was Strehlen (present-day Strzelin in south-west Poland). It is not far from Wroclaw (Breslau).

the Vienna *Oswald* has the same basic pattern as the Munich Oswald, it differs so much from the latter in its details that it is regarded as a separate branch of the tradition.[22]

The third branch is a prose text in a German collection of short prose saints' Lives, *Der Heiligen Leben*, often called the 'Wenzel-passional'. This collection dates from the end of the fourteenth century. It exists in a number of manuscripts and was printed several times. The Oswald legend it contains, derived from the Munich Oswald, gives the Oswald story in a simplified form.[23] This text, meant for wide circulation, became very popular around the middle of the fifteenth century. It differs in its details from both the Munich Oswald and the Vienna Oswald. There is, moreover, an Old Icelandic version of this text, probably written in the second half of the fifteenth century. Although this text has enough in common with the German text to justify its inclusion in the same group, it is also rather independent, combining elements from the Munich Oswald, Bede, and Reginald.[24] What is especially interesting about this third branch of the tradition is that it shows, by its inclusion in ecclesiastical legendaries, that the Oswald story produced on the continent had come to be accepted by the church there as Christian legend.

It is also interesting to compare the ways in which Oswald is presented in these various branches of the tradition. In the Munich *Oswald* and the prose texts derived from it Oswald is introduced as 'king of England'.[25] These texts still associate Oswald with his native country. According to the Vienna *Oswald*, however, Oswald was king of Germany.[26] In a fragment of one Oswald text which falls outside the tradition just described, Oswald is presented as king of Norway.[27] In the prose text included in legendaries Oswald is not of royal descent; he is described as a very good Christian upon whom God bestowed kingship as a reward for his outstanding virtues.[28]

---

[22] Ed. G. Baesecke, *Der Wiener Oswald* (Heidelberg 1912); ed. G. Fuchs, *Der Wiener Oswald* (Germanistische Abhandlungen, vol. 53; Breslau 1920). On dating and localisation see also Curschmann, *MODSE*, pp. 213-21.

[23] *Der Heiligen Leben und Leiden anders genannt das Passional*, ed. S. Rüttgers (2 vols, Leipzig 1913), II, pp. 287-94.

[24] The Old Icelandic version has been edited by J. Sigurdsson, 'Saga Ósvalds Konúngs hins Helga', in *Annaler for nordisk Oldkyndighed og Historie* (Copenhagen 1854), pp. 34-91.

[25] Baesecke, *MO*, lines 935, 1090-1230.

[26] *Der Wiener Oswald*, lines 226-8.

[27] This fragment, preserved at Linz, has been published by M. Curschmann, '"Sant Oswald von Norwegen": ein Fragment eines Legendenepos', *Zeitschrift für deutsches Altertum und deutsche Literatur* 102 (1973), pp. 101-14.

[28] *Der Heiligen Leben*, ed. Rüttgers, II, p. 287.

On the continent, therefore, Oswald underwent a process of dissociation from his native soil and original kingdom, from his royal ancestry, and from his whole historical context. He became rooted in continental soil, where he was vested with the kind of kingship that belongs to the realm of myth and legend. In the Alpine countries Oswald became the patron saint of cattle, of the harvest, and of the weather.[29] He controlled the natural forces, on the benevolence of which a rural population depended for its existence.

In the nineteenth and early twentieth centuries several scholars supported the theory that this role of Oswald was a survival of the cult of Woden.[30] According to this theory Oswald's name, the meaning of which is 'ruler of the gods', had led to his being merged with the figure of Woden, some of whose properties were transferred to Oswald. This would also account for Oswald's being linked with a raven, for Woden had two ravens which he sent to the earth each day to bring him information, and is often portrayed with one or two ravens (see Pl. 24).

This theory is rejected by the majority of modern scholars. Peter Clemoes, however, says in his Jarrow Lecture that the raven is 'doubtless of remote Teutonic ancestry'.[31] Earlier, E. P. Baker had related how, each year on 5 August (Oswald's feast day), men and boys climbed to a chapel high in the Alps. Here, they prayed to a King Oswald of the Tyrol, in whose reign there was much prosperity, and who, with his raven, made the weather.[32] In lower Bavaria the figure of Oswald was linked with ancient customs in connection with the harvest: the last sheaf on the last field was fashioned into a figure, called the 'Wode' or 'Waude' elsewhere in Germany, but the 'Aswald' or 'Oswald' in Bavaria. It was decorated with flowers and became the focus of prayer, dancing, and festivity.[33]

Iconographical representations of Oswald commonly depict him with one or more attributes, most of which go back to Bede. These are: the crown, sceptre, and orb, as symbols of his kingship (Pl. 12); the ciborium, as a

---

[29] A. Berger, 'Die Oswaldlegende in der deutschen Literatur, ihre Entwicklung und ihre Verbreitung', *Beiträge zur Geschichte der deutschen Sprache und Literatur* 11 (1886), pp. 365-469 at pp. 432-7.

[30] See, for example, I. V. Zingerle, *Die Oswaldlegende und ihre Beziehung zur deutschen Mythologie* (Stuttgart and Munich 1856), pp. 87-103, who was followed by C. A. Bernoulli, *Die Heiligen der Merowinger* (Tübingen etc. 1900), pp. 202-3.

[31] Clemoes, p. 11.

[32] E. P. Baker, 'The cult of St Oswald in northern Italy', *Archaeologia* 94 (1951), pp. 167-94, at p. 191. Cf. Zingerle, op. cit. pp. 71-4.

[33] Zingerle, *Die Oswaldlegende*, pp. 78-83; Berger, 'Die Oswaldlegende', pp. 434-6. Cf. K. H. Göller and J. Ritzke-Rutherford, 'St Oswald in Regensburg: a reconsideration', in *Bavarica Anglica*, vol. I: *A Cross-Cultural Miscellany presented to Tom Fletcher* (= *Forum Anglicum*, ed. O. Hietsch, vol. 8; Frankfurt am Main 1979), pp. 98-118, at pp. 109, 118.

symbol of his charity towards the poor (Pls 13, 20-1); the sword, which is a symbol of his battle against the pagans, while it also reminds us of his martyrdom, as does the palm-branch, which is another of his attributes, perhaps also because the palm-branch was symbolically associated with pilgrims to the Holy Land. In the late thirteenth or fourteenth century the raven made its appearance in the iconography of St Oswald, initially in a secular context (Pls 16, 20-1). Oswald was more and more frequently depicted with his raven until, by the middle of the fifteenth century, the bird had become a regular attribute, even in ecclesiastical contexts (Pl. 22).[34]

From the fact that the raven first appeared in the iconography of St Oswald in the late thirteenth or fourteenth century, many scholars conclude that the raven is of literary origin, and that its use as an attribute was due to the spread and increasing popularity of the Oswald story.[35] It is indeed most likely that, as far as iconography is concerned, the raven is of literary origin. But what was its ultimate origin? Why did it suddenly appear in the Munich *Oswald* as Oswald's companion? It seems odd to suppose that the appearance of this bird in the German poem should have been the result of deliberate choice on the part of the author. One of the characteristics of medieval literature is that it sticks to traditional patterns. The bird acting as messenger of love in medieval folk-song is usually small and white, and traditionally associated with love, such as the dove. The raven, on the other hand, is commonly regarded as a bird of ill omen, and in Christian thought it was associated with the devil and with vice. It is true that we meet with ravens of a helpful nature now and then, as in the cases of Elijah and of St Benedict.[36] In such cases, however, the raven normally acts as an intermediary between heaven and earth, and this, in fact, is also the function of Woden's ravens. In the Oswald story we find a perhaps unique example of a raven acting as an intermediary between earthly lovers.[37] That this role played by a raven was

---

[34] Vizkelety gives an interesting survey of the iconography of St Oswald on the continent, c.1050-1650: art. cit., pp. 130-46. See also Berger, 'Die Oswaldlegende', pp. 425-30; and above, pp. 4-12.

[35] So Baesecke, *MO*, pp. 264, 292ff., 381; Curschmann, *MODSE*, p. 15f.; W. Lampen, 'De vereering van St Oswald bijzonder in de Nederlanden', *Ons Geestelijk Erf* 1 (1927), pp. 142-57.

[36] For Elijah being fed by ravens see I Kings (= Vulgate III *Reges*) 17: 2-6. St Benedict used to feed a raven, which obeyed the saint's command to dispose of poisoned bread in a safe place: Gregory the Great, *Dialogi* II, 8, 3; ed. A. de Vogüé, *Grégoire le Grand, Dialogues* (3 vols, Sources Chrétiennes 251, 260, 265; Paris 1978-80), vol. II, p. 162.

[37] In *MODSE*, Curschmann mentions various examples of speaking birds acting as go-betweens (p. 15f.), but in none of these cases does a raven act as intermediary between lovers, nor is there any example of a raven acting in that capacity in S. Thompson, *Motif-Index of Folk-Literature* (revised edition, 6 vols, Copenhagen 1955-58).

felt to be incongruous appears from a local Oswald tradition in Carinthia and Slovenia. A folk-song sung in these regions tells how a white dove comes flying to Oswald, who lives as a hermit in the wood, and asks him to give it a ring for a bride across the sea. Oswald gives the ring; however, when the dove is flying across the sea it nearly loses the ring, though it catches it again at the last moment. The dove turns black with fright and becomes a raven. In this song an explanation is given for the colour and species of the bird, which were apparently felt to be most unusual for a messenger of love.[38]

How should we explain this departure from conventional practice? The answer may be that the raven was indeed a survival of the Woden cult, and that the uncharacteristic role of love messenger was forced upon the raven because there was already a link between Oswald and this bird in popular imagination. That the raven did not appear in the iconography of St Oswald until the late thirteenth or fourteenth century is no proof that the association between Oswald and the raven does not date from long before that time. We may assume that the raven, belonging to the popular, semi-pagan Oswald tradition, was not depicted by earlier church artists because they were still able to distinguish between Christian and popular traditions. Therefore these artists, working in the service of God, not of Woden, depicted the holy king they knew from Christian legend, adorning him with the symbols of his royal rank and Christian virtues.

By the time the raven began to appear in the iconography of St Oswald the story of Oswald and his raven was accepted as Christian legend, for the dividing line between Christian legend and popular tradition must have become increasingly vague as the Munich Oswald grew in size, popularity, and influence, and more and more pious details were added to it. As we have seen, from the middle of the fifteenth century the Oswald story was widely dispersed in Christian circles through its inclusion in legendaries, and it was around the same time that the raven became a regular attribute in the iconography of St Oswald. Although the raven as an attribute is undoubtedly of literary origin, we may suppose a pre-literary tradition with regard to the raven to explain its introduction into literature and the uncharacteristic role assigned to it.

In this connection it is interesting to note the different ways in which the various texts account for the presence of the raven. In both the Munich *Oswald* and the Vienna *Oswald*, Oswald has had the raven for many years, but neither text tells us where the bird came from.[39] On the other hand, the Budapest *Oswald* and the Swabian prose version of the Munich Oswald tell

---

[38] Berger, 'Die Oswaldlegende', pp. 431-2. Cf. also *Slovenske Ljudske Pesmi*, ed. Z. Kumer, M. Matičetov and V. Vodušek, vol. II (Ljubljana 1981), pp. 426-7.

[39] Baesecke, *MO* lines 342-4, and 410. *Der Wiener Oswald*, ed. Baesecke, lines 110-11.

us that Oswald had inherited the raven from his father.[40] Finally in the third, ecclesiastical, branch of the Oswald tradition, where the Life of St Oswald occurs amongst the Lives of other saints, we find a new motif to account for the raven's origin: the raven comes flying down from heaven, carrying a letter from St Peter and a little container of chrism for the anointing of Oswald – a scene which lent itself readily to illustration (Pl. 23).[41] As has been pointed out elsewhere, the same motif occurs in a legend about the Merovingian king Clovis, at whose coronation a dove came flying from heaven, carrying the chrism in a phial.[42] This motif was conveniently introduced into the ecclesiastical version of the Oswald story, to give a Christian explanation for the presence of the raven.

The raven and the ring, though of continental origin, eventually found their way to England. For instance, they are carved on the recent organ case in St Oswald's church, Durham.[43] They may seem out of place there; for, historically, there is nothing to connect them with the Northumbrian king. On a symbolic level, however, they are highly appropriate, since in the Munich *Oswald* they symbolise Oswald's efforts to win paganism over to his side, the side of Christianity. For the raven in the poem is instrumental in bringing about a union between Oswald and a heathen princess whom he converts; and Oswald's attempt to win a bride is symbolic of his divine mission to convert the pagans.[44] In this way, the iconographic representation of Oswald deriving from the continental tradition tallies with an actual trait of the historical Oswald, his concern to spread Christianity. And it is this same zeal for the Christian faith that earned Oswald his reputation as a saint far beyond the confines of his native land.

---

[40] Vizkelety, 'Der Budapester Oswald', lines 7-8 (p. 151) – though cf. lines 144-5, which seem to suggest that the raven had been reared by Oswald himself. The Swabian prose version, lines 33-4; ed. Curschmann, *MO*, p. 197.

[41] *Der Heiligen Leben*, ed. Rüttgers, II, p. 287. The woodcut illustrating the scene in this edition is apparently taken from the Lübeck Passional: Curschmann, *MODSE*, p. 208. A different woodcut, taken from the Oswald Life in *Dat duytsche Passional*, published at Cologne in 1485, is illustrated by Baker, 'Cult', *Archaeologia* 94, p. 174, fig. 4 and n. 3.

[42] See Baker, 'Zug', p. 116, n. 4.

[43] Built in 1988, case designed by Henry Moss: see *The New Organ at St Oswald's Durham*, ed. B. de la Mare (Durham 1988), p. 13. The raven makes an earlier appearance in County Durham in a late 19th-century stained-glass window in the chapel of Auckland Palace, Bishop Auckland, and in a stained-glass window of c.1910 in the north aisle of St Oswald's, Durham. Cf. also above, p. 10.

[44] Baesecke, *MO* lines 246-9.

Pre-Reformation Dedications to St Oswald in England and Scotland: a Gazetteer

ALISON BINNS

I

Introduction

It is notoriously difficult to determine the precise age of the majority of pre-Reformation parish church dedications. Inevitably therefore, any study of dedications which seeks to explain their origin and to uncover chronological, regional, or other trends, will be characterised by tentative conclusions and guesswork. For sites in England the starting point in the compilation of the gazetteer has been the list of medieval Oswald dedications in Frances Arnold-Forster's *Studies in Church Dedications of England's Patron Saints*.[1] The value of her work is, however, severely compromised by its extensive dependence on eighteenth-century antiquarian information first added to the fourth edition (1742) of John Ecton's *Thesaurus Rerum Ecclesiasticarum*, and later substantially incorporated into the *Liber Regis* of 1786 edited by John Bacon. These sources have recently been subjected to a devastating critique by Richard Clark in an analysis of church dedications in Derbyshire.[2] Clark has demonstrated that more than two-fifths of the dedications of medieval Derbyshire churches recorded in sixteenth-century or earlier sources have changed since that time. What is more, most of them had changed by the time of their appearance in these eighteenth-century sources, and can be attributed to the carelessness or ill-founded guesswork of the antiquaries who attempted to supply information which was apparently becoming lost from local tradition before the end of the sixteenth century. If the Derbyshire evidence is at all typical of the country as a whole (and there is no reason to think otherwise), it clearly follows that the general presumption of continuity of dedication from the middle ages to the present day, hitherto widely accepted, can no longer be taken for granted, and that only dedications attested by a sixteenth-century or earlier source can be regarded

---

[1]   Arnold-Forster; for monastic dedications, see A. Binns, *Dedications of Monastic Houses in England and Wales 1066-1216* (Woodbridge 1989). Two important articles on methodology are: H. Delehaye, 'Loca sanctorum', *AB* 48 (1930), pp. 5-64; and W. Levison, 'Medieval church dedications in England: some problems', *Transactions of the Architectural and Archaeological Societies of Durham and Northumberland* 10 (1946), pp. 57-79.

[2]   R. Clark, 'The dedications of medieval churches in Derbyshire: their survival and change from the Reformation to the present day', *Derbyshire Archaeological Journal* 112 (1992), pp. 48-61.

as securely founded.[3]

The difficulties involved in establishing the pre-Reformation dedicatees of Scottish medieval churches are even greater than in England; nevertheless, for the sake of completeness, an attempt has been made to cover the Scottish material, the starting point for which is J. M. Mackinlay's *Ancient Church Dedications in Scotland*.[4]

The evidence of place-names provides a useful (though limited) source of information about dedications to Oswald, as well as a clue to their possible antiquity. At least four place-names incorporate Oswald's name, the Kirkoswalds in the north-west (two in Ayrshire, one in Cumberland, possibly also one in Kirkcudbrightshire) and the Oswaldkirk in Yorkshire. Three questions have to be clearly distinguished in evaluating the implications of these for the antiquity of the Oswald dedications they perpetuate: the date of the first recorded documentary evidence of the name; the period during which names of these forms are likely to have been coined; and the actual dates of the dedications themselves. Clearly the first two together only supply a *terminus ante quem* for the currency of the dedication, which might have been in existence long before being incorporated into a place-name. The first documentary record of each name is noted in the gazetteer.[5]

Precise evidence for the year of dedication survives in only a handful of cases. Ashbourne, Derbyshire, was dedicated in Oswald's honour in 1241, Fulford, Yorkshire, in 1349, and Dean, Cumberland, in 1447.[6] It seems that Oswaldkirk, Yorkshire, was in need of rededication in 1287. In each case there is good reason to suppose that this was a rededication or a dedication of a new building on an old site, a point worth noting in itself, for it implies both that the dedication to Oswald may well pre-date the written record, and

---

3   The inescapable implication of Clark's appendix (ibid., pp. 57-9) is that mistakes in the 18th-century attributions have frequently determined the present-day dedications.

4   J. M. Mackinlay, *Ancient Church Dedications in Scotland. Non-Scriptural Dedications* (Edinburgh 1914).

5   I am most grateful to Dr D. Craig and Mr V. Watts for their advice on the published sources and the derivation of particular names respectively. (For a discussion of the likely dates of these dedications, see Cambridge, pp. 129-30.)

6   The high altar of Durham Cathedral was dedicated 'in honore sanctae Mariae Virginis et beati Oswaldi martyris, et sanctissimi patris nostri Cuthberti...' in 1380 (*Historiae Dunelmensis Scriptores Tres. Gaufridus de Coldingham, Robertus de Graystanes, et Willelmus de Chambre*, ed. J. Raine (SS 9, 1839), p. 136). Yet, in a tract compiled by John Wessington (prior of Durham 1414-46), the cathedral itself is described as dedicated to St Mary and St Cuthbert only: see A. Hamilton Thompson, 'The MS list of churches dedicated to St Cuthbert, attributed to Prior Wessyngton', *Transactions of the Architectural and Archaeological Society of Durham and Northumberland* 7 (1935), pp. 151-77, at pp. 164, 172 (m. 4v).

that Oswald continued in popularity as a patron saint throughout the medieval period. In 1483 John Bradburn founded a chantry in honour of God and St Oswald in Ashbourne church. In 1502 an Indulgence granted by Archbishop Thomas Savage of York refers to the chapel of Saints Cuthbert and Oswald at Winksley cum Grantley, Yorkshire, recently built by Abbot Marmaduke Huby of Fountains. It is likely that this too replaced an earlier chapel under Oswald's invocation. Oswald's cult, though localised, proved tenacious.

Some churches originally dedicated to Oswald now have other patron saints. Some changes may have coincided with the rebuilding of the church, for example, at Warton, Lancashire. In other cases, evidence from wills suggests an alternative dedication to Oswald (for example, at Finningley and Ragnall in Nottinghamshire), though firm conclusions are hard to draw because the dedication given may be that of a side-chapel or altar rather than that of the church as a whole. Occasionally Oswald seems to have usurped other saints, as at Dunham in Nottinghamshire, which may originally have been dedicated to Saints Peter and Paul. Clearly this whole area needs further research in the light of Clark's work in Derbyshire.

Dedications to Oswald are found primarily in the north of England and the north midlands, particularly Yorkshire, Lincolnshire, and Nottingham-shire (Fig. 8).[7] Dedications in the south of the country are rare, though Old St Paul's Cathedral in London contained an altar dedicated in Oswald's honour,[8] and there is an outlying group in Gloucestershire (Fig. 9). Several parish churches with Oswald dedications were connected with the monastic foundations under his patronage: Compton Abdale, Gloucestershire, and Widford, Oxfordshire, belonged to Gloucester Priory; Winwick, Lancashire, and Lythe, Yorkshire, belonged to Nostell Priory; Howell, Lincolnshire, belonged to Bardney Abbey. In some cases, however, notably Winwick, it appears that the Oswald dedication pre-dated the link with the monastic church. The Lincolnshire dedications may reflect either the presence of

---

[7] Local studies of church dedications include: J. Brownbill, 'Ancient church dedications in Cheshire and south Lancashire', *Transactions of the Historic Society of Lancashire and Cheshire*, new series 54 (1902), pp. 19-44; J. Raine, 'The dedications of the Yorkshire churches', *Yorkshire Archaeological Journal* 2 (1871-2), pp. 180-96; T. H. B. Graham and W. G. Collingwood, 'Patron saints of the diocese of Carlisle', *Transactions of the Cumberland and Westmorland Antiquarian and Archaeological Society*, new series 25 (1925), pp. 1-27; E. Venables, 'The dedications of the churches of Lincolnshire, as illustrating the history of the county', *Archaeological Journal* 38 (1881), pp. 365-90; J. Raine, 'The dedications of the Nottinghamshire churches', *Associated Architectural Societies Reports and Papers* 16 (ii) (1881), pp. 231-42. See also Butler, 'Dedications'.

[8] *The Peterborough Chronicle of Hugh Candidus*, ed. W. T. Mellows (Peterborough 1966), p. 59.

Oswald's relics at Bardney between the late seventh and early tenth centuries, or the abbey's later claim to Oswald's body after its refoundation in 1087.[9] Three of them are in the north of the county, where the Northumbrian influence on church dedications was far stronger than the Mercian, and of these there are reasons for thinking that at least one, Crowle, might be ancient. The Gloucestershire dedications must surely postdate the translation of Oswald's relics there in 909, as indeed does the dedication of Gloucester Priory itself to St Oswald.[10]

In addition to being a popular dedicatee for churches, Oswald gave his name to wells or springs at Astbury, Cheshire[11] (on which the church of St Oswald at Brereton with Smethwick was originally dependent), Burneside and Grasmere in Westmorland, Elvet, County Durham, Oswestry, Shropshire, and Warton and Winwick in Lancashire. In addition, the church at Kirkoswald in Cumberland contains a well.[12]

The following gazetteer of pre-Reformation parish and monastic church dedications to St Oswald attempts to provide, for each entry, the earliest extant documentary evidence for the dedication: it cites, when available, any pre- or early post-Reformation records where Oswald is actually named as patron saint, or which state when the church was dedicated in his honour. In a few cases, evidence of this kind indicates that the tradition of a pre-Reformation dedication to Oswald is spurious. In the absence of documentary evidence pointing either way, evidence indicating the possible antiquity and character of the church is noted. The gazetteer is arranged in alphabetical order of the pre-1974 counties, and alphabetically within each county. All certain and possible dedications to St Oswald are mapped in Figures 8 and 9 (pp. 268-71, below), with the exceptions of Durham Cathedral (see above, p. 242 n. 6) and *Scythlescester* (below, p. 255). The keys to Figures 8 and 9 list the counties in order to facilitate cross references to the gazetteer. Individual entries can also be located via the book's index.

9   Butler, 'Dedications', p. 45.
10 In three cases (Oswaldkirk, Yorkshire; Paddlesworth, Kent; and Shipton Oliffe, Gloucestershire) it has been suggested that the dedication to Oswald may in fact be to St Oswald of Worcester; in none of them is the case compelling (see gazetteer, ad loc.).
11 *A Descriptive Catalogue of Ancient Deeds in the Public Record Office* (6 vols; London 1890-1915), VI, C.4898 (p. 145).
12 Morris, *Churches*, p. 87; cf. Rollason, above, pp. 170-1.

II

Gazetteer

AYRSHIRE

KIRKOSWALD (alias Balmaknele) (Fig. 8, no. 3)
Unidentified place within the parish of Ballantrae (formerly Kirkcudbright-Innertig).[13] A charter of 1541 mentions the place-name;[14] the former existence of a church or chapel dedicated to Oswald may be inferred. A possible early context for this dedication is suggested by Cambridge, above, pp. 129-30.

KIRKOSWALD (of Turnberry) (Fig. 8, no. 2)
The place-name, first attested in 1324,[15] implies that the medieval parish church was dedicated to Oswald, and this is borne out by the holding of an annual fair on St Oswald's day 'from time immemorial'.[16] A possible early context for this dedication is suggested by Cambridge, above, pp. 129-30.

CHESHIRE

BACKFORD (Fig. 8, no. 47)[17]
Situated three miles to the north of Chester, the church was given by the Mascys during Henry II's reign to the priory of Birkenhead.[18] The township of Backford is not recorded in Domesday Book and the date of the foundation of the church is not known. In 1291 it was valued at £5 6s. 8d. The parish of Backford was carved out of the older parish of Chester, and it has been suggested that it took as its patron saint that of the mother-church.[19] The oldest parts of the present fabric are early fourteenth century.[20]

BIDSTON (Fig. 8, no. 46)
Bidston is not recorded in Domesday Book; like Backford (see previous entry) it was granted by the Mascys to the priory of Birkenhead at its

---

[13] I. B. Cowan, *The Parishes of Medieval Scotland* (Scottish Record Society 93; Edinburgh 1967), p. 120.

[14] Mackinlay, *Ancient Church Dedications*, p. 233, citing *Registrum Magni Sigilli Regum Scottorum*, ed. J. M. Thomson *et al.*, *1513-46*, p. 549.

[15] D. Brooke, 'Kirk-compound place-names of Galloway and Carrick', *Transactions of the Dumfriesshire and Galloway Natural History and Antiquarian Society*, 3rd series 58 (1983), pp. 56-71, at p. 71.

[16] Mackinlay, *Ancient Church Dedications*, p. 233.

[17] *LR*, p. 1220.

[18] W. Dugdale, *Monasticon Anglicanum* (6 vols in 8; revised edn by J. Caley, H. Ellis, and B. Bandinel; London 1817-30), IV, p. 239.

[19] Brownbill, 'Dedications', p. 28.

[20] N. Pevsner and E. Hubbard, *The Buildings of England, Cheshire* (Harmondsworth 1971), p. 69.

foundation.[21] Evidence for its early history is scant; the marriage of William Pulle and Isabel Boteler at the 'parish kirk of Bidstone' is recorded in 1436.[22] It has been suggested that the dedication to St Oswald is modern and followed the rebuilding of the church in 1856, though this must be conjectural as, despite effort at the time to trace the original dedication, this remains unknown.[23] In 1550 there were three bells in the church, one of which was inscribed with St Oswald's name, and according to tradition had been brought from Hilbre, which had itself acquired it from St Oswald's Chester. Brownbill states that this prompted the nineteenth-century dedication to Oswald.[24] The oldest surviving part of the fabric is early sixteenth century.[25] A possible early context for this dedication is suggested by Cambridge, above, pp. 147-8.

BRERETON (WITH SMETHWICK) (Fig. 8, no. 51)

A deed of Ralph de Brereton granted Smethwick 'to God, and St Oswald and the chapel of Brereton, to be held therefrom by his nephew Orme, son of Thurstan de Smethwick, and his heirs'.[26] Though undated, the *floruit* of the persons named appears to have been the late twelfth century,[27] so the dedication to Oswald must date from at least that time.[28] The church was originally dependent on Astbury, where there was a well associated with St Oswald,[29] but it became parochial during the reign of Richard I.[30] A possible early context for this dedication is suggested by Cambridge, above, pp. 147-8.

CHESTER (Fig. 8, no. 48)

An early religious community here was refounded as a community of clerks, probably by Æthelflæd of Mercia in the early tenth century; by then it housed the relics of St Werburg. After it was again refounded in the late eleventh century, this time as a Benedictine abbey, its parochial responsibilities were discharged by a secular vicar attached to the altar in the nave of the abbey church. By the early thirteenth century, this altar was dedicated to St Oswald.[31] It is likely, however, that Oswald's cult at Chester dates back to the time of Æthelflæd, who was responsible for refortifying Chester at the

21 *Monasticon*, IV, p. 239.
22 J. Brownbill, 'History of the old parish of Bidston, Cheshire', *Transactions of the Historic Society of Lancashire and Cheshire* 88 (1936), pp. 1-60, p. 1.
23 Brownbill, 'Bidston', p. 19.
24 Loc. cit.
25 Pevsner and Hubbard, *Cheshire*, p. 95.
26 G. Ormerod, *The History of the County Palatine and City of Chester*, ed. T. Helsby (3 vols; 2nd edn, London 1875-82), III, p. 90.
27 Ibid., III, p. 82.
28 Ibid., III, p. 92.
29 See above, p. 244.
30 Ormerod, *Chester*, III, p. 90.
31 VCH *Cheshire*, III, pp. 132-3, 138.

same time as she was engaged in recovering the relics of St Oswald from Bardney and installing them at Gloucester.[32]

LOWER PEOVER (Fig. 8, no. 50)

In 1269 the parishioners of Lower Peover and Richard Grosvenor of Hulme of Allstocke agreed that the prior and convent of Norton should find them a chaplain to say mass in their chapel every Sunday and Wednesday and on specified saints' days, including 'die sancti Oswaldi in cuius honorem fundata est praedicta capella'.[33]

MALPAS (Fig. 8, no. 52)[34]

In origin the church may have been an Anglo-Saxon minster church, and its dedication to St Oswald pre-Conquest.[35] The oldest parts of the present fabric date only from the early fourteenth century, however.[36]

WORLESTON (Fig. 8, no. 49)

Arnold-Forster regarded the dedication to Oswald as nineteenth-century, and it is not listed among Oswald dedications in Cheshire noted by Sir Stephen Glynne.[37] The tithes of Worleston were granted to Chester in the eleventh century by Ralph, son of Eremwine, but a dispute apparently arose with the abbey of Combermere.[38] This was settled after 1266, but the wording of the charter is unclear as to whether or not a chapel had actually been built at Worleston by this time, and there is no mention of its dedication.[39] The present church is nineteenth-century.[40]

CUMBERLAND

DEAN (Fig. 8, no. 12)[41]

Rectors of the early thirteenth-century church of Dean are recorded in the St Bees cartulary, though the church's patron saint is not named.[42] The church is supposed to have been reconsecrated in 1447.[43] The south arcade of the

[32] VCH *Cheshire*, II, p. 252; A. T. Thacker, 'Chester and Gloucester', *Northern History* 18 (1982), pp. 199-211, at pp. 203-4. Cf. Thacker, above, pp. 120-1; and see below, pp. 253, 250.

[33] Ormerod, *Chester*, I, p. 607.

[34] *LR*, p. 1215.

[35] VCH *Cheshire*, I, p. 269; Thacker, above, pp. 122-3.

[36] Pevsner and Hubbard, *Cheshire*, p. 273.

[37] Arnold-Forster, III, 316; S. Glynne, *Notes on the Churches of Cheshire*, ed. J. A. Atkinson (Chetham Society, new series, 32; Manchester 1894).

[38] *The Chartulary or Register of the Abbey of St Werburgh, Chester*, ed. J. Tait (2 vols, Chetham Society, new series, 79, 82; Manchester 1920, 1923), I, no. 3.

[39] Ibid., II, no. 495.

[40] Pevsner and Hubbard, *Cheshire*, p. 391; Arnold-Forster, III, 316.

[41] *LR*, p. 1252.

[42] *The Register of the Priory of St Bees*, ed. J. Wilson (SS 126, 1915), nos. 98, 102.

[43] Graham and Collingwood, 'Patron saints' (as n. 7), p. 15.

present church is of *c*.1200, and there is a Romanesque font.[44] A possible early context for this dedication is suggested by Cambridge, above, p. 147.

KIRKOSWALD (Fig. 8, no. 11)

The first extant reference to the place-name occurs in the Pipe Roll for 1167.[45] In the sixteenth century Thomas, Lord Dacre, established a short-lived collegiate foundation here, the *Valor Ecclesiasticus* of 1535 referring to 'the master or provost of the Collegiate church of St Oswald of Kyrkoswald and Dacre'.[46] A possible early context for this dedication is suggested by Cambridge, above, p. 147.

WETHERAL (Fig. 8, no. 10)

During the thirteenth century at least there was apparently a chapel to St Oswald near the priory, for a charter of 1292 refers to 'crucem quae est juxta capellam Sancti Oswaldi ex parte aquae de Eden versus Corkeby [i.e. Corby]'.[47] Its exact location remains uncertain. A possible early context for this dedication is suggested by Cambridge, above, p. 143, and cf. Fig. 5, p. 141.

DERBYSHIRE

ASHBOURNE (Fig. 8, no. 55)

An original inscription on the south transept wall of the present church records that in 1241 'dedicata est hec ecclesia et hoc altare consecratum in honore sancti Oswaldi regis et martyris a venerabili patre domino Hugone Patishul Coventrensi episcopo'.[48] A chantry in honour of God and St Oswald was founded here in 1483 by John Bradburn of Hough and his wife, Ann.[49]

[44] N. Pevsner, *The Buildings of England, Cumberland and Westmorland* (Harmondsworth 1967), p. 119.

[45] A. M. Armstrong, *The Place-Names of Cumberland* (3 vols; English Place-Name Society 20-22; Cambridge 1950-2) p. 215. Fellows-Jensen raises the possibility that the generic may have replaced the Old English equivalent (G. Fellows-Jensen, *Scandinavian Settlement Names in the North-West* (Copenhagen 1985), pp. 195-6).

[46] VCH *Cumberland*, II, p. 209.

[47] *Register of the Priory of Wetheral*, ed. J. E. Prescott (Cumberland and Westmorland Antiquarian and Archaeological Society, Charter Series, 1; 1897), p. 429.

[48] J. C. Cox, *Notes on the Churches of Derbyshire* (4 vols; Chesterfield 1875-79), II, p. 371.

[49] F. Jourdain, 'Chantries founded in the parish church of Ashbourne, Co. Derbyshire', *Derbyshire Archaeological and Natural History Society* 14 (1892), pp. 141-57, at pp. 155-6.

DURHAM
ELVET (DURHAM CITY) (Fig. 8, no. 9)
Early documentary evidence of the patron saint is found in a charter of 1189 in which Bishop Hugh confirmed the composition between the prior and convent of Durham and the hospital of St Giles with regard to the tithes of Clifton, 'quae usque ad illud tempus reddi solebat ecclesiae sancti Oswaldi de Elveta'.[50] The church had been granted to the prior and monks of Durham 'ad nutrimentum eorum' in a charter purporting to be of c.1084, but which was in fact a forgery probably dating to the 1170s.[51] A possible early context for this dedication is suggested by Cambridge, above, pp. 148-54. Just to the west of the churchyard, halfway down the steep bank of the river Wear, is a well associated with St Oswald.

EAST LOTHIAN
WHITTINGEHAME (Fig. 8, no. 6)
The church was claimed as an Oswald dedication by Mackinlay who, however, states no evidence in its support.[52] The church was anciently a chapelry of the parish of Dunbar.[53] No traces of the medieval church survive above ground,[54] and its precise site remains uncertain. A possible early context for this dedication is suggested by Cambridge, above, pp. 155-6.

GLOUCESTERSHIRE
COMPTON ABDALE (Fig. 9, no. 76)[55]
The manor was probably an ancient possession of St Oswald's Gloucester. It was alienated to Stigand, archbishop of Canterbury, in the late pre-Conquest period, and at the time of the Domesday Survey was held by Archbishop Thomas I of York.[56] The date of the foundation of the church is not known; it was appropriated to St Oswald's Gloucester.[57] Arnold-Forster suggests that the date of the village feast in early August supports a dedication to

---

[50] J. Barmby, *Memorials of St Giles, Durham* (SS 95, 1896), p. 213.
[51] *Durham Episcopal Charters 1071-1152*, ed. H. S. Offler (SS 179, 1968), pp. 27, 32-3.
[52] Mackinlay, *Ancient Church Dedications*, pp. 234-5.
[53] Cowan, *Parishes* (as n. 13), p. 210.
[54] C. McWilliam, *The Buildings of Scotland, Lothian Except Edinburgh* (Harmondsworth 1978), p. 469.
[55] *LR*, p. 328.
[56] A. Hamilton Thompson, 'The jurisdiction of the archbishops of York in Gloucestershire with some notes on the history of the priory of St Oswald at Gloucester', *Transactions of the Bristol and Gloucester Archaeological Society* 43 (1921), pp. 85-180, at p. 94.
[57] Ibid., pp. 95, 105, 124.

Oswald.[58] The oldest parts of the present fabric are thirteenth century.[59]

GLOUCESTER, Augustinian Priory (Fig. 9, no. 73)

William of Malmesbury described the founding and endowing of this house by Æthelflæd, Lady of the Mercians, and her husband Æthelred, c.900.[60] The initial dedication seems to have been to St Peter.[61] In 909 Oswald's body was brought here from the ruined monastery of Bardney in Lincolnshire.[62] The church was served by secular canons until 1152 or 1153, when Henry Murdac, archbishop of York, refounded it as a priory of Augustinian canons.[63] Like Nostell,[64] St Oswald was part of the common designation of the monastery, so references to the saint's name are numerous. For a reference specifically indicating Oswald as the dedicatee of the church, see, for example, a letter of 1281 from the archbishop of York concerning the appointment of a prior, addressed 'Suppriori et canonicis ecclesie nostre de Sancto Oswaldo Gloucestrie'.[65]

LASSINGTON (Fig. 9, no. 72)

Arnold-Forster lists the dedication as uncertain, though Hamilton Thompson gives Oswald (the present-day dedication). The manor was probably a pre-Conquest possession of St Oswald's Priory, and was held by the archbishop of York in 1062, the archbishop being tenant-in-chief in Domesday Book. The church remained within the peculiar archiepiscopal jurisdiction of York.[66] The oldest parts of the present church are Romanesque.[67]

ROCKHAMPTON (or St Leonard) (Fig. 9, no. 74)[68]

There seems to be no early documentation. At the time of the Domesday Survey the manor was held by Osbern Giffard from the king; there is no record of a church. The alternative dedication to Leonard is given by

58 Arnold-Forster, I, 315-16.
59 D. Verey, *The Buildings of England, Gloucestershire, I, The Cotswolds* (Harmondsworth 1970), p. 200.
60 *Willelmi Malmesbiriensis Monachi De Gestis Pontificum Anglorum Libri Quinque*, IV, 155; ed. N. E. S. A. Hamilton (RS; 1870), p. 293.
61 M. Hare, *The Two Anglo-Saxon Minsters of Gloucester* (Deerhurst Lecture 1992; Deerhurst 1993), p. 6.
62 See below, p. 253, and Thacker, above, p. 120.
63 Hamilton Thompson, 'Jurisdiction', pp. 98-9, 112-13.
64 See below, p. 264.
65 *The Register of William Wickwane, Lord Archbishop of York 1279-1285*, ed. W. Browne (SS 114, 1907), p. 234.
66 Arnold-Forster, III, 176; Thompson, 'Jurisdiction', pp. 104-5.
67 D. Verey, *The Buildings of England, Gloucestershire, II, The Vale and the Forest of Dean* (Harmondsworth 1970), p. 283.
68 *LR*, p. 329 (*s.v.* Rockington).

Arnold-Forster, who regards it as probably a later development, though no supporting evidence is cited.[69] The oldest parts of the present church date from the fourteenth century.[70]

SHIPTON OLIFFE (Fig. 9, no. 75)[71]

The manor, adjacent to Compton Abdale,[72] was probably an ancient possession of St Oswald's Gloucester, but was in the hands of the archbishops of York from 1062, and had been alienated by the late twelfth century.[73] The church is documented before 1100.[74] It has been suggested that the dedication was to St Oswald the archbishop, but in view of the close and ancient connection with St Oswald's Gloucester Arnold-Forster was surely right in supposing this to be a later misunderstanding of an original dedication to Oswald king and martyr.[75] The oldest parts of the present structure are the Romanesque piers of the chancel arch.[76]

KENT

PADDLESWORTH (Fig. 9, no. 79)

The will of Robert Regge (1484) refers to the churchyard of St Oswald of Paddlesworth.[77] Its dedication to St Oswald, unusual in the south of England,[78] may have been influenced by its proximity to Lyminge, of which it was formerly a chapelry. A nunnery had been founded at Lyminge in the seventh century by St Æthelburh, widow of King Edwin, Oswald's predecessor in Northumbria. The church was in existence by the late eleventh century when it is mentioned in the *Domesday Monachorum*.[79]

---

[69] Arnold-Forster, I, 415, note.
[70] Verey, *Gloucestershire*, II, p. 329.
[71] *LR*, p. 351.
[72] See above, p. 249.
[73] Hamilton Thompson, 'Jurisdiction', pp. 91-2, 102.
[74] C. Heighway, *Anglo-Saxon Gloucestershire* (Gloucester 1987), p. 170.
[75] Arnold-Forster, II, 316.
[76] Verey, *Gloucestershire*, I, p. 400.
[77] *Testamenta Cantiana: a Series of Extracts from Fifteenth and Sixteenth Century Wills relating to Church Building and Topography*, ed. A. Hussey (London 1907), p. 244.
[78] Everitt claims that the dedication was to Oswald the archbishop, though his grounds are not stated (A. Everitt, *Continuity and Colonization. The Evolution of Kentish Settlement* (Leicester 1986), p. 256).
[79] T. Tatton-Brown, 'The churches of the Canterbury diocese in the 11th century', in *Minsters and Parish Churches. The Local Church in Transition 950-1200*, ed. J. Blair (Oxford University Committee for Archaeology, monograph 17; Oxford 1988), pp. 105-18, at p. 115. Late seventh-century Northumbrian influence at Lyminge is a possibility: see P. Wormald, *Bede and the Conversion of England* (Jarrow lecture; Jarrow 1984), pp. 17-18.

KIRKCUDBRIGHTSHIRE

KELTON (Fig. 8, no. 4)

A confirmation of William the Lion, king of Scots, dated January 1210, includes land granted 'Deo et Ecclesie Sancti Oswaldi martiris de Kelletun'.[80]

KIRKCARSWELL (Fig. 8, no. 5)

This name has been claimed as deriving from an original form Kirkoswald.[81] The earliest recorded forms of the name, which are fourteenth-century,[82] leave the matter in some doubt, however.[83]

LANCASHIRE

WARTON (or Holy Trinity) (Fig. 8, no. 44)

The dedication has been claimed to be to the Holy Trinity.[84] The advowson of the church is first recorded in 1246. The case for an ancient dedication to Oswald rests on the observance of the village feast day on 5 August, and may receive some support from the presence of a St Oswald's well nearby.[85] It has been suggested that the dedication was changed to the Holy Trinity during the reign of Henry VII or Henry VIII, when the church was almost entirely rebuilt.[86] The oldest part of the present church is early fourteenth-century.[87]

WINWICK (alias Makerfield) (Fig. 8, no. 45)

According to Domesday Book, in Winwick 'St Oswald had two ploughlands exempt from all taxation'. Shortly afterwards, Stephen Count of Mortain gave 'ecclesiam sancti Oswaldi de Macrefeld' to the Augustinian priory at Nostell in Yorkshire. The grant to Nostell Priory may imply a more ancient

---

80   *Regesta Regum Scottorum* vol. II: *The Acts of William I*, ed. G. W. S. Barrow (Edinburgh 1971), no. 489 (pp. 446-7). I am most grateful to Dr D. Brooke for drawing my attention to this reference.

81   D. Brooke, 'The Northumbrian settlements in Galloway and Carrick: an historical assessment', *Proceedings of the Society of Antiquaries of Scotland* 121 (1991), pp. 295-327, at p. 304; G. Fellows-Jensen, 'The Vikings' relationship with Christianity in the British Isles: the evidence of place-names containing the element *kirkja*', in *Proceedings of the Tenth Viking Congress, Larkollen, Norway*, ed. J. E. Knirk (Oslo 1987), pp. 295-307, at pp. 302, 304; eadem, 'Scandinavians in Dumfriesshire and Galloway: the place-name evidence', in *Galloway: Land and Lordship*, ed. R. D. Oram and G. P. Stell (Edinburgh 1991), pp. 77-95, at p. 90.

82   See Brooke, 'Kirk-compounds' (as n. 15), p. 69.

83   I am grateful to Victor Watts for his advice on this name.

84   *LR*, p. 1256.

85   VCH *Lancashire*, VIII, p. 153, note 12.

86   F. Gastrell, *Notitiae Cestriensis, or Historic Notices of the Diocese of Chester*, vol. II, part iii, ed. F. R. Raines (Chetham Society 22; Manchester 1850), p. 558.

87   N. Pevsner, *The Buildings of England, Lancashire, II. The Rural North* (Harmondsworth 1969), p. 255.

association with Oswald.[88] There is a well associated with St Oswald here.[89]

LINCOLNSHIRE

ALTHORPE (Fig. 8, no. 65)[90]

There was a church here at the latest by 1223, when Bishop Hugh of Lincoln settled a dispute between Adam, rector of Althorpe, and Oliver, parson of Bottesford.[91] The oldest parts of the present church are fourteenth century.[92]

BARDNEY (Anglo-Saxon monastery, later Benedictine abbey) (Fig. 8, no 68)

A monastery was in existence before the translation of Oswald's relics there some time before 697.[93] In 1087 Gilbert de Gaunt, earl of Lincoln, refounded it as the monastery of Saints Peter, Paul and Oswald.[94]

BLANKNEY (Fig. 8, no. 69)[95]

Domesday Book records a church here, and a priest. Around 1130 the church was granted by Ralph de Ayncourt to the Augustinian priory of Thurgarton in Nottinghamshire.[96] The oldest parts of the present fabric date from the thirteenth century.[97]

CROWLE (Fig. 8, no. 63)[98]

A church was recorded here in Domesday Book. Evidence for its early history is scant; in 1239 Robert de Esingwaud was instituted to the church of Crowle.[99] The oldest parts of the present fabric are Romanesque.[100] The site has produced important Viking-age sculpture, however.[101]

---

[88] *EYC*, III, no. 1428. See further below, under Nostell Priory, and cf. Rollason and Thacker, above, pp. 121-2, 173-4.

[89] See Thacker and Rollason, above, pp. 102, 170.

[90] *LR*, p. 454.

[91] *The Registrum Antiquissimum of the Cathedral Church of Lincoln* (10 vols, Lincoln Record Society; Lincoln 1927-1973), I, no. 513.

[92] N. Pevsner and J. Harris, *The Buildings of England, Lincolnshire* (Harmondsworth 1964), p. 169.

[93] *HE* III, 11, and Thacker, above, pp. 104-7; for their translation to Gloucester in 909, see above, Gloucester Priory, and Thacker, above, pp. 120-1.

[94] *Monasticon* (as n. 18), I, pp. 628-9. On the date of the Oswald dedication, cf. Cambridge, above, p. 139.

[95] *LR*, p. 444.

[96] *Monasticon*, VI, p. 191. See also *The Thurgarton Cartulary*, ed. T. Foulds (Stamford 1994), pp. 3-4.

[97] Pevsner and Harris, *Lincolnshire*, p. 459.

[98] *LR*, p. 454.

[99] *Rotuli Roberti Grosseteste Episcopi Lincolniensis AD MCCXXXV-MCCLIII*, ed. F. M. Davis (Lincoln Record Society, 2; 1914), p. 140.

[100] Pevsner and Harris, *Lincolnshire*, pp. 223-4.

[101] D. S. Davies and A. W. Clapham, 'Pre-conquest carved stones in Lincolnshire', *Archaeological Journal* 83 (1926), pp. 1-20, at pp. 5, 11-12, fig. 1.

HOWELL (Fig. 8, no. 71)[102]

Domesday Book records a church and a priest here. There is little documentary evidence for its early history; in 1239, when Ralph de Benigworth was instituted at the church, it belonged to Bardney Abbey.[103] The oldest part of the present fabric is Romanesque, and there is a pre-Conquest grave-cover from the site.[104]

LUDDINGTON (Fig. 8, no. 64)[105]

The date of the foundation of the church is not known. In 1262 the church was granted to the abbey of Selby by Richard Gravesend, bishop of Lincoln.[106] The present structure dates from the nineteenth century.[107]

RAND (Fig. 8, no. 66)[108]

The date of the foundation of the church is not known. The oldest parts of the present fabric are twelfth-century,[109] though remains of what are probably earlier structures have been found in recent excavations.[110]

STRUBBY (Fig. 8, no. 67)

Arnold-Forster regarded the dedication to Oswald as ancient.[111] The early history of the church is unknown; a reference occurs c.1200, when William of Cornhill granted it to the canons of Lincoln Cathedral; the earliest part of the present fabric dates from a century or so later.[112]

WALCOT (Fig. 8, no. 70)[113]

The church was formerly a chapelry of Billinghay.[114] In 1291 its net value was assessed at £12 13s. 4d.[115] The date of its foundation is not known; the present structure dates from the mid nineteenth century.[116]

---

[102] *LR*, p. 402.

[103] *Rotuli Grosseteste*, p. 58.

[104] Pevsner and Harris, *Lincolnshire*, p. 581.

[105] *LR*, p. 455.

[106] *The Coucher Book of Selby*, ed. J. T. Fowler (2 vols; Yorkshire Archaeological and Topographical Association, Record Series, 10, 13 (1891-3)), I, p. 299.

[107] Pevsner and Harris, *Lincolnshire*, p. 308.

[108] *LR*, p. 464.

[109] Pevsner and Harris, *Lincolnshire*, pp. 338-9.

[110] S. M. Youngs, J. Clark, and T. B. Barry, 'Medieval Britain and Ireland in 1982', *Medieval Archaeology* 27 (1983), pp. 161-229, at pp. 190-1.

[111] Arnold-Forster, III, 271.

[112] *Registrum Antiquissimum*, III, no. 1045; Pevsner and Harris, *Lincolnshire*, p. 383.

[113] *LR*, p. 446.

[114] Loc. cit.

[115] *Taxatio Ecclesiastica Angliae et Walliae Auctoritate P. Nicholai IV, circa A.D. 1291* (Record Commission; London 1802), p. 61.

[116] Pevsner and Harris, *Lincolnshire*, pp. 701-2.

NORTHUMBERLAND

BAMBURGH (Fig. 8, no. 7)

Bamburgh became an early centre of Oswald's cult when the saint's arm was enshrined there in the church of St Peter between 642 and 670.[117] Between 1121 and 1127 the churches of St Oswald and St Aidan of Bamburgh were granted by King Henry I to Nostell Priory, a grant which may reflect the ancient associations of Bamburgh with Oswald.[118] The problems of determining the location of this church and the antiquity of its dedication are discussed by Cambridge, above, pp. 134-9.

ST OSWALD IN LEE (HEAVENFIELD) (Fig. 8, no. 8)

The chapel of St Oswald was subordinate to the priory and parish church of Hexham, as is made clear in a charter of William Greenfield, archbishop of York (1310), which speaks of 'ecclesiam parochialem de Hextildesham, cum capellis sancti Johannis de Lega, sanctae Mariae de Hextildesham, sancti Oswaldi, Byngefeld, et Alwenton'.[119] It is presumably to be identified with the chapel described by Bede as having been 'recently' erected by the monks of Hexham at the site of the battle of Heavenfield.[120]

SCYTHLESCESTER

A church built at this place, where King Ælfwald of Northumbria had been assassinated in 788, is said to have been dedicated to Saints Cuthbert and Oswald: '...in honore Dei et sanctorum Cuthberti episcopi et Oswaldi regis et martyris consecrata'.[121] The location remains unidentified, but the above reference describes it as 'iuxta murum' (that is, close to the Roman Wall), and it was presumably also fairly near Hexham, to which the king's body was taken for burial.[122] (The current dedication of Halton church, Northumberland, to St Oswald, St Cuthbert and King Alfwald is of nineteenth-century origin.)

NOTTINGHAMSHIRE

BROUGHTON SULNEY (or St Luke) (Fig. 9, no. 62)

Little is known of the early history of the church. An *inspeximus* of 1317 records Richard de Bussell's grant of the church of *Brocton* to the priory of Lenton.[123] Though recording an alternative dedication to St Luke, Arnold-

---

[117] *HE* III, 6. For the problems associated with the later history of Oswald's relics at Bamburgh, see Bailey, above, pp. 197-9.

[118] *EYC*, III, no. 1428; see Rollason, above, pp. 173-4.

[119] *The Priory of Hexham, its Chroniclers, Endowments and Annals*, ed. J. Raine (SS 46, 1865), p. 123.

[120] *HE* III, 2. See Thacker, above, pp. 107-8.

[121] *HR, s.a.* 788 (p. 52).

[122] Loc. cit.

[123] *Monasticon* (as n. 18), V, p. 112.

Forster states that York records evidenced its dedication to Oswald.[124]

BULCOTE (or Holy Trinity) (Fig. 8, no. 60)
This church was formerly a chapel of Burton Joyce (see below). Arnold-Forster notes the possibility that it was dedicated to Oswald, though no supporting evidence is cited.[125] Elsewhere, however, she states that the dedication to the Holy Trinity occurs in York records,[126] which implies that the attribution to Oswald is erroneous.

BURTON JOYCE (alias Burton on Trent; now St Helen) (Fig. 8, no. 61)
Evidence of the church's dedication to St Oswald is found in Nottingham borough records for 1440/41 and the will of Henry Jonson (1471).[127] The dedication had changed to St Helen by the second half of the eighteenth century.[128]

DUNHAM (or St Peter) (Fig. 8, no. 57)
The original dedication was apparently either to St Peter or Saints Peter and Paul, for the will of Robert Jackson (1499) refers to the parish church of the Apostles Peter and Paul of Dunham-on-Trent, and the village feast was observed on August 1 (St Peter ad vincula).[129] The attribution of the dedication to Oswald in the *Liber Regis* is presumably therefore mistaken: there was a chapel of St Nicholas in the fifteenth-century church; possibly there was also a chapel of St Oswald.[130] If so, this may have given rise to the later tradition of a dedication to Oswald.

EAST STOKE (Fig. 8, no. 59)
Evidence for its dedication to St Oswald is found in the will (1480) of John Colyngham, vicar of Stoke, who wished to be buried 'in choro ecclesiae S Oswaldi de Stoke'.[131]

FINNINGLEY (or Holy Trinity) (Fig. 8, no. 56)
The present-day dedication is to St Oswald, and this dedication is also given by the *Liber Regis*.[132] The medieval dedication, however, was to the Holy Trinity, as evidenced by the will of Brian Sampall of Finninglay (1479) which

[124] Arnold-Forster III, 69.
[125] Arnold-Forster, III, 369.
[126] Arnold-Forster, III, 71, note.
[127] *Burton Joyce and Bulcote – Studies in the History of Two Trent Valley Villages* (Burton Joyce 1978), pp. 31-2.
[128] *LR*, p. 1176.
[129] H. Chadwick, *History of Dunham on Trent* (Cambridge Massachusetts, 1924), p. 209.
[130] *LR*, p. 1186; ibid., p. 209.
[131] *Testamenta Eboracensia: A Selection of Wills from the Registry at York*, ed. J. Raine (6 vols.; SS 4, 30, 45, 53, 79 106; 1855-1902), III, p. 218.
[132] *LR*, p. 1180 (*s.v.* Fenningley).

refers to 'ecclesia S Trin. de Fynningley'.[133]

RAGNALL (or St Leonard) (Fig. 8, no. 58)
The present-day dedication is to St Oswald, which is also given by the *Liber Regis*.[134] The evidence of fourteenth- and fifteenth-century wills, however, indicates that the medieval dedication of this church, originally a chapelry of Dunham (*q.v.*), was to St Leonard; there are also references to an altar of St Mary, but no extant references to St Oswald.[135]

OXFORDSHIRE (formerly Gloucestershire)

WIDFORD (or St Mary) (Fig. 9, no. 77)
According to the Domesday Survey for Gloucestershire, in Barrington Hundred, St Oswald of Gloucester held Widford (although there is no mention of a church here). The manor was probably an ancient possession of the priory; it had been alienated by the late twelfth century.[136] It appears that the church was built by or for the monks of St Oswald's Priory in Gloucester (see above, p. 250). Arnold-Forster gives an alternative dedication to St Mary without, however, citing any evidence in support of that or of that to St Oswald, the present-day dedication.[137] The oldest parts of the existing fabric date from the thirteenth century.[138]

RENFREWSHIRE

CATHCART (Fig. 8, no. 1)
A will of 1550 requested burial 'in choro Sancti Oswaldi in Cathcart'.[139] There was allegedly a well associated with Oswald near the site of the pre-Reformation church.[140]

SHROPSHIRE

HINSTOCK (Fig. 9, no. 54)[141]
Perhaps originally a small chapel, founded by lords of the manor of Hinstock.[142] The first extant written record of the church dates from 1306, when William le Butler granted 'the parish church of the vill of Hinstock' to

---

[133] *Testamenta Eboracensia*, V, p. 26.
[134] *LR*, p. 1188.
[135] Chadwick, *Dunham*, p. 127.
[136] Hamilton Thompson, 'Jurisdiction' (as n. 56), pp. 94, 102.
[137] Arnold-Forster, III, 305.
[138] J. Sherwood and N. Pevsner, *The Buildings of England, Oxfordshire* (Harmondsworth 1974) p. 841.
[139] Mackinlay, *Ancient Church Dedications*, pp. 233-4.
[140] Ibid., p. 234.
[141] *LR*, p. 187.
[142] R. W. Eyton, *Antiquities of Shropshire* (12 vols; London 1854-60), VIII, p. 22.

Alcester Abbey.[143] The oldest parts of the present fabric date from the early eighteenth century.[144]

OSWESTRY (Fig. 9, no. 53)[145]

A confirmation of Henry I in favour of Shrewsbury Abbey dated 1121 mentions that 'Rainaldus...et Hugo filius Warini dederunt... ecclesiam sancti oswaldi'; the original grant probably dates to between 1086 and 1102.[146] During the twelfth and thirteenth centuries the church was known as 'album monasterium' (alternatively 'blancmonasterium'), that is, the white minster.[147] For the identification of the two, see, for example, a quitclaim dating from between 1186 and 1210, referring to 'ecclesie sancti oswaldi de Albo monasterio'.[148] Nearby lies a well associated with St Oswald, a focus of popular devotion in the middle ages.[149]

SUSSEX

HOOE (or All Saints) (Fig. 9, no. 78)

Two sixteenth-century wills refer to the church of All Saints.[150] The attribution of the dedication to either St Oswald or St James[151] appears therefore to be erroneous.

WESTMORLAND

BURNESIDE (Fig. 8, no. 14)

The present church is modern,[152] but stands on the site of a much older chapel a short distance from which is a well, known as the Miller's Well; this was previously known as St Oswald's Well, and is the only evidence in favour of a dedication of the chapel to Oswald.[153]

GRASMERE (Fig. 8, no. 13)[154]

This church was originally a chapel dependent on Kendal; the first extant documentary evidence dates from 1254.[155] In 1302 it was appropriated, with

---

[143] Ibid.

[144] N. Pevsner, *The Buildings of England, Shropshire* (Harmondsworth 1958), p. 150.

[145] For the case for identifying this site with *Maserfelth*, the place of Oswald's death, see Stancliffe, above, pp. 84-96.

[146] *Ctl. Shrewsbury*, I, no. 35 (p. 33); p. 38.

[147] Ibid., p. 281. Reginald records a similar tradition: see Tudor, above, pp. 190-1.

[148] *Ctl. Shrewsbury*, II, no. 301 (pp. 280-1).

[149] See Stancliffe, Rollason and Tudor above, pp. 86, 170-1, 190-1.

[150] *Transcripts of Sussex Wills*, ed. W. H. Godfrey (4 vols, Sussex Record Society, 41-3, 45; Lewes 1937-41), vol. II, pp. 331-2.

[151] Arnold-Forster, III, 155, the latter alone being given in *LR* (p. 142).

[152] Pevsner, *Cumberland and Westmorland*, p. 236.

[153] Arnold-Forster I, 313.

[154] *LR*, p. 1256.

[155] J. F. Curwen, 'The church of St Oswald, Grasmere', *Transactions of the Cum-*

the church of Kendal, to the abbot and convent of St Mary's York.[156] Armitt suggests that the original foundation may have been much earlier; a well in the Grasmere valley also bore the name of St Oswald, and the ceremony of rush bearing is still observed on the Sunday next to August 5,[157] but allegedly was formerly held on Oswald's feast day.[158] The back-plate of the poor-box, which bears the date 1648, carries the inscription 'S. OSWALDVS'.[159] The oldest parts of the present church date from the fourteenth century, and sculpture apparently of the twelfth century is also recorded from the site.[160]

RAVENSTONEDALE (Fig. 8, no. 15)[161]

During Henry II's reign, the church was granted by Thorphin to the priory of Watton in Yorkshire, but it was not appropriated fully until the fourteenth century.[162] The earliest parts of the present (largely eighteenth-century) structure are of c.1200.[163]

YORKSHIRE

ARNCLIFFE, West Riding (Fig. 8, no. 18)[164]

The date of the building of the church is not known; possibly it was founded by the De Arches, lords of the manor of Arncliffe, but the manor was soon alienated to the Percies.[165] In 1291 the church was valued at £33 6s. 6d.[166] The oldest extant fabric is late Gothic.[167]

ASKRIGG, North Riding (Fig. 8, no. 19)[168]

Uctred, priest of Askrigg, occurs between 1175 and 1204.[169] This is the largest church in Wensleydale; its early history is uncertain. The only known

berland and Westmorland Archaeological and Antiquarian Society, new series 14 (1913), pp. 312-24, at p. 312.

[156] M. L. Armitt, *The Church of Grasmere: A History* (Kendal 1912), p. 54.

[157] Ibid., p. 14.

[158] Mackinlay, *Ancient Church Dedications*, p. 233, n. 5.

[159] Curwen, 'Grasmere', p. 317, fig. on p. 318.

[160] Pevsner, *Cumberland and Westmorland*, p. 247.

[161] *LR*, p. 1202.

[162] J. F. Curwen, *The Later Records of the Church of North Westmorland* (Cumberland and Westmorland Archaeological Society Record Series 7; 1932), p. 214.

[163] Pevsner, *Cumberland and Westmorland*, p. 285.

[164] *LR*, p. 1127.

[165] G. Lawton, *Collectio Rerum Ecclesiasticarum de Diocesi Eboracensi, or Collections Relative to the Churches and Chapels within the Diocese of York to which are added Collections Relative to the Churches and Chapels within the Diocese of Ripon* (London 1842), p. 244.

[166] *Taxatio Ecclesiastica* (as n. 115), p. 300.

[167] N. Pevsner, *The Buildings of England, Yorkshire, the West Riding*, revised E. Radcliffe (Harmondsworth 1967), p. 84.

[168] *LR*, p. 1247.

[169] *EYC*, IV, no. 115.

date is the foundation of a chantry of St Anne in 1467 by James Metcalf.[170] The oldest extant fabric dates from the fifteenth century, but the north arcade piers are apparently reused from a thirteenth-century predecessor.[171]

BROUGHTON IN CRAVEN, West Riding (or All Saints) (Fig. 8, no. 34)
There is early documentary evidence of the dedication to All Saints: in 1152-3, William, son of Duncan, nephew of the king of Scotland, and Alice de Rumilly his wife gave 'ecclesiam Omnium Sanctorum de Broctune' with its lands and tithes to Embsay Priory.[172] Lawton also gives All Saints as the dedication.[173] There seems therefore to be no basis for the claim in antiquarian sources that it had supplanted an ancient dedication to St Oswald.[174]

CASTLE BOLTON, North Riding (Fig. 8, no. 20)
The first extant documentary evidence of the chapel of St Oswald at Castle Bolton occurs in 1399, when licence was granted to Richard le Scrope of Bolton to turn the parish church of Wensley into a college, which was to find a chaplain to serve in the chapel of St Anne in the castle of Bolton and a chaplain to serve the chapel of St Oswald in Bolton.[175]

COLLINGHAM, West Riding (Fig. 8, no. 37)[176]
The church lacks early documentation. Gladwin, priest of Collingham, was witness to a charter of William Percy II, between 1147 and 1154.[177] In 1258 the church was given to the chapel of St Mary and the Holy Angels in York by Richard de Morville.[178] The material evidence implies an earlier origin, however, for the nave shows traces of side-alternate quoining possibly of late pre-Conquest date,[179] and both Anglian and Viking-age sculpture have been recovered from the site.[180] A possible early context for this dedication is suggested by Cambridge, above, p. 145.

---

[170] *The Certificates of the Commissioners Appointed to Survey the Chantries, Guilds, Hospitals, etc. in the County of York*, ed. W. Page (2 vols; SS 91, 92, 1894-5), I, pp. 105-6.

[171] N. Pevsner, *The Buildings of England, Yorkshire, the North Riding* (Harmondsworth 1966), p. 66.

[172] *EYC*, VII, no. 15.

[173] Lawton, *Collections*, p. 249.

[174] T. D. Whitaker, *The History and Antiquities of the Deanery of Craven in the County of York* (3rd edn; Leeds and London 1878), p. 113; Raine, 'Dedications' (as note 7), p. 184.

[175] *CPR 1396-9*, p. 489.

[176] *LR*, p. 1108.

[177] *EYC*, XI, no. 14.

[178] Lawton, *Collections*, p. 59.

[179] H. M. and J. Taylor, *Anglo-Saxon Architecture* (2 vols; Cambridge 1965), I, pp. 166-7.

[180] See Cambridge, above, p. 144, n. 55.

EAST HARLSEY, North Riding (Fig. 8, no. 24)

Explicit reference to Oswald as patron saint is found in the will of John Gristwhate (1539), who was curate at the church.[181] An earlier indication appears in a charter dating from between 1239 and 1257, in which Prior John of Guisborough granted to William de Sawcock the chapel of Harlsey: 'Idem vero Willelmus capellanum et omnia alia ad hoc necessaria propriis sumptibus inveniet, et respiciet capellam de Herleseye in una libra cerae, vel sex denariis, singulis annis die S. Oswaldi, nomine recognitionis'.[182]

FARNHAM, West Riding (Fig. 8, no. 28)

There seems to be no early documentation specifically relating to the church, though a popular cult of St Oswald at Farnham is attested as early as the twelfth century.[183] In 1291 the church was valued at £26 13s. 4d.[184] It was appropriated to the Carthusian house of Beauvale in 1355.[185] Lawton gives the patron saint as not known;[186] Arnold-Forster gives Oswald, but without citing any supporting evidence.[187] The oldest part of the surviving fabric is the twelfth-century chancel.[188]

FILEY, East Riding (Fig. 8, no. 31)

Evidence for the dedication to St Oswald occurs in the will (1502) of William Blackburne of Filey.[189] A possible early context for this dedication is suggested by Cambridge, above, p. 143.

FLAMBOROUGH, East Riding (Fig. 8, no. 32)

It is uncertain when the dedication to St Oswald dates from, but it appears in thirteenth-century charters in the cartulary of Bridlington Priory,[190] to which the church had been given in the twelfth century.[191] A possible early context for this dedication is suggested by Cambridge, above, p. 155.

FULFORD, East Riding (Fig. 8, no. 38)

The first explicit reference to a dedication to Oswald is on 10 July 1349, when Hugh, archbishop of Damascus, was charged with dedicating the chapel and burial ground of St Oswald at Fulford.[192]

---

[181] *Cartularium Prioratus de Gyseburne*, ed. W. Brown (SS 86, 89, 1889-94), II, p. 296, n. 4.

[182] Ibid., II, no. MCVIII.

[183] See Rollason, above, pp. 166, 171.

[184] *Taxatio Ecclesiastica*, p. 307.

[185] *Monasticon* (as n. 18), VI, p. 12.

[186] Lawton, *Collections*, p. 553.

[187] Arnold-Forster, III, 122.

[188] Pevsner, *Yorkshire West*, p. 195.

[189] *Testamenta Eboracensia* (as n. 131), IV, p. 202.

[190] F. Brearley, *A History of Flamborough* (Driffield 1971), p. 30.

[191] *EYC*, IV, pp. 440-1.

[192] *The Fabric Rolls of York Minster*, ed. J. Raine (SS 35, 1859) p. 237 (quoting the

GUISELEY, West Riding (Fig. 8, no. 35)

Evidence for the dedication to St Oswald occurs in the will (1548) of Anne Hawkesworth of Esholt, who left 'my bodie to be buried in the quere of the church of Sancte Oswaldes at Gyesley'.[193] A possible early context for this dedication is suggested by Cambridge, above, pp. 144-6.

HAUXWELL, North Riding (Fig. 8, no. 21)[194]

The church and a carucate of land were given by Ulf Fornesson to St Mary's Abbey, York, between 1097 and 1137,[195] the grant being confirmed by King Henry II in 1156 or 1157.[196] The oldest parts of the present fabric are late eleventh-century,[197] and Viking-age sculpture survives from the site.[198]

HORTON IN RIBBLESDALE, West Riding (or Thomas à Becket) (Fig. 8, no. 17)

There is no record of the founding of the church; in 1249 the archbishop of York appropriated the church of Horton to the nuns of St Clement, York, the advowson having been granted by Alicia de Staveley.[199] Lawton gives the dedication as St Oswald or St Thomas à Becket, followed by Arnold-Forster, though neither cites any supporting evidence.[200] The oldest parts of the surviving fabric are Romanesque.[201]

HOTHAM, East Riding (Fig. 8, no. 39)[202]

The first extant reference dates from 1261, when patronage of the church was disputed between Geoffrey, son of Jordan, and John of Hotham.[203] The oldest part of the existing fabric is the early twelfth-century west tower.[204] A possible early context for this dedication is suggested by Cambridge, above, pp. 154-5.

---

register of Archbishop Zouche).

193 *Testamenta Eboracensia*, VI, p. 266.

194 *LR*, p. 1245.

195 VCH *Yorkshire, North Riding*, I, p. 250.

196 *EYC*, I, no. 354.

197 VCH *Yorkshire, North Riding*, I, pp. 249-50; Pevsner, *Yorkshire North*, p. 183.

198 W. G. Collingwood, 'Anglian and Anglo-Danish sculpture in the North Riding of Yorkshire', *Yorkshire Archaeological Journal* 19 (1907), pp. 267-413, at p. 330, figs. on p. 331.

199 *The Register of Walter de Gray, Lord Archbishop of York*, ed. J. Raine (SS 56, 1872), no. 490; *EYC*, I, no. 359.

200 Lawton, *Collections*, p. 255; Arnold-Forster, III, 158.

201 W. A. Shuffrey, *The Churches of the Deanery of North Craven* (Leeds 1914), p. 236; Pevsner, *Yorkshire West*, pp. 269-70.

202 *LR*, p. 1143 (*s.v.* Holtham).

203 VCH *Yorkshire, East Riding*, IV, p. 120.

204 N. Pevsner (with J. Hutchinson), *The Buildings of England, Yorkshire: York and the East Riding* (Harmondsworth 1972), p. 257.

KIRK SANDALL, West Riding (Fig. 8, no. 43)

A thirteenth-century reference to the church's patron saint occurs in a quitclaim of 1230 of Thomas, son of Hugh of Sandal, in favour of the prior of Lewes, to whom the church had been granted in the twelfth century: '...quietum clamavi Hugoni priori de Lewes...totum jus et clamium quod habui et habere potui in ecclesia sancti Oswaldi de Sandale'.[205]

LEATHLEY, West Riding (Fig. 8, no. 36)

The precise date of the foundation is not known. The church, together with two bovates of land, was given to the priory of Healaugh Park by Hugh, son of William de Leathley,[206] sometime before 1310, when it is mentioned in an *inspeximus*;[207] but the dedication is not indicated. Lawton gives the patron saint as not known; Arnold-Forster gives St Oswald, though neither cites any supporting evidence.[208] The oldest parts of the present fabric are early Romanesque.[209]

LYTHE, North Riding (Fig. 8, no. 26)

Explicit reference to a dedication to St Oswald is contained in the will (1499) of Thomas Artas, rector of Lythe, which mentions 'Ecclesia S. Oswaldi de Lith'; the fact that the church was granted to Nostell Priory in the early twelfth century suggests a more ancient association with Oswald, however.[210] The tower contains two bells, one of which is inscribed 'Sanctus Oswel Deo'.[211] A possible early context for this dedication is suggested by Cambridge, above, pp. 140-3.

METHLEY, West Riding (Fig. 8, no. 40)

In 1357 a commission was appointed to enquire into the dedication of the church.[212] Explicit evidence of a dedication to Oswald occurs in the will of Sir John Colne, rector of Methley (1407-21), who directed that his body be buried 'in ecclesia sancti Oswaldi de Methlay'.[213] A possible early context for this dedication is suggested by Cambridge, above, p. 147.

---

[205] *EYC*, VIII, no. 129.

[206] *The Chartulary of the Augustinian Priory of St John the Evangelist of the Park of Healaugh*, ed. J. S. Purvis (Yorkshire Archaeological Society, Record Series, 92; 1936), p. 20.

[207] *Calendar of the Charter Rolls Preserved in the Public Record Office, 1226-1516* (6 vols, London 1903-27), vol. III, *AD 1300-1326*, mem. 11, item 20, and cf. 21 (p. 164).

[208] Lawton, *Collections*, p. 88; Arnold-Forster, III, 178.

[209] Pevsner, *Yorkshire West*, pp. 301-2.

[210] *Testamenta Eboracensia*, IV, p. 162; *EYC*, II, no. 1012, III, nos. 1466, 1467; see Rollason, above, p. 173 and n. 44.

[211] VCH *Yorkshire, North Riding*, II, p. 398.

[212] *The History of Methley*, ed. H. S. Darbyshire and G. D. Lumb (Thoresby Society 35; Leeds 1937), p. 131.

[213] York, Borthwick Institute, Probate Register II (1396-1464), fol. 53ᵛ. On the

NEWTON IN CLEVELAND, North Riding (Fig. 8, no. 25)

The church was originally a dependent chapel of Great Ayton, and was given with the latter to Whitby Abbey during the reign of Henry I.[214] There are several references to 'capella de Newton' in the Whitby cartulary, though none names its patron saint.[215] Lawton gives the patron saint as not known; it is attributed to Oswald (the present-day dedication) by Arnold-Forster who, however, cites no supporting evidence.[216] The oldest parts of the present fabric are Romanesque.[217] A carved stone sometimes claimed as Anglo-Saxon is in fact early Romanesque.[218]

NOSTELL, West Riding (Augustinian Priory) (Fig. 8, no. 41)

Though the priory's foundation has been dated to as early as 1109, it appears likely that Archbishop Thurstan of York was responsible for introducing Augustinian canons to Nostell some time between 1114 and 1119 and that Henry I actively supported the new foundation shortly afterwards.[219] Like St Oswald's Gloucester (see above), Nostell was a centre of Oswald's cult and St Oswald's name was part of the common designation of the monastery; for an early reference explicitly naming Oswald as the dedicatee of its church, see Henry I's confirmation, dating from between 1121 and 1127 (probably 1121-2), which mentions: 'ecclesiam Beati Oswaldi regis et martiris ... in loco qui dicitur Nostlay'.[220] Nostell was early endowed with several churches which may already have had (or as a result of being given to the priory, acquired) dedications to St Oswald: see under Bamburgh (Northumberland); Winwick (Lancashire); Lythe and Wragby (both in Yorkshire).[221]

OSWALDKIRK, North Riding (Fig. 8, no. 30)

The place-name is first mentioned in Domesday Book.[222] Smith takes the reference to be to St Oswald the archbishop on the unconvincing grounds

---

iconographical representations of St Oswald at Methley see above, p. 7, n. 15, p. 8 and n. 20.

[214] VCH *Yorkshire, North Riding*, II, p. 275.

[215] *Cartularium Abbathiae de Whiteby*, ed. J. C. Atkinson (2 vols; SS 69, 72, 1879-81), nos. 6, 121, 164-5, 358-9, 399.

[216] Lawton, *Collections*, p. 495; Arnold-Forster, III, 210.

[217] Pevsner, *Yorkshire North*, p. 268.

[218] G. Zarnecki, *English Romanesque Sculpture 1066-1140* (London 1951), pp. 14-15, 27, pl. 13.

[219] T. N. Burrows, 'The foundation of Nostell Priory', *Yorkshire Archaeological Journal* 53 (1981), pp. 31-5.

[220] *EYC*, III, no. 1428 (p. 130). For Nostell as a cult-centre, see Rollason, above, pp. 169, 173-4.

[221] For further discussion, see Rollason, loc. cit.

[222] A. H. Smith, *The Place-Names of the North Riding of Yorkshire* (English Place-Name Society 5; Cambridge 1928), p. 55.

that the estate belonged to York Minster in the late pre-Conquest period.[223] Fellows[-]Jensen interprets the name as almost certainly a Scandinavian-isation of an older English name.[224] The first extant reference to Oswald as patron saint occurs in 1240, when Peter of Jarpenvill and Maud his wife granted the advowson of the church of St Oswald to William of Barton and Emma his wife.[225] In 1287 the dean of Ryedale stated that the church of Oswaldkirk was not dedicated.[226] This is unlikely to indicate that the church was newly built, however, but rather that it had been polluted by the shedding of blood, or that a new high altar had been erected, or that the dedication feast had fallen into disuse.[227] A possible early context for this dedication is suggested by Cambridge, above, pp. 143-4.

SOWERBY, North Riding (Fig. 8, no. 29)
Lawton gives the dedication as St Oswald.[228] The church was originally a dependent chapel of Thirsk. The earliest extant documentary reference dates from between 1143 and 1147, when the prior and convent of Newburgh tried to substantiate their claims to various churches, including the church of Thirsk with its chapels of Sowerby, Hulton, and Carlton.[229] The oldest part of the present fabric is the twelfth-century south doorway.[230]

THORNTON IN CRAVEN, West Riding (now St Mary) (Fig. 8, no. 33)
The will of James Carr (1526) names the church of St Oswald of Thornton,[231] but at some later date the patron saint changed to St Mary, the dedication given by the *Liber Regis*, Lawton, and modern authorities.[232]

THORNTON IN LONSDALE, West Riding (Fig. 8, no. 16)
Lawton gives the dedication as St Oswald.[233] The oldest parts of the present fabric, before twentieth-century fire damage, were twelfth-century.[234]

[223] Loc. cit.

[224] G. Fellows[-]Jensen, *Scandinavian Settlement Names in Yorkshire* (Copenhagen 1972), p. 246; cf. pp. 133-4, 149.

[225] *Yorkshire Feet of Fines. Feet of Fines for the County of York, 16-30 Henry III*, ed. J. Parker (Yorkshire Archaeological Society, Record Series 67, 1925), no. 847.

[226] *The Register of John le Romeyn, Lord Archbishop of York, 1286-1296*, ed. W. Brown (2 vols; SS 123, 128, 1913-16), I, no. 463.

[227] Ibid., I, p. xvii.

[228] Lawton, *Collections*, p. 446.

[229] *English Episcopal Acta*, vol. V, *York 1070-1154*, ed. J. Burton (Oxford 1988) no. 95.

[230] Pevsner, *Yorkshire North*, p. 351.

[231] *Testamenta Eboracensia*, V, pp. 219-20, where the context makes it clear that this Thornton is meant.

[232] LR, p. 1127; Lawton, *Collections*, p. 269.

[233] Lawton, *Collections*, p. 588.

[234] Pevsner, *Yorkshire West*, p. 513.

THORNTON STEWARD, North Riding (Fig. 8, no. 22)[235]
Domesday Book records a church here. This, with half a carucate of land, was given by Wymar the steward to the monks of St Mary's York.[236] The oldest parts of the present fabric are at latest Romanesque,[237] and Viking-age sculpture has been recovered from the site.[238]

WEST ROUNTON, North Riding (Fig. 8, no. 23)
Explicit evidence of the dedication occurs in a charter datable to between about 1174 and 1186 in which Ranulf, son of William of Surtees, granted 'Deo et ecclesie Sancti Oswaldi de Rungeton unum masuagium quod est inter cimiterium ejusdem ecclesie et viam quae ducit ad molendinum...';[239] the present-day dedication is to St Oswald. The *Liber Regis* and Lawton, however, give the dedication as St James.[240] It remains unclear whether this alternative dedication is ancient or due to more recent confusion.

WINKSLEY (CUM GRANTLEY), West Riding, SS Cuthbert and Oswald (Fig. 8, no. 27)
Built by Abbot Marmaduke Huby of Fountains (1495-1526), it is a very late instance of a dedication to Oswald, and its existence is recorded in an Indulgence granted by Archbishop Thomas Savage of York in 1502: '...ob magnam et sinceram devocionem quam erga Sanctum Cuthbertum episcopum et beatum martirum Oswaldum gerit, unam capellam apud Wynkesley infra parochiam Ripon ... in honore Dei et Sanctorum praedictorum, ubi, ut dicitur, idem Sanctus Cuthburtus aliquamdiu personaliter conversando et religiose vivendo sanctum ducebat vitam...'[241] Both the *Liber Regis* and Lawton give the dedication as St Oswald only.[242] Fragments of the medieval chapel survive, built into the present early twentieth-century one.[243]

WRAGBY, West Riding (or St Michael) (Fig. 8, no. 42)
Wragby was close to the Augustinian priory of St Oswald, Nostell, and the canons were responsible for the parochial chapel, which was possibly a

---

[235] *LR*, p. 1247.
[236] VCH *Yorkshire, North Riding*, I, p. 267; *EYC*, I, no. 354.
[237] Pevsner, *Yorkshire North*, p. 372.
[238] Collingwood, 'North Riding', p. 402, figs. on p. 403.
[239] *EYC*, II, no. 946.
[240] *LR*, p. 1123; Lawton, *Collections*, p. 505.
[241] *Memorials of the Abbey of St Mary of Fountains*, ed. J. Walbran and J. T. Fowler (3 vols; SS 42, 47, 130, 1863-1918), I, pp. 421-3.
[242] *LR*, p. 2163; Lawton, *Collections*, p. 547. Cf. Arnold-Forster, III, 134, *s.v.* Grantley ('SS Cuthbert and Oswald, or St Oswald').
[243] Pevsner, *Yorkshire West*, pp. 554-5. For other aspects of Huby's promotion of the cult of St Oswald, see Rollason, above, p. 164.

successor to the early church of St Oswald at the 'old place'.[244] Robert de Lacy's grant to Nostell included St Oswald's wood and two churches, one at Featherstone and the other possibly at Wragby.[245] The *Liber Regis* and Lawton both give the dedication as St Michael, however, while Arnold-Forster gives St Mary and St Michael, all without citing supporting evidence.[246] The existing fabric is late Gothic. The current dedication is to St Michael and Our Lady. St Oswald, flanked by two bishops, figures prominently in the east window of 1533; but this may reflect the concerns of the prior of Nostell, who was responsible for installing it.[247]

[244] A. Hamilton Thompson, *History and Architectural Description of the Priory of St Mary, Bolton-in-Wharfedale, with Some Account of the Canons Regular of the Order of St Augustine and their Houses in Yorkshire* (Thoresby Society Publication 30; Leeds 1928), p. 30.

[245] *EYC*, II, p. 133.

[246] *LR*, p. 1159; Lawton, *Collections*, p. 168; Arnold-Forster, III, 317.

[247] Pevsner, *Yorkshire West*, p. 560.

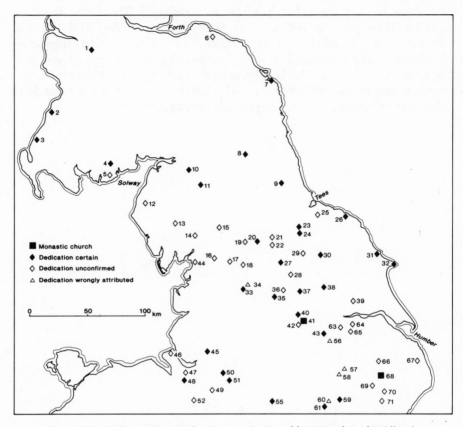

Figure 8: Pre-Reformation Dedications to St Oswald, I: North and Midlands

1. Cathcart, Renfrewshire
2. Kirkoswald (of Turnberry), Ayrshire
3. Kirkoswald (alias Balmaknele), Ayrshire
4. Kelton, Kirkcudbrightshire
5. Kirkcarswell, Kirkcudbrightshire
6. Whittingehame, East Lothian
7. Bamburgh, Northumberland
8. St Oswald in Lee (Heavenfield), Northumberland
9. Elvet (Durham City), County Durham
10. Wetheral, Cumberland
11. Kirkoswald, Cumberland
12. Dean, Cumberland
13. Grasmere, Westmorland
14. Burneside, Westmorland
15. Ravenstonedale, Westmorland
16. Thornton in Lonsdale, Yorkshire
17. Horton in Ribblesdale, Yorkshire
18. Arncliffe, Yorkshire
19. Askrigg, Yorkshire
20. Castle Bolton, Yorkshire
21. Hauxwell, Yorkshire
22. Thornton Steward, Yorkshire
23. West Rounton, Yorkshire
24. East Harlsey, Yorkshire
25. Newton in Cleveland, Yorkshire
26. Lythe, Yorkshire
27. Winksley (cum Grantley), Yorkshire
28. Farnham, Yorkshire
29. Sowerby, Yorkshire
30. Oswaldkirk, Yorkshire
31. Filey, Yorkshire
32. Flamborough, Yorkshire
33. Thornton in Craven, Yorkshire
34. Broughton in Craven, Yorkshire
35. Guiseley, Yorkshire
36. Leathley, Yorkshire
37. Collingham, Yorkshire
38. Fulford, Yorkshire
39. Hotham, Yorkshire
40. Methley, Yorkshire
41. Nostell Priory, Yorkshire
42. Wragby, Yorkshire
43. Kirk Sandall, Yorkshire
44. Warton, Lancashire
45. Winwick, Lancashire
46. Bidston, Cheshire
47. Backford, Cheshire
48. Chester, Cheshire
49. Worleston, Cheshire
50. Lower Peover, Cheshire
51. Brereton (with Smethwick), Cheshire
52. Malpas, Cheshire
53. Oswestry, Shropshire
54. Hinstock, Shropshire
55. Ashbourne, Derbyshire
56. Finningley, Nottinghamshire
57. Dunham, Nottinghamshire
58. Ragnall, Nottinghamshire
59. East Stoke, Nottinghamshire
60. Bulcote, Nottinghamshire
61. Burton Joyce, Nottinghamshire
62. Broughton Sulney, Nottinghamshire
63. Crowle, Lincolnshire
64. Luddington, Lincolnshire
65. Althorpe, Lincolnshire
66. Rand, Lincolnshire
67. Strubby, Lincolnshire
68. Bardney Abbey, Lincolnshire
69. Blankney, Lincolnshire
70. Walcot, Lincolnshire
71. Howell, Lincolnshire

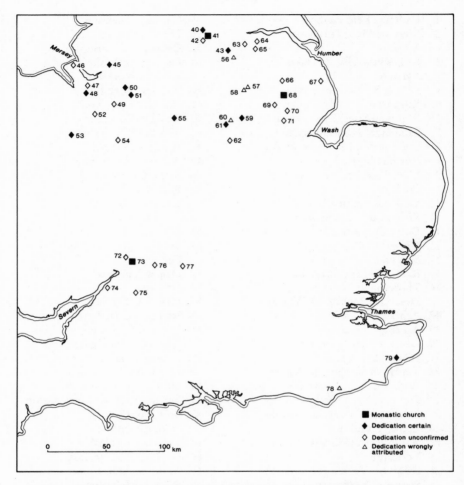

Figure 9: Pre-Reformation Dedications to St Oswald, II: Midlands and South

270

40. Methley, Yorkshire
41. Nostell Priory, Yorkshire
42. Wragby, Yorkshire
43. Kirk Sandall, Yorkshire
44. Warton, Lancashire
45. Winwick, Lancashire
46. Bidston, Cheshire
47. Backford, Cheshire
48. Chester, Cheshire
49. Worleston, Cheshire
50. Lower Peover, Cheshire
51. Brereton (with Smethwick), Cheshire
52. Malpas, Cheshire
53. Oswestry, Shropshire
54. Hinstock, Shropshire
55. Ashbourne, Derbyshire
56. Finningley, Nottinghamshire
57. Dunham, Nottinghamshire
58. Ragnall, Nottinghamshire
59. East Stoke, Nottinghamshire
60. Bulcote, Nottinghamshire
61. Burton Joyce, Nottinghamshire
62. Broughton Sulney, Nottinghamshire
63. Crowle, Lincolnshire
64. Luddington, Lincolnshire
65. Althorpe, Lincolnshire
66. Rand, Lincolnshire
67. Strubby, Lincolnshire
68. Bardney Abbey, Lincolnshire
69. Blankney, Lincolnshire
70. Walcot, Lincolnshire
71. Howell, Lincolnshire
72. Lassington, Gloucestershire
73. Gloucester Priory, Gloucestershire
74. Rockhampton, Gloucestershire
75. Shipton Oliffe, Gloucestershire
76. Compton Abdale, Gloucestershire
77. Widford, Oxfordshire
78. Hooe, Sussex
79. Paddlesworth, Kent

Further Reading

The following, very selective, suggestions are intended for those with no prior knowledge of the subject, who may wish to explore the wider context to the studies in the present volume, or to follow up for themselves the sources on Oswald, or the story of the spread of his cult abroad. (Those who wish to pursue more detailed subjects arising from individual papers are recommended to follow up the references in the relevant footnotes.)

The Context for Oswald

James Campbell (ed.), *The Anglo-Saxons* (Oxford 1982) – the best general introduction, embracing both a chronological survey and thematic 'picture essays', which introduce much archaeological and other non-literary evidence; splendidly illustrated.

Henry Mayr-Harting, *The Coming of Christianity to Anglo-Saxon England* (3rd edn, London 1991) – strongly recommended.

Barbara Yorke, *Kings and Kingdoms of Early Anglo-Saxon England* (London 1990) – good up-to-date survey, with chapters both on individual kingdoms (including Northumbria) and on kingship.

Peter Hunter Blair, *Northumbria in the Days of Bede* (London 1977) – an enjoyable, well-written introduction to various themes, for the interested general reader, written by a scholar and a Northumbrian; strong on the cultural side.

Nick Higham, *The Northern Counties to AD 1000* (London and New York 1986) – for those wanting a more conventional, chronologically-based regional history.

The Sources for Oswald

A) Bede: the fundamental source

Translations

Bede's Ecclesiastical History of the English People, edited and translated by Bertram Colgrave and R. A. B. Mynors (Oxford 1969) – the most reliable (though not infallible) translation available, with a helpful Introduction.

Bede: The Ecclesiastical History, translated by Bertram Colgrave, with additional works edited by Judith McClure and Roger Collins (Worlds Classics series; Oxford and New York 1994) – Colgrave's translation as an inexpensive paperback.

Bede, *Ecclesiastical History of the English People*, translated by L. Sherley-Price, edited with new Introduction by D. H. Farmer (Penguin Classics series; revised edn. Harmondsworth 1990) – included here because of its widespread popularity; but even in the revised 1990 edition, some misleading mis-translations remain. Beware especially that of the chapter heading to book III, ch. 2, which implies – wrongly – that the British army which Oswald fought at Heavenfield was a pagan army. ('Barbarians' have been rendered as 'heathen'!)

Interpretation

A starting point might be Mayr-Harting, *Coming*, ch. 2, taken in tandem with the 'Historical Introduction' in Colgrave and Mynors's edition. Then turn to James Campbell, 'Bede I', in his *Essays in Anglo-Saxon History* (London 1986), pp.

1-27, which challenges the reader to engage critically with Bede's *History*. Other essays in the same book are also of interest.

Commentaries

Charles Plummer ('Carolus Plummer'), ed., *Venerabilis Baedae Opera Historica* (2 vols., Oxford 1896) – do not be deterred by the formidable Latin title: vol. II consists of excellent notes in English, a veritable goldmine of information, which has dated astonishingly little.

J. M. Wallace-Hadrill, *Bede's Ecclesiastical History of the English People: A Historical Commentary* (Oxford 1988) – written to accompany Colgrave and Mynors, op. cit., which it occasionally corrects. Intended as a supplement to Plummer, not to replace him. Full bibliography.

B) Adomnán's *Life of Columba*, book I, ch. 1: brief extract only on Oswald's exile and the battle of Heavenfield.

Translations

Adomnán's Life of Columba, edited and translated by A. O. and M. O. Anderson (revised edn, Oxford 1991).

Adomnán of Iona, *Life of St Columba*, translated with exemplary introduction and notes by Richard Sharpe (Penguin Classics series, Harmondsworth 1995).

Interpretation

Máire Herbert, *Iona, Kells and Derry: The History and Hagiography of the Monastic Familia of Columba* (Oxford 1988), ch. 12 – discussion of Adomnán's work, its aims and audience.

The Cult of St Oswald

David Rollason, *Saints and Relics in Anglo-Saxon England* (Oxford 1989) – for the general context.

Peter Clemoes, *The Cult of St Oswald on the Continent* (Jarrow Lecture; Jarrow 1983) – brief general survey. (Jarrow Lectures are available, at a reasonable price, direct from St Paul's Church, Jarrow, Tyne and Wear.)

E. P. Baker, 'St Oswald and his church at Zug', in *Archaeologia* (Society of Antiquaries of London) vol. 93 (1949), pp. 103-23 – excellent detailed survey of spread of Oswald's cult in Switzerland, good on iconography, well illustrated.

E. P. Baker, 'The cult of St Oswald in northern Italy', *Archaeologia* vol. 94 (1951), pp. 167-94 – takes the story from medieval beginnings down to modern times.

Those willing to read French and German should not miss:

Robert Folz, 'Saint Oswald roi de Northumbrie: étude d'hagiographie royale', in *Analecta Bollandiana* (Société des Bollandistes, Brussels), vol. 98 (1980), pp. 49-74 – detailed, wide-ranging survey; includes some information on the liturgical material.

Michael Curschmann, *Der Münchener Oswald und die deutsche spielmännische Epik* (Münchener Texte und Untersuchungen zur deutschen Literatur des Mittelalters, vol. 6; Munich 1964) – includes a discussion of the continental iconography and cult.

Index

The index aims to be comprehensive. It was compiled by the publisher, Shaun Tyas. References to the work of contemporary historians within the text have not been indexed. References to British counties are to the pre-1974 boundaries. The footnotes are included if they contain comments which supplement the main text, but not if they contain only bibliographical references. '219 + n.43' means that both the main text and the note are relevant. '219: n.43' means that only the note is relevant. References to notes are followed by a semi-colon (;) to minimise any confusion with the page numbers. References to the plates are in the style 'Pl. 6' or 'Pls 6-8'.

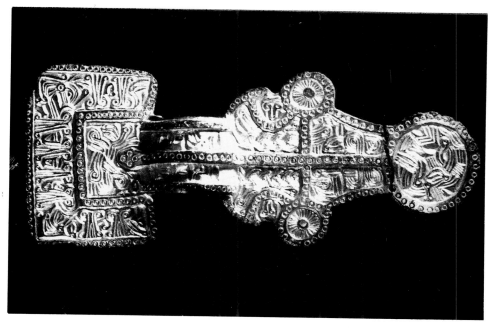

1. Square-headed brooch from Catterick, North Yorkshire (British Museum)

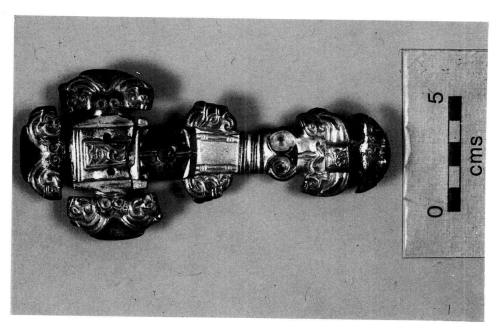

2. Florid cruciform brooch from a late sixth-century female grave from Norton, Cleveland
(Cleveland County Council)

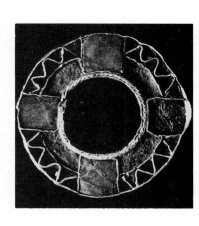

3 (above). Penannular brooch with bird's head terminals from Clogh, Co. Antrim (British Museum)

4 (top right). Decorative pyramid with filigree and garnet decoration from Dalmeny, East Lothian (National Museum of Scotland)

5 (right). Gold, garnet and amber disk brooch from Ripon (Dean and Chapter of Ripon)

6. Whalebone casket (the 'Franks Casket'), panel from the lid depicting a battle scene (British Museum)

7. Sword hilt, with filigree and garnet decoration, from Cumberland
(British Museum)

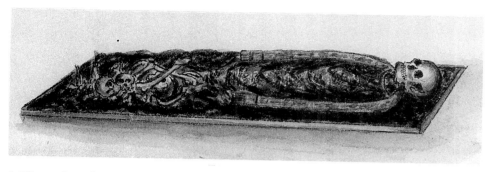

8. Watercolour showing St Cuthbert's body and other remains as excavated at Durham in 1827 (Dean and Chapter of Durham)

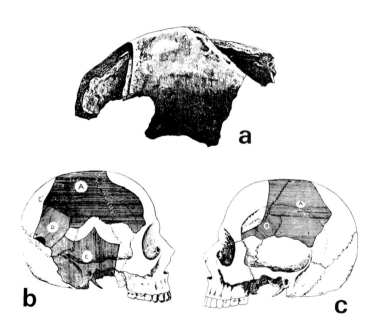

9. Oswald's skull as excavated at Durham in 1899, showing: large fragment with weapon cut (a); and reconstruction incorporating other fragments (b-c)

10. Hildesheim head-reliquary of Oswald opened to show relics wrapped in textiles
(Dom- und Diözesanmuseum, Hildesheim)

11. Utrecht head-relic of Oswald, perhaps from Zeddam
(Rijksmuseum Het Catharijneconvent, Utrecht)

12. Hildesheim head-reliquary with head of Oswald and (below left) panel depicting him enthroned: late 12th C. (Dom- und Diözesanmuseum, Hildesheim)

13. Oswald's charity when feasting with Bishop Aidan, from the Berthold Missal: Weingarten, 1200-32 (Pierpont Morgan Library, New York, M. 710, fol. 101ᵛ)

14. Statue of Oswald holding dish, from west front of Wells Cathedral, *c.*1220-40 (photograph before restoration, the Conway Library, Courtauld Institute of Art)

15. Oswald with bird, stained-glass window in York Minster: 1285-1300
(Chapter House vestibule, no. CH n. IX (or no. 50), right-hand light, top)

16. King with bird, probably Oswald with raven, statue: 14th C.
(Museum der Stadt, Regensburg)

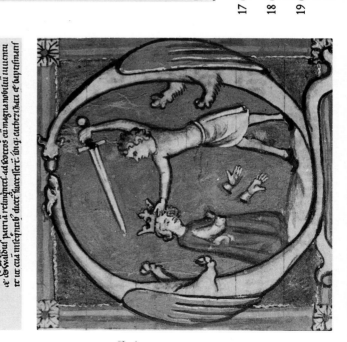

17 (top left). Oswald, initial from a collection of saints' Lives: 2nd half of 12th C. (Munich, Universitätsbibliothek 2° Cod. MS 312, fol. 104ᵛ)

18 (left). Oswald's 'martyrdom', from a collection of saints' Lives: Trier, 14th C. (Darmstadt, Hessische Landesbibliothek MS 2766, fol. 44ᵛ)

19 (above). St Cuthbert holding Oswald's head, initial from Nicholas of Lyra's commentary on the Pentateuch: Durham Priory, 1386 (Durham, Dean and Chapter Library, MS A.I.3, fol. 1ʳ)

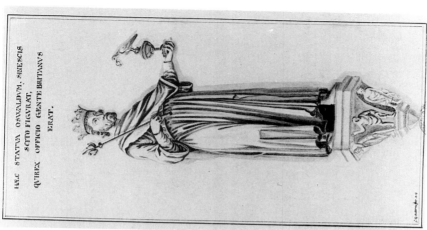

HAC STATVA OSVALDVM, SNESCIS
SCITO FIGVRAT,
QVIREX OFFICIO GENTE BRITANVS
ERAT.

21. The same statue before restoration: drawing
by J. G. Ostermeyer, 1812
(Museum der Stadt, Regensburg)

20. Oswald holding a covered cup, statue from the
Dollingersaal, Regensburg, Bavaria: late 13th C.
(Museum der Stadt, Regensburg)

22. Oswald with raven on his orb holding ring, wing of an altarpiece by the Styrian Master: Styria, Austria, mid 15th C. (Steiermärkisches Landesmuseum Joanneum, Graz)

23. Raven arriving from heaven with letter and chrism for Oswald's coronation: Salzburg school, 2nd half of 15th C. (Bayerisches Nationalmuseum, Munich)

24. Óðin (Woden) struggling with the wolf Fenrir, with a raven on his shoulder: fragment of stone cross-slab from Kirk Andreas, Isle of Man, 10th C. (The Manx Museum, Douglas)